GW00691884

Corporate Tax Base in the Light of the IAS/IFRS and EU Directive 2013/34

EUCOTAX Series on European Taxation

VOLUME 48

Series Editors

Prof. Dr Peter H.J. Essers, Fiscal Institute Tilburg/Center for Company Law, Tilburg University

Prof. Dr Eric C.C.M. Kemmeren, Fiscal Institute Tilburg/Center for Company Law, Tilburg University

Prof. Dr Dr h.c. Michael Lang, WU (Vienna University of Economics and Business)

Introduction

EUCOTAX (European Universities Cooperating on Taxes) is a network of tax institutes currently consisting of eleven universities: WU (Vienna University of Economics and Business) in Austria, Katholieke Universiteit Leuven in Belgium, Corvinus University of Budapest, Hungary, Université Paris-I Panthéon-Sorbonne in France, Universität Osnabrück in Germany, Libera, Università Internazionale di Studi Sociali in Rome (and Università degli Studi di Bologna for the research part), in Italy, Fiscaal Instituut Tilburg at Tilburg University in the Netherlands, Universidad de Barcelona in Spain, Uppsala University in Sweden, Queen Mary and Westfield College at the University of London in the United Kingdom, and Georgetown University in Washington DC, United States of America. The network aims at initiating and coordinating both comparative education in taxation, through the organization of activities such as winter courses and guest lectures, and comparative research in the field, by means of joint research projects, international conferences and exchange of researchers between various countries.

Contents/Subjects

The EUCOTAX series covers a wide range of topics in European tax law. For example tax treaties, EC case law, tax planning, exchange of information and VAT. The series is well-known for its high-quality research and practical solutions.

Objective

The series aims to provide insights on new developments in European taxation.

Readership

Practitioners and academics dealing with European tax law.

Frequency of Publication

2-3 new volumes published each year.

The titles published in this series are listed at the end of this volume.

Corporate Tax Base in the Light of the IAS/IFRS and EU Directive 2013/34

A Comparative Approach

Edited by
Mario Grandinetti

Published by:
Kluwer Law International B.V.
PO Box 316
2400 AH Alphen aan den Rijn
The Netherlands
Website: www.wklawbusiness.com

Sold and distributed in North, Central and South America by:
Wolters Kluwer Legal & Regulatory U.S.
7201 McKinney Circle
Frederick, MD 21704
United States of America
Email: customer.service@wolterskluwer.com

Sold and distributed in all other countries by:
Turpin Distribution Services Ltd
Stratton Business Park
Pegasus Drive, Biggleswade
Bedfordshire SG18 8TQ
United Kingdom
Email: kluwerlaw@turpin-distribution.com

Printed on acid-free paper.

ISBN 978-90-411-6745-3

© 2016 Kluwer Law International BV, The Netherlands

Printed in the United Kingdom.

Editor

Mario Grandinetti is a Researcher of Tax Law at the University of Turin (Italy). He is also Lecturer of Tax Law and has been Lecturer of International, European and Comparative Tax Law at the University of Turin. He holds a PhD in Public and Tax Law in the European dimension from the University of Bergamo (Italy). He was visiting researcher at the Max Planck Institute in Intellectual Property and Tax Law, Munich (Germany) and at the University of Valencia (Spain). He was the winner of the "Giovanni Goria Foundation" scholarship (2010) dedicated to young researcher. His areas of expertise are domestic company taxation (accounting and taxation in particular), European and International Taxation, VAT and Group taxation.

Contributors

Nina Aguiar is Adjunct Professor of Law at the Polytechnic Institute of Bragança. She has been Integrated CIJE member since 2006. She obtained a European doctorate from the University of Salamanca (2006) in the Financial Law, Rights and Guarantees for Taxpayers area. She holds a Law degree from the Faculty of Law of Lisbon.

Marco Barassi is Associate Professor of Tax Law in the Department of Law at the University of Bergamo, Italy. He is a member of the European Association of Tax Law Professors and of "Associazione dei Professori di Diritto Tributario" His main area of research is comparative tax law. He has published a book (*La comparazione nel diritto tributario*) and many articles on this subject.

Gianluigi Bizioli is Associate Professor of Tax Law and International and EU Tax Law in the Department of Law at the University of Bergamo, Italy; *Of Counsel* at Ludovici and Partners (Milan-Rome-London) and member of the Board of Professors of the PhD in Business & Law. Author of numerous publications in the field of International and EU Tax Law as well as of the fiscal federalism.

Donatella Busso is Associate Professor of Economics and Business Administration in the Department of Management at the University of Turin, Italy, where she teaches consolidated financial statements and IFRS and Affiliate Professor of Financial Accounting at the École Supérieure de Commerce de Paris (ESCP Europe). She is the author of many publications on the subject of financial statements, consolidated financial statements and IFRS. She is a qualified Italian Chartered Accountant and a consultant, working with many companies in the role of director in listed companies and statutory auditor in non-listed companies.

Maurizio Cisi is Associate Professor of Business Administration in the Department of Management at the University of Turin, Italy. He is a chartered accountant and auditor and also is a financial analysis expert. One of his main field of research is International Accounting Standards and the evolution of financial reporting for unlisted companies.

Andreas Eggert is an attorney at law at the Munich office of Hogan Lovells International LLP and a member of its tax practice group. After his law studies in Augsburg and his clerkship at the Higher Regional Court in Munich, Andreas worked as a research associate at the Max Planck Institute for Tax Law and Public Finance in Munich where he wrote his dissertation on the proposed CCCTB.

Peter H.J. Essers is Professor of Tax Law at Tilburg University, specializing in national and international personal and corporate income tax. He is director of the European Tax College and coordinator of EUCOTAX (European Universities Cooperating on Taxes). He has been a visiting professor at the Université Panthéon-Sorbonne, the University of Bologna, Universidad de Barcelona, the University of Osnabrück, Northwestern University Chicago, LUISS University Rome, the University of Turin and WU Vienna. He has been chairman of the Academic Committee of the European Association of Tax Law Professors (EATLP) and also member of the Netherlands Senate and chairman of the Finance Committee of the Senate.

Simon James is an Associate Professor of Economics in the Department of Organisation Studies at the University of Exeter Business School, a Fellow of the Chartered Institute of Taxation and an Honorable Member of the Society for the Advancement of Behavioral Economics. He has held visiting positions at six universities overseas and has published many research papers and sixteen books.

Renaud Jaune, French Civil Servant – Ministry of Finance – General Directorate for Public Finances. Conseil d'Etat (administrative Supreme Court) as Judge, 2013-2014. Ministry of Finance – Tax Legislation Directorate – Head of Unit E1 (Bilateral Treaty Negotiations, Competent Authority on Mutual Agreement Procedures as regards Elimination of Double Taxation, 2009-2012. PhD candidate at the Paris Sorbonne University – Doctoral Study on The Law and the Transfer Pricing Regulation.

Andrés Báez Moreno is Associate Professor of Tax Law at Universidad Carlos III in Madrid, Spain and lawyer at the Madrid bar association and postdoctoral research fellow at IBFD on selected issues of the UN Model. He has been a visiting pre and postdoctoral researcher at the Universities of Münster and Cologne, Germany and Padova, Italy and at IBFD. His areas of expertise are domestic company taxation (in particular, commercial and tax accounting) and international taxation, fields in which he has published two books and more than thirty articles and contributions in Spanish, English and German. He has participated as a tax expert in several administrative and judicial proceedings collaborating with various Spanish and international law firms in the field of international and European taxation.

Maria Lucia Passador is a PhD candidate in Legal Studies, Business and Social Law, at Bocconi University in Milan, where she graduated *magna cum laude* in July 2014, and Visiting Researcher at Harvard Law School. Her active research interests relate to Corporate Law, Financial Markets and Securities Regulation, and she published articles in these areas of law, especially from comparative perspective.

Steven Peeters is active as an affiliated researcher at the Institute for Tax Law of the KU Leuven and is a Senior Attorney at Liedekerke (Brussels). His research focuses on the intersection between corporate taxation and corporate law, and on the impact of EU law on corporate taxation.

Victor Borges Polizelli has PhD and LLM degrees in Economic, Finance and Tax Law, from the School of Law at the University of São Paulo, 2006-2013. He graduated with a Bachelor of Science degree in Accounting from the University of São Paulo, 2008 and a Bachelor of Law degree from the University of São Paulo, 2001. Victor has written books, chapters and other publications in the areas of corporate taxation, accounting and tax planning. At present, he is working as a Professor of Tax Planning and Tax Law for post graduation courses at the Brazilian Tax Law Institute (IBDT) and at the São Paulo School of Economics (FGV - EESP). He is also tax advisor at KLA – Koury Lopes Advogados, dedicated to the Tax Planning and Mergers and Acquisitions groups of the firm.

Giovanni Strampelli is Associate Professor of Commercial Law at Bocconi University in Milan, where he teaches Company Law and Accounting Law. He is Faculty Member of the PhD in Legal Studies at Bocconi University. He is author of monographs and articles in the fields of company law, accounting law, financial market law and insolvency law.

Júlio Tormenta is a Senior Tax Manager of the Corporate Tax division of PricewaterhouseCoopers. He graduated in Management and Business Administration from the Catholic University of Lisbon. He graduated in Economics from the Catholic University of Lisbon and in Law from the Autónoma University of Lisbon. He completed his post-graduation in Management and Taxation at IESF and earned a Master's in Tax Law from the Autónoma University of Lisbon. He enrolled on a PhD programme in Tax Law at the Autónoma University of Lisbon. His areas of expertise are general corporate tax issues and compliance taxation.

Edoardo Traversa is Professor of Tax Law at the University of Louvain (UCL) and Of Counsel at Liedekerke (Brussels). His interest mainly focuses on the European tax integration (EU directives, EU freedoms and Fiscal State aid) and international taxation, as well as fiscal and financial federalism and the interaction between taxation and public policies. He regularly advises various EU and Belgian public authorities on those issues. As a lawyer, he advises and assists corporate, non-profit and individual clients in these areas, and represents them in litigation before domestic and European courts.

Charlène van Eysinga is a postdoctoral research fellow at the Catholic University of Louvain (FNR Luxembourg). She is senior lecturer at the Universities of Luxembourg (Grand Duchy of Luxembourg) and Nancy II (France).

Steven J. Willis is Professor of Law at the Levin College of Law, University of Florida in Gainesville, FL. His main areas of research concern U.S. tax law, accounting and finance. In particular, he focuses on the time value of money and its effects in various legal areas. He is a member of the Florida and Louisiana Bars and is a Certified Public Accountant in Louisiana.

Summary of Contents

Table of Contents

CHAPTER 7
Accounting and Taxation: Germany
Andreas Eggert   115

Acknowledgments

This research project began two years ago and now the reader has the chance to keep in his/her hands the result: a book!

The topic of the book is the subject of my first monograph that has not yet been finished, although it is now nearing completion. During the study, I felt the need to move beyond the national perspective and, consequently, follow a comparative approach as well.

For that reason, I decided to contact many authoritative authors who have published essays and monographs on this issue.

My first acknowledgment is dedicated to all those who accepted my invitation and replied patiently and with attention to my continual requests.

Moreover, while undertaking this work I have benefited greatly from the help and support of a number of people.

I am grateful to Professor Gianluigi Bizioli and Professor Marco Barassi, of the University of Bergamo, for their invaluable support, encouragement and guidance and not only for this project. I would also like to thank Professor Claudio Sacchetto, my mentor since starting my academic career and head of our common School of Tax Law in Bergamo and Turin.

I would also like to thank Professor Peter Essers for his support with this project.

Last, but not least, I wish to thank the Department of Management of the University of Turin and Dr. Susan Jane Kingshott for, respectively, their financial support and insights and comments. Without them, the book that reader keeps in his/her hands would have another form and another content!

On a personal level, I am deeply indebted to my family and friends for their moral support.

This book is dedicated to them and, in particular, to my wife and to my three daughters (Sofia, Francesca and the baby that is on the way).

Foreword

The history of science, including human sciences which encompass the science of taxation, is marked by facts and events, some of which, although accidental, have proven to be effective in providing theoretical stimuli for research and investigation in the advancement of knowledge. An emblematic and universal example is the famous apple that enabled Isaac Newton to verify the existence of the principle of universal gravitation.

On the subject of taxation, the events triggering such a progress of knowledge, do not occur in the same way, but in presenting this collective study, it seemed appropriate to the writer of this foreword to give account of the background behind the origin and existence of this work today.

The research presented in this book derives from a meeting and an exchange of ideas and is based on the insight of three young researchers, Mario Grandinetti from Turin University, Andreas Baez Moreno from Carlos III University of Madrid and Nina Aguiar from the Polytechnic Institute of Bragança who, encouraged perhaps by the environment and context of the annual congress of the European Association of Tax Law professors in Lisbon in 2013, undertook this interdisciplinary research project together with scholars from various European countries. It set out to be an experiment that today has come to fruition and many of the hypotheses outlined during the afore-mentioned academic event, have, three years later, been confirmed. The project was encouraged by the fact that the three authors happened for some time to have cultivated an interest in the same topic, writing numerous articles published in leading scientific journals and monographs on the subject of the relationship between determining the tax base of a company in the tax context and the result as determined according to company rules from the balance sheet, the so-called dependence principle.

This foreword is, deliberately, instrumental to underline that, on one side, the scope of the research was not just on a national but also a European and non EU level and performed intentionally according to a method that is strictly comparative, as required of scholars nowadays, not only to know *tout court* the analogous experiences of other countries, but also to understand one's own national model, in compliance with the suggestion of the first chairman of the EATLP, Prof. Moessner who upheld, "A first step in developing coordinated tax systems within the European Union is therefore to develop a common language in taxation within Europe" J. Moessner, Association of European Tax Law Professors: A common Language in Taxation within Europe in EC Tax Review, 1999, p. 158.

As is well-known, the topic dealt with has been the focus of the European authorities for some time, given the relevance of company taxation and, consequently, the business income and the search for a harmonized model, an unavoidable objective if a true common or single market is to be achieved within a European and globalised economic system. It is no coincidence that even in a time of relative economic stagnation, the objective of harmonizing company tax has been prioritized on the agenda of the European Union Authorities.

What better opportunity for the aforementioned Authors, having independently concluded analyses on the topic with their results published in monographs, to perform a comparison and examine the results. Together with the contribution and support of the Department of Management of the University of Turin, the idea was further developed as a result of the initiative and persistence of Mario Grandinetti who wished to extend participation to other scholars from various European and non-EU countries, the all-important criterion for their participation being their research into the topic.

Each of the participants was asked not only to describe their own national model, but also to express their views according to the comparative method and, in particular, a logical order typical of the questionnaire, thus highlighting the theoretical assumptions, the reference models taken as a comparison and specifying the reasons and solutions for the doctrine and for the law.

The research topic dealt with in this book has always been the object of particular attention of legislators and scholars of tax law due to the importance of the interests at stake but, as stated above, for some years, interest on this topic has also involved scholars of related disciplines such as accounting and commercial law. As far as tax law is concerned, specific attention has been dedicated to this matter since the approval of the European ruling n. 1606/2002 concerning the consolidated and general balance sheet discipline according to the IAS/IFRS accounting principles and, lately, with Directive 2013/34/EU. To this must be added the fact that for some time the European Union has been focusing on the proposal for the Directive on the Common Consolidated Corporate Tax Base (CCCTB) that has recently been reproposed by the European Commission under Common Corporate Tax Base (the acronym 'CCTB'), the removal of one "C" means excluding the consolidation of the tax bases, which draws inspiration, for many elements of the future tax base, from what has been established in accounting.

The topic is interwoven with tax law because, as is highlighted by the various chapters in the collective volume, the prevalent model for determining the company's tax base is that of derivation or dependency on the result of the balance sheet. Furthermore, this aspect confirms (underlines) a prejudice in systematic tax theory, in other words this sector of the legal system is purported to be "second class", because as a rule and, as in this case, it adopts notions and concepts as pre-defined by other disciplines.

This foreword explains the logical sequence of the chapters in the book which are dealt with, first and foremost, by scholars in commercial law and business administration. The opening chapter of the book, written by Prof. Giovanni Strampelli and by Dr. Passador and dedicated to the legal aspects of accountancy harmonization in Europe and the future prospects (trends) for development, acts as a foreword for the subsequent reports and even for the specific part written by tax law scholars. This first chapter is followed by an investigation by Prof. Donatella Busso and Prof. Maurizio Cisi which is more strictly linked to accounting. The first of the two chapters investigates the peculiarities and differences between the main principles underpinning IAS/IFRS and the similar or different ones established by Directive 2013/34/EU, which have recently been implemented in the Member States of the European Union. The second chapter, which is in line with the first, furthers this investigation, concentrating on the individual balance sheet entries.

The book continues with the presentation of the individual national reports that cover most countries of the European Union, as well as federal tax systems such as those of Brazil and the United States.

Amongst the greatest merits ascribable to this research is, as previously mentioned, the application of the comparative method and, therefore, the opportunity to highlight the similarities and the differences between the various foreign models with an explanation of the underlying reasons for such differences. Apart from the in-depth examination of the individual scholars, the topic has also been studied by a comparatist, Prof. Marco Barassi, for the very purpose of seizing the potential offered by comparison which, as mentioned, goes well beyond a simple illustration of the national frameworks. Finally, the US and the Brazilian models provide a number of points for consideration *de jure condendo* linked to the European CCTB project and the distinctive nature of this model compared with that of north (and south) America. This analysis was conducted by Prof. Gianluigi Bizioli.

In conclusion, there is good reason to believe that the "*experiment*" has been a success and the merit goes to the person whose intuition has enabled the implications to be converted into interesting analyses with a result that will be of certain theoretic and scientific validity. Moreover, the result will also serve as a parameter for those who will be called to translate such results into regulatory requirements on both a European and national level.

Claudio Sacchetto
University of Turin

PART I   IAS/IFRS and the New Directive
2013/34/EU from the Commercial Law
Perspective

CHAPTER 1

The Unfinished Harmonization of the Accounting Law in the EU

Giovanni Strampelli & Maria Lucia Passador

§1.01   INTRODUCTION

"Accounting's Tower of Babel creates a severe barrier for cross-border business":[1] this is the first and foremost reason why the harmonization of the accounting law represents one of the most important, ambitious and worthy aims constantly pursued by the legislator in the field of company law. That prime purpose was initially furthered by accounting guidelines and also, at a later stage, by the adoption of International Accounting Standards (IAS)/International Financial Reporting Standards (IFRS) (Regulation (EC) No. 1606/2002 of the European Parliament and of the Council of July 19, 2002 on the application of international accounting standards). Furthermore, the European Legislator, according to Directives 2003/51/EC, 2001/65/EC and 2013/34/EU, reduced the sharp and striking differences among the Accounting Directives on the one hand and the IAS/IFRS principles on the other hand. Notwithstanding the clear developments in the European legislation, it cannot be denied that the true objective – which is complete accounting harmonization – has not been truly achieved yet. Regulation (EC) 1606/2002 and Directive 2013/34/EU grant considerable powers

---

1. B. Grossfeld, *Comparative Accounting*, in *Texas International Law Journal*, vol. 28, n. 2, 1993, 233 ff., at 236 and note 12. Accordingly, B.S. Thomas, *International Accounting and Reporting. Developments Leading to the Harmonization of Standards*, in *New York University, Journal of International Law and Politics*, vol. 15, n. 3, 1983, 517 ff., D. Chalmers, *Accounting for Europe*, in *Oxford Journal of Legal Studies*, vol. 19, n. 3, 1999, 517 ff. A fiscal perspective of accounting harmonization is adopted in S.D. Selbach, *The Harmonization of Corporate Taxation and Accounting Standards in the European Community and Their Interrelationship*, in *Connecticut Journal of International Law*, vol. 18, n. 2, 2003, 523 ff. and G. Leo, *European Accounting Harmonization: Achievements, Prospects and Tax Implications*, in *EC Tax Review*, vol. 1, n. 3, 1992, 178 ff.

to Member States and, consequently, wide diversities exist regarding the application of accounting rules in different countries. The differences between the sets of applicable accounting norms in each State result in a non-uniform functioning of the so-called *legal capital system*, provided for in Directive 2012/30/EU.

The essay proceeds as follows. First, sections §1.02, §1.03 and §1.04 will explain the sweeping and far-reaching changes in the EU accounting legislation. Second, section §1.05 will illustrate the strong effects of *fair value* and other valuation methods, which are alternatives to the historical cost method. Third, section §1.06 will address the problems arising from the complex interaction between *fair value accounting* (and the detection of unrealized gains) and the system of creditors' protection based on share capital. Finally, we will conclude by formulating some closing remarks.

§1.02   THE FIRST STEP OF THE EU ACCOUNTING LAW HARMONIZATION: THE FOURTH DIRECTIVE

As the European Economic Community (EEC) became increasingly important and influential, a growing need for a coherent regulatory framework was also felt with regard to the accounting law. Moreover, such a compelling need was expressed in Article 54, paragraph 3, letter g), of the 1957 Rome Treaty, based on the fact that coordination and harmonization among national disciplines[2] are essential to allow the application of the "right of establishment", in order to "reach an economic equal level playing field within the Community"[3] and, consequently, to gradually develop a common market.

The European legislator used legal instruments, mainly Directives and Regulations, to reach such goals, being perfectly aware that "harmonization does not necessarily mean uniformity": in other words, it is relevant in order to achieve financial information that is, as far as possible, equivalent and comparable although it is still not uncommon for Member States and/or for companies[4] to have options. While Directives bind only Member States to which they are addressed regarding the result to be

---

2. *"Financial accounting [...] is an important language of commerce. Like all languages, its effectiveness as a means of communication is aided by a precise definition of words and rules as to its structure. Moreover, users' costs may be reduced, and the value of the data for comparative purposes enhanced [...]"*, in P. THORELL & G. WHITTINGTON, *The Harmonization of Accounting within the EU. Problems, Perspectives and Strategies*, in *The European Accounting Review*, vol. 3, n. 2, 1994, 215-239, at 215.

3. A. HALLER, *Financial Accounting Developments in the European Union: Past Events and Future Prospects*, in *The European Accounting Review*, 2002, vol. 11, n. 1, 153-190, at 155. *See also* B. CARUSO, *Armonizzazione dei diritti e delle legislazioni della Comunità Europea*, in *Enc. Giur*, vol. II, Roma, 1993; K. VAN HULLE, *Harmonization of Accounting Standards. A View from the European Community*, in *Accounting in Europe*, 1992, vol. 1, n. 1, 161 ff., especially at 165 ff. and, for empirical considerations, L. CANIBANO & A. MORA, *Evaluating the Statistical Significance of de facto Accounting Harmonization: A Study of European Global Players*, in *European Accounting Review*, vol. 9, n. 3, 2000, 305-348.

4. K. VAN HULLE, *Harmonization of Accounting Standards. A View from the European Community*, in *Accounting in Europe*, vol. 1, n. 1, 1992, 161 ff., at 161, where the Author underlines the advantages and disadvantages of using directives as legal instruments for Member States in the implementation process.

achieved, leaving the national authorities to choose the most suitable forms and means, Regulations have general application and are binding and directly applicable in their entirety to all Member States. In other words, while Directives provide Member States with various options to reach the shared goal, Regulations are applied directly, without being subject to a peculiar *iter* in order to be recognized and adopted by national codes.

Even though the accounting directives initially aimed at reaching full comparability among European balance sheets, the regulation only led to a formal equivalence of the optional accounting norms.[5] Directive 78/660/EEC, also known as the Fourth Directive,[6] certainly provides relevant guidelines that Member States may use and it contains the *minimum* legal conditions to be applied by all EU countries.[7]

The regulation contained in the above-mentioned document allows national laws great freedom of choice in the national implementation of the provisions. National legislators may consider the application of more stringent or complete evaluation criteria more suitable to the needs of national companies. Indeed, Member States are allowed to choose from a vast number of options when deciding the most appropriate standards to be applied, defining the relevant measures to depict the situation of the company in the most consistent way. Even though, at first sight, such a flexible

---

5. Indeed, this consequence is due to the fact that directives *"are normative acts, in essence principle norms, suspected of a different application in the Member States [...] [which] amplify the interpretations given by each Member State [and] reducing the convergence degree of the national accounting norms"*. See E. HLACIUC, M. SOCOLIUC & D. MATES, *The IAS/IFRS Standards System between Harmonization and Deformity*, in *The Journal of the Faculty of Economics*, 2010, 868-874, at 868 and note 586, for the references in B.M. CRASBERG, *The Role and Future Plans of the International Accounting Standards Committee*, Quaderni di Finanza Consob, n. 31, 1998, at 20 and S. FORTUNATO, *Armonizzazione contabile fra sovranità e globalizzazione*, in *Riv. soc.*, 1999, 329.
6. Given such a general introduction on the topic, from this point on, a narrower focus will shift towards annual accounts, due to their pivotal role within corporate law. Needless to say, a clearly intelligible annual account provides considerable insights into the actual operating results and allows the true extent of the assets of a company to be appreciated. If we were asked to cite a leading example to prove such a statement, it would be worth recalling that, prior to the corporate law reform, a reading of annual accounts without considering the notes to financial statements might have led to an incomplete protection of minority shareholders (e.g., in the event of a complete lack of dividend payments) resulting from an improper application of fiscal norms. *See*, on the topic, at a national level, M. TIEGHI, *Il bilancio d'esercizio dopo la riforma del diritto societario*, Bologna, 2004 and OIC, *I principali effetti della riforma del diritto societario sulla redazione del bilancio di esercizio*, Milan, 2004, while, at an international level, R.G. RAJAN & L. ZINGALES, *The Influence of the Financial Revolution on the Nature of Firms*, in *The American Economic Review*, 2001, 206 ff.
7. *"The main features of the Fourth Directive requirements are as follows: 1 Format rules for the balance sheet (Articles 9 and 10) and the profit and loss account (Articles 23-26). [...] 2 Disclosure requirements (Article 43) which represent an averaging of existing practice within EU member countries, with options where there is a possibility of serious conflict. 3 Valuation rules (Articles 31-42) based upon historical cost but with alternative rules allowing current values. [...] 4 The true and fair view (Article 2) prevails over specific provisions, where [exceptional] circumstances justify it. [...] This is, of course, inevitable, if member countries are to work towards a common system derived from their existing practices. It does however, raise the possibility that, by advocating the lowest common denominator of current practice with options where no common denominator could be found, the Fourth Directive was not increasing harmonization at all, but simply window-dressing existing practice"*, in P. THORELL & G. WHITTINGTON, *The Harmonization*, at 218 f.

disposition may appear to be inconsistent with the mission assigned to – and carried out by – the Fourth Directive, in the light of the considerable difficulties and obstacles that Member States had and still have to face in order to merge their national legal systems with the European one, the prescribed pliancy of the regulation fulfills the stated intention to reconcile the various existing positions as much as possible, by converting practical divergences into concrete legislative options.

The Fourth Directive introduced vital principles in the field of accounting, such as "clarity" and "true and fair" representation (or an *image fidèle* or *ein den tatsächlichen Verhältnissen entsprechendes Bild*)[8] of the economic and financial position of companies: key rules to be favored over other norms. In addition, it expressed postulates of indisputable importance (Article 31), among which it is worth mentioning the principle of prudence (or *Imparität Prinzip*)[9] and of *going concern*; the unitary structure of the documents connected to the financial valuation (balance sheets, income statements and integrative notes), whose contents are precisely set out (albeit with several options); the immutability of valuation criteria used to elaborate them yearly (also "consistency principle"); the separate assessment of each budget item (or *Einzelbewertungsprinzip*) and the charge of incomes and expenses in close connection with their relative period, irrespective of the date of their collection or payment (or *Realisation Prinzip*).

Both English connotations, such as a greater emphasis on the principles of truthfulness and competence (the "matching principle"), as well as German ones, in the light of several references to the principle of prudence, are taken into account in the final version of the Directive. In fact, accounting entries represent a guarantee to protect the rights of third parties, as proven by accounts on dividends, profits gained, foreseeable risks and eventual future losses. In view of these considerations, it seems clear that the Directive is not characterized by revolutionary technical innovations, as it simply reiterates some pre-existing principles of good accounting. Nevertheless, it takes a step forward in terms of advertising and disclosure, as well as strongly

---

8. For a comparative linguistic analysis, *see* S. AISBITT & C. NOBES, *The True and Fair View Requirement in Recent National Implementations*, in *Accounting and Business Research*, vol. 31, n. 2, 2001, 83-90, in particular Table 1, *Signifiers for a true and fair view*, and Appendix 3.

9. As to prudence, there is no doubt that the negotiators of the Fourth Directive considered it as an accounting principle and wanted to place it in a pre-eminent position, due also to the close relationship between accounting and taxation in most Member States and to protect creditors. "*There can be no doubt that the prudence concept in the Fourth Directive is an important valuation principle which was intended to play a key role. This was a logical consequence from the situation that existed in most Member States prior to the adoption of the directive. The different status of the prudence principle as opposed to the other valuation principles results already from the fact that it is the only valuation principle which is defined in the directive*", as stated in K. VAN HULLE, *Prudence: A Principle or an Attitude?*, in *The European Accounting Review*, vol. 5, n. 2, 1996, 375-382, at 375 and 381. The paper also makes reference to: COMMISSION OF THE EUROPEAN COMMUNITIES, *Explanatory Memorandum to the 1971 Proposal for a Fourth Council Directive on Company Law*, *Bulletin of the European Communities*, Supplement 7/71, November 10, 1971, 35-67; COMMISSION OF THE EUROPEAN COMMUNITIES, *Explanatory Memorandum to the 1974 Amended Proposal for a Fourth Council Directive on Company Law*, *Bulletin of the European Communities*, Supplement 6/74, February 26, 1974, 5-9; EUROPEAN COMMISSION, *Communication on Accounting Harmonisation: A New Strategy vis-a-vis International Harmonisation*, 1995, Brussels, COM 95(508).

contributing towards a significant growth in a genuine and shared European culture. It is significant that this drafting technique does not represent a mere transposition or expansion of one given national system, but rather a real synthesis of prevalent national approaches.

Unfortunately, even if the deadline for the transposition of the Fourth Directive was originally set for December 31, 1981, several countries – *inter alia*, Italy – waited more than a few years, due to their economic contexts, before transposing the Fourth Directive, through the enactment of Legislative Decree No. 127/1991, by which the Seventh Directive was also transposed.

§1.03   THE FOLLOWING STEPS: DIRECTIVE 2003/51/EC AND DIRECTIVE 2013/34/EU

In the following years, the Fourth Directive[10] underwent a series of additions and modifications.

A particularly relevant innovation introduced by Directive 2001/65/EC was the possibility for Member States to provide all companies (or only certain types) with the chance to assess financial instruments according to the method of fair value or a different method.[11] In particular, the Directive required the inclusion of a specific section ("7-*bis*"), in which the use of such a method of valuation is specifically regulated, indicating the financial instruments to which it is applicable, the rules determining the fair value and the classification in the balance sheet of eventual changes which might occur to the originally determined amount. The option to allow Member States to opt for drafting a Note in an abbreviated form for small and medium enterprises (SMEs) represented another relevant innovation. Lastly, the 2001 Directive integrated the content of the Note and the Report on the Management to mould them

---

10. Apart from these directives, which specifically relate to accounting, *"there are a number which relate to the background of accounting and the context in which it is carried out. Notable amongst these are the Eighth Directive on the qualifications of auditors and several directives in the area of financial market regulation. The latter are concerned with the access of securities to the market. They include directives on the co-ordination of listing requirements (79/279), the public offering of securities (80/390) (listing prospectuses), interim reports (82/121) and public offering prospectuses (89/298). They demonstrate that the EU's accounting requirements are part of a broader system of harmonization of financial markets and institutions"*, in P. Thorell & G. Whittington, *The Harmonization*, at 221.

11. *See Consideranda 6-9*, Directive 2001/65/EC: *"(6) The dynamic nature of international financial markets has resulted in the widespread use of not only traditional primary financial instruments such as shares and bonds, but also various forms of derivative financial instruments such as futures, options, forward contracts and swaps. (7) Leading accounting standard setters in the world are moving away from the historical cost model for the valuation of these financial instruments towards a model of fair value accounting. (8) The Communication of the Commission on Accounting harmonisation: a new strategy vis-à-vis international harmonisation called for the European Union to work to maintain consistency between Community accounting directives and developments in international accounting standard setting, in particular within the International Accounting Standards Committee (IASC). (9) In order to maintain such consistency between internationally recognised accounting standards and Directives 78/660/EEC, 83/349/EEC and 86/635/EEC, it is necessary to amend these Directives in order to allow for certain financial assets and liabilities to be valued at fair value. This will enable European companies to report in conformity with current international developments".*

to the new provisions on the valuation of financial instruments. The discipline of the valuation of financial instruments according to the fair value was also made potentially applicable to consolidated financial statements. Over the years, amendments to the Fourth Directive introduced substantial changes within a process of accounting modernization,[12] such as the possibility for Member States to require or to permit the elaboration of models based on fair value with regard to the accounting of commodities, financial instrument derivatives, real estate investments and non-agricultural products.

Almost a decade later, the Fourth Directive was amended by Directive 2003/51/EC. The main changes made to the Fourth Directive were: (i) the option that Member States have to authorize (or even prescribe) the inclusion of additional sheets among the annual accounts; (ii) the possibility of adopting a Report and Account which differs compared to the financial statements set out in Articles 9-10 and to the income statements mentioned in Articles 23-26; (iii) the chance of valuating specified categories of assets other than financial instruments, at amounts determined by reference to fair value (Article 42e), limiting the authorization to consolidated financial statements and allowing eventual variations in terms of values which should be registered within the annual accounts. In addition, should an asset be valued according to such a rule, Member States may permit or require a change in the value to be included in the profit and loss account in respect of all companies or any classes of company (Article 42f); (iv) the request for clear information on the content of the Report on Auditing (Article 51); (v) the request for extra information, needed to prepare the Report on the Management according to the size and complexity of the business, using financial and/or non-financial indicators (with the only exception of SMEs, which can be exempted from mentioning non-financial information), as well as a balanced and comprehensive analysis of the *status* of the corporation and (vi) the obligation of Member States to impede companies, which are admitted to trading on a regulated market, from taking advantage of the exemptions provided together Articles 11, 27, 46, 47 and 51 (respectively regarding SMEs, the Report on the Management, advertising and the Report on Auditing) (Article 53a).

In July 2007, the European Commission issued a Communication on the need to elaborate a simplified business regulation in the area of company law, accounting and auditing, in which questions about the need to reduce administrative burdens, especially for SMEs, and about the adequacy of the current regulatory systems in relation to the peculiar structure of the market were expressed. The Commission concretely identified measures for the simplification of the procedures required for SMEs, calling for their introduction within Member States. As a consequence, it suggested several steps to be taken:

– extending of the limits for a company to be included in a different category, according to its size. According to the Fourth and Seventh Directive, it may

---

12. *See* both L. De Angelis, *Quale "modernizzazione" per il diritto contabile italiano?*, in Aa.Vv., *Studi in onore di Umberto Belviso*, Bari, vol. I, 389 ff. and in *Giur. comm.*, vol. 37, n. 4, 561 ff., in particular, para. 6 and S. Fortunato, *La modernizzazione delle direttive contabili e i principi contabili internazionali (IAS/IFRS)*, in *Soc.*, 2006, 1070 ff.

happen if limits are exceeded for two consecutive years, without paying attention to the current economic cycles of small enterprises and the fact that they may require more than two years to consolidate their growth;

- creating of a category among corporations, labeled "Microentities", including the companies which could be exempted from the European accounting Directive[13] since the obligations raised under the Fourth Directive would be particularly burdensome to them due to the uneasy balance between benefits and costs incurred;
- introducing a new possibility for some SMEs: the extension of the regime applicable to "Small entities" to include them too;
- reducing the obligations on the publication of financial statements for SMEs. According to the Commission, these corporations often deal with a small group of stakeholders who can gain easy and direct access to financial statements by requesting them from the company itself.

On the grounds of such a Communication, a lengthy review process of the Directives was undertaken and two Consultation papers were prepared. These steps aimed at highlighting different issues related to the Accounting Directives, at profitable discussions with stakeholders and at simplifying the context in which businesses operate in the fields of company law, accounting and auditing, confirming the intention of the EU legislator to reduce the administrative burden imposed on EU businesses. As to the most relevant financial statement, two major discussions are worth recalling. On the one hand, the proposal of the European Commission to reduce the number of documents available for the balance sheet and income statement compared to the options envisaged by the Fourth Directive is welcomed by the majority of respondents to the Consultation. On the other hand, the Commission proposed to adapt the contents of the supplementary note to the differences in size of the companies, as well as to align the information required to that requested by IFRS.

In the light of the results of the two Consultations, the European Commission published a legislative proposal. It consisted of the new Directive and a document ("Impact Assessment"), summarizing the previously raised issues and highlighting the expected impact deriving from the implementation of the new European legislation. *Inter alia*, such an impact might entail an enhanced clarity and comparability of financial statements, especially in comparison with international and widely-held corporations; a simplification of legislation and a significant cost reduction, especially with regard to companies of minor size; a protection of the interests of creditors, shareholders and other third parties through the maintenance of a *minimum* level of financial information. In addition, it should also be highlighted that numerous contributions of the doctrine expressed doubts on the adequacy of the contents of the text under consultation, compared to the objectives pursued by the European legislator.

---

13. S. CEUSTERMANS & D. BREESCH, *Financial Reporting Regulation: Valuable or Burdensome? An Exploratory Test-Case for Microentities*, in *European Financial Reporting Research Group (EU-FIN)*, Prague, September 6, 2012.

On June 26, 2013, the new Directive 2013/34/EU on financial statements issued consolidated financial statements and related reports of certain types of companies,[14] amending Directive 2006/43/EC and repealing the Fourth (and Seventh) Directive. It aimed at giving *"a coherent response to the shortcomings of the internal market [through] a sustainable and inclusive growth model, [modernizing the existing] legislative framework in order to arrive at a balanced policy sustaining the demand for environmentally friendly, socially responsible and innovative goods and services, provide contracting authorities with simpler and more flexible procedures, and give SMEs easier access".*[15] In comparison with the 2011 proposal, its text highlights significant amendments[16] suggested by an in-depth analysis conducted by the European Council and European Parliament as well as from the systematic dialogue among institutions to draw up shared dispositions.[17] The result of the *iter* described above is a newly structured Directive, providing the operators in the field with a set of rules that offers new options to Member States and showing the utmost care, as well as a protective attitude, for the necessities of SMEs, which is also evident from the "bottom-up" perspective emerging from it.

Its undeniable relevance is derived from the indisputable fact that the 2013 Directive merges dispositions applicable to financial statements, on the one hand, and governing consolidated financial statements, on the other hand. Its initial fifty-eight "Whereas", in which the scope of the new rules and the choices made in the subsequent Articles are clarified, are absolutely essential for a full understanding of its principal parts. The main issues debated therein concern: the criterion of evaluation of alternative fixed assets based on revaluated amounts, the alternative criterion based on fair value, the provisions applicable to income statements, notes, reports and financial statements, the rules applicable to the publication of documents and to the promotion of transparency in payments to governments (which is particularly awkward for extractive industries and logging of primary forests), and the dispositions on exemptions.

Beneficiaries of Directive 2013/34/EU are grouped on the basis of both quantitative data reported under assets and of the average number of employees, distinguishing between individual businesses and business realities which are part of a group. The identification of these clusters intends to identify the beneficiaries of the simplification of administrative requirements in terms of the preparation and publication of the financial statements. In this regard, Article 3 defines the quantitative parameters to distinguish them, in the case of individual companies, microenterprises and SMEs, while, in the case of groups, small groups are separated from medium-sized groups and

---

14. *See* generally H. BECKMAN, *The New EU-Directive on Annual and Consolidated Financial Statements and Related Management Reports*, in *European Company Law*, 2013, 199-212.
15. EUROPEAN COMMISSION, *Twelve Projects for the 2012 Single Market: Together for New Growth*, April 13, 2011, Document IP/11/469.
16. On the inconsistencies between the Commission's Proposal and the Accounting Directive, *see* C. THOLE, *Die Reform der Europäischen Insolvenzverordnung. Zentrale Aspekte des Kommissionsvorschlags und offene Fragen*, in *Zeitschrift für europäisches Privatrecht*, 2014, 39-76, at 68.
17. M. VENUTI, *The Proposal For Updating The EU Accounting Directives: The Adequacy of The Proposal Versus The Legislative Targets*, Financial Reporting 41-2012, 65 ff.

large ones. Articles 4 and 6 report the general principles for preparing the financial statements. The former states the principle of "clarity", "truth" and "fairness" in drafting prospectuses and documents, underlining the need for consistency and for regulating any opportunistic behavior, therefore ensuring a certain degree of reliability of the values mentioned in the accounting statements. The latter, instead, presents additional principles, such as the principle of "prudence", "continuity" in a "going concern" perspective, "competence", "separate valuation of heterogeneous elements", "consistent application of accounting policies" and "materiality". In order to ensure compliance with the postulates of the financial statements and to facilitate stakeholders inside and outside the company in reading and comparing balance sheets and the financial income of domestic enterprises, the new Directive insists on the non-modifiability of the structure of income statements and balance sheets. Member States may even require further in-depth reports (Article 4, paragraph 1, second sentence), as well as additional information (Article 4, paragraphs 5-6), for SMEs.

As to the valuation of financial statement items, the recent Directive claims that it should primarily be based on the purchase price or on the cost of production (Article 6, paragraph 1, letter i). Special attention is even devoted to fixed assets and financial instruments (Articles 7 and 8, where some exceptions to the general principles are set out).

In some cases, it is possible to use criteria that are alternative to the historical cost method.

In respect of all undertakings or any classes of undertaking, Member States may also permit or require the measurement of fixed assets at revalued amounts. In this case, the difference between measurement on a purchase price or production cost basis on the one hand and measurement on a revaluation basis on the other hand, shall be entered in the balance sheet in the non-distributable revaluation, either directly or indirectly, under capital and reserves. Such a reserve, adjusted in case of need on the basis of the revalued amount, may be capitalized and shall be reduced where the amounts transferred to it are no longer necessary for the implementation of the revaluation basis of accounting.

Furthermore, Member States shall permit or require, in respect of all undertakings or any classes of undertaking, the measurement of financial instruments, including derivative financial instruments (as commodity-based contracts), at fair value; and the measurement of specified categories of assets other than financial instruments at amounts determined by reference to it.[18] Such a measurement shall not apply in some cases, as stated in Article 8, section 4. The fair value shall be determined by reference to the *Market Value*, according to the value detected by the prices on active markets, characterized by transactions that are easily and regularly available to operators. In the

---

18. This change in the valuation also occurred, with the same kind of problems, in the Unites States of America, as shown in FASB, *Statement No. 157 "Fair Value Measurements"*, September 2006, available at http://www.fasb.org. *See also* R.C. ADKERSON, *Discussion of DAAM: The Demand for Alternative Accounting*, in *Journal of Accounting Research*, 1978, 31 ff. and L. REVSINE, *Replacement Cost Accounting*, Englewood Cliff, 1973.

absence of active markets, it is necessary to refer to normal transactions or, possibly to current market values related to similar activities or, alternatively, even to the technique of the present value of cash flows generated by the element under valuation.

Such different criteria lead to different measurements of the income and assets, the fairness of which is evaluated in terms of concrete goals that corporate and legal science are determined to achieve.[19]

§1.04   A DIFFERENT STRATEGY OF (INCOMPLETE) HARMONIZATION OF ACCOUNTING LAW IN EUROPE: THE INTRODUCTION OF IAS/IFRS

The accounting system based on the above-mentioned Directives was not considered appropriate by the European Commission since it did not meet the requirements linked to the increasing integration of financial markets at an international level.

Since 2000, following the Lisbon European Council, the European Commission has shown a remarkable improvement in the comparability of accounts, representing favorable preconditions for creating a single market for financial services within the EU.[20] The creation of a unique market was imposed by globalization and the development of new information technologies (mainly through electronic trading platforms) that allowed operators to act globally, thanks especially to a continual and standardized flow of information. Moreover, relevant, timely, reliable and comparable information assumes a leading role in the protection of investors' interests, creditors and other stakeholders, as well as in ensuring that all operators act on a level playing field, under equal conditions.[21]

Consistent with this objective, the European Commission introduced the use of IAS/IFRS in the accounting discipline through the European Regulation (EC) 1606/2002.

The Commission set up the endorsement of IAS/IFRS, structuring it on a double – political and technical – level, through the establishment of two separate organs: The

---

19. S. Fortunato, *Dal costo storico al* "fair value": *al di là della rivoluzione contabile*, in *Riv. soc.*, 2007, I, 941 ff. and *Ibid.*, *Le valutazioni per il bilancio*, in *Giur. comm.*, 2015, I, 42 ff.
20. *See* Recital 4 of the *Regulation (EC) No 1606/2002 of the European Parliament and of the Council of 19 July 2002 on the application of international accounting standards,* according to which "[t]*he reporting requirements set out in these Directives cannot ensure the high level of transparency and comparability of financial reporting from all publicly traded Community companies which is a necessary condition for building an integrated capital market which operates effectively, smoothly and efficiently. It is therefore necessary to supplement the legal framework applicable to publicly traded companies*". G. Strampelli, *Distribuzioni ai soci e tutela dei creditori. L'effetto degli IAS/IFRS*, Torino, 2009, 81 ff.
21. In this sense, *see Recital 4* of Regulation (EC) 1606/2002, stating that the introduction of IAS/IFRS (at least as to the consolidated financial statements of listed companies) "*aims at contributing to the efficient and cost-effective functioning of the capital market. The protection of investors and the maintenance of confidence in the financial markets is also an important aspect of the completion of the internal market in this area. This Regulation reinforces the freedom of movement of capital in the internal market and helps to enable Community companies to compete on an equal footing for financial resources available in the Community capital markets, as well as in world capital markets*".

Accounting Regulatory Committee (ARC), in charge of judging the Commission's proposals on the adoption of IAS, and the *European Financial Reporting Advisory Group* (EFRAG), which is responsible for providing the Commission with technical support in the IAS adoption procedure. According to Article 3 of Regulation (EC) No. 1606/2002, IAS/IFRS principles can be adopted only if they are fully consistent with the objective of a "true and fair view" (already mentioned in Recital 9) and they "meet the criteria of understandability, relevance, reliability and comparability required of the financial information needed for making economic decisions and assessing the stewardship of management" (paragraph 3, second point).

At the outcome of the procedure, the principles issued by the International Accounting Standards Board (IASB) were accepted by the European Commission through Regulation (EC) No. 1725/2003 and its subsequent amendments,[22] therefore assuming force of law. More precisely, the IAS/IFRS, once endorsed through Regulation, are directly applicable in the Member States and prevail over any national rule that may conflict with them. Therefore, national rules relating to annual accounts and consolidated financial statements cannot prevent the full and correct application of the IAS/IFRS.

Nevertheless, the adoption of IAS/IFRS did not guarantee the harmonization of European accounting law.[23] Regulation (EC) 1606/2002 requires the consolidated financial statements of listed companies only to be drawn up according to IAS/IFRS. As to the individual accounts of listed companies and to the individual and consolidated financial statements of all other companies, Member States might opt for imposing or, rather, permitting the use of IAS/IFRS. This decision is consistent with the European Commission's aim: fostering the integration of European financial markets. In fact, the decisions of investors are normally based on consolidated financial statements, since the information offered in them is deemed more important than that contained in the individual financial statements of a corporation. The options granted to Member States regarding the application of IAS/IFRS to individual accounts of listed companies and to the individual and consolidated financial statements of all other companies have led to their non-uniform application in the EU. Only a limited number of Member States have provided listed and unlisted companies with the possibility or the obligation to draw up

---

22. Up to now, the European Commission has adopted all the IAS/IFRS principles, with the sole exclusion of IFRS 9 on the assessment of financial instruments. Following the amendments made by the IASB to IFRS 9, however, even this standard is currently being implemented. The latest steps in the endorsement process of the most recent IAS/IFRS are available at http://www .efrag.org, while a full list of the Community regulations adopted to date for the implementation of the IAS/IFRS is available at http://ec.europa.eu/finance/accounting/legal_framework/ regulations_adopting_ias/original_text_en.htm.
23. See N. VÉRON & G.B. WOLFF, *Capital Markets Union: A Vision for the Long Term*, Bruegel Policy Contribution, presented to informal ECOFIN, 2015/05, available at http://www.bruegel.org, at 12. The Authors observe that "*the EU adoption of International Financial Reporting Standards (IFRS), decided in 2002 and implemented in 2005-06, was a huge step in this direction, but more needs to be done. There remain wide differences between member states in IFRS implementation and enforcement and in other aspects of financial disclosure. Two main reforms should be considered in this area*".

(individual and/or consolidated) financial statements in accordance with the newly introduced principles.[24] This fact makes the comparison of all individual financial statements of companies located in different Member States particularly difficult,[25] and it affects the application of a system of creditors' protection based on the notion of share capital as provided for in Directive 2012/30/EU. According to the so-called legal capital system, individual annual accounts constitute the real ground for the determination of distributable income, for the assessment of capital losses and for the purchase of treasury shares or the granting of financial assistance.[26]

As a partial result of the recent financial crisis, in the last few years, the European Commission has launched several initiatives to assess the adequacy of IAS/IFRS principles and the arrangements regarding their transposition into EU legislation. In March 2013, the European Commission appointed Philippe Maystadt to examine the best ways to strengthen the contribution of the EU to their development and to improve governance bodies contributing to the process of implementing them. In addition, on June 18, 2015, the European Commission published a *Report on the Evaluation of Regulation (EC) No. 1606/2002*, a document that showed a positive assessment of both the IAS Regulation and the effects produced by its norms.

Although in its assessment of the IAS Regulation, the European Commission considered extending the scope of the mandatory application of IAS/IFRS, notwithstanding the issues arising from the interaction of the latter with the legal capital system, no legislative changes occurred. According to the European Commission:

> [c]onsultations showed that a majority of stakeholders regarded the options for national governments as appropriate. The fact that Member States have a great diversity in their use of options was seen by some as proof that the system works well and does not need to be changed. It may also be that, due to the diversity of legal frameworks in the EU, it would be difficult to achieve more consistency.[27]

In view of the creation of a Capital Markets Union, however, the European Commission ruled that the application of IAS/IFRS principles might have turned out to

---

24. See *Overview of the use of options provided in the IAS Regulation (1606/2002) in the EU* (December 2013 version) drawn up by the European Commission, available at http://ec.europa .eu/internal_market/accounting/docs/legal_framework/20140718-ias-useofoptions_en.pdf.
25. Regulation (EC) No. 1606/2002 favored the comparison among consolidated financial statements of listed companies domiciled in various Member States. See, on the topic, EUROPEAN COMMISSION, *Report on the evaluation of Regulation (EC) No. 1606/2002 (the IAS Regulation)*, published on June 18, 2015, available at http://ec.europa.eu/finance/accounting/docs/ias-evaluation/20150618-report_en.pdf.
26. EUROPEAN COMMISSION, *Report on the evaluation of Regulation (EC) No. 1606/2002 (the IAS Regulation)*, at 7: "[a]*lthough IFRS-based financial information is the starting point for much prudential regulation, the IASB does not include prudential supervisors or regulators on its list of users. Nevertheless, there is a need to ensure that financial information is fit for that purpose whilst recognising that prudential regulators can demand other information to meet their different objectives*".
27. See the Commission Staff Working Document concerning the Report Evaluation of Regulation (EC) No. 1606/2002, dated July 19, 2002 on the application of International Accounting Standards, available at http://eur-lex.europa.eu/legal-content/EN/TXT/PDF/?uri = CELEX:520 15SC0120&from = EN, at 23.

be too burdensome for small and medium-sized enterprises (SMEs). So, in order to facilitate their access to capital markets, according to the Commission:

> the development of a simplified, common, and high quality accounting standard tailored to the companies listed on certain trading venues could be a step forward in terms of transparency and comparability, and if applied proportionally, could help those companies seeking cross-border investors to be more attractive to them.[28]

§1.05   THE ADOPTION OF *FAIR VALUE* AND THE RECOGNITION OF UNREALIZED PROFITS: FROM REALIZED TO "OVERALL" INCOME

The IAS/IFRS assign a merely informative role to annual accounts, without considering the previously established objectives of the annual determination of the distributable income and without attributing to them a wider organizational relief (compared to the one that financial statements assume), while acting as "legal ground" for shareholders' decisions concerning the reduction of capital for losses, the increase of share capital by capitalization of reserves, the share buyback or the granting of financial assistance. The purpose of the "IAS/IFRS financial statements" is only to provide information that is relevant to investors' choices, as financial statements meeting the need for information are considered appropriate for handling the needs of all users.[29]

In line with such objectives, annual accounts complying with IAS/IFRS principles shall represent the actual value of the entire business (and, therefore, the shares representing the entire share capital) and an income expressing the "overall" result for the reference period. This period should also take into account the not yet realized income components notwithstanding the fact that they are derived from the variations in the value of the assets.

In line with the tasks assigned to annual accounts, IAS/IFRS require the (optional or mandatory, depending on the various asset classes) use of fair value as a criterion of evaluation. Its definition, according to the words used in the various IAS/IFRS principles, is represented by the amount for which an asset could be exchanged, or a liability settled, between knowledgeable, willing parties in an arm's length transaction. Therefore, compared to the historical cost, it allows a representation of the actual value of these elements that are included in the company's assets.

As it constitutes an approximation of the current value of the assets – determined by assuming the market value of the property or, if the assets are not traded on an active market or, at least in a significant number of transactions, the market value of similar assets as a reference – adjusted fair value takes all differences with respect to

---

28. European Commission, *Green Paper. Building a Capital Markets Union*, COM(2015) 63 final, available at http://eur-lex.europa.eu/legal-content/EN/TXT/PDF/?uri=COM:2015:63:FIN&from=EN.
29. E. Ferran, *The Place for Creditor Protection on the Agenda for Modernisation of Company Law in the European Union, ECGI Law Working Paper n. 51/2005*, 2005, available at http://www.ecgi.org, 18 ff.

asset valuation into account. Finally, should it not be possible to determine the fair value based on the market value, it will be necessary to use alternative valuation techniques and models.

Regardless of the fact that it is determined referring to market values or to alternative valuation techniques, the use of fair value implies the recognition of values which are only estimated and whose realization and conversion into cash receipts is only probable (and unsure).

Despite the accounting convention based on the historical cost method, where any revaluation compared to book value is only permitted in limited (previously considered) cases, the fair value criterion provides that, at the end of each financial year, the assets of the company are reassessed in order to adjust the book value to fair value: if the latter have increased during the year, it will lead to unrealized capital gains, corresponding to the amount of the revaluation itself. The adoption of the fair value method, rather than that of historical cost, clearly marks the overcoming of the realization principle, since it permits the recognition of unrealized gains.[30]

The trend towards the recognition of unrealized profits in annual accounts and the representation of the so-called overall income (including gains and losses both realized and unrealized) not only relates to the drafting of financial statements in accordance with the IAS/IFRS principles. As previously affirmed,[31] Directive 2013/34/EU permits Member States to opt for requiring or for allowing the assessment of evaluation criteria that are alternative to those of historical cost, in order to make accounting information relevant.[32] While, on the one hand, Article 7 – although in the absence of an express reference to the notion of fair value – allows for the evaluation of fair assets on the ground of alternative measurement techniques which are substantially identical to the fair value technique, on the other hand, Article 8 offers the chance to evaluate certain classes of assets and, in particular, the financial instruments at fair value.

§1.06   THE RECOGNITION OF UNREALIZED GAINS AND THE DECLINING HARMONIZATION OF THE CREDITORS' PROTECTION SYSTEM BASED ON LEGAL CAPITAL

Member States are granted the possibility to require or to allow the evaluation of certain classes of assets at fair value or, alternatively, at a revalued amount. Such an option, granted by Directive 2013/34/EU, represents an adjustment of the Directive on the IAS/IFRS, without leading to an effective harmonization between these two accounting regimes.

---

30. A. MOXTER, *Gewinnrealisierung nach den IAS/IFRS: Erosion des HGB-Realisationsprinzip*, in *ZVgIRWiss*, 2004, at 279; J. BAETGE, *Fair Value-Accounting versus Realisations- Imparitäts- und Vorsichtsprinzips*, in *Rechnungswesen*, 2003, at 230 ff.
31. *See* section §1.03.
32. According to *considerandum* n. 18 of Directive 2013/34/EU, *"Member States should be allowed to permit or require undertakings to revalue fixed assets in order that more relevant information may be provided to the users of financial statements"*.

First, the Directive only offers an option which is not uniformly used by Member States. For instance, the Italian Legislative Decree 139/2015 (which transposed Directive 2013/34/EU) requires the measurement of derivative financial instruments at fair value, but it does not allow the adoption of alternative criteria to the historical cost in order to valuate other asset classes. Second, the scope of both fair value and revalued amount does not match the requirements of the IAS/IFRS, as national legislators may limit the application of the criteria set out in Directive 2013/34/EU (Articles 7 and 8) only to defined categories of activities.

The fair value method and the recognition of unrealized profits technique have a considerable impact on the organizational function of annual accounts in the EU where financial statements represent the basis of the entire legal capital system, as provided for in Directive 2012/30/EU. The recognition of unrealized profits arising from the use of fair value or from the adoption of criteria that are alternative to the historical cost required under Article 7, affects some relevant issues: the determination of profits, the detection of capital losses and the composition of equity which is deemed to be relevant for other operations, such as the purchase of treasury shares.

The interaction between the accounting discipline and the legal capital system is slightly different according to Directive 2013/34/EU and IAS/IFRS. In fact, the latter do not legally regulate distributable profits, with the only exception of expressed prohibitions stated in national legislations. Article 7 of Directive 2013/34/EU, instead, states that the *"difference between measurement on a purchase price or production cost basis and measurement on a revaluation basis shall be entered in the balance sheet in the revaluation reserve under 'Capital and reserves'"* and, as a consequence, gains raised from revaluation cannot be distributed until finally realized. Furthermore, Article 8 provides that increases and decreases in the fair value of financial instruments shall be included in the profit and loss account, with rare exceptions, and that Member States may permit or require a change in the value of an available for sale financial asset, other than a derivative financial instrument, to be included directly in the fair value reserve. In conclusion, it is evident that Directive 2013/34/EU, on the one hand, and IAS/IFRS principles, on the other hand, regulate the treatment of gains and revaluation losses differently.

Due to such a difference, the functioning of the legal capital rule varies in accordance with the fact that financial statements are prepared according to IAS/IFRS principles or on the basis of national rules aligned with Directive 2013/34/EU. Member States may also independently adjust the treatment of unrealized gains resulting from annual accounts, in order to limit their effects on the functioning of the legal capital system.

When the evaluation criteria that have been used result in the recognition of unrealized profits, Member States are obliged to dictate the necessary provisions needed in order to make financial statements suitable to determine distributable profits and, from a wider perspective, the function of capital maintenance.[33] More precisely,

---

33. D. Cairns, *Applying International Accounting Standards*, London, 1999, at 107.

national legislators are required to introduce measures which are needed to "neutral-ize" unrealized gains (and losses) derived from valuation methods and to ensure that the annual account and the net equity resulting from annual accounts represent the suitable basis for the legal capital system.[34]

In 2008, the European Commission commissioned a study[35] from the German branch of KPMG that showed the different regimes of unrealized gains provided by Member States requiring or providing for the preparation of financial statements in accordance with IAS/IFRS principles. Some Member States (including Italy) set up specific limits on the distribution of unrealized gains derived from the fair value while others do not dictate any provision on this matter and, consequently, allow the distribution of unrealized profits. This different approach results in a non-uniform functioning of the legal capital system in Member States and in a resulting divergence in the treatment of companies located in different nations.

§1.07   CONCLUDING REMARKS

The adoption of IAS/IFRS principles with Regulation (EC) 1606/2002 and the Account-ing Directives have not led to an effective harmonization of accounting rules in the EU, with the sole exception of the consolidated financial statements of listed companies (which must be prepared in accordance with the IAS/IFRS). The numerous choices granted to Member States under the IAS/IFRS Regulation and Directive 2013/34/EU give rise to significant differences in the criteria to be used in the preparation of financial statements in Member States. Such differences also lead to a non-uniform application of the system of creditors' protection based on share capital, required by Directive 2012/30/EU that considers financial statements as a baseline.

In order to achieve harmonization of accounting rules in the EU, it does not seem possible to simply eliminate the currently provided power of choice. In particular, it would not be appropriate to extend the scope of the mandatory application of IAS/IFRS principles. In fact, such a choice might impose excessive burdens on minor corpora-tions, given the complexity of IAS/IFRS.[36] The proposal made by the European Commission in this regard seems appropriate: a simplified (if compared to that of IAS/IFRS) and qualitatively higher bookkeeping system could be elaborated for minor listed companies and for those intending to go public in specific venues (such as multilateral trading facilities – MTF).[37] An incentive towards accounting harmoniza-tion could be derived from a project for a Common Consolidated Corporate Tax Base

---

34. A similar problem also arises in relation to the determination of the taxable income. In fact, in that field too, legislators of Member States have to establish the *criteria* for the assessment of the relevant income for tax purposes.
35. KPMG Deutsche Treunhand Gesellschaft AG, *Feasibility study on an alternative to the capital maintenance regime established by the Second Company Law Directive 77/91/EEC of 13 December 1976 and an examination of the impact on profit distribution of the new EU accounting regime*, 2008, available at http://ec.europa.eu.
36. European Commission, *Green Paper. Building a Capital Markets Union*.
37. European Commission, *Green Paper. Building a Capital Markets Union*.

(CCCTB), promoted by the European Commission,[38] as a *"move towards harmonisa-tion of the corporate income tax base would have obvious spillovers in terms of harmonisation of single-entity accounting requirements".*[39]

In addition, in order to harmonize the functioning of the *legal capital system* in the Member States, the European legislator should consider the possibility of regulating the treatment of profits (and losses) arising from the use of *fair value* and other alternative *criteria* to historical price in Directive 2012/30/EU. This would reduce the variations in treatment amongst companies from different Member States and amongst those preparing their financial statements in accordance with the IAS/IFRS or national rules complying with Directive 2013/23/EU.

---

38. In June 2015, as previously announced in the Action Plan for Fair and Efficient Corporate Taxation, the Commission presented a strategy to re-launch the Common Consolidated Corporate Tax Base (CCCTB).
39. *See* N. VÈRON & G.B. WOLFF, *Capital Markets*, at 12. However, the Authors observe that the present project on CCCTB *"would be only an option for companies, and its adoption would thus not have obvious impact in terms of accounting frameworks".*

PART II IAS/IFRS and the New EU Directive 2013/34 from the Accounting Perspective

CHAPTER 2

IAS/IFRS and the New Directive 2013/34/EU from the Accounting Perspective

Donatella Busso

§2.01   INTRODUCTION

Since 2005, European companies' financial statements can be drawn up according to two different accounting models: either according to International Reporting Accounting Standards (IFRS) issued by the International Accounting Standard Board (IASB) and endorsed by the European Union or according to national laws which derived from European Directives (Fourth Directive – Annual accounts and Seventh Council Directive – Consolidated accounts).

The differences between these two accounting models are significant, one reason being they are addressed to different types of companies: large public companies (IFRS) and small-medium private enterprises (national laws). Over the last fifteen years, the European Union has amended the Fourth and the Seventh Directive many times. In particular, the two directives were amended in 2001 (Directive 65/2001/EC) and in 2003 (Directive 51/2003/EEC), in order to maintain consistency between Community Accounting Directives and developments in the international accounting standard setting. Then in 2013, the European Union issued Directive 2013/34/EU that replaces both the Fourth Directive (Directive 78/660/EEC) and the Seventh Directive (Directive 83/349/EEC). This time, the changes aimed at simplifying accounting requirements for certain types of companies and reducing administrative burdens, in particular for SMEs.

After all these modifications, IFRS compliant financial statements and financial statements drawn up according to the new Directive share some principles but remain at variance in other parts where the two accounting models still continue to show differences.

It is worth highlighting that both IFRS and Directive are defined "principle based" compared to U.S. GAAP that are considered "rule based". However, even if IFRS are considered "principle based" they are accompanied by many examples, application guidance, basis for conclusions and so on. The Directive is really "principle based" because there are no examples, no application guidance and no basis for conclusions. Therefore, in comparing the two models even when there are similarities, in IFRS it is always possible to find a more thorough analysis and explanation.

§2.02 DIFFERENCES AND SIMILARITIES BETWEEN IAS/IFRS REGULATION AND THE NEW DIRECTIVE. A GENERAL OVERVIEW

The topics analyzed are the following:

(1) purpose of financial statements;
(2) statements of annual report;
(3) hierarchy of general provisions and principles;
(4) balance sheet and profit and loss account;
(5) notes;
(6) simplifications for small and medium undertakings.

[A] Purpose of Financial Statements

IAS 1 (paragraph 7) states that "general purpose" financial statements are those intended to meet the needs of users who are not in a position to require an entity to prepare reports tailored to their particular information needs. The Conceptual Framework for Financial Reporting specifies that the objective of financial statements is to provide financial information that is useful to existing and potential investors, lenders and other creditors in making decisions about providing resources to the entity. Therefore, even if IAS 1 seems to broaden financial statement users, the Conceptual Framework highlights that users are subjects that provide resources to the entity. Even if it is not explicitly stated, the typical entity considered by IFRS is a large public company that has to provide information first and foremost to all its investors, lenders and creditors.

According to Directive 2013/34/EU, annual financial statements pursue various objectives and "*do not merely provide information for investors in capital markets but also give an account of past transactions and enhance corporate governance*".

Moreover, according to recital (4), the European Union tries to find an appropriate balance between users' interest and companies' interest; in particular, companies' interest in not being unduly burdened with reporting requirements. It is worth remembering that Directive 2013/34/EU deals not only with financial statements but also with the management report and corporate governance statement. Consequently, if we focus only on financial statements, companies whose instruments are listed in a European market are out of the scope of the Directive, since they have to prepare IFRS compliant financial statements.

Therefore, the purposes are different because the scope is different: large public entities for IFRS and small and medium private companies for the Directive.

[B] Statements of Annual Report

According to IAS 1 (paragraph 9), the objective of financial statements is to provide information about the financial position, financial performance and cash flows of an entity and to show the results of the management's stewardship of the resources entrusted to it. To meet this objective, financial statements provide information about:

– assets, liabilities and equity;
– income and expenses;
– contributions by and distributions to owners in their capacity as owners;
– cash flows.

In order to meet this goal, an entity's financial statements consist of (IAS 1, paragraph 10):

– a statement of financial position as at the end of the period (balance sheet);
– a statement of profit or loss and other comprehensive income for the period (profit or loss-income statement and other comprehensive income);
– a statement of changes in equity for the period;
– a statement of cash flows for the period;
– notes, comprising a summary of significant accounting policies and other explanatory information.

It is mandatory to provide comparative information at least for the preceding period.

According to the Directive 2013/34/EU (Article 3) the annual financial statements must give a true and fair view of the undertaking's assets, liabilities, financial position and profit or loss. Cash flows are not explicitly mentioned nor are contributions by and to owners. The consequence is that Article 4 declares that the minimum statements of an annual report are:

– balance sheet;
– profit and loss account;
– notes.

The cash flow statement and the statement of changes in equity are not mandatory documents. For companies other than small and micro undertakings, Member States are allowed to require additional statements.

[C]   Hierarchy of General Provisions and Principles

In IFRS, general provisions are dealt with by the Conceptual Framework and IAS 1 – Presentation of financial statements.

In Figure 2.1, a summary of the hierarchy of general provisions in IFRS is reported.

Figure 2.1   General Features of Financial Statements under IFRS

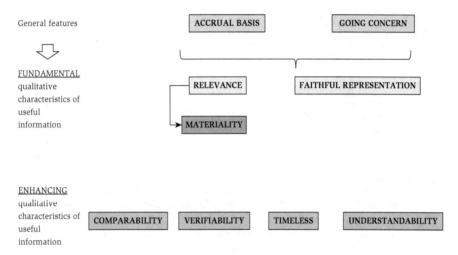

At a first level, the underlying assumptions for IFRS compliant financial statements are "going concern" and "accrual basis accounting". Then, in order to provide useful information, two fundamental qualitative characteristics must be presented: the information must be relevant and it must give a faithful presentation.

Moreover, there are four other "enhancing" qualitative characteristics: a piece of information must be comparable, verifiable, timeless and understandable.

The hierarchy in the Directive is different and is reported in Figure 2.2.

Figure 2.2   *General Feature of Financial Statements under European Directive*

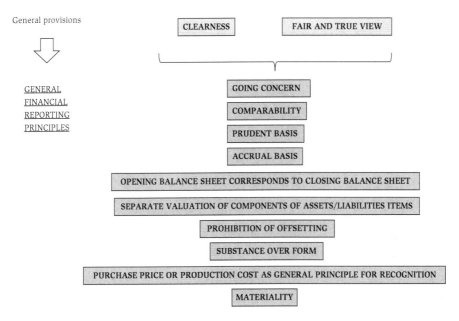

As general provisions, financial statements must present a "clear" and "true and fair" view of the company's assets, liabilities, financial position and profit or loss. In order to obtain a "clear" and "true and fair" view, each company must apply some general financial reporting principles (Article 6). There are many general financial reporting principles, above all "going concern", "comparability", "prudent basis" and "accrual basis".

Some provisions are present in both models and they are applied in the same way (e.g., "going concern"). Other provisions are present in both models, but their relevance and application is different (e.g., "accrual basis"). Other provisions are present in both models, but there are some differences (e.g., "faithful representation" in the IFRS and "true and fair view" in the Directive). Other provisions are present only in one model (e.g., "prudence basis" is not present in the IFRS while "verifiability" is not present in the Directive).

These differences are consistent with the different purposes of the financial statements under the two models: mainly large public companies for IFRS and small-medium private companies for Directive.

The main general provisions are examined as follows.

[1]   *True and Fair View*

IFRS compliant financial statements must present the financial position, financial performance and cash flows of an entity fairly (IAS 1, paragraph 15). Fair presentation means a faithful representation of the effects of transactions, other events and conditions in accordance with the definition and recognition criteria for assets, liabilities, income and expenses set out in the Conceptual Framework. IAS 1 states that in virtually all circumstances, when an entity is compliant with IFRS the entity is able to provide a fair presentation. In any case, a fair presentation requires an entity to select and apply accounting policies and to present information in a way that provides relevant, reliable, comparable and understandable information (IAS 1 paragraph 17). The Conceptual Framework considers the faithful representation as one of the two fundamental qualitative characteristics that information must have in order to be useful. According to paragraph QC12-QC16 of the Conceptual Framework, in order to obtain a perfect and faithful representation, a depiction should have three character-istics: it should be complete, neutral and free from error. Moreover, even if it is not explicitly stated, a fair presentation implies the use of "substance over form" (Concep-tual Framework, paragraph BC3.26).

In the Directive (Article 4.3), there is a similar provision in Article 4: "*the annual statements shall give a true and fair view*". As many authors have highlighted since 1978, the adjective "true" must be read together with "fair". In fact, since drawing up financial statements means making estimates, it does not make sense to expect the "truth" since an estimate always needs judgment. Therefore, it is necessary to estimate all the items of the financial statements in a fair way, because a "true view" is a consequence of "fair" estimates.

When a company applies provisions of the Directive, it is supposed to present a "true and fair view". In fact, Article 4 states that if, in exceptional cases, the application of a provision of the Directive is incompatible with the true and fair view, that provision shall be disapplied.

From this point of view, IFRS and the Directive are similar because:

– complying with IFRS (or the Directive) is sufficient in almost all cases to achieve a faithful presentation (or a true and fair view);
– when in extremely rare circumstances (or exceptional cases) applying an IFRS (or a provision of the Directive) would generate a conflict with general purposes, a company must depart from such a requirement, but it is obliged to provide information about the reasons for this departure together with its effect on the financial statements.

[2]   Clearness

According to the Conceptual Framework (paragraph QC30) "classifying, characterising and presenting information clearly and concisely makes it understandable". In para-graph QC32, the Conceptual Framework specifies that financial statements are pre-pared for users who have a reasonable knowledge of business and economic activities and who review and analyze the information diligently. Therefore, "understandable" does not mean everyone must be able to understand, but only those who have knowledge of the business and economic activities of the company. Sometimes, it is not even sufficient because transactions are so complex that professional advice is needed.

The Directive (Article 4.2) states *"the annual financial statements shall be drawn up clearly"*. However, the Directive does not provide any other explanation about the meaning of "clearly". There are some requirements regarding the balance sheet and the profit and loss account that force companies to provide "clear" statements (e.g., the requirement of a non-flexible layout for financial statements, prohibition of offsetting assets/liabilities, revenues/costs), but there are specific paragraphs about the general meaning of "clear".

[3] Going Concern

Going concern is an assumption both for IFRS and for the Directive. Under IFRS, going concern is an underlying assumption of financial statements: only if a company is likely to continue to operate in the foreseeable future, shall it use IFRS (Conceptual Framework (CF), paragraph 4.1). IAS 1 requests companies to demonstrate the existence of going concern for at least twelve months from the end of the reporting period and provides some examples of situations to be analyzed carefully (unsatisfactory current and expected profitability, debt repayment schedules and so on). Moreover, companies are requested to disclose situations of material uncertainties that may lead either to the preparation of financial statements on a going concern basis in any case or on another basis.

Under the Directive, going concern is the first general financial reporting principle (Article 5.1.a.): the undertaking shall be presumed to be carrying on its business as a going concern. Also for this general reporting principle, there are no other specific requirements or explanations.

[4] Comparability: Consistency

Comparability is one of the four enhancing qualitative characteristics of financial information. According to the Conceptual Framework (paragraph QC20) "information about a reporting entity is more useful if it can be compared with similar information about other entities and with similar information about the same entity for another period or another date". The Conceptual Framework points out that consistency and comparability are different, even if consistency is related to comparability. In fact "consistency refers to the use of the same methods for the same items, either from period to period within a reporting entity or in a single period across entities. Comparability is the goal; consistency helps to achieve that goal".

IAS 1 (paragraph 38) prescribes at least one year of comparative information for all amounts reported in the financial statements for the current period. For narrative and descriptive information, comparative information must be included when relevant to understand the financial statements of the current period.

In IFRS there are many requirements about consistency:

- a company must present and classify an item of its financial statements consistently from one period to the next, unless a change is more appropriate or it is requested by another IFRS;
- when a company changes an accounting policy, it must apply it retrospectively, unless it is impracticable;
- when a company changes the presentation or classification of items of financial statements, the company must reclassify comparative amounts, unless it is impracticable.

In the Directive, the second general financial reporting principle is "consistency". In particular, Article 6.1.b states "accounting policies and measurement bases shall be applied consistently from one financial year to the next". Moreover, Article 9.5 requests companies to show for each balance sheet and profit and loss the corresponding item for the preceding financial year. Member States are allowed to request the adjustment of the figure for the preceding financial year when those figures are not comparable. So while IFRS require them to be adjusted, the Directive allows Member States to do so: basically, it depends on the option adopted by the different European countries.

[5]   Prudent Basis

In IFRS, "prudence" is not a general provision. Financial statements must be prepared on an accrual basis and, in accordance with the single standards, companies are obliged (or allowed) to recognize profits even if they have not been made at the reporting date. In the previous version of the Framework (effective until 2009), prudence was included, but the meaning of prudence was "the inclusion of a degree of caution in the exercise of the judgments needed in making the estimates required under conditions of uncertainty, such that assets or income are not overstated and liabilities or expenses are not understated". Consequently, also in the old version, the presence of prudence did not mean the prohibition of including profits that have not yet been made at the reporting date, but only the need for a certain caution in making estimates. In fact, paragraph 37 stated that "However, the exercise of prudence does not allow, for example, the creation of hidden reserves or excessive provisions, the deliberate understatement of assets or income, or the deliberate overstatement of liabilities or expenses, because the financial statements would not be neutral and, therefore, not have the quality of reliability."

Most probably, prudence will soon reappear in IFRS. In fact, in 2015, IASB published an Exposure Draft for public comment proposing a revised Conceptual Framework for Financial Reporting. In the Exposure Draft, there is again explicit reference to prudence, described as caution when making judgments under conditions of uncertainty.

In the Directive, prudence is the pillar of recognition and measurement. In fact, the third general financial reporting principle (Article 6.1.c) is prudence. The Directive does not simply state that recognition and measurement must be done on a prudent basis: it emphasizes this concept giving some more details:

- only profits made at the date of the balance sheet may be recognized;
- all liabilities arising in the course of the financial year concerned or in the course of a previous financial year must be recognized, even if such liabilities become apparent only between the date of the balance sheet and the date on which the balance sheet is drawn up;
- all negative value adjustments shall be recognized, whether the result of the financial year is a profit or a loss;
- a Member State (Article 6.5) can permit or require the recognition of all foreseeable liabilities and potential losses arising in the course of the financial year concerned or in the course of a previous financial year, even if such liabilities or losses become apparent only between the date of the balance sheet and the date on which the balance sheet is drawn up.

Presumably, this is the most important difference between IFRS and the Directive due to the different purposes of the two accounting models. IFRS are addressed to large public companies where users are mainly investors, interested in financial statements in order to take economic decisions: for them, any deliberate over- or under-statement is likely to lead to suboptimal decisions and a misallocation of capital (Steve Cooper, A tale of "prudence"). The Directive is addressed to small-medium private companies where users are not only investors but also subjects who provide resources. Financial statements are also used in order to distribute dividends or to verify whether the company is maintaining a minimum amount of capital. For these reasons, financial statements under the Directive are based on "conservative accounting", where the meaning of prudence is as described above.

However, it is necessary to point out that even if in the Directive recognition and measurement must be performed on a prudent basis, there are many explicit exemptions: for example, for financial instruments. On the contrary, in IFRS there are many assets for which the subsequent measurement must be done at cost, with an explicit prohibition against recognizing profits that are not made at the reporting date.

[6] Accrual Basis

Accrual basis is a general financial reporting principle both for IFRS and for the Directive. To be more precise, under IFRS the accrual basis is an underlying assumption, at the same level of going concern. That means that according to IFRS it does not make sense to draw up financial statements considering another basis of accounting (e.g., on a cash basis). However, accrual basis is a very general principle: IFRS do not specify anything more about the principle, but IAS 1 (paragraph 28) states that when accrual basis is used, an entity recognizes items as assets, liabilities, equity, income and expenses when they satisfy the definitions and recognition criteria for those elements in the Framework. These criteria are then recalled in the different standards when they define assets, liabilities and equity. It is worth remembering that in 2014, the

IASB issued a new standard about revenue recognition (IFRS 15), defining a core principle in order to recognize a revenue from contracts with customers. According to this new standard, "an entity shall recognize revenue to depict the transfer of promised goods or services to customers in an amount that reflects the consideration to which the entity expects to be entitled in exchange for those goods or services". The new IFRS 15 represents an important driver for accrual basis, since it establishes when a company must recognize a revenue from a contract with customers.

In the Directive, accrual basis is a general statement (Article 6.1.d) but there are no other specific details. Moreover, accrual basis is always subject to prudent basis.

[7]   Opening Balance Sheet Corresponds to Closing Balance Sheet

Article 6.e states that the opening balance sheet for each financial year shall correspond to the closing balance sheet for the preceding financial year. This is a general principle in order to be sure that assets, liabilities and equity recognized in the balance sheet at the end of the reporting period are the same as those recognized at the beginning of the subsequent period. It means that it is not possible to change assets, liabilities or equity amounts in the opening process.

In IFRS, there are no such requirements. On the contrary, IAS 8 requires companies to apply changes in accounting policies and the correction of material errors of prior periods retrospectively. Companies must adjust the opening balance of each affected component of equity for the earliest prior period presented and the other comparative amounts disclosed for each prior period presented as if the new accounting policy had always been applied (or as if the error had not occurred). The adjustment is usually made to retained earnings. According to IFRS, it is mandatory to modify the opening balance when retrospective accounting is required. However, users can understand the impact by reading the statement of changes in equity, where it is mandatory to disclose "*for each component of equity, the effects of retrospective application or retrospective restatement recognised in accordance with IAS 8*". Consequently, modifications due to changes in accounting policies or the correction of errors do not affect profit and loss and they are disclosed in the statement of changes in equity.

[8]   Components of Assets and Liabilities to Be Valued Separately

In IFRS, each standard defines the "unit of account" that is the level at which an asset or a liability is aggregated or disaggregated in an IFRS for recognition purposes.

In particular, IFRS 13 – Fair value measurement deals with this topic providing many indications about the unit of account when a company must determine an asset or a liability fair value.

The Directive has a specific principle in Article 6.1.f that states components of assets and liabilities shall be valued separately. This requirement aims at obliging companies not to avoid the prudent basis application. In fact, in this way it is

32

impossible to offset profits that are not made at the end of the reporting period with losses due to the prudent basis.

[9]   Offsetting of Assets/Liabilities and Revenues/Costs

IFRS and Directive requirements are consistent. In fact, IAS 1, paragraph 32 states: "An entity shall not offset assets and liabilities or income and expenses, unless required or permitted by an IFRS". Article 6.1.g of the Directive states that any set-off between asset and liability or between income and expenditure items shall be prohibited. However, Member States may require or permit offsetting of a particular asset/liability or income/expenditure provided that the amounts offset are disclosed as gross amounts in the notes (Article 6.2).

[10]   Substance over Form

The general "substance over form" principle was removed in 2010 from the Conceptual Framework. According to the Conceptual Framework Basis for Conclusions, substance over form is not considered a separate component of faithful representation because it would be redundant. Faithful representation means that financial information represents the substance of an economic phenomenon rather than merely representing its legal form. Representing a legal form that differs from the economic substance of the underlying economic phenomenon would not result in a faithful representation. However, the IASB is considering re-introducing "substance over form" in the Conceptual Framework.

Article 6.1.h states that items in the profit and loss and balance sheet must be accounted for and presented having regard to the substance of the transaction or arrangement concerned. However, Member States can exempt a company from doing so.

Finally, even if IFRS do not explicitly mention "substance over form", financial statements cannot be considered IFRS compliant without applying the "substance over form" principle. On the contrary, European Member States can exempt companies from being compliant with this principle.

[11]   Principle of Purchase Price or Production Cost

When an IFRS deals with an asset or a liability, it identifies different situations:

- – Initial recognition
- – Initial measurement
- – Subsequent measurement.

The concept of "measurement" is different according to its timing: the initial measurement is related to the amount to be recognized in the balance sheet when the asset or liability is initially recognized (e.g., when the asset is purchased or the liability assumed). Then, at the balance sheet date, the measurement is called "subsequent measurement" and it relates to the amount to be disclosed in the balance sheet.

Speaking of the initial measurement, all IFRS state an asset or liability to be initially recognized at its initial fair value. Fair value is defined as "the price that would be received to sell an asset or paid to transfer a liability in an orderly transaction between market participants at the measurement date" (IFRS 13, paragraph 9). In many cases, the initial fair value coincides with the transaction price, i.e., the purchase price or the production price. When initial fair value and transaction price do not coincide, IFRS require the use of fair value and that the difference between the amounts is recognized according to the "nature" of this difference.

Subsequent measurement in IFRS can either be at cost or at fair value, depending on the various assets and liabilities.

Directive 2013/34 is not so precise and Article 6.1.i states that "items recognized in the financial statements shall be measured in accordance with the principle of purchase price or production cost". So it is possible to affirm that the general principle for both initial and subsequent measurement is cost. However, Articles 7 and Article 8 provide some important exceptions, analyzed in the following chapter written by Prof. Cisi.

[12]   Materiality

Relevance is one of the two fundamental qualitative characteristics of the information reported in financial statements. In particular, the Conceptual Framework states that relevant financial information is capable of making a difference in the decisions made by users (paragraph QC6) and that financial information is capable of making a difference in decisions if it has predictive value, confirmatory value or both (paragraph QC7).

Consequently, in the Conceptual Framework materiality is an addition to relevance: information is material if omitting it or misstating it could influence decisions that users make on the basis of financial information about a specific reporting entity (paragraph QC11). Materiality is also present in IAS 1 with the same meaning. Recently, IAS 1 has been amended in some parts related to materiality in order to clarify that each company must assess if a piece of information is or is not material. The topic is so important that IASB issued an exposure draft of a document called "Practical Statement: Application of materiality to financial statements" in order to give advice about how to assess whether a piece of information is material or not. In this Practical Statement, the IASB highlights that materiality applies to all aspects of financial statements: recognition, measurement, presentation and disclosure.

The Directive has a similar requirement in Article 6.1.j when it states a company is not requested to comply with requirements set out in the Directive when the effect of complying with them is immaterial. Companies are exempt from applying recognition, measurement, presentation, disclosure and consolidation requirements if they are immaterial. In the Directive, the meaning of "immaterial" is not provided. Moreover,

Member States can limit the scope of the exemption to presentation and disclosure, obliging companies to apply all the requirements of recognition and measurement.

[D] Balance Sheet and Profit and Loss Account

[1] General Provisions

The balance sheet (statement of financial performance) and profit and loss account (statement of profit or loss and comprehensive income) are dealt with in IAS 1. For both documents, IAS 1 does not prescribe a specific layout, but only a minimum content. Moreover, the recent amendments to IAS 1 clarify that a company is not obliged to present all the items considered as the minimum content if they are not material. Accordingly, companies are free to decide the balance sheet and income statement layout, to present totals and subtotals and so on. They only have to comply with some minimum requirements. The assumption is that each company is different and for the investors it is interesting to have the management's view when possible. So it would not make sense to oblige all companies to provide the same balance sheet and income statement layout. On the contrary, each company must use the layout suitable for depicting a faithful representation.

Directive 2013/34/EU has a completely different approach. Companies are obliged to present the balance sheet and profit and loss according to a precise layout. Companies are obliged to show balance sheet and profit and loss items separately and in the order indicated. The assumption is that if all the companies present the same layout comparability should improve.

Both IFRS and the Directive oblige companies to maintain the same layout year after year. When a company departs from this principle, IFRS require the comparative amounts to be restated, whereas the Directive only requires the departure to be disclosed in the notes.

Since IFRS do not require a specific layout, IAS 1 states "an entity shall present separately each material class of similar items. An entity shall present separately items of a dissimilar nature or function unless they are immaterial".

The Directive distinguishes adaptations according to the level of items involved. So it is not possible to adapt (aggregate or disaggregate) items preceded by capital letters and Roman numerals whereas it is possible to aggregate or adapt items preceded by Arabic numerals.

[2] Balance Sheet Presentation

According to IAS 1, an entity can present its balance sheet with assets and liabilities classified as either current or non-current items (IAS 1 paragraph 61). This presentation is considered the most useful when an entity supplies goods or services within a clearly identifiable operating cycle. IAS 1 states that only for some companies (as, for example, financial institutions) it is more useful to present assets and liabilities in accordance with a liquidity order, i.e., in an increasing or decreasing order of liquidity. According to IAS 1, paragraph 64, an entity is permitted to present some of its assets and liabilities using a current/non-current classification and others in order of liquidity when this provides information that is reliable and more relevant. The need for a mixed basis of presentation might arise when an entity has diverse operations.

The Directive provides a specific layout presented in Annex III and Annex IV. The two layouts present the same categories preceded by the same capital letters and the same Roman numerals. The difference is the layout: horizontal in Annex III and vertical in Annex IV. On the asset side, the main categories are fixed assets and current assets. The presentation of an asset as fixed or current depends on the purpose for which it is intended. Even if this distinction may not be completely consistent with the one used by IFRS (non-current and current) they are very close. On the liability side, the classification criterion is not so clear. In fact, the main categories are equity, provisions and creditors. Creditors are presented together, irrespective of their function (financial or non-financial) and their maturity.

Consequently, if we compare the asset side, it is possible to find a certain similarity between IFRS and the Directive whereas the liability side is not comparable. In fact, IFRS compliant financial statements must present the same distinction (current and non-current) for both assets and liabilities whereas in the Directive the liabilities are not classified in a consistent way.

Under IFRS, entities are requested to disclose the amount expected to be recovered or settled after more than twelve months for each asset and liability line item that combines amounts expected to be recovered or settled no more than twelve months after the reporting period and more than twelve months after the reporting period.

According to Annex III and IV, companies are requested to show amounts falling due and payable within one year separately from amounts falling due and payable in more than one year. However, this requirement applies only for Debtors included in Current Assets and Creditors.

Under IFRS, own shares and unpaid subscribed capital are considered as a transaction with equity owners (IAS 32) and so they are presented within the equity. According to the Directive, it is possible to present these items either as investments (i.e., as assets) or as equity.

[3]   Profit or Loss Account Presentation

In the IFRS, the statement of profit or loss and comprehensive income is part of the financial statements. If we consider only the statement of profit or loss, IFRS and the Directive are comparable, otherwise they are not, since the Directive does not require the statement of other comprehensive income.

IAS 1 encourages companies to present an analysis of expenses recognized in profit or loss using a classification based on either their nature or their function within the entity in the profit or loss. The choice between the two classifications must be made according to the one which provides information that is reliable and more relevant.

IAS 1 does not prescribe specific subtotals, since the entity must present additional line items, headings and subtotals when such a presentation is relevant to an understanding of the entity's financial performance.

The Directive also allows two layouts, based on nature classification and function classification and it does not prescribe any specific subtotals.

[E]   Notes

Notes are part of the financial statements for both IFRS and Directive.

IAS 1 states some generic provisions about their structure. In particular, the notes must present information about the basis for the preparation of the financial statements and the specific accounting policies, disclose the information required by IFRS that is not presented elsewhere in the financial statements and provide information that is not presented elsewhere in the financial statements, but is relevant to an understanding of them. Every standard requires the disclosure of the topic dealt with in the standard. For example, IAS 16 – Property, plant and equipment deals with tangible assets and contains some paragraphs dedicated to their disclosure. Moreover, there are other standards whose content only concerns disclosure (e.g., IFRS 7 – Financial Instruments: Disclosures). IASB is discussing a project (Disclosure Initiative) to force entities to provide information that is relevant, since many entities simply comply with all the requirements even if the information is not material.

The Directive includes some articles about disclosure in which there is a list of information to be provided by companies. Comparing the information requested by IFRS with that requested by the Directive, it is clear that the latter is less analytic even if the macro-topics are all covered.

[F]   Simplifications for Small and Medium Undertakings

In 2009, the IASB issued the IFRS for SMEs. The IFRS for SMEs is a self-contained Standard, designed to meet the needs and capabilities of small and medium-sized entities.

Compared with the full IFRS, the IFRS for SMEs is less complex in a number of ways:

- topics that are not relevant for SMEs are omitted. For example: earnings per share, interim financial reporting and segment reporting, topics relevant only to listed companies;
- many principles for recognizing and measuring assets, liabilities, income and expenses in full IFRS are simplified. For example, goodwill is amortized and

not impaired, all borrowing and development costs are recognized as expenses, for associates and jointly-controlled entities the cost model is required;
– significantly fewer disclosures are required (roughly a 90% reduction).

One of the Directive's goals is to simplify requirements for small and medium companies. As a result, there are many simplifications regarding balance sheet and profit and loss layout as well as about disclosure.

CHAPTER 3

Differences and Similarities between IAS/IFRS Regulation and the New Directive

Maurizio Cisi

§3.01 INTRODUCTION

The Directive 2013/34/EU of the European Parliament and the Council modifies the stipulations of the Directive 2006/43/CE and repeals the stipulations of Directives 78/660/EEC (Directive IV) and 83/349/EEC of the Council (Directive VII).

The publication of this Directive aims to meet both the provisions on the individual financial statements, as well as those on the consolidated financial statements.

The introduction of the new Directive aims to improve the coverage information of the accounting document and to begin a process of simplification of administrative burdens and standards for the preparation and publication of the financial statements (Provasi R., Sottoriva C., 2015).

On the one hand, the new Directive does not bring any significant changes to the structure of the reporting documents, but it clarifies the prescriptions regarding the simplifications for certain categories of entities (micro- and SMEs) and the additional information requirements imposed on others (large entities and groups).

Nevertheless, the introduction of the new European Directive could be considered as a step forward for the financial reporting of European Union business entities, mainly because of the updating and modernization of the contents of the Directives. The result is a clearer and more comparable structure of companies' financial statements, with specific focus on undertakings that develop their activities on an international level and have a greater number of stakeholders (Socoliuc & Grosu, 2015).

On the other hand, the Directive is a step forward in the process of convergence towards an internationally accepted common framework for financial reporting based on updated high quality principles and evaluation approaches that define the most appropriate way to achieve that 'true and fair view' that any financial statement is required to provide for the benefit of its stakeholders (Corbella et al., 2013; Combarros, 2000; Deac, 2014).

In this context, the Directive is a 'bridge' towards the IFRS that are clearly designed for the purpose of reflecting the economic substance more than the legal form as well as providing a more timely representation of economic gains and losses. Compared with the accounting standards that have historically typified Continental Europe, the new features deriving from the Directive are intended to make the determination of the earnings more informative even on the basis of a lower discretionary power, although the path towards IFRS has not yet been completed (Paoloni, 2005; Azzali, 2005; Di Carlo & Potito, 2008).

This chapter aims to investigate such arguments more deeply on a comparative basis considering the main differences and similarities between IAS/IFRS regulation and the new Directive.

§3.02   FROM ACCOUNTING PRINCIPLES TO IMPACT ON INCOME REPRESENTATION

The new Directive closes the gap existing between accounting systems and overcomes the incisive differences affecting the comparability of the accounting items provided by companies applying IFRS and companies using national rules based on EU Directive application.

The ongoing process of convergence between the EU system and IFRS is primarily based on the use (even under option) of accounting measures other than cost. Even if the pillar of the Directive system is the recognition[1] in the financial statements in accordance with the principle of purchase price or production cost,[2] the Directive

---

1. According to Article 6 (General financial reporting principles), items presented in the annual and consolidated financial statements shall be recognized and measured on a prudent basis, and in particular:

    (i) only profits made at the balance sheet date may be recognized;
    (ii) all liabilities arising in the course of the financial year concerned or in the course of a previous financial year shall be recognised, even if such liabilities become apparent only between the balance sheet date and the date on which the balance sheet is drawn up; and
    (iii) all negative value adjustments shall be recognised, whether the result of the financial year is a profit or a loss.

2. According to Article 6 (General financial reporting principles), items presented in the annual and consolidated financial statements shall be recognized and measured on a prudent basis, and in particular:

    (i) only profits made at the balance sheet date may be recognized;
    (ii) all liabilities arising in the course of the financial year concerned or in the course of a previous financial year shall be recognised, even if such liabilities become apparent only between the balance sheet date and the date on which the balance sheet is drawn up; and
    (iii) all negative value adjustments shall be recognised, whether the result of the financial year is a profit or a loss.

40

defines alternative measurement basis for specific assets. By way of derogation from point (i) of Article 6(1), it gives Member States the power to permit or require, in respect of all undertakings or any classes of undertaking, the measurement of fixed assets at their revalued amount, as well as introducing Fair Value accounting for financial instruments and derivatives.

The innovation consists in the recognition at fair value of financial instruments which, based on the old rules, were valued at cost or were not even recorded in the financial statements (i.e., derivative instruments).

It is clear that one of the main advantages of the fair value accounting is the market-based representation. This measurement contemplates a hypothetical transaction between market participants at a specific date and, therefore, 'captures the essence' of the company's performance in its dynamic and continuous process of evolution. It has been noted that where the cost is not suitable for representing the economic and financial situation of enterprises properly, it will be useful for identifying alternative measurement techniques (Fortunato, 2007).

Fair value accounting should aim to assure the reliability of the accounting representation of the performance that evolves continuously along with the process of business management. In this context a financial information system based on fair value can assure consistency between the characteristics of the continuous process of business management and its accounting representation.

This accounting approach can effectively represent the results already achieved and draw attention to the expected results of on-going operations by making reference to fair values, whether in-use or in exchange (Corbella et al., 2013).

The main aspects analysed below concern:

– the revaluation model option for fixed assets;
– the fair value model adoption.

§3.03   EU DIRECTIVE'S NEW ACCOUNTING OPTIONS: FROM COST TO REVALUATION MODEL

The Directive defines the 'revalued amount' as an alternative measurement basis for fixed assets rather than cost.

The revaluation option in general is consistent with the measurement basis allowed by the IFRS Framework. However, differences emerge following a detailed analysis.

Under IFRS, using the revaluation model, after being recognized as an asset, an item whose fair value can be measured reliably shall be carried at a revalued amount, that being its fair value at the date of the revaluation less any subsequent accumulated depreciation and subsequent accumulated impairment losses.

In order to define the fair value, IFRS clarify that it is uncommon for an active market to exist for an intangible asset, although this may happen. For example, in some jurisdictions, an active market may exist for freely transferable taxi licences, fishing licences or production quotas. However, an active market cannot exist for brands, newspaper mastheads, music and film publishing rights, patents or trademarks, because each such asset is unique. Also, although intangible assets are bought and sold, contracts are negotiated between individual buyers and sellers, and transactions are relatively infrequent. For these reasons, the price paid for one asset may not provide sufficient evidence of the fair value of another.

Within the IFRS framework, the frequency of revaluations depends on the volatility of the fair values of the intangible assets being revalued. If the fair value of a revalued asset differs materially from its carrying amount, a further revaluation is necessary. Some intangible assets may experience significant and volatile movements in fair value, thus necessitating annual revaluation. Such frequent revaluations are unnecessary for intangible assets with only insignificant movements in fair value.

When the fair value of a revalued asset differs materially from its carrying amount, a further revaluation is required.

Both Directive and IFRS allow revaluation accounting for all classes of intangible assets and Property, plant and equipment.[3]

According to the Directive, the revaluation can be applied to all fixed assets.

Under the IFRS framework, if an asset's carrying amount is increased as a result of a revaluation, the increase shall be recognized in other comprehensive income and accumulated in equity under the heading of revaluation surplus. However, the increase shall be recognized in the profit or loss to the extent that it reverses a revaluation decrease of the same asset previously recognized in the profit or loss.

If an asset's carrying amount is decreased as a result of a revaluation, the decrease shall be recognized in the profit or loss. However, the decrease shall be recognized in other comprehensive income to the extent of any credit balance in the

---

3. If an item of intangible asset, property, plant and equipment is revalued, the entire class to which that asset belongs shall be revalued. A class of property, plant and equipment is a grouping of assets of a similar nature and use in an entity's operations. The following are examples of separate classes:

    (a) land;
    (b) land and buildings;
    (c) machinery;
    (d) ships;
    (e) aircraft;
    (f) motor vehicles;
    (g) furniture and fixtures; and
    (h) office equipment.

Under IFRS, PPE does not include biological assets related to agricultural activity or mineral rights and mineral reserves, such as oil, natural gas and similar non-regenerative resources.

    A class of intangible assets is a grouping of assets of a similar nature and use in an entity's operations. Examples of separate classes may include:

    (a) brand names;
    (b) mastheads and publishing titles;
    (c) computer software;
    (d) licences and franchises;
    (e) copyrights, patents and other industrial property rights, service and operating rights;
    (f) recipes, formulae, models, designs and prototypes; and
    (g) intangible assets under development.

revaluation surplus in respect of that asset. The decrease recognized in other comprehensive income reduces the amount accumulated in equity under the heading of revaluation surplus.

According to the Directive, value adjustments shall be calculated each year on the basis of the revalued amount. However, by way of derogation from Articles 9 and 13, Member States may permit or require that only the amount of the value adjustments arising as a result of the purchase price or production cost measurement basis be shown under the relevant items in the layouts set out in Annexes V and VI and that the difference arising as a result of the measurement on a revaluation basis be shown separately in the layouts.

The Directive does not provide a specific basis of measurement. In some countries (i.e., Italy) specific revaluation laws allowed the revaluation of certain types of assets (buildings and land) taking into account the real current value.

According to the Directive, the fair value method is an alternative method that can be applied to different types of assets. It is governed by Article 9, according to which Member States authorize or prescribe, for all companies or any classes of companies, the assessment of the fair value of financial instruments, including derivative financial instruments, and assets other than financial instruments. These factors include fixed assets, which are measured according to the restating method.

[A]   Revaluation of Property, Plant and Equipment

Under IFRS, as a general rule, an item of property, plant and equipment shall be measured at initial recognition at its cost.[4] According to IAS 16, after recognition an entity shall choose either the cost model or the revaluation model as accounting policy and shall apply that policy to an entire class of property, plant and equipment.

Using the cost model, all items of property, plant and equipment are measured, after initial recognition, at cost less any accumulated depreciation and any accumulated impairment losses.

Revaluations shall be made with sufficient regularity to ensure that the carrying amount does not differ materially from that which would be determined using fair value at the end of the reporting period.

According to paragraph 34 of the IAS 16, the frequency of revaluations depends upon the changes in fair values of the items of property, plant and equipment being revalued. When the fair value of a revalued asset differs materially from its carrying

---

4. The cost of an item of property, plant and equipment comprises all of the following:

    (a) its purchase price, including legal and brokerage fees, import duties and non-refundable purchase taxes, after deducting trade discounts and rebates;

    (b) any costs directly attributable to bringing the asset to the location and in the condition necessary for it to be capable of operating in the manner intended by management. These can include the costs of site preparation, initial delivery and handling, installation and assembly, and testing of functionality;

    (c) the initial estimate of the costs of dismantling and removing the item and restoring the site on which it is located, an obligation incurred by an entity either when the item is acquired or as a consequence of having used the item during a particular period.

amount, a further revaluation is required. Considering that some items of property, plant and equipment experience significant and volatile changes in fair value, an annual revaluation is required. However, such frequent revaluations are unnecessary for items with only insignificant changes in fair value. Instead, it may be necessary to revalue the item only every three or five years.

When an item is revalued, the carrying amount of that asset is adjusted to the revalued amount. At the date of revaluation, the asset is treated in one of the following ways:

(a) the gross carrying amount is adjusted in a manner that is consistent with the revaluation of the carrying amount of the asset. For example, the gross carrying amount may be restated by reference to observable market data or it may be restated proportionately to the change in the carrying amount. The accumulated depreciation at the date of the revaluation is adjusted to equal the difference between the gross carrying amount and the carrying amount of the asset after taking into account accumulated impairment losses; or

(b) the accumulated depreciation is eliminated against the gross carrying amount of the asset.

In order to avoid selective revaluation of assets and the reporting of amounts in the financial statements that are a mixture of costs and values as at different dates, the revaluation option is available only on the basis of an entire class or PPE. If an item of property, plant and equipment is revalued, the entire class of property, plant and equipment to which that asset belongs shall be revalued.

In any case, where the option is applied, the amount of the difference between measurement on a purchase price or production cost basis and measurement on a revaluation basis shall be entered in the balance sheet in the revaluation reserve under 'Capital and reserves'.

Under the Directive, the revaluation reserve may be capitalized in whole or in part at any time and it shall be reduced where the amounts transferred to that reserve are no longer necessary for the implementation of the revaluation basis of accounting.

Article 7, paragraph 2 states that Member States may lay down rules governing the application of the revaluation reserve, provided that transfers to the profit and loss account from the revaluation reserve may be made only where the amounts transferred have been entered as an expense in the profit and loss account or reflect increases in value which have actually been realized.

According to the Directive, no part of the revaluation reserve may be distributed, either directly or indirectly, unless it represents a gain actually realized and it may not be reduced.

Under IFRS, when the revaluation option is exercised and an asset's carrying amount is increased as a result of a revaluation, the increase shall be recognized in other comprehensive income and accumulated in equity under the heading of revaluation surplus. However, the increase shall be recognized in the profit or loss to the extent that it reverses a revaluation decrease of the same asset previously recognized in the profit or loss.

At the same time, if an asset's carrying amount is decreased as a result of a revaluation, the decrease shall be recognized in the profit or loss. However, the decrease shall be recognized in other comprehensive income to the extent of any credit balance existing in the revaluation surplus in respect of that asset. The decrease recognized in other comprehensive income reduces the amount accumulated in equity under the heading of revaluation surplus.

Paragraph 41 of IAS 16 clarifies that the revaluation surplus included in equity in respect of an item of property, plant and equipment may be transferred directly to retained earnings when the asset is derecognized. This may involve transferring the whole of the surplus when the asset is retired or disposed of. However, some of the surplus may be transferred as the asset is used by an entity. In such a case, the amount of the surplus transferred would be the difference between depreciation based on the revalued carrying amount of the asset and the depreciation based on the asset's original cost. Transfers from revaluation surplus to retained earnings are not made through the profit or loss.

Table 3.1 shows the main aspects described comparing IFRS and Directive principles.

Table 3.1   The Revaluation Option

Revaluation Option	Dir 2013/34/EU	IFRS
All fixed assets	x	X
Only for entire classes of assets	x	X
Value adjustments calculated	Each year	Revaluations shall be made with sufficient regularity
Basis for measurement	Value adjustments calculated on the basis of the revalued amount.	Fair value at the end of the reporting period
Increase as a result of revaluation	the amount of the difference between measurement on a purchase price or production cost basis and measurement on a revaluation basis shall be entered in the balance sheet in the revaluation reserve under "Capital and reserves"	In OCI and in equity as a revaluation surplus or in profit or loss to the extent that it reverses a revaluation decrease
Decrease of an asset's carrying amount as a result of a revaluation		Recognised in the profit or loss or in other comprehensive income to the extent of any credit balance in the

Revaluation Option	Dir 2013/34/EU	IFRS
		revaluation surplus and corrisponding reduction in the amount accumulated in equity as revaluation surplus
Capitalization or transfer within the equity of the revaluation reserve/surplus	Revaluation reserve may be capitalised in whole or in part at any time	Transfers from revaluation surplus to retained earnings are not made through profit or loss.
Reduction of the revaluation reserve/surplus	When the reserve is no longer necessary for the implementation of the revaluation basis of accounting	The revaluation surplus may be transferred directly to retained earnings when the asset is derecognised
Distribution of the revaluation reserve/surplus	No part of the revaluation reserve may be distributed, whether directly or indirectly, unless it represents a gain that has actually been realized.	

§3.04   THE EU DIRECTIVE'S NEW ACCOUNTING OPTIONS: SWITCHING FROM COST TO FAIR VALUE

The need for comparability of financial information throughout the Union makes it necessary to require Member States to allow a system of fair value accounting for the accounting of certain financial instruments and derivatives.

By way of a derogation from point (i) of Article 6(1) (that states that items recognized in the financial statements shall be measured in accordance with the principle of purchase price or production cost), the Directive requires the measurement of financial instruments, including derivative financial instruments and of specified categories of assets other than financial instruments, at fair value. Such permission or requirement may be restricted by single states to consolidated financial statements.

According to the Directive, the fair value method is an alternative measurement basis that can be applied to different types of assets: financial instruments, including derivative financial instruments and assets other than financial instruments. That means that the field of applicability includes current assets and non-fixed assets which are measured according to the restating method.

The valuation based on the fair value also applies to the following liabilities:

– Liabilities held as part of the trading portfolio.
– Derivative financial instruments.

According to Article 8, paragraph 4 the fair value measurement does not apply to:

– Non-derivative financial instruments held-to-maturity.
– Loans and receivables originated by the enterprise and not held for trading purposes.
– Investments in subsidiaries, associates and interests in joint ventures, equity instruments issued by the company and contracts that provide for contingent consideration as part of a business combination, as well as other financial instruments whose special characteristics, according to what is generally accepted, should be accounted for differently from other financial instruments.

These requirements are consistent with IFRS rules that state that, after initial recognition, an entity shall measure financial assets, including derivatives that are assets, at their fair values, without any deduction for transaction costs that may be incurred on the sale or other disposal, except for the following financial assets:

(a) loans and receivables which shall be measured at amortized cost using the effective interest method;
(b) held-to-maturity investments which shall be measured at amortized cost using the effective interest method; and
(c) investments in equity instruments that do not have a quoted price on an active market and whose fair value cannot be reliably measured and derivatives that are linked to and must be settled by the delivery of such equity instruments which shall be measured at cost.

Table 3.2 shows the main aspects described, comparing IFRS and Directive principles.

Table 3.2   The Fair Value for Financial and Non-financial Assets

	Dir 2013/34/EU	IFRS
Financial Instruments		
Available For Sale financial assets	-	Fair Value - reserve
Financial assets or liabilities held for trading	-	Fair Value tpl
Financial asset	Fair Value tpl	
with reliable market	FV = Market value	FV
without reliable market	FV = Evaluation techniques or Purchase price or production cost	no FV
Derivatives (no hedge)	FV	FV tpl
Hedging instruments	Fair Value - reserve	FV

	Dir 2013/34/EU	IFRS
Derivatives that are linked to and must be settled by delivery of equity instruments without a reliable market	-	Cost
Liabilities as a part of a trading portfolio	FV	-
Financial instruments held to maturity (non derivative)	No FV	No FV - Amortized cost
Loans and receivables	No FV	No FV - Amortized cost
Investments in subsidiaries, associates, and interests in joint ventures	No FV	No FV
Equity instruments issued by the company	No FV	no FV
Contracts that provide for contingent consideration as part of a business combination	No FV	-
Other financial instruments whose special characteristics that, according to what is generally accepted, should be accounted for differently from other financial instruments.	No FV	-
Assets other than financial instruments	FVTPL only for Consolidated FS	Inv. properties FV tpl Biological assets FV tpl

According to Article 8, Paragraph 7 of the Directive, the fair value shall be determined by reference to one of the following values:

(a) the market value, in the case of financial instruments for which a reliable market can readily be identified. Where the market value is not readily identifiable for an instrument but can be identified for its components or for a similar instrument, the market value may be derived from that of its components or of the similar instrument;

(b) in the case of financial instruments for which a reliable market cannot be readily identified, a value resulting from generally accepted valuation models and techniques, provided that such valuation models and techniques ensure a reasonable approximation of the market value.

Financial instruments that cannot be measured reliably by any of the methods described in points (a) and (b) of the first subparagraph shall be measured in accordance with the principle of purchase price or production cost insofar as measurement on that basis is possible.

On the topic of fair value determination, IFRS are more detailed compared with the Directive and state that (IFRS 11) the objective of a fair value measurement is to estimate the price that would be received to sell an asset or paid to transfer a liability in an orderly transaction on the principal (or most advantageous) market at the measurement date under current market conditions (i.e., an exit price) regardless of whether that price is directly observable or estimated using another valuation technique.

According to IFRS 11, Fair value is a market-based measurement, not an entity-specific measurement. At the same time, fair value measurement is for a particular asset or liability, given that when measuring fair value an entity shall take into account the characteristics of the asset or liability if market participants would take those characteristics into account when pricing the asset or liability at the measurement date. Such characteristics include, for example, the following:

(a) the condition and location of the asset; and
(b) restrictions, if any, on the sale or use of the asset.

The measurement of the fair value of an asset or a liability is made using the assumptions that market participants would use when pricing the asset or liability, and assuming that market participants act in their economic best interest.[5]

Under IFRS rules, a valuation technique that maximizes the use of relevant observable inputs and minimizes the use of unobservable inputs is used when a price for an identical asset or liability is not observable. Three widely used valuation techniques are the market approach, the cost approach and the income approach. In the fair value evaluation process, an entity's intention to hold an asset or to settle or otherwise fulfil a liability is not relevant.

The Directive states that the changes in value are included in the income statement. Changes are recognized directly in a fair value equity reserve when:

(1) the instrument accounted for is a hedging instrument, as part of a hedging transaction that allows all or part of the change in value not to be entered in the income statement;
(2) the change in value relates to an exchange difference arising on a monetary item that forms part of an investment entity's net investment in a foreign entity.

---

5. According to IFRS 11, in developing these assumptions, an entity does not need to identify specific market participants. Rather, the entity shall identify characteristics that distinguish market participants generally, considering factors specific to all the following:

(a) the asset or liability;
(b) the principal (or most advantageous) market for the asset or liability; and
(c) market participants with whom the entity would enter into a transaction in that market.

For the purpose of measuring a financial asset after initial recognition, IFRS classify financial assets into the following four categories:

– financial assets at fair value through profit or loss;
– held-to-maturity investments;
– loans and receivables; and
– available-for-sale financial assets.
– Financial assets or financial liabilities classified as held for trading are accounted at fair value through profit or loss.[6]
– Held-to-maturity investments such as non-derivative financial assets with fixed or determinable payments and fixed maturity that an entity has the positive intention and ability to hold to maturity, other than:
  (a) those that the entity upon initial recognition designates as at fair value through profit or loss;
  (b) those that the entity designates as available for sale; and
  (c) those that meet the definition of loans and receivables.
– Loans and receivables are non-derivative financial assets with fixed or determinable payments that are not quoted on an active market, other than:
  (a) those that the entity intends to sell immediately or in the short-term, which shall be classified as held for trading and those that the entity upon initial recognition designates as at fair value through profit or loss;
  (b) those that the entity upon initial recognition designates as available for sale; or
  (c) those for which the holder may not substantially recover all of its initial investment, other than because of credit deterioration, which shall be classified as available for sale.
– Available-for-sale financial assets: those non-derivative financial assets that are designated as available for sale or are not classified as (a) loans and receivables, (b) held-to-maturity investments or (c) financial assets at fair value through profit or loss.

To summarize, the fair value criterion applied to financial instruments is based on one of the following values:

(a) the market value, in the case of financial instruments for which a reliable market can readily be identified or the market value of a similar instrument;

---

6. A financial asset or financial liability is classified as held for trading if it meets the following:
  (i) it is acquired or incurred principally for the purpose of selling or repurchasing it in the near term;
  (ii) on initial recognition it is part of a portfolio of identified financial instruments that are managed together and for which there is evidence of a recent actual pattern of short-term profit-taking; or
  (iii) it is a derivative (except for a derivative that is a financial guarantee contract or a designated and effective hedging instrument).

(b) the value resulting from generally accepted valuation models and techniques, as they allow for the reasonable approximation of the market value;

(c) the purchase price principle or the production cost where the (a) and (b) methods do not apply.

[A] Fair Value for Non-financial Assets

As clarified, the Directive requires the measurement of financial instruments, including derivative financial instruments. Such permission is also extended to specified categories of assets other than financial instruments. No specification is given and the rules should be derived from IFRS 11 that state that the fair value measurement of a non-financial asset takes into account a market participant's ability to generate economic benefits by using the asset in its highest and best use or by selling it to another market participant that would use the asset in its highest and best use.[7]

IFRS 11, paragraph 32 states that the fair value measurement of a non-financial asset assumes that the asset is sold consistently with the unit of account specified in other IFRS (which may be an individual asset). That is the case even when that fair value measurement assumes that the highest and best use of the asset is for it to be used in combination with other assets or with other assets and liabilities because a fair value measurement assumes that the market participant already holds the complementary assets and the associated liabilities.

§3.05 THE EU DIRECTIVE'S AND IFRS'S ACCOUNTING PRINCIPLES: ASSESSMENT OF MAIN SIMILARITIES AND DIFFERENCES

From exploring differences existing between, on the one hand EU accounting rules and on the other IFRS, it is clear that distances are shrinking. Differences in specific items however, still remain. Table 3.3 shows the main differences and similarities.

---

7. The highest and best use of a non-financial asset takes into account the use of the asset that is physically possible, legally permissible and financially feasible, as follows:

(a) A use that is physically possible takes into account the physical characteristics of the asset that market participants would take into account when pricing the asset (e.g., the location or size of a property).

(b) A use that is legally permissible takes into account any legal restrictions on the use of the asset that market participants would take into account when pricing the asset (e.g., the zoning regulations applicable to a property).

(c) A use that is financially feasible takes into account whether a use of the asset that is physically possible and legally permissible generates adequate income or cash flows (taking into account the costs of converting the asset to that use) to produce an investment return that market participants would require from an investment in that asset put to that use.

Table 3.3   Comparison of the Main Accounting Principles

	Dir 2013/34/EU	IFRS	
Intangible Assets			
Goodwill	Amortization over useful life (or 5-10 ys)	No depreciation - Impairment	
Research costs	No capitalization	No capitalization	
Development costs	Amortization over useful life (or 5-10 ys)	Amortization over useful life	
Advertising costs	No capitalization	No capitalization	
Fixed assets			
PPE	Cost or revaluated amount	Cost or revaluated amount	
Investment properties	Cost or revaluated amount	Fair value or cost	
Financial Leases	-	Fair value / present value of the minimum lease payments (if lower)	
Biological assets	-	Fair value less costs to sell	
Investments in	Individual / consolidated	Consolidated or individual	Separate
subsidiaries	Cost or equity	-	Cost/Fair Value/Equity
associates	Cost or equity	Equity	Cost/Fair Value/Equity
joint ventures	Cost or equity / Proportional	Equity	Cost/Fair Value/Equity
other	Cost	Cost or Fair Value	Cost or Fair Value
Joint Operations	-	Interest method	Interest method

Focusing on the evaluation criteria for assets and liabilities, similarities and differences arise in the following specific aspects:

(1) Intangible assets;
(2) Value adjustments to assets;
(3) Amortized cost;
(4) Equity method for participating interests;
(5) Inventory evaluation.

[A]   Intangible Assets

According to IFRS, intangible assets (other than goodwill) are all identifiable non-monetary assets without physical substance. An asset is identifiable when:

(a) it is separable, i.e., capable of being separated or divided from the entity and sold, transferred, licensed, rented or exchanged, either individually or together with a related contract, asset or liability; or

(b) it arises from contractual or other legal rights, regardless of whether those rights are transferable or separable from the entity or from other rights and obligations.

An intangible asset should be recognized if, and only if:

(a) it is probable that the expected future economic benefits that are attributable to the asset will flow to the entity;

(b) the cost or value of the asset can be measured reliably; and

(c) the asset does not result from expenditure incurred internally on an intangible item.

An entity shall assess the probability of expected future economic benefits using reasonable and supportable assumptions that represent management's best estimate of the economic conditions that will exist over the useful life of the asset.

According to the Directive, the class of Intangible Assets, in line with IFRS, comprises only the following items:

(1) Costs of development (insofar as national law permits their being shown as assets);

(2) Concessions, patents, licences, trademarks and similar rights and assets;[8]

(3) Goodwill, to the extent that it was acquired for valuable consideration;

(4) Payments on account.

Formation expenses may be capitalized when permitted by national law.

Compared with the previous accounting Directive's requirements, the elimination of research costs reduces the relevance of subjective values in financial statements, due to the assumptions related to the capitalization of possible indirect costs and to the estimates related to the recoverable value of assets reported in the balance sheet.

---

8. The Directive clarifies that these assets should be:

(a) acquired for valuable consideration and need not be shown under tangible assets C (I) (3); or

(b) created by the undertaking itself, insofar as national law permits their being shown as assets.

Comparing rules for intangible assets under IFRS and the Directive, issues may arise, relating to the amortization process.

The Directive clarifies that intangible assets shall be written off over the useful economic life of the intangible asset itself. In exceptional cases, where the useful life of goodwill and development costs cannot be reliably estimated, such assets shall be written off within a maximum period set by the Member State. That maximum period shall not be shorter than five years and shall not exceed ten years.[9] Where national law authorizes the inclusion of formation expenses under 'Assets', they shall be written off within a maximum period of five years. Under European rules, once capitalized, intangible assets are tested for long-lasting value reductions.

The Directive's general rule on the depreciation of intangible assets is consistent with IFRS where they state that the depreciable amount of an asset shall be allocated on a systematic basis over its useful life.[10]

Differently, IAS 38 distinguishes between intangible assets with a definite useful life, which shall be amortized and tested for impairment according to IAS 36 (Impairment of Assets) whenever there is an indication that the intangible asset itself may be impaired, and intangible assets with indefinite useful life, which should not be amortized but tested for impairment annually, even though there is no indicator of impairment.

For the purpose of impairment testing, goodwill acquired in a business combination shall, from the acquisition date, be allocated to each of the acquirer's cash-generating units, or groups of cash-generating units, that are expected to benefit from the synergies of the combination, irrespective of whether other assets or liabilities of the acquiree are assigned to those units or groups of units.

Goodwill sometimes cannot be allocated on a non-arbitrary basis to individual cash-generating units, but only to groups of cash-generating units. Each unit or group of units to which the goodwill is so allocated shall:

(a) represent the lowest level within the entity at which the goodwill is monitored for internal management purposes; and
(b) not be larger than an operating segment as defined by IFRS 8.

If on the one hand, the IFRS's accounting approach allows the use of abstraction in the calculation for the amortization of assets to be avoided – thus decreasing the relevance of subjective values in the profit and loss account and the degree of

---

9. According to the Directive, an explanation of the period over which goodwill is written off shall be provided within the notes to the financial statements.
10. The useful life is determined considering:
    (a) the expected usage of the asset, assessed by reference to the asset's expected capacity or physical output;
    (b) expected physical wear and tear, which depends on operational factors such as the number of shifts for which the asset is to be used and the repair and maintenance programme and the care and maintenance of the asset while idle;
    (c) technical or commercial obsolescence arising from changes or improvements in production, or from a change in the market demand for the product or service output of the asset.
    (d) legal or similar limits on the use of the asset, such as the expiry dates of related leases.

subjectivity of the financial information – on the other hand, the impairment test, which must be carried out, generates a few significant considerations as to the degree of subjectivity (Pieri, 2010).

Sometimes, the impairment test does not concern a single asset, but a Cash Generating Unit (CGU) or a group of CGUs. In such a case, the determination of the carrying amount pursuant to IAS 36 involves several 'choices', including – but not limited to:

(i)   the identification of the assets which must be included in the accounting value of the CGU;

(ii) the allocation to the CGU of only those assets that can be directly attributed to it;

(iii) the accounting treatment of corporate assets which must also be tested for impairment;

(iv) the role of start-up costs in the assessment of the value of CGUs.

The Directive specifies that where national law authorizes the inclusion of costs of development under 'Assets' and the costs of development have not been completely written off, Member States shall require that no distribution of profits takes place unless the amount of the reserves available for distribution and profits brought forward is at least equal to that of the costs not written off.

IFRS clarify that given the history of rapid changes in technology, computer software and many other sectors, intangible assets are susceptible to technological obsolescence. Therefore, it is often the case that their useful life is short.[11]

[B]   Value Adjustments to Assets

Under IFRS, after recognition as an asset, an item of property, plant and equipment or an intangible asset shall be carried at its cost less any accumulated depreciation and any accumulated impairment losses.

As a general definition, an impairment loss is the amount by which the carrying amount of an asset exceeds its recoverable amount.

To determine whether an item of property, plant and equipment is impaired, an entity applies IAS 36 Impairment of Assets. That Standard explains how an entity reviews the carrying amount of its assets, how it determines the recoverable amount of an asset and when it recognizes, or reverses the recognition of, an impairment loss.[12]

---

11. See Amendments to IAS 16 and IAS 38 – Clarification of Acceptable Methods of Depreciation and Amortisation issued in May 2014.

12. According to IAS 36, para. 12, in assessing whether there is any indication that an asset may be impaired, an entity shall consider, as a minimum, the following indications:

External sources of information:

(a) there are observable indications that the asset's value has declined during the period significantly more than would be expected as a result of the passage of time or normal use.

The Directive is not far from this approach and intends value adjustments to take account of changes in the values of individual assets established at the balance sheet date. It distinguishes:

- value adjustments to fixed assets;
- value adjustments to current assets.

The Directive clarifies that the purchase price or production cost or revalued amount of fixed assets with limited useful economic lives shall be reduced by value adjustments calculated to write off the value of such assets systematically over their useful economic lives.

According to the Directive, value adjustments to fixed assets shall be subject to the following rules:

(a) value adjustments to be made in respect of financial fixed assets, so that they are valued at the lower figure to be attributed to them at the balance sheet date;

(b) value adjustments shall be made in respect of fixed assets, whether their useful economic lives are limited or not, so that they are valued at the lower figure to be attributed to them at the balance sheet date if it is expected that the reduction in their value will be permanent.

These value adjustments shall be charged to the profit and loss account and disclosed separately in the notes to the financial statements if they have not been shown separately in the profit and loss account.

Value adjustments shall be made in respect of current assets with a view to showing them at the lower market value or, in particular circumstances, another lower value to be attributed to them at the balance sheet date.

(b) significant changes with an adverse effect on the entity have taken place during the period, or will take place in the near future, in the technological, market, economic or legal environment in which the entity operates or in the market to which an asset is dedicated.

(c) market interest rates or other market rates of return on investments have increased during the period, and those increases are likely to affect the discount rate used in calculating an asset's value in use and decrease the asset's recoverable amount materially.

(d) the carrying amount of the net assets of the entity is more than its market capitalisation.

Internal sources of information:

(e) evidence is available of obsolescence or physical damage of an asset.

(f) significant changes with an adverse effect on the entity have taken place during the period, or are expected to take place in the near future, to the extent to which, or manner in which, an asset is used or is expected to be used. These changes include the asset becoming idle, plans to discontinue or restructure the operation to which an asset belongs, plans to dispose of an asset before the previously expected date, and reassessing the useful life of an asset as finite rather than indefinite.

(g) evidence is available from internal reporting that indicates that the economic performance of an asset is, or will be, worse than expected.

Measurement at the lower of the values may not continue if the reasons for which the value adjustments were made have ceased to apply. According to the Directive, this provision shall apply to value adjustments of all assets other than goodwill.

[C]   Amortized Cost

The Directive (Article 12, paragraph 10) states that where the amount repayable on account of any debt is greater than the amount received, the difference may be shown as an asset.[13] The principle states that the amount of that difference shall be written off by a reasonable amount each year and completely written off no later than the time of repayment of the debt.

As a general rule, IFRS state that after initial recognition, all financial liabilities shall be measured at amortized cost, using the effective interest method.[14]

According to IAS 39, the amortized cost of a financial asset or financial liability is the amount at which the financial asset or financial liability is measured at initial recognition minus principal repayments, plus or minus the cumulative amortization using the effective interest method of any difference between that initial amount and the maturity amount, and minus any reduction (directly or through the use of an allowance account) for impairment or uncollectibility.

[D]   Equity Method for Participating Interests

In respect of the treatment of participating interests, the Directive clarifies that Member States may permit or require participating interests to be accounted for using the equity method in annual financial statements.

The adoption of this accounting option (i.e., requested for associates' undertakings in the consolidated financial statements by Article 27 of the Directive) should take account of the essential adjustments resulting from the particular characteristics of annual financial statements as compared to consolidated financial statements.

Under IFRS, according to IAS 28 investments in associates are accounted for using:

- the equity method in the consolidated financial statements and in the consolidated financial statements prepared by a entity without investment in subsidiaries;

---

13. The difference shall be shown separately in the balance sheet or in the notes to the financial statements.
14. The following instruments shall not be measured using amortized cost:
    (a) financial liabilities at fair value through profit or loss. Such liabilities, including derivatives that are liabilities, shall be measured at fair value except for a derivative liability, which is linked to and must be settled by delivery of an equity instrument that does not have a quoted price in an active market for an identical instrument, whose fair value cannot otherwise be reliably measured, that shall be measured at cost.

– the cost method (or fair value) or the equity method[15] in the separate financial statement.

The equity method is also requested by IFRS for investments in joint ventures.[16] This is not completely consistent with the EU rules that allow the proportional method for joint ventures in the consolidated financial statements (Article 26).

Using the Cost model, an investor shall measure investments in associates, other than those for which there is a published price quotation, at cost less any accumulated impairment losses. The investor shall recognize dividends and other distributions received from the investment as income regardless of whether the distributions are from accumulated profits of the associate arising before or after the date of acquisition.

Using the equity method of accounting, an equity investment is initially recognized at the transaction price (including transaction costs) and is subsequently adjusted to reflect the investor's share of the associate's profit or loss.

Although no problems arise with the distributability of the positive net result by applying this method to the consolidated financial statements, its application in annual stand-alone legal entities may create misleading situations. In this regard, the Directive states that Member States may permit or require that the proportion of the profit or loss attributable to the participating interest be recognized in the profit and loss account only to the extent of the amount corresponding to dividends already received or for which payment can be claimed. Moreover, where the profit attributable to the participating interest recognized in the profit and loss account exceeds the amount of the dividends already received or for which payment can be claimed, the amount of the difference shall be placed in a reserve which cannot be distributed to shareholders.

[E]   Inventory Evaluation

Member States may permit the purchase price or production cost of stocks of goods of the same category and all fungible items including investments to be calculated either on the basis of weighted average prices, on the basis of the 'first-in, first-out' (FIFO) method, the 'last-in, first-out' (LIFO) method, or a method reflecting generally accepted best practice.

According to IAS 2, inventories shall be measured at the lower of cost and net realizable value (determined as the selling price less completion and selling costs).

The cost of inventories is determined by using the FIFO or weighted average cost formula for all inventories having a similar nature and use to the entity.

---

15. The use of the Equity Method in Separate Financial Statements was approved through an Amendment to IAS 27 issued in August 2014.
16. A jointly controlled entity is a joint venture that involves the establishment of a corporation, partnership or other entity in which each venturer has an interest.
    The entity operates in the same way as other entities, except that a contractual arrangement between the venturers establishes joint control over the economic activity of the entity.
    According to IFRS 11, a venturer shall measure its investments in jointly controlled entities by the equity method.

The LIFO method is not permitted by IFRS.

According to IAS 2, techniques such as the standard cost method, the retail method or the most recent purchase price for measuring the cost of inventories are valid if the result approximates the cost.

IAS 2 requires an entity to assess, at the end of each reporting period, whether the carrying amount of the inventories is not fully recoverable (i.e., because of damage, obsolescence or declining selling prices). If an inventory item (or group of items) is impaired, the entity shall measure the inventory at its selling price less completion and selling costs, recognizing an impairment loss.

§3.06   EU DIRECTIVE VERSUS IFRS: ISSUES NOT COVERED

Comparing the Directive and IFRS principles, some aspects emerge that are not covered. In particular, no specific accounting option is stated by the Directive concerning the following aspects that are, conversely, defined by IFRS:

– Financial leases;
– Investment property;
– Biological assets;
– Joint Operations.

[A]   Financial Leases

The Directive states that the presentation of items in financial statements should take into account the economic reality or commercial substance of the underlying transaction or arrangement. This rule seems to acquire crucial importance in analysing the (impact of accounting for leases) in a context in which no specific accounting principles are defined. Moreover, the accounting practice had already adopted the IFRS accounting principles for leasing representation in the financial statements.

The classification of leases adopted by IFRS is based on the extent to which risks and rewards incidental to ownership of a leased asset lie with the lessor or the lessee.[17] Therefore, a lease that substantially transfers all the risks and rewards incidental to ownership of an asset is classified as a finance lease.[18] A lease is classified as an

---

17. According to IAS 17, risks include the possibilities of losses from idle capacity or technological obsolescence and of variations in return because of changing economic conditions, as well as rewards that may be represented by the expectation of profitable operation over the asset's economic life and of gain from appreciation in value or realization of a residual value.

18. Examples of situations that individually or in combination would normally lead to a lease being classified as a finance lease are:

   (a) the lease transfers ownership of the asset to the lessee by the end of the lease term;
   (b) the lessee has the option to purchase the asset at a price that is expected to be sufficiently lower than the fair value at the date the option becomes exercisable for it to be reasonably certain, at the inception of the lease, that the option will be exercised;
   (c) the lease term is for the major part of the economic life of the asset even if title is not transferred;

operating lease if it does not substantially transfer all the risks and rewards incidental to ownership.

The accounting criteria for lessees is based on the recognition of finance leases at the commencement of the term of the lease as assets and liabilities in their statements of financial position at amounts equal to the fair value of the leased property or, if lower, at the current value of the minimum lease payments, each determined at the inception of the lease.

A finance lease gives rise to depreciation expenses for depreciable assets as well as finance expenses for each accounting period. The depreciable amount of a leased asset is allocated to each accounting period during the period of expected use on a systematic basis consistent with the depreciation policy adopted by the lessee for depreciable assets owned. If there is a reasonable certainty that the lessee will obtain ownership by the end of the lease term, the period of expected use is the useful life of the asset; otherwise, the asset is depreciated over the shorter of the lease term and its useful life.

The depreciation policy for depreciable leased assets shall be consistent with that for depreciable owned assets, and the depreciation recognized shall be calculated in accordance with IAS 16 Property, Plant and Equipment and IAS 38 Intangible Assets.

At the same time, for operating leases, lease payments are recognized as an expense on a straight-line basis unless another systematic basis is representative of the time pattern of the user's benefit, even if the payments are not on that basis.

[B]   Investment Properties

Specific evaluation principles for investment properties are defined under IFRS. Conversely, no specific accounting rule is defined by the Directive.

According to IAS 40, an entity shall choose as its accounting policy either the fair value model or the cost model and shall apply that policy to all of its investment property.[19]

The international standards state that, after initial recognition at cost, an entity shall measure investment property whose fair value can be measured reliably without undue cost or effort on an ongoing basis, at fair value through profit or loss.[20]

(d) at the inception of the lease, the present value of the minimum lease payments amounts to at least almost all of the fair value of the leased asset; and

(e) the leased assets are of such a specialized nature that only the lessee can use them without major modifications.

19. Investment property is property (land or a building, or part of a building, or both) held by the owner or by the lessee under a finance lease to earn rentals or for capital appreciation or both, rather than for:

   (a) use in the production or supply of goods or services or for administrative purposes; or
   (b) sale in the ordinary course of business.

20. An entity is encouraged, but not required, to measure the fair value of investment property on the basis of a valuation by an independent valuer who holds a recognized and relevant professional qualification and has recent experience in the location and category of the investment property being valued.

All other investment properties are accounted for as property, plant and equipment using the cost-depreciation-impairment model.

[C]   Biological Assets

The evaluation of biological assets is not defined under the Directive. Conversely, IFRS define specific accounting rules. Under IFRS 41 (Agriculture), a biological asset is defined as a living animal or plant. The same principle clarifies that the biological transformation comprises the processes of growth, degeneration, production and procreation that cause qualitative or quantitative changes in a biological asset and states that an entity shall recognize a biological asset when and only when:

(a) the entity controls the asset as a result of past events;[21]
(b) it is probable that future economic benefits associated with the asset will flow to the entity;
(c) the fair value or cost of the asset can be measured reliably.

A biological asset shall be measured on initial recognition and at the end of each reporting period at its fair value less selling costs, except in the case where the fair value cannot be measured reliably.

[D]   Joint Operations

Specific evaluation principles for interests in a joint arrangement whereby the parties that have joint control of the arrangement have rights to the assets and obligations for the liabilities, relating to the arrangement (joint operations), are defined under IFRS. Conversely, no specific accounting rule is defined by the Directive. The IFRS 11 establishes principles for financial reporting by entities that have an interest in arrangements that are controlled jointly by two or more joint venturers. According to this principle, in relation to an interest in a joint operation, a joint operator shall account both in its consolidated and in its separate financial statements for:

(a) its assets, including its share of any assets held jointly;
(b) its liabilities, including its share of any liabilities incurred jointly;
(c) its revenue from the sale of its share of the output arising from the joint operation;
(d) its share of the revenue from the sale of the output by the joint operation;
(e) its expenses, including its share of any expenses incurred jointly.

---

21. In agricultural activity, control may be proven, for example, by legal ownership of cattle and the branding or otherwise marking of the cattle on acquisition, birth, or weaning. The future benefits are normally assessed by measuring significant physical attributes.

§3.07   CONCLUSIONS

As described, the new Directive closes the gap between EU accounting rules and IFRS as far as previous key differences are concerned such as the evaluation of non-current based assets only at their historical cost and the evaluation of financial assets and derivatives. These differences are overcome on the basis of the fair value alternative or mandatory accounting criteria providing information that can be of more relevance to the users of financial statements than purchase price or production cost-based information.

It should be noted that the literature underlines that an extensive use of 'mark to market' accounting, based on fair values, will probably increase the volatility of reported income, as well as the gap between income and cash flows (Gwilliam & Jackson, 2008). Moreover, historical cost valuations are seen as reliable but may be considered as irrelevant, while market valuations may be seen as more relevant but less reliable, while little benefit and high costs were expected for marked-to-model valuation, suggesting that the costs and benefits associated with the revaluation model for property, plant and equipment depend largely on the existence of current market prices (Di Pietra et al., 2008).

According to the new accounting rules introduced by the Directive, some advantages will arise for the readers of the financial statements due to the Fair Value method which provides the latest data on the value of the assets, thus offering more accurate information, and the objectivity of the same, as determined by reference to the market value (Quagli, 2006).

Some limitations, however, exist primarily concerning aspects such as (Provasi & Sottoriva, 2015):

(1) The lack of accuracy when there are no markets on which to base values derived from models and measurement techniques for the estimation.
(2) The great variability of the value, linked to the difficulty in applying the fair value method rather than the purchase price or the cost.
(3) Greater difficulty in applying the fair value method rather than the purchase price or the cost.

More in general, the disadvantages deriving from a broader adoption of fair value accounting lead to a higher degree of subjectivity due to the assessment of an asset's or liability's value based not only on an 'objective' value determined by the cash out-flow. As a matter of fact, the assessment of fair value involves choosing between different approaches (market approach, cost approach, income approach) using directly or indirectly observable data (values on active markets, observable inputs or non observable inputs) and this allows a degree of subjectivity that is higher than that allowed under the cost model.

On the other hand, a regulation based on greater fair value measurement and disclosures should improve the information environment, the relevance of accounting information and predictability (Amhed et al., 2013; Devalle et al., 2010).

Some open aspects in terms of the differences between IFRS and Directive rules still remain. These concern aspects such as:

– Impairment test for goodwill, where the Directive does not provide for goodwill or other intangible assets with indefinite useful lives to be tested for impairment annually. Such assets are amortized on the basis of a definite number of years.
– Financial leases, where the Directive does not provide for different accounting treatments for operating and finance leases and does not require the adoption of the IFRS method for representing finance leases.
– LIFO method for inventories, where the Directive still allows the use of this method.

Therefore, misalignments occur in the representations of such transactions.

REFERENCES

Ahmed, K., Chalmers, K., & Khlif, H. (2013). A Meta-analysis of IFRS Adoption Effects. The International Journal of Accounting, 48, 2013, 173-217.

Azzali, Stefano. (2005) L'informativa di bilancio secondo i principi contabili nazionali e internazionali. Torino, Giappichelli.

Combarros, J.L. (2000). Accounting and Financial Audit Harmonization in the European Union. The European Accounting Review, 2000, 9:4, 643-654.

Corbella, S., et al., (2013). IFRS Adoption in Italy: Which Effects on Accounting Figures and Subjectivity? Accounting and Finance Research, 2(4).

Deac, M. (2014). The New EU Accounting Directive – A Comparison of Reporting Requirements. Annals of the 'Constantin Brâncuşi' University of Târgu Jiu, Economy Series.

Devalle, A., Onali, E., & Magarini, R. (2010). Assessing the Value Relevance of Accounting Data after the Introduction of IFRS in Europe. Journal of International Financial Management and Accounting, 21(2) 85-119.

Di carlo A., Potito L. (a cura di) (2008) *Financial Reporting: The Evolution in Progress.* Torino, Giappichelli.

Di Pietra R. et al., (2008). Comment on the IASB's Exposure Draft 'IFRS for Small and Medium-Sized Entities' Accounting in Europe, 5(1) 27-47.

Fortunato, S. (2007). Dal costo storico al 'fair value': al di là della rivoluzione contabile. Rivista delle società, 941-964.

Gwilliam, D., & Jackson, R.H.G. (2008). Fair Value in Financial Reporting: Problems and Pitfalls in Practice – A Case Study Analysis of the Use of Fair Valuation at Enron. Accounting Forum, 32(3) 240-259.

Paoloni, M. (a cura di) (2005). Il bilancio d'esercizio nel contesto nazionale ed internazionale. Torino, Giappichelli.

Pieri, V. (2010). The Relevance and the Dynamics of Goodwill Values Under IAS/IFRS: Empirical Evidences from the 2005-2009 Consolidated Financial Statements of the Major Companies Listed in Italy. University of Rome III – Department of Business Studies. http://ssrn.com/abstract = 1695892.

Provasi, R., & Sottoriva, C. (2015). Preliminary Considerations About the Transposition of Directive 2013/34/EU Into Italian Accounting System. Journal of Modern Accounting and Auditing, 11(6) 302-312.

Quagli, A. (2006). *Bilancio di esercizio e principi contabili*. Torino, Giappichelli.

Socoliuc, M., & Grosu, V. (2015). The consequences of the new EU accounting Directive on financial reporting. Annals of the 'Constantin Brâncuşi' University of Târgu Jiu, Economy Series.

PART III   Accounting and Taxation:
Reports from Different Countries

CHAPTER 4

Accounting and Taxation: Belgium

Edoardo Traversa & Steven Peeters

§4.01 INTRODUCTION

This contribution addresses various issues with respect to the relationship between the determination of the financial results and the corporate income tax base under Belgian law.

First, the general principles with respect to this so-called Book-Tax Relationship in Belgium will be set out. Second, an overview will be provided of the main differences between the result of a company from a financial reporting and a tax perspective. Third, the extent to which the determination of the corporate income tax base in Belgium differs from the CCCTB will be examined. Finally, the impact of the implementation of Accounting Directive 2013/34/EU on the existing legislative framework will be discussed.

§4.02 GENERAL PRINCIPLES WITH RESPECT TO THE BOOK-TAX RELATIONSHIP[1]

[A] Determination of the Tax Base: Principles

The Belgian Income Tax Code ('*BITC*') does not contain an encompassing definition of the 'taxable profits'.

Hence, the starting point to determine the taxable income of companies is the variation of the net worth of the company during a financial year as reflected in the annual accounts of the company in accordance with Belgian Generally Accepted Accounting Principles ('*Belgian GAAP*'). Then, by application of express tax law provisions, that book result is either increased (e.g., by means of the non-deductibility of certain disallowed expenses and the taxation of granted abnormal or gratuitous advantages) or decreased (e.g., by means of the exemption of certain realized capital gains on shares and the Notional Interest Deduction (NID)) for tax purposes.

Belgium thus applies a principle of 'unity of annual accounts', which means that tax law does not provide its own set of rules to determine annual statements for tax purposes, but rather uses the annual accounts established for accounting purposes and subsequently adapts the result in accordance with specific tax law provisions.

This principle is not explicitly enshrined in the BITC, but the latter contains a few references to accounting law:

- The annual accounts of the company have to be added to the corporate income tax declaration of the company (Article 307, §3 BITC *jo.* declaration forms determined by royal decree).
- Certain tax law definitions refer to accounting law: '*The notions "intangible, tangible or financial fixed assets", "establishment costs" and "stocks and contracts in progress" have the meaning attributed thereto in the legislation on accountancy and annual accounts of companies.*' (Article 2, §1, 9°, BITC).

---

1. Interesting contributions in this respect: J. KIRKPATRICK, 'L'influence du nouveau droit comptable sur le droit fiscal des sociétés en Belgique', *J.T.* 1982, 193-197; G. GELDERS, 'Droit comptable et fiscalité', *Bull. contr.* 1984, 1246-1269; J.-P. SERVAIS, 'Dissociation ou connexion entre le droit comptable et le droit fiscal? Examen critique à l'aune de vingt ans d'expérience belge', *Bull. Commission for Accounting Norms* 1997, 100-171; M. DE WOLF, 'Droit comptable et droit fiscal: deux amants inséparables?', *Liber Amicorum Henri Olivier*, Brugge, Die Keure, 2000, 201-210; D. GARABEDIAN, 'Bénéfice imposable et droit comptable' (noot onder Cass. 20 februari 1997), *RCJB* 2000, 530-557; J. KIRKPATRICK and D. GARABEDIAN, *Le régime fiscal des sociétés en Belgique*, Brussels, Bruylant, 2003, pp. 110-116; B. COLMANT, 'Verband tussen het boekhoudrecht en het fiscaal recht van ondernemingen: enige aanknopingspunten en bedenkingen', *Accountancy & Tax* 2006/1, 23-31; H. LAMON and A. VAN BAVEL, 'IAS/IFRS pour les comptes sociaux de toutes les sociétés belges?', *DAOR* 2006, 348-383; A. HAELTERMAN, *Vennootschapsbelasting doorgelicht*, Brugge, Die Keure, 2012, 53 *e.s.*; H. LAMON and A. VAN BAVEL, *Aspects fiscaux de la comptabilité et technique de déclaration fiscale*, Brussels, Larcier, 2013, 23-39; L. PINTE, 'Droit comptable et droit fiscal: rétrospective et perspectives', in C. DOCCLO (ed.), *Alabaster 1938-2013*, Limal, Anthemis, 2013, 395-417; K. VAN HULLE, N. LYBAERT and J.-P. MAES, *Handboek Boekhoud- en Jaarrekeningrecht*, Brugge, Die Keure, 2015, 32-35.

When reference is made to Belgian accounting law, it concerns the non-consolidated financial statements of a Belgian company in accordance with Belgian GAAP. The Belgian corporate income tax is calculated at the level of each company individually and no intragroup consolidation is allowed.

[B] Determination of the Tax Base: Two Methods[2]

From a more technical perspective, the BITC itself provides two methods for calculating the corporate income tax base: one which is based on the origin of the income, and the other on the allocation thereof. These two methods lead as a rule to the same result.

According to the *first method,* the tax base of a company is determined *in accordance with the origin of the income* acquired by a company. In this respect, Article 183 BITC provides that the taxable income of a company is the same as the taxable income of individuals and that the amount thereof is determined in accordance with the personal income tax rules applicable to profits earned by unincorporated undertakings.

It is generally accepted in Belgian law that all income generated by Belgian companies (whether such income arises from a commercial exploitation or from movable or immovable property) is considered as professional income and is thus in principle taken into account for the determination of the tax base of the company.[3]

The *second method* does not take into account the origin of the income, but the *allocation* thereof. This method defines the tax base as the sum of (i) the increase of the taxed reserves; and (ii) the distributed dividends.

Article 185 BITC explicitly provides that corporate income tax is due on the total amount of the profits, including distributed dividends. The express inclusion of distributed dividends does not materially change the scope of the taxable income, but was added to underline the difference compared to the system prior to the 1964 tax reform.

[C] Link between Belgian GAAP Financial Accounts and Tax Accounts

As stated above, the taxable income of companies is based on the financial results, adapted in accordance with tax specific exceptions.

The decision to link accounting law and tax law was made at the time of the adoption of the comprehensive accounting rules in Belgium in 1975-1976 and remained valid as from then on. Prior to the adoption of these accounting rules, tax regulations were an important tool for the determination of acceptable accounting practices (in the absence of a comprehensive set of accounting rules).[4]

---

2. A. Haelterman, *Vennootschapsbelasting doorgelicht*, Brugge, Die Keure, 2012, 52-58.
3. Cass. 28 January 1969, *Pas.* 1969, I, 489.
4. K. Van Hulle, N. Lybaert and J.-P. Maes, *Handboek Boekhoud- en Jaarrekeningrecht*, Brugge, Die Keure, 2015, pp. 32-35.

At the time of the introduction of the accounting regulation, the following important principles were set out in the preparatory works of the accounting law of 17 July 1975 and the implementing Royal Decree of 8 October 1976.

First, the *dependency*[5] *of tax law on accounting law* as regards the determination of the taxable base for corporate income tax. This principle was referred to in the preparatory works of the Royal Decree of 8 October 1976 regarding the annual accounts: '*The rules with respect to evaluations, amortization, capital reductions and provisions for contingencies set out in this royal decree will be accepted by the tax administration for the determination of the tax base, except to the extent that tax laws explicitly derogate therefrom*'.[6] However, it took until 20 February 1997 before the Belgian Supreme Court[7] confirmed that this generally accepted relation had to be recognized as a legal principle.[8] Companies thus have to determine their taxable profits in accordance with Belgian accounting law, and are only allowed to deviate therefrom if explicitly provided for by Belgian tax law.[9] On the contrary, the tax administration is bound by a result that is in conformity with accounting law if no deviating tax provision exists.

Second, it was decided on a political level that the reform of the accounting norms should be *neutral,* which means that it should not have a direct or indirect tax impact. In the preparatory works of the accounting law of 17 July 1975, it was in this respect clarified that: '*The Government does not intend to indirectly modify, by the provision to be adopted, to change the scope of the current tax legislation. It will ensure this neutrality and will take, if need be, the necessary legislative, regulatory or administrative initiatives.*'[10] In practice, due to the dependency principle, changes in the interpretation of accounting concepts inevitably have an impact on tax rules. In some instances,

---

5. In Belgium, this principle is often referred to as '*primacy* of accounting law over tax law'. The use of the term 'dependency' is preferable to avoid misunderstanding, as the financial accounts are only the reference point, from which tax law can deviate. This term is also used by EU institutions (see for example the Communication of 24 November 2003 from the Commission to the Council, the European Parliament and the European Economic and Social Committee, 'An Internal Market without company tax obstacles: achievements, ongoing initiatives and remaining challenges', COM(2003) 726 final).

6. Report to the King accompanying the Royal Decree of 8 October 1976 concerning the annual accounts of companies, *Belgian Official Gazette* 19 October 1976.

7. Cass. 20 February 1997, *Pas.* 1997, I, 253. In this case, the Court followed a three-step reasoning. First, the Supreme Court states explicitly the principle of dependency of tax law on accounting norms except express derogation in tax law: 'Considering that companies' taxable gains are determined in accordance with accounting rules, unless tax law provides for an explicit deviation therefrom'. Second, the Court controlled whether the accountancy treatment of the taxpayer was in conformity with applicable accountancy rules. Third, the existence of an explicit derogation in tax law was examined. This method was also set out by the Commission for Accountancy Norms in its Bulletin of March 1998, p. 2.

8. The Supreme Court refused in 1995 to accept that there is a general principle of law that accountancy law 'rules' tax law, see Cass. 5 May 1995, *Pas.* 1995, 457.

9. For example, the Court of Appeals of Ghent decided on 5 October 2004 that a taxpayer was not allowed to deduct a business expense in a certain financial year, as that business expense should already have been accounted for in the previous financial year in accordance with accounting law: Ghent, 5 October 2004, *TFR* 2005, 341, commented on by I. Van de Woesteyne, 'Tijdstip van aftrek van beroepskosten overeenkomstig artikel 49 WIB 1992', *TFR* 2005, 344-349.

10. Explanatory memorandum to the law of 17 July 2015 with respect to accountancy and annual accounts of companies, *Doc. parl.* Senat 1976-1975, nr. 436/1, 4.

it appeared that certain changes in the interpretation of accounting law had clear tax consequences.[11]

[D] Annual Accounts and Their Binding Effect

[1] Annual (Non-consolidated) Accounts in Accordance with Belgian GAAP

The financial accounts that constitute the basis for the calculation of the Belgian corporate tax base, are the annual (non-consolidated) accounts of the company. These statements have to be established in accordance with Belgian GAAP.

Based on Article 4 of EC Regulation nr. 1606/2002 of 19 July 2002 on the application of International Accounting Standards (IAS), Belgian publicly traded companies are, however, required to prepare their *consolidated* accounts in conformity with the IAS. In general, Belgium has not used its power under Article 5 of that regulation to require the use of IAS for (i) publicly traded companies with respect to their annual (non-consolidated) accounts; or (ii) other companies with respect to their consolidated[12,13] or annual (non-consolidated) accounts.[14]

There is thus currently no link between the IAS/IFRS norms and the determination of the corporate income tax base in Belgium.

The potential influence of the general introduction of IAS/IFRS on tax law has already been addressed in doctrine:[15]

> B. COLMANT explained that the change to IAS/IFRS with respect to the annual (non-consolidated) accounts would automatically lead to a change of several tax rules, unless it were considered to break the link between accounting law and tax law. He is of the opinion that the IAS/IFRS would be inappropriate to determine the corporate tax base because of the different viewpoints compared to Belgian GAAP, and more in particular (i) the valuation of assets and liabilities on the basis of their fair value instead of on the basis of historical cost; (ii) the different meaning that is given to the realization principle; and (iii) the substance over form approach. He also pointed out that, in order to ensure that the equality principle would be respected, a transfer (for tax purposes) to IAS/IFRS would only be

---

11. Reference is made to Advice nr. 126/17 of the Commission for Accounting Standards regarding the acquisition of assets for no consideration. Regarding this issue, see also section §4.02[C][2].
12. All Belgian companies that have to establish consolidated accounts, may opt to establish them in accordance with IAS/AFRS norms. Such a decision is irrevocable.
13. An exception is provided for Belgian credit institutions and investment undertakings, which have to draw up their consolidated accounts in accordance with IFRS/IAS as from 1 January 2006 (Royal Decree 5 December 2004).
14. M. WYCKAERT indicated that Belgium is resisting the pressure to further implement IFRS/IAS because of the existing link with tax law, but that the resistance will not continue forever. M. WYCKAERT, 'Het vennootschaps- en het fiscaal recht: een gedwongen huwelijk of natuurlijke bondgenoten', in *Liber Amicorum Frans Vanistendael*, Herentals, Knops Publishing, 2007, (567) 571-572.
15. Regarding the impact of IAS/IFRS on Belgian company law, see D. SAFRAN, 'Quelques incidences en droit de sociétés de l'application des norms comptables internationals IAS/IFRS', *T.B.H.* 2006, 379-403.

possible if all Belgian companies were obliged to establish their statements in accordance with IAS/IFRS.[16]

H. Lamon and A. Van Bavel argue that the impact of a potential change to IAS/IFRS norms would not be insurmountable, basing themselves on a study performed in 2005[17] which came to the conclusion that the differences between the tax rates of states are a consequence of the difference in nominal tax rate rather than a consequence of the difference in tax base.[18]

[2]   Binding Effect of the Annual Accounts

The annual accounts are in principle *binding vis-à-vis the company* for tax purposes. This means that the tax liabilities of a company can be determined based on the annual accounts as approved by the annual meeting of shareholders, and that the company may in principle not amend these accounts subsequently in order to avoid or mitigate tax liabilities deriving from the financial situation that they reflect. In this respect, the commentary of the tax administration to the BITC mentions: '*the annual accounts approved by the general meeting of shareholders irrevocably binds the company, except when it concerns material mistakes or errors.*'[19]

The binding effect does not apply in the event that the annual accounts are affected by an error. This was confirmed by the Belgian Supreme Court.[20] This is a logical conclusion in the light of the principle that tax liability arises from the law and is based on the actual situation of the taxpayer, beyond what is reflected in accounting documents.[21] In a recent note, the Belgian Commission of Accountancy Norms[22] explained that there are two types of errors that may be corrected in order to ensure that that the annual accounts give a true and fair view of the company:

- Material (clerical) errors (e.g., typos, a profit that is erroneously entered on a wrong account, calculation errors and other manifest errors that are independent from any legal assessment).
- Errors in law or in fact, which may even contain a certain element of assessment, or even a valuation error.

---

16. B. Colmant, 'Verband tussen het boekhoudrecht en het fiscaal recht van ondernemingen: enige aanknopingspunten en bedenkingen', *Accountancy & Tax*, nr. 1/2006, pp. 23-31.
17. O. Jacobs, Ch. Spengel, Th. Stetter and C. Wendt, 'EU Company Taxation in Case of a Common Tax Base: A Computer-based Calculation and Comparison Using the Enhanced Model of the European Tax Analyser', *Intertax* 2005, pp. 414-428.
18. H. Lamon and A. Van Bavel, 'IAS/IFRS pour les comptes sociaux de toutes les sociétés belges?', *DAOR* 2006, (348) 370.
19. Commentary to the Belgium Income Tax Code, nr. 340/31.
20. Cass. 12 May 1989, *Pas.* 1989-1990, II, nr. 521, commented on by J. Kirkpatrick and D. Garabedian, 'La rectification du bilan de la société anonyme en droit privé et en droit fiscal', *RCJB* 1992, pp. 317-347.
21. A. Haelterman, *Vennootschapsbelasting doorgelicht*, Brugge, Die Keure, 2012, p. 64.
22. Commission for Accountancy Norms, Advice 2014/4 of 23 April 2014: 'Correction of the annual accounts'.

An error has to be distinguished from a judgment call of the company in an area where applicable accountancy rules leave some margin of appreciation (e.g., with respect to the valuations of assets where a margin of appreciation exists, the distribution of a dividend) and where the decision is in itself not illegal.[23] The company is not allowed to revise such judgment calls.[24]

Moreover, the annual accounts are not binding vis-à-vis the company when they are in contradiction with applicable accounting standards.

In section §4.02[B] of this contribution, we already stated that the *tax administration has to respect the decisions* made by the taxpayer in the annual accounts to the extent that (i) the accountancy treatment is in compliance with applicable accountancy laws; and (ii) tax law does not provide for an explicit derogation of accountancy law.

A recent application of this binding link between accounting law and tax law for the tax administration is the case *Bloomsbury v. Belgian State*, in which the Court of Justice of the European Union (*'CJEU'*) issued an order on 6 March 2014.[25]

That case concerned the transfer of shares for no consideration between two Belgian companies.[26] Bloomsbury, the acquirer of the shares, had not included this acquisition in its annual accounts in accordance with the Belgian GAAP principle that the value of assets has to be determined based on their historical cost (i.e., acquisition price minus depreciations and capital reductions). The tax administration was of the opinion that the participation should have been included in Bloomsbury's annual accounts in accordance with the principle that the annual accounts shall give a true and fair view of the company's assets, liabilities, financial position and profits and loss (provided for in Article 2, paragraph 3 of the Fourth Directive nr. 78/660/EEC of 25 July 1978). The tax administration argued this with the aim of taxing the real value of the asset at the ordinary corporate income tax rate, as it has the power to include undervaluations of assets in the corporate income tax base if such undervaluations are inconsistent with accounting law.

In its judgment, the CJEU first recalls that, although the Fourth Directive does not aim at establishing the conditions under which the annual accounts of companies may or must serve as a basis for the determination of the corporate income tax base by the tax authorities, it is in no way excluded that annual accounts can be used by Member States as a reference base for tax purposes (as is the case in Belgium), and that the Fourth Directive does not prohibit the Member States from correcting the effects of the accounting rules to determine their taxable profit.[27] Afterwards, the CJEU decided that the fact that an asset is undervalued is a necessary corollary of the choice to value

---

23. With respect to the difference between a 'material error' and a 'judgment call', see W. D'HAESE, 'Het boekhoudrecht in relatie tot de vennootschapsbelasting', in M. DE JONCKHEERE (ed.), *Een reis doorheen de fiscale basisbeginselen*, Brugge, Die Keure, 2011, pp. 191-195 and S. HUYSMAN, *Fiscale winst. Theorie en praktijk van het fiscale winstbegrip in België*, Kalmthout, Biblo, 1994, 249 e.s.
24. Cass. 2 February 1977, *JDF* 1977, 129.
25. Order in *Bloomsbury NV v. Belgian State*, C-510/12, ECLI:EU:C:2014:154 (only in French and Dutch), in which the Court confirmed its judgment in *Belgian State v. GIMLE*, C-322/12, ECLI:EU:C:2013:632.
26. In the GIMLE case, it concerned the acquisition of assets for a low consideration.
27. Bloomsbury, para. 16 and GIMLE, para. 28.

assets on the basis of their historical cost rather than on their true value, and that the principle that the annual accounts have to give a true and fair view does not permit a derogation from this first principle when the acquisition price is manifestly lower than the true value of the assets.[28] As a consequence of this judgment, the Court of Appeals of Ghent decided on 21 April 2015 that the tax administration could not tax the undervaluation of the shares because the undervaluation was not inconsistent with the applicable accounting provisions.[29]

§4.03   DIFFERENCES BETWEEN THE FINANCIAL INCOME AND TAXABLE INCOME

[A]   Introduction

As mentioned before, the annual variation of the net worth of a company is the reference point for determining the Belgian corporate income tax base of that company, except if expressly provided for in tax law.

Below is an overview of some important differences between the income for accounting purposes and for tax purposes.

[B]   Tax Provisions Decreasing the Corporate Income Tax Base

[1]   Dividend Received Deduction ('Participation Exemption')

In accordance with the EU Parent-Subsidiary Directive,[30] Belgium grants a deduction from the corporate income tax base of 95% of the dividend income received on shares in resident and non-resident companies (not limited to the EEA) subject to the following requirements: (i) holding at least 10% of the equity of the company or shares with an acquisition value of at least EUR 2.5 million; (ii) holding the shares for an uninterrupted period of at least one year in full ownership; and (iii) satisfaction of the 'subject-to-tax' condition at the level of the distributing entity.

As a consequence of the CJEU *Cobelfret*[31] case, excess deductions in a taxable period from an EEA company and some tax-treaty countries may be carried-forward.

The 5% of the dividends that is not exempt, may be offset by (deductible) costs incurred by the company.

---

28. Bloomsbury, paras 17-30 and GIMLE, paras 29-42.
29. H. Putman, 'Verkrijging volledig om niet: evenmin waardering aan werkelijke waarde', *Fiscoloog* 2014, nr. 1382, p. 8; S. Van Crombrugge, 'Verkrijging activa ten kostelozen titel: fiscus verliest achterhoedegevecht', *Fiscoloog* 2015, pp. 7-8; H. Putman en J. Vanhecke, 'Verkrijging activa beneden marktwaarde: altijd, soms of nooit onmiddelijke winsterkenning?', *TFR* 2015, pp. 575-590.
30. Council Directive 2011/96/EU of 30 November 2011 on the common system of taxation applicable in the case of parent companies and subsidiaries of different Member States.
31. Judgment in *Belgian State v. Cobelfret*, C-138/07, ECLI:EU:C:2009:82.

[2] Exemption for Capital Gains on Shares

Capital gains on shares realized by a Belgian company are tax exempt if the following conditions are met: (i) the subject-to-tax condition is met at the level of the company whose shares are sold; (ii) the seller holds the shares for at least one year in full ownership; and (iii) the seller qualifies as a 'small company'.[32]

If the subject-to-tax condition is not met, capital gains on shares are subject to ordinary corporate income tax at a rate of 33.99%.

If the subject-to-tax condition is met, but the shares were not held for a minimum duration of one year, the so-called short-term capital gain is taxed at a separate rate of 25.75%, irrespective of whether the company qualifies as a small company.

If the subject-to-tax condition is met, the shares were held for at least one year and the company does not qualify as a small company, the capital gain is subject to a separate tax of 0.412%. This is a minimum tax against which no tax assets can be offset.

[3] Notional Interest Deduction (NID)

The NID, which is officially called 'deduction for risk capital' (better known in literature as 'allowance for corporate equity', allows a company to decrease its corporate income tax base with a fictitious interest for its equity. The equity that is taken into account equals the net assets of the company at the end of the previous financial year, corrected with certain adjustments.[33] The rate of the NID is determined yearly on the basis of the Belgian Government Bonds over ten years. The NID rate is increased by 0.5% for small companies. For the taxable period 2015 (tax year 2016), the NID rate equals 2.13% for small companies and 1.63% for other companies.

Initially, excess NID could be carried-forward over seven years. Due to budgetary constraints, the government decided to abolish this possibility as from tax year 2012.

According to the explanatory memorandum of the law of 22 June 2005 introducing the NID, the main objective of this measure was to put debt financing and equity financing on an equal footing. However, the introduction of this mechanism also needs to be understood as an attempt to create an attractive alternative for the favourable tax

---

32. A small company is a company that does not fulfil more than one of the following criteria: (i) average employees (FTE): 50, (ii) average turnover (excl. VAT): EUR 9,000,000 and (iii) balance sheet total: EUR 4,500,000. For tax purposes, the criteria mentioned above have to be considered on a consolidated basis together with their affiliated companies. See also Chapter 5 below.
33. Among others, the difference between the net book value of the assets and the liabilities attributable to a foreign permanent establishment had to be excluded if the income from that permanent establishment was not taxable in Belgium pursuant to a double taxation convention. This exclusion was considered inconsistent with the freedom of establishment by the CJEU in *Argenta Spaarbank NV v. Belgian State*, C-350/11, ECLI:EU:C:2013:447. See also: R. NEYT and S. PEETERS, 'Balanced Allocation and Coherence: Some Thoughts in Light of Argenta and K', *EC Tax Review* 2014, pp. 64-75.

regime of coordination centres, which was abolished because of its incompatibility with state aid rules.[34]

The utilization of the NID is restricted by the so-called *Fairness Tax* as of tax year 2014. This is a separate corporate income tax of 5.15%, which is, broadly speaking, due on an amount of dividends that is declared during a certain taxable period on profits that benefited from NID or carried-forward tax losses.[35] This rule is not applicable to small companies.

[4]   Other Significant Measures Decreasing the Corporate Income Tax Base

- Carry-forward of tax losses without time limitation.
- Deduction of 80% of the income derived from patents that are (partly or fully) self-developed or improved in the company's Belgian or foreign research centre. For small companies, the benefit of the deduction is no longer subject to the condition that the patent is developed or improved in a research centre of that company. The remaining part of the income can still be offset by costs or other tax assets.
- Investment deduction.[36]

[C]   Tax Provisions Increasing the Corporate Income Tax Base

[1]   Disallowed Expenses: General Provision

In general, professional expenses are deductible by companies in Belgium if the following conditions are satisfied: (i) the cost must be linked to the exercise of the business; (ii) the cost must be incurred or borne during that taxable period; (iii) they must be made to obtain or retain taxable income; and (iv) the existence and the amount of the cost must be justified by the taxpayer. Costs that do not satisfy these conditions are disallowed and have to be added to the tax base.

[2]   Disallowed Expenses: Express Provisions

The BITC also expressly disallows certain expenses made by a company. Some examples:

---

34. Advocate General Mengozzi included a short description of the tax regime applicable to coordination centres and the state aid procedures related to it in his opinion in the case *Argenta Spaarbank NV v. Belgian State*, C-350/11, ECLI:EU:C:2012:580.
35. M. Dhaene and A. Brohez, 'De fairness tax: een grondige analyse en enkele bedenkingen omtrent de verenigbaarheid met hogere rechtsnormen', *TFR* 2013, 897-914.
36. For a description of the investment deduction, please see the brochure of the Belgian Federal Public Service of Finances: http://financien.belgium.be/nl/binaries/brochure-investment-deduction-2014_tcm306-260937.pdf.

- corporate income tax itself and certain other taxes;
- losses on shares, except to the extent that these losses are incurred at the time of a full distribution of the capital of a company and that the losses cover the capital that is represented by those shares;
- payments to blacklisted jurisdictions and jurisdictions that are considered to be non-compliant by the OECD Global Forum on Transparency and Exchange of Information for Tax Purposes if (i) those payments are not listed in an annex to the corporate income tax return;[37] or (ii) even if the payments are listed, if the taxpayer does not prove that they are made in the framework of real and genuine transactions and to other entities than wholly artificial arrangements;
- Interest above certain thresholds (thin-cap rules, see below).

[3] Thin-Cap Rules

Belgian tax law provides for a 5 to 1 thin-cap rule with respect to (i) loans whereby the beneficial owner is not subject to income taxes, or, with regard to interest income, is subject to a tax regime which is substantially more advantageous than the Belgian tax regime; and (ii) intragroup loans.

The interest paid on qualifying debt is not deductible for Belgian tax purposes to the extent that the qualifying debt exceeds five times the equity. In this respect, equity is the sum of (i) the taxed reserves at the beginning of the taxable period; and (ii) the paid-up capital at the end of the taxable period.

A similar refusal of interest deduction exists for interest paid to individuals that are shareholders or directors of the company as well as to (non-resident) corporate directors. In that case, the acceptable debt-equity ratio is 1 to 1.

[4] Excess Depreciations

[a] Introduction: Depreciations in Belgium[38]

Tangible and intangible assets having a limited lifetime may be depreciated or amortized, and such depreciations (amortizations) are in principle tax deductible. In accordance with Article 61 BITC, depreciations (amortizations) are considered as deductible business expenses to the extent (i) that they are based on the acquisition value or investment value; and (ii) that they coincide with a decrease in value that has occurred during the taxable period.

Depreciations (amortizations) are calculated either on a straight-line basis or on a declining basis.

---

37. The tax administration stated in a circular letter that the sanction on non-deductibility cannot apply solely because of the absence of a declaration if the payment is made to an entity in the EU or in a country with which Belgium has concluded a double convention with a non-discrimination clause.
38. For a more detailed discussion of depreciations in Belgium, see Cl. CHEVALIER, *Vademecum Vennootschapsbelasting*, Brussels, Larcier, 2013, 420-520.

According to the *straight-line method*, a fixed annual amount is deducted over the asset's useful life.

Tax law provides certain specific indications in this respect, for example:

– Intangible assets (e.g., goodwill, patents) have to be depreciated over a period of at least five years. As an exception, intangible assets relating to research and development can be deducted over a period of at least three years.
– The tax administration has given certain indications in its commentary of what it considers reasonable depreciations, e.g., 3% for industrial buildings or 5% for commercial buildings or offices.

The *method for calculating depreciations on a declining basis* allows the company to opt for accelerated depreciations on certain assets.[39] Pursuant to this method, the depreciation percentage of the first year is, at most, double the percentage that would apply if the straight-line depreciation method were used. As from the second year, the depreciation amount is determined annually by multiplying the remaining value after the deduction of the previous year by the same percentage in the first year. However, as from the year in which the result of this multiplication is lower than the amount that would have been allowed if the straight-line depreciation method were used, the amount of the straight-line depreciation method may be used for depreciation. The depreciation value may not be higher than 40% of the acquisition value of the asset.

This accelerated method is provided for in tax law, but Belgian accounting law accepts the application thereof in the financial statements. However, the difference between the accelerated depreciations and the justified amount from an economic perspective has to be disclosed in the explanatory notes to the financial statements.

[b]   Disallowed Excess Depreciations

If the depreciations exceed the amount that is acceptable from a tax perspective, the excess amount has to be added to the corporate income tax base of the company for that year. The disallowed 'excess depreciations' may, however, be recovered by the company in the following years.

§4.04   CCCTB

[A]   Introduction

On 16 March 2011, the European Commission launched its proposal for a Council Directive on a Common Consolidated Corporate Tax Base ('CCCTB Draft Directive').[40]

---

39. This method may not be used for (i) cars, cars for dual use, minibuses and certain light trucks, and (ii) fixed assets if the use of such assets has been ceded by the taxpayer applying the depreciations to a third party.
40. Proposal of 16 March 2011, for a Council Directive on a Common Consolidated Corporate Tax Base (CCCTB), COM(2011) 121/4.

The CCCTB Draft Directive contains a set of rules that are independent from the accounting and tax rules of the Member States to determine the corporate tax base of companies or groups of companies in the European Union.

The implementation of the CCCTB in Belgium would have a significant impact on the corporate income tax base. In this respect, A. Roggeman concluded in her Ph.D. dissertation that such an implementation would lead to an increase in the average tax burden of a large company of 16% and of an SME of 14%.[41] This study disregarded the effect of potential consolidation, and thus limited itself to the assessment of the Common Consolidated Tax Base (CCTB).

The main reasons for such a difference will be set out in the next section.

[B] Main Differences between CCCTB and Belgian Corporate Income Tax Base[42]

[1] *Absence of Link with Accounting Rules: Definition of Profit*

From a structural viewpoint, it is striking that the CCCTB is not based on the income of the company determined in accordance with applicable accounting rules, but rather contains an independent set of rules to establish the corporate income tax base.

Accordingly, the CCCTB Draft Directive contains a definition of tax base referring to the independent definition of revenues (Article 10 *jo.* 4(8) of the Draft CCCTB Directive). Such an encompassing definition does not exist in Belgian corporate income tax law (see section §4.02[A] above).

[2] *Tax Consolidation*

A very remarkable difference in the two systems is the mandatory tax consolidation between group members, a feature which is included in the CCCTB Draft Directive (Articles 54-60), but is currently not provided for in Belgian income tax law. The introduction of consolidation in Belgium would have a significant impact as it would enable groups to compensate losses on a group level.

As a consequence of group tax consolidation, transactions entered into between group members may be disregarded (Article 59(1) of the Draft CCCTB Directive). This renders transfer pricing in an intragroup context within the European Union less sensitive.

---

41. A. Roggeman, *Essays on the Common Consolidated Corporate Tax Base*, Ph.D. dissertation U. Gent Faculty of Economics and Business Administration (supervisor Prof. dr Ph. Van Cauwenberge), http://hdl.handle.net/1854/LU-5857306. The study was based on the European Tax Analyzer ('ETA'):Ch. Spengel, M. Ortmann-Babel, B. Zinn and S. Matenaer, 'A Common Corporate Tax Base for Europe: An Impact Assessment of the Draft Council Directive on a CC(C)TB', *World Tax Journal*, 2012, pp. 185-221.
42. The aim of this part is to give a short description of the main differences between the CCCTB and the Belgian corporate income tax base. For an extensive discussion: S. Mertens, 'De Common Consolidated Corporate Tax Base: een revolutie inzake vennootschapsbelasting?', *AFT* 2015/1, pp. 33-59.

In this respect, it is of note that no thin-capitalization rule is included in the CCCTB Draft Directive (either for consolidated group companies or for group companies outside the EU).

In June 2015, the Commission re-launched the CCCTB project. On that occasion, it was suggested to start with a CCTB and postpone the consolidation until a second phase. Postponing the consolidation on an EU level leads to a later introduction of the concept of tax consolidation in Belgium.

[3]   Belgian Tax Incentives

The introduction of the CCCTB would significantly reduce the power of Belgium to design its own tax incentives. The most important tax incentive that does not fit within the CCCTB as proposed by the Commission is the NID (see section §4.03[B][3] above), given the considerable effect of that measure on the effective tax rate of companies. Besides, more specific tax incentives such as the patent box deduction and the tax shelter for the audio-visual industry are also not included in the CCCTB.

[4]   Income from Dividends and Capital Gains on Shares

The CCCTB Draft Directive provides for a general exemption of income received from profit distributions and for proceeds from a disposal of shares (Article 11(c)). From a Belgian perspective (and in the light of the Parent-Subsidiary Directive), it is remarkable that these exemptions are not subject to minimum requirements with respect to the size of the participation and the minimum holding period. On the contrary, the CCCTB Draft Directive does require the satisfaction of a subject-to-tax condition, in the absence of which exemption is not granted (see the so-called Switch-over clause provided for in Article 73).

Although a full exemption is granted, Article 14(g) provides that the costs incurred to lead to such an exempt income are not deductible and that such costs shall be fixed at a flat rate of 5% of that income unless the taxpayer demonstrates that the actual cost incurred is lower. With respect to dividend exemption, the (rebuttable) 5% rate is reminiscent of the Belgian participation exemption, which allows a 95% deduction plus the possibility to deduct the remaining 5% following normal rules on business expenses (see section §4.03[B][1] above). With respect to capital gains on shares, a similar rule does not currently exist in Belgian corporate income tax law.

[5]   Depreciations (Amortizations)

The depreciation rules provided for in the CCCTB Draft Directive differ significantly compared to the rules that are currently applicable in Belgium. Some examples:

– Buildings: depreciation over 40 years is considerably longer than 20 years or 33 years, as is acceptable in Belgium.

- Intangible assets: depreciation over 15 years if the period of grant or legal protection cannot be determined, while the general rule in Belgium is 5 years.
- Depreciations of most other assets are calculated on the basis of an asset pool, of which a yearly 25% can be depreciated. In Belgium, the depreciation of assets has to be determined on an individual basis and not pooled.

§4.05 ACCOUNTANCY DIRECTIVE

Belgian tax law contains several specific rules or exceptions for 'small companies' compared to large companies. Some examples: (i) the NID percentage for small companies is 0.5% higher compared to the one applicable to other companies; (ii) small companies are not subject to the long-term capital gains tax of 0.412%; (iii) the Fairness Tax is not applicable to small companies; and (iv) proceeds paid out to shareholders of small companies are, under certain circumstances, subject to lower withholding tax rates.[43]

Belgian tax law does not contain a separate definition of 'small company', but refers to the definition used in company and accounting law.

The definition of a 'small company' used in company and accounting law (Article 15 Company Code) was recently changed to meet the requirements of Directive 2013/34/EU of the European Parliament and of the Council of 26 June 2013 on the annual financial statements, consolidated financial statements and related reports of certain types of undertakings ('*Accounting Directive*')

Prior to the implementation of the Accounting Directive, a small company was defined as a company that does not satisfy more than one of the following criteria: (i) average employees (FTE): 50; (ii) average turnover (excl. VAT): EUR 7,300,000; and (iii) balance sheet total: EUR 3,650,000. A company that has more than 100 employees (FTE) qualified in any event as a small company. The criteria mentioned had to be considered on a consolidated basis with all affiliated companies.

The following changes were made by the law of 18 December 2015 that implemented the Accounting Directive into Belgian law:[44]

- The turnover and balance sheet total *thresholds* were indexed, leading to the following criteria: (i) average employees (FTE): 50: (ii) average turnover (excl. VAT): EUR 9,000,000; and (iii) balance sheet total: EUR 4,500,000. Moreover, the additional criterion providing that any company having at least 100 employees is a large company, was abolished.
- The *change of status* from a small company to a large company or vice versa will only have effect if, based on the criteria, a company should be classified differently on the basis of the balance sheets of two subsequent financial years.

---

43. For an overview of all specific measures applicable to small companies: C. DE BACKERE, 'Standpunt. Naar een autonome fiscale kmo-definitie? De kleine vennootschap als kmo in fiscalibus: stand van zaken en toekomstperspectieven', *TRV* 2014, 758-772.
44. Law of 18 December 2015 regarding the implementation of the Accounting Directive, *Belgian Official Gazette* 30 December 2015.

In that case, the rules of the other regime will apply to that company as of the financial year following those two years. In other words, a company does not change its status because it qualifies only one financial year for another regime.

- The thresholds no longer have to be examined on a *consolidated basis*, except for parent companies (including companies constituting a consortium) and companies that are established with the sole aim of circumventing the obligation to report certain information.

In principle, these changes also have an effect on the application of the specific tax rules applicable to 'small companies'. Accordingly, the amended thresholds and the amended rules regarding the change of status of 'small company' are also relevant for tax law purposes.

However, the rule that the criteria have to be determined on a consolidated basis with all affiliated companies will remain valid for tax purposes. This means that the definition of small company for corporate and accountancy purposes will no longer be exactly the same as the one applicable for tax purposes. Accordingly, certain companies can qualify as a small company for corporate and accounting purposes, while they are considered large companies from a tax perspective.

With regard to the link between accounting and tax, it is interesting to note that the Central Economic Council[45] stated the following in its advice regarding the implementation of the Directive: '*The council indicates that there is a close connection in Belgium between accountancy and tax. The council wants to keep this as it is. Thus, simplifications of the accounting obligations may only be implemented to the extent that the connection with tax is not put into danger and that financial reporting remains to constitute the basis for correct tax calculations of companies.*'[46]

Moreover, the Belgian legislator introduced a separate category of 'micro-companies'. A micro-company is a company that does not exceed one of the following criteria: (i) average employees (FTE): 10; (ii) average turnover (excl. VAT): EUR 700,000; and (iii) balance sheet total: EUR 350,000. In the *tax shift* negotiations of summer 2015, the government decided in this respect to provide more beneficial tax regimes already to start-up companies qualifying as micro-companies compared to the regime that applies to small companies.

§4.06   CONCLUSION

According to Belgian law, the (non-consolidated) financial results of a company pursuant to Belgian GAAP constitute the reference point for the determination of the corporate income tax base. Deviations from the financial results are, in principle, only permissible if provided for by express tax provisions. As the determination of the tax base is linked to Belgian GAAP accounts, IAS/IFRS does not affect the tax base.

---

45. The central council in which representatives of employers and employees are represented.
46. Advice regarding the implementation of the new accounting directive, CCE/CRB 2015-0600, http://www.ccecrb.fgov.be/txt/fr/doc15-600.pdf.

From a Belgian perspective, the remarkable features of the CCCTB are group consolidation and the absence of a link between the determination of the tax base and the corporate income tax base. Moreover, the non-existence of the NID and the different depreciation rules are highly relevant.

Accounting Directive 2013/34/EU is implemented in Belgian law by the law of 18 December 2015. From a Belgian tax perspective, the amendments to the definition of 'small companies' are the most interesting, as this concept is also referred to in tax law. In this respect, it is of note that a (limited) difference is made between the concept of 'small companies' within accounting/corporate law and tax law.

CHAPTER 5

Accounting and Taxation: Brazil

Victor Borges Polizelli

This chapter will address fundamental attributes of the Brazilian book-tax relationship that was set before the adoption of IFRS,[1] highlighting its main features and details of day-to-day practice that caused an unplanned dominance of tax over financial accounting. IFRS will then be focused on to present how Brazilian tax law was adapted to allow an immediate elective disruption of the connection with IFRS and to implement a complex system with three books of account (tax accounting, old financial accounting and new financial accounting). This examination of the impacts of IFRS adoption will ultimately underline the format of the new book-tax relationship in Brazil, and the method chosen to bind tax accounting and IFRS together in a controlled manner, aiming to avoid future unexpected tax consequences derived from changes in financial accounting changes.

Attention will be given to the main differences of the proposed CCCTB and the Brazilian computation of the corporate tax base and also to the procedural changes recently effected in Brazil to achieve full convergence with IFRS (even for SMEs) in an effort comparable to that of the new EU accounting directive.

§5.01 MAIN FEATURES OF THE BRAZILIAN BOOK-TAX RELATIONSHIP

This first section will point out the general characteristics of the Brazilian book-tax relationship that prevailed over the last decades and depict the major factors of the pre-IFRS scenario.

---

1. The acronym IFRS is used as a reference to both types of pronouncements: IFRSs, issued by IASB, and IASs, issued by its predecessor, the IASC, and their corresponding interpretative acts.

[A]   Source of Financial Accounting Rules and Brazilian GAAP

Tax law makes reference to concepts described in commercial accounting rules. However, commercial accounting in Brazil has traditionally been a field with a short supply of regulations. Common practice of accountants has always played a major role in the past rather than legally codified rules.[2] It was not until the late 1970s that a broad range of specific rules regarding the criteria for drawing up financial statements was established by purely commercial statutes.

Law 6,404 ("Law of Corporations") was published in 1976 and replaced the few accounting rules of the previous commercial law by adding detailed guidance on the required financial statements, with a specification of the layout and the standardized chart of accounts, and also the establishment of a variety of valuation criteria for assets/liabilities and guiding principles for recognition of revenue/expense, etc.

Until today, such Law 6,404 can still be seen as the fundamental legal source of accounting rules in Brazil. Nonetheless, there is certain controversy as to its binding-ness to all companies. Law 6,404 aimed at providing extensive regulation to corpora-tions (especially listed companies) did not address Limited Liability Companies (LLCs).[3] LLCs – the most commonly used corporate form in Brazil – are regulated by the Civil Code, which contains very rudimentary accounting rules that cannot be treated seriously.[4]

The outcome is that, from a practical standpoint, most Brazilian companies (LLCs) are also subject to the same set of accounting rules provided for in the Law of Corporations, but there are no precise boundaries as to which specific rules can be selectively avoided.[5] Notwithstanding that, as explained below, Brazil adopted IFRS-SME in 2009 and today the national accounting law applicable to LLCs is mostly derived from this statute.

---

2. Pronouncements of professional bodies and writings of scholars contributed to form "generally accepted" accounting practices in those years. See Hercules Boucher, *Estudos de impôsto de renda e contabilidade*, Saraiva, 1950, pp. 131-175.
3. The whole set of accounting rules provided in this Law, and also the regulations set forth by the Brazilian Securities and Exchange Commission (CVM), are mandatory for listed corporations, large sized companies (total assets over BRL 240 million or annual gross revenue over BRL 300 million), financial institutions and insurance companies. Non-listed corporations are obliged to follow Law 6,404 and may choose to apply CVM regulations (Article 177, paragraph 6 of Law 6,404).
4. The present Civil Code is the result of a bill proposed in the early 70s which was finally debated in Congress in 2000 and 2001 without the reformulation of such old-fashioned accounting rules. They prescribe incomplete requirements, do not address several types of financial statements and require the use of an antiquated type of P&L account that does not display the net profit explicitly for the year. See Eliseu Martins, *Atrocidades contábeis no novo Código Civil: (1ª e 2ª partes)*, in Boletim Temática Contábil e Balanços, n° 40-41, IOB, 2002.
5. For instance, recent amendments were made in the Law of Corporations to remove two accounts from the statutory chart of balance sheet accounts, namely "retained earnings" and "revaluation reserve". The intention, in the first case, is to force companies to justify expressly the reasons for not making profit distributions. The application of this obligation to LLCs is, however, an unsettled matter. An official ruling drafted by the Brazilian Accounting Pronouncements Com-mittee (CPC) endorsed the selective application of this obligation to corporations only, releasing

[B] Fundamental Rules for the Computation of Corporate Tax Base

Moving back to the original setting of the Brazilian book-tax connection, attention must be drawn to the modifications made in the tax law at the same time as the enactment of the Law of Corporations.

The fundamental rules for defining the tax base were established in 1977, when a specific tax statute (Decree-law 1,598/1977)[6] not only shaped the basic connection with financial accounting, but also filled several gaps in the financial accounting statutes with regard to legal definitions of revenue, expense and details of the valuation of inventories. From the beginning, financial accounting statutes were fewer in number compared to tax statutes. Given the absence of congressional initiative to update accounting statutes, this process of a soft reverse influence of tax over financial accounting would continue for several years.

The above mentioned Decree-law 1,598 employs legal concepts derived from financial statements – net income, operating profit, non-operating results, etc. – and also states that these factors will be calculated in accordance with the principles of commercial law.[7] Taxation is based on individual financial statements and there is no tax consolidation: each legal entity of a group of companies is considered a separate taxpayer.

Taxable profit is called "real profit"[8] and is determined according to a profit and loss method instead of a balance sheet approach. Such a calculation of the profit is directly linked to the annual net profit ascertained in the commercial accounts of the company, but adjustments with an exclusive tax nature are made in a specific tax book,[9] without interfering with the financial accounting.[10] The real profit is based on the books and records the taxpayer must keep in compliance with commercial and tax laws[11] and the computation of the annual net profit must follow the provisions of Law 6,404.[12] All types of income, except certain real estate activities, are subject to income tax at the same rate.[13]

LLCs from compliance (OCPC 02, item 115), whilst the same legal document intends to extend the general prohibition of the use of revaluation mechanisms to both corporations and LLCs (OCPC 02, items 127-132).

6. This Decree-law is a "sister" statute of the Law of Corporations, as it clearly intended to adapt the tax statutes to the, by then, newly implemented improvements of commercial law.

7. DL 1,598/77, section 6, paragraph 1, which makes precise reference to elements of the profit and loss statement, as regulated by Article 187 of the Law of Corporations.

8. All comments made in this article refer to the "real profit" taxation regime, which is computed on the basis of commercial profit adjusted by inclusions and exclusions. A great number of companies (those with annual gross revenue below 78 million) elect taxation based on "deemed profit" regime.

9. The "book for the computation of real profit" (*LALUR – livro de apuração do lucro real*).

10. See more details below in section §5.01[C][1].

11. DL 1,598/77, head of sections 6 and 7. Real profit is "net income adjusted by additions, exclusions or compensations prescribed or authorized by the tax laws" and is "determined based on the bookkeeping that the taxpayer must keep, in compliance with commercial and tax laws".

12. DL 1,598/77, section 67, item XI.

13. The corporate tax rate of 34% is a combination of two quite similar taxes: a 25% corporate income tax (*IRPJ – imposto de renda de pessoas jurídicas*) and a 9% social contribution on net

87

It is unfair to say that the tax legislation of the 1960s and 1970s was lacking legal definitions of accounting concepts which were then filled by the new Law of Corporations. Quite the opposite. The tax law was already ahead of the accounting law in terms of detailed regulations, and, therefore, when the innovations of such commercial Law came about, the changes enshrined by Decree-law 1,598 were, in several cases, destined to adapt the calculation of the tax base to the already existing formula of prior tax law (Law 4,506 of 1964).[14]

Many types of book-tax differences continued to exist and the enactment of these "sister" statutes did not result in the unification of book and tax accounting. The main source of permanent differences lies in non-deductible expenses and exempt income. Main examples of the latter comprise subsidies linked directly to investment in business assets, income attributable to participation exemption and damage recoveries.

With respect in particular to the participation exemption, Brazilian tax law contains a broad and encompassing provision that relieves the income tax on dividend payments to all kinds of shareholders (individuals and companies, nationals and foreigners, even if they are domiciled in low tax jurisdictions).[15] No taxes are imposed on income registered under the equity pick-up method, or dividends received, nor is there any withholding tax for dividends paid out. One important aspect is that even though financial and taxable profit rarely coincided, the participation exemption of Brazilian law imposed no restriction for the untaxed distribution of dividends based on unadjusted financial profit, even when the financial profit was higher than the tax profit.[16]

On the expenses side, there is a general clause allowing deductibility of expenses that can be considered usual, normal and necessary for the preservation of the source of income.[17] Some types of expenses are subject to limitations, such as royalties and promotional product sampling. Fines and penalties are not deductible. The same for gifts and donations, except some specific donations to charitable entities. Payments to directors are deductible as long as they are considered benefits in kind and taxed as such.

---

profits (*CSLL – contribuição social sobre o lucro líquido*). There are some minor differences in the taxable bases of these two taxes which will be ignored in this study for purposes of simplification.

14. See comments on the Decree-law by F. Nepomuceno, *"Lucro real": o novo lucro tributável*, Editora Ipanema, São Paulo, 1978, p. 15. See comments on this foundational book-tax relationship by José Luiz Bulhões Pedreira, *Imposto sobre a renda: Pessoas jurídicas*, Vol. I, Justec, 1979, pp. 223-224 (item 126.3).

15. Law 9,249, section 10: "The profits or dividends based on the results reported as of the month of January 1996, paid or credited by companies taxed on the basis of real, deemed or arbitrated profit, will not be subject to the levy of income tax at source, or integrate the basis of calculation of the beneficiary's income tax, be it an individual or a company, domiciled in Brazil or abroad".

16. The discrepancies could result in higher financial profit than tax profit in some initial periods and can be explained by temporary differences. The total effect is neutral, as financial and tax profit tend to coincide in the long run.

17. Income Tax Regulation (Decree 3,000/1999), section 299.

Revenue recognition is based on the accrual principle and oriented by a conservative version of the realization principle.[18] Hence, transactions are registered when they occur from a legal standpoint, which is generally based on criteria set forth by civil law rules for determining the point in time when the most significant risks and rewards are transferred. Exceptions are made for long-term construction contracts and long-term arrangements for the supply of goods and services with predetermined prices, the taxable profit of which may be calculated under the percentage-of-completion method.[19] Unsettled currency gains/losses may also be subject to taxation on an accrual basis upon election.

[C] The Original Book-Tax Linkage: Two Books Became One

Even though the intention of the Law of Corporations and Decree-Law 1,598/77 was to create a simplified two-book-system, allowing the segregation of financial and tax accounting, the reality observed in the subsequent years showed an increasing influence of tax rules over accounting practice and, as a result, two-books practically became one.[20]

Bearing in mind that classification models for book-tax connections are normally driven by the strength of influence of tax rules over financial accounting practice and vice-versa, it is possible to say, in the expression recently adopted by Essers and Russo, that the Brazilian book-tax relationship of these early years fits the definition of a system with "practically formal dependence".[21]

Using the terminology proposed by Lamb, Nobes and Roberts,[22] the Brazilian book-tax linkage can be seen as a case of "leadership of tax accounting", as tax

---

18. The realization principle is a general guideline the effective application of which depends on several types of realization criteria provided for in the law. When the law applies a very conservative version, the cash event is the ultimate relevant criterion. A moderate conservative version defines as a "critical event" the point of the passage of risks according to civil law. A value-based approach would favor the accretion of income as the triggering event and in this case an effective market transaction would be substituted for a "broad sense" market transaction. V. Polizelli, *O princípio da realização da renda: reconhecimento de receitas e despesas para fins do IRPJ,* IBDT / Quartier Latin, 2012, pp. 240-253, 263-266. T. Schröer, *Das realisationsprinzip in Deutschland und Grossbritannien: eine systematische Untersuchung und ihre Anwendung auf langfristige Auftragsfertigung und Währungsumrechnung,* Peter Lang, 1998, pp. 200-205.
19. This method is elective. The realization in this case is driven by a criterion of value accretion rather than the critical event of the passage of risk according to the civil law.
20. See Tatiana Lopes, *Custos políticos tributários: o impacto do tamanho na alíquota tributária efetiva,* Dissertation, FEA-USP, available at www.teses.usp.br, pp. 70-73.
21. In this system no separate tax accounts are allowed and fiscal option rights must be exercised in accordance with options made in financial accounting. Furthermore, only explicit tax legislation can create differences between financial and tax accounting. See P. Essers & R. Russo, *The Precious Relationship between IAS/IFRS, National Tax Accounting Systems and the CCCTB,* in P. Essers, T. Raaijmakers, R. Russo, P; Schee, L. Tas & P. Zanden (eds), The Influence of IAS/IFRS on the CCCTB, Tax Accounting, Disclosure, and Corporate Law Accounting Concepts: "A Clash of Cultures", Wolters Kluwer, 2009, p. 32.
22. See M. Lamb, C. Nobes & A. Roberts, *International Variations in the Connections between Tax and Financial Reporting,* in Accounting and Business Research, 28(3), 174-175.

rules/options are in practice followed for both tax and financial reporting purposes.[23] This happens not only due to the absence of sufficiently specific financial reporting rules, but mainly because of the adoption of the financial conformity rule by Brazilian law in some cases, as explained below in section §5.01[C][1].

From a practical standpoint, Brazil is, therefore, more aligned with a "continental approach", by reason of the high strength of tax influence on accounting policy choices.[24] One possible explanation for such a format can be seen in the way companies are financed and the lack of a self sufficient financial and legal culture. Countries like Brazil, that have traditionally been financed through debt/equity of insiders (partners, family members and creditors with long-term relationships) show no demand for investor-oriented reporting and will have developed accounting systems that serve traditional functions of calculating prudently distributable profit and taxable income.[25]

Theoretical justifications for a linkage with financial accounting include the simplicity of using a more developed and organized system of registration of facts. As mentioned above, tax rules prior to 1978 already comprised a complete set of definitions necessary for the computation of the tax base. The great advantage of linking with the newly enacted Law of Corporation was the use of a more detailed set of rules for bookkeeping, the preparation of financial statements and the calculation of results.[26] The main reason mentioned in the Congressional memorandum was the need to adapt tax law to the more detailed commercial rules and avoid possible controversies in the interpretation of prior tax law.[27]

Such new national accounting legislation brought about advanced rules on the use of the accrual principle. In addition, national GAAP plays an important role in the prescription of rules regarding bookkeeping, with detailed guidance on: (i) classification of accounts in the balance sheet; (ii) principles and criteria for the evaluation of assets and liabilities; (iii) breakdown of the income statement. Tax legislation does not regulate bookkeeping and does not provide criteria for revenue/expense recognition. These matters are resolved by reference to commercial/civil law.[28]

The legal source of such book-tax linkage, its particularities and also the main deviations observed in financial statements by reason of tax influence will be examined in further detail below.

---

23. In the list of arenas proposed by these authors to diagnose the book-tax linkage, Brazil would show more Case IV ("Tax leads") situations and also a significant number of Case V ("Tax dominates").
24. See M. Lamb, C. Nobes & A. Roberts, *International Variations in the Connections between Tax and Financial Reporting*, in Accounting and Business Research, 28(3), 186.
25. See C. Nobes, *International Variations in IFRS Adoption and Practice*, Research Paper from Association of Chartered Certified Accountants, 2011, pp. 10-12.
26. See José Luiz Bulhões Pedreira, *Imposto sobre a renda: Pessoas jurídicas*, Vol. I, Justec, 1979, pp. 223-224 (item 126.3).
27. Items 3 and 5 of the Memorandum of Justification that accompanied the Decree-law 1,598/77.
28. See José Luiz Bulhões Pedreira, *Imposto sobre a renda: Pessoas jurídicas*, Vol. I, Justec, 1979, pp. 289-290 (item 165.7), 328-339 (item 175).

[1] Tax Conformity and Financial Conformity

The Brazilian statutes referred to above as "sister" statutes clearly structured the computation of taxable profit under a "dependency" model that includes both attributes of tax conformity and a soft version of financial conformity.[29] However, it is not necessarily a strong dependence that would also allow the application of a reverse authoritative principle,[30] such as in Germany.

The Brazilian type of connection can be labeled as "tax conformity", meaning the adoption of a general presumption that taxable profit is computed on the basis of Generally Accepted Accounting Principles (GAAP).[31] Accordingly, tax conformity is simply a normative reference made by tax law to concepts provided for in purely commercial statutes and it holds true in those areas where specific tax law does not provide a precise rule or does not conflict with accounting rules.

In its turn, financial conformity refers to the exercise of tax options and, more precisely, to the fact that such tax-driven choices cause a mandatory inclusion of particular items in the financial reporting as a necessary precondition for the granting of tax relief.[32] Brazilian tax law does not contain an express formulation of financial conformity such as the well-known case of the German tax law provision,[33] but the exercise of tax options, particularly for the claiming of tax deductions, generally depends on the prior inclusion of expenses in the financial profit, and this fact highlights the presence of a certain degree of financial conformity.[34] Claiming the deduction of expenses for tax purposes without prior registration of these expenses in financial accounting is prohibited. Case law has consistently repealed the argument that tax deductions can be freely exercised.[35]

Brazilian financial conformity is flexible in certain cases, as occurs with tax deductions/reliefs that are exclusive of tax accounting. Tax deductions/reliefs that

---

29. "Tax conformity" is used here as a reference to the "authoritative principle", corresponding to the *materielle Massgeblichkeitsprinzip*. "Financial conformity" corresponds to the *formelle Massgeblichkeitsprinzip*.
30. This expression refers to the *umgekehrte Massgeblichkeitsprinzip*.
31. G. Radcliffe, G. *The Relationship between Tax Law and Accounting Principles in the United Kingdom and France*, in the Irish Journal of Taxation, 1993, 1, *apud* M. Lamb, C. Nobes & A. Roberts, *International Variations in the Connections between Tax and Financial Reporting*, in Accounting and Business Research, 28(3), 173.
32. G. Radcliffe, G. *The Relationship between Tax Law and Accounting Principles in the United Kingdom and France*, in the Irish Journal of Taxation, 1993, 1, *apud* M. Lamb, C. Nobes & A. Roberts, *International Variations in the Connections between Tax and Financial Reporting*, in Accounting and Business Research, 28(3), 173.
33. Second sentence of section 5 of the German income tax law (EStG, 5 Abs., 1 S. 2), before the recent BilMoG reform act.
34. The mechanism of calculation of taxable profit allows exclusions, but these normally refer to the exclusion of exempt income and not the exclusion of expenses (which, despite having been allowed for tax purposes, may have not been computed in the accounting profit).
35. See reference to case law since the early 20s and also the few divergent cases on this matter in V. Polizelli, *Balanço comercial e balanço fiscal: Relações entre o direito contábil e o direito tributário e o modelo adotado pelo Brasil*, in Revista de Direito Tributário Atual, v. 24, 2010, Dialética, pp. 594-599.

diverge from financial accounting criteria are normally treated as independent exclusions for tax purposes and do not affect financial accounting.[36] The original configuration of book-tax linkage provided specific mechanisms for the implementation of such a simplified "two-book" system: the purpose of the tax book used for the computation of real profit ("LALUR") is to record those adjustments that bear an "exclusive tax nature" and "are not comprised by commercial bookkeeping".[37] Notwithstanding that, tax rules eventually began to influence financial accounting, causing the deviations mentioned in section §5.01[C][2] below.

One cannot say, however, that Brazilian law adopted the reverse authoritative principle.[38] The Brazilian tax statutes do not allow a conclusion similar to that of the German Financial Court,[39] in the sense that optional commercial rights must be exercised in a manner that increases taxable profit.[40] This is a conclusion that, in our view, cannot be drawn automatically from the equality principle, especially in a legal system that does not pursue the ideal of a "single balance sheet" (*Einheitsbilanz*).[41] Tax differences caused by an election of the taxpayer and most likely classifiable as temporary differences would hardly be seen as unfair. An illustration of how tax and accounting option rights work together in Brazil will be shown in section §5.01[C][3] below.

[2]   Deviations (Reverse Authoritativeness)

As the Brazilian book-tax system was originally designed to avoid the fiscal "pollution" of financial statements, deviations of financial statements are not legally allowed. However, this legally designed segregation of financial and tax accounting did not last long. Practice rapidly ignored the theory and deviations eventually started to occur. Tax rules dominated accounting practice and prevented companies from applying legally valid (and sometimes more appropriate) accounting valuation criteria when these were not accepted for tax purposes.

The most common cases of deviations perceived in financial statements include depreciation and bad debt provision accounting, the underlying reasons for which are explained in further detail below. Other types of deviations comprise market valuation

---

36. This is valid e.g., for cases of accelerated depreciation.
37. Decree-law 1,598/77, section 8, item I, sub-item "c" and paragraph 2. A detailed explanation of this mechanism was provided by Normative Opinion CST 96/1978.
38. Some examples of the reluctance of tax authorities to apply tax conformity resulted in a practical reverse authoritativeness in Brazil. These situations will be commented below in section §5.01[C][3].
39. BFH GrS 2/68, of 3 February 1969.
40. The outcome in Germany was that options given by commercial law are not valid for tax purposes when tax law is silent about the relevant consequence. Since taxation is based on the total profit and the entrepreneur cannot depict himself as being poorer than he really is, it follows that commercial options for capitalization become mandatory capitalization for tax purposes, and options for recognition of liabilities become prohibited in the tax computation. See S. Mayer, *Entwicklung der Massgeblichkeit in Deutschland*, in W. Schön (Ed.), Steuerliche Massgeblichkeit in Deutschland und Europa, Otto Schmidt, 2005, pp. 158-159.
41. See V. Polizelli, *O princípio da realização da renda: reconhecimento de receitas e despesas para fins do IRPJ*, IBDT / Quartier Latin, 2012, pp. 93-94, 121-122.

of agricultural products and accounting of financial leasing: accounting rules that did not have a corresponding tax command were broadly ignored.[42]

Taking the depreciation example, tax rules allow a straight-line depreciation method irrespective of the level of actual usage of the asset. If a company opted to compute depreciation for accounting purposes in a more faithful manner and showed lower depreciation in any given year, this would anticipate taxation in that year, since the option made for accounting purposes would automatically bind the taxable profit.[43]

Bad debt provision was allowed as a deduction until 1996, however, the tax rules imposed certain ceilings (ranging from 1.5% to 3% depending on the relevant year) and these were also respected in the commercial accounting for the sake of simplification. After 1997, such tax allowance was revoked and with it went the practice of most companies for accounting for bad debt provisions.[44]

As noted by Tatiana Lopes, whenever options were available to taxpayers, they would easily forgo the faithful representation of economic reality in their financial statements in favor of a lower tax burden. If the use of an accounting option was necessary to enable a tax reduction, the choice would be tax-driven to the detriment of duly accounting the essence of the transactions.[45]

[3]   Assessment of Financial Income by Tax Authorities

Although financial profit is the starting point for assessing taxable income, the tax authorities are not allowed to interfere in financial accounting to change criteria used therein, even when the latter are not allowed for tax purposes. Hence, tax adjustments are to be made off-the-books in a special tax book (LALUR).

The prohibition of interference of tax administration in the assessment of financial income was clarified thoroughly in regulations issued during the same period when book-tax linkage was developed.[46] They provided expressly that "tax rules governing the collection of taxes on income do not govern the accounting procedures. Bookkeeping methods are freely chosen by the taxpayers and will only be challenged when they do not comply with accounting standards". Even in the presence of a clear tax rule prohibiting the use of challengeable accounting procedures,[47] no authorization was given to tax authorities to make corrections to financial accounting.

---

42. The leasing example is interesting, as new regulations set forth by Brazilian Securities and Exchange Commission (to demand a different treatment of financial and operating leases) were rebutted even in financial accounting, as discussed in a famous article by Prof. Comparato. See F. Comparato, *O irredentismo da "nova contabilidade" e as operações de "leasing"*, in Revista de Direito Mercantil, Industrial, Econômico e Financeiro. year XXVI, n° 68, RT, 1987, pp. 50-62.
43. S. Iudícibus, E. Martins, E.R. Gelbcke, A. Santos, *Manual de contabilidade societária, aplicável a todas as sociedades de acordo com as normas internacionais e do CPC*, Atlas, 2010, 2nd ed., p. 14.
44. S. Iudícibus, E. Martins, E.R. Gelbcke, *Manual de contabilidade das sociedades por ações (aplicável às demais sociedades)*, Atlas, 2003, 6th ed, pp. 97, 102.
45. See Tatiana Lopes, *Custos políticos tributários: o impacto do tamanho na alíquota tributária efetiva*, Dissertation, FEA-USP, available at www.teses.usp.br, p. 72.
46. Normative Opinions 347/1970 and 23/1977.
47. In times of monetary correction, taxpayers could make use of accounting reclassification of assets (e.g., from fixed assets to current assets account) to avoid adverse tax effects. Tax law

A thorough examination of this matter involves a wide variety of situations concerning what is allowed or compulsory in both financial and tax accounting, as illustrated in the chart below. The consequences shown in the last column reflect the statutory mechanism of book-tax linkage and do not consider the practical deviations commented on above in section §5.01[C][2].

Figure 5.1

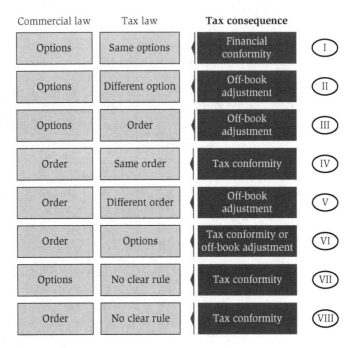

When accounting rules outline a number of acceptable approaches which coincide with the options given in tax law (Case I), financial conformity will be necessary to allow the intended tax effect. In those cases where tax law provides a divergent option (II, VI) or order (III, V), the deviating tax effect must be recorded in the tax book (LALUR) in an off-book adjustment.[48]

Special consideration must be given to those cases where no clear rule is available and a purely commercial treatment might affect the taxable result due to the automatic tax linkage (Cases VII and VIII). The broad and encompassing coverage of financial accounting allows the application of commercial rules/options in the absence

---

7,799/1989 forbids the use of financial accounting procedures to reduce taxable profit. However, even in this case, tax authorities could only claim off-the-book adjustments for tax purposes. See Normative Opinion 2/1996.

48. For instance, while accounting rules impose the accrual basis for the recognition of expenses, tax law may impose actual payment as a condition for deduction. Even in such a case of conflicting orders, there is no need to change the financial accounting. The tax effect is an off-book adjustment (See Normative Opinion CST 34/1981).

of specific tax rules.[49] Nevertheless, tax authorities have constantly shown a reluctance to apply innovative accounting rules automatically[50] and even purported a practical form of reverse authoritativeness.[51] This, however, is not the prevailing mechanism in Brazil and tax conformity should make its way to being properly applied.

§5.02 IMPACT OF IFRS ADOPTION ON FINANCIAL AND TAX ACCOUNTING

Legislative changes for the adoption of IFRS in Brazil were made unexpectedly at the very end of 2007 and affected the computation of corporate taxes of years 2008 and 2009. It was almost the end of the year, when Brazilian Congress decided to move forward a long -shelved project to change the Law of Corporations[52] in order to align the Brazilian accounting rules with international standards. Even though the intention was to leave tax rules untouched and allow the segregated development of financial accounting, the lawmaker struck one of the most precious basic concepts of tax accounting: the linkage with financial accounting.

[A] Full Conversion with IFRS

The implementation of IFRS in Brazil has been carried out by modifying the legal core of Brazilian accounting rules, sending a strong message for the need for a practical disruption of the linkage with tax accounting. The Law of Corporations was modified by virtue of the enactment of Law 11,638 on December 28, 2007 and later legal changes were implemented in 2009.

A special committee of experts was set up: the Brazilian Accounting Pronouncements Committee (CPC), with a mission to study, adapt and draft rules for harmonizing the Brazilian accounting regulations with IFRS. During 2008 and 2009, the whole set of IFRS was duly translated and transformed into locally binding regulations. Brazilian GAAP has been amalgamated with IFRS. Full conversion took place in 2010.[53]

---

49. Such inevitable tax conformity was sustained in Normative Opinion CST 11/1976.
50. When provisions were allowed as a tax deduction and a new type of provision was made mandatory by commercial law, tax authorities sustained the need for the requalification of the underlying transaction/event in order to remove it from the tax computation. Normative Opinion CST 23/1977 stated that provisions and reserves included in the financial statements can only result in tax relief if clearly provided for in tax statutes.
51. When the Brazilian Securities and Exchange Commission (CVM) issued regulations in the 90s to require present value adjustments in financial statements of listed companies, tax authorities sustained the mandatory taxation of the corresponding revenues and disallowance of expenses. Cf. H. Higuchi; F. H. Higuchi, *Imposto de renda das empresas: Interpretação e prática,* 18th ed., Atlas, 1993, p. 95.
52. Law 6,404/76. See more details on the preexisting Brazilian accounting situation in section §5.01[A] above.
53. Under such "full conversion method", the Brazilian regulating bodies amended the IFRS, deleting some options and giving them a Brazilian number. The outcome is still regarded as a full conversion. Nobes, *International variations in IFRS adoption and practice,* Research Paper from Association of Chartered Certified Accountants, 2011, p. 17.

The IFRS for SMEs was implemented in full in the second half of 2009. Brazil assumed a leading position in the conversion to IFRS, becoming possibly the first country to fully converge with such standards.[54] After 2010, IFRS was made obligatory for all types of companies, listed or not, large or small companies (including subsidiaries of foreign companies). IFRS is mandatory not only for consolidated, but also for individual accounts.[55] Such annual individual financial statements, prepared in compliance with IFRS, are valid for purposes of profit distribution, the measurement of the financial position and performance of a company, cash flow analysis, etc.

There are some areas of financial accounting where conflicts arise between criteria set forth in the Law of Corporations and IFRS. This leads to the persistence of practices based on national accounting rules, such as the method of accounting for gross revenue and inventories (in order to include value added taxes),[56] and also investments in controlled entities.[57]

[B]   Tax Consequences: Three Books on the Table

As noted above, the core of Brazilian financial accounting rules was suddenly modified at the end of 2007. And tax rules – especially those that are based on accounting concepts – were left alone. The consequences for financial accounting were enormous: the definition of legal ownership was radically changed and new valuation mechanisms such as adjusted present value, impairment, mark-to-market accounting were finally introduced as mandatory measures for financial statements. A whole new scenario was created by reason of the adoption of IFRS and significant controversies arose as to the immediate and inevitable tax effects of such changes.

Convergence with IFRS brought legal uncertainty, as indirect changes in the corporate tax base could lead straight to an unplanned tax increase. Such changes complied with all constitutional requirements for rising taxes: they were introduced by a Law and published the year before. If the adoption for example of adjusted present value mechanism caused a reduction of the 2008 expense for a certain company, this reduction would inevitably lead to higher taxable profit and more taxes.

However, it was extremely difficult to measure precisely the overall impact of IFRS adoption in the computation of taxes. In the aim of facilitating the process of IFRS adoption with less tax disruption, a Provisional Measure was issued by the end of

---

54. See Patrícia de Souza Costa, *Implicações da adoção das IFRS sobre a conformidade financeira e fiscal das companhias abertas brasileiras,* Dissertation, FEA-USP, available at www.teses.usp. br, p. 92.
55. Full IFRS applies for listed companies, large sized companies (total assets above BRL 240 million or annual gross revenue above BRL 300 million), financial institutions, insurance companies and those subject to public accountability. Moreover IFRS-SME applies to non-listed corporations and all other types of companies.
56. Due to the Brazilian mechanism of calculation of value added taxes, the current practice is that inventories purchased are accounted net of VAT and gross revenues include VAT.
57. Brazilian national Law requires the net equity pick up method and IFRS allows only the cost of acquisition or fair value.

2008,[58] allowing taxpayers to use old accounting rules for the computation of taxes. Such "Transitional Taxation Regime" gave rise to a complicated system of three books. Every company would need to prepare: (i) financial statements based on IFRS; (ii) financial statements based on Brazilian GAAP of 2007 (pre-IFRS); and (iii) the tax book used for computation of real profit ("LALUR") linked with the financial statements of Brazilian GAAP of 2007.

Such a transitional regime was planned to last for at least two years (2008-2009), or until a new national law was issued to establish a connection with IFRS. As expressly provided in the relevant legal statute, the future law would target "tax neutrality", probably meaning that no tax changes would be caused by IFRS.

Despite its complexity, this three-book system promoted certainty and was adhered to by virtually all companies. The most controversial matter of this period involves the extent of participation exemption: should it be based on dividends calculated under old accounting rules or IFRS? IFRS was the governing rule for the calculation of distributable dividends and tax law never formulated any obstacle for the exemption of dividends based on financial profit (even when these profits were higher than tax profit).[59] Fortunately, this point was eventually clarified in 2014, when a new tax law was passed to adapt the computation of taxes to IFRS and confirmed the exemption of financial profits based on IFRS.[60]

[C] Tax Adaptation in 2015: Peaceful Coexistence of Two Books

2015 marks the beginning of a new era of the book-tax relationship in Brazil being the first time there has been a mandatory application of a tax law linking the calculation of taxable profit to IFRS accounting.[61] The original linkage was frozen over the past seven years and a newly designed book-tax relationship now makes tax accounting presumably independent from future changes in the IFRS environment. One significant intention of such a mechanism is to emancipate financial accounting, which will then be free to pursue commercial purposes without the fear of any unintended tax consequences.

The "tax neutrality" promised by the previous tax law[62] was accomplished to a great extent, as no tax effect was given to many of the innovations brought by IFRS.[63]

---

58. Provisional Measure 449/2008, later converted into Law 11,941/2009. A Provisional Measure is a Decree that temporarily has the same legal force as a Law.
59. See comments above on paragraph §5.01[B] (*supra* note 16).
60. A similar discussion involved the calculation of interest on net equity (a deductible dividend provided in Brazilian tax law) and the dilemma consisted in choosing the IFRS net equity or the net equity calculated on the basis of old accounting rules.
61. Law 12,973/2014.
62. Provisional Measure 449/2008 commented in section §5.02[B] above.
63. A good summary of the major changes of Law 12,973/2014 can be found in C.L.P.M.Silva *et alli*, *Tributação e IFRS no Brasil: Alterações na legislação do IRPJ, CSLL, PIS/PASEP e da COFINS, trazidas pela Lei n° 12.973/2014*, in Revista de estudos tributários e aduaneiros, Brasília-DF, year I, n° 01, 2014, available at http://www.revistadareceitafederal.receita.fazenda.gov.br, pp. 393-422.

Focusing on some significant items of discrepancy between IFRS and prior tax law, the following is a list of topics that will not affect taxation:

- *Depreciation*: taxpayers may adopt straight-line depreciation for tax purposes irrespective of the method used for book purposes.
- *Present value adjustments:* no tax effect (e.g., long term sales revenue will be taxed upfront).
- *Fair value measurement:* no tax effect (e.g., gains derived from fair value measurement of financial assets, investment properties or also those from business combinations) will not be taxed, as long as they are highlighted and controlled in separate subaccounts of the financial books and records.
- *Impairment of assets:* no tax effect until the relevant asset is disposed of.

One topic that was the subject of great change and attracted a lot of attention in Brazil was the criterion for purchased goodwill accounting. The previous tax law of the 1990s granted a tax benefit in relation to purchased goodwill and the criterion of price allocation did not require the allocation of value to intangibles or other acquired assets, so that taxpayers could allocate almost all the price paid in a business acquisition to goodwill.[64] A great deal of litigation took place on this matter in the last decade (prior to IFRS adoption), as tax authorities did not agree with such price allocation and used non-binding IFRS guidance as a basis for their contention. Now, with the issuance of Law 12,973/2014 the IFRS criteria for purchase price allocation have been adopted for tax purposes, reducing the potential of tax amortization in future business acquisitions.

For the future changes in financial accounting, the book-tax relationship in Brazil will no longer admit tax conformity. The newly issued rule on this matter provides that:

> The modification or adoption of accounting methods and criteria, through administrative acts issued after the publication of this law and based on powers conferred on commercial law will have no effect in the determination of federal taxes until further specific tax law governing the matter is issued.

§5.03   CCCTB AND FISCAL ASPECTS OF THE NEW ACCOUNTING DIRECTIVE

Discussions around a CCCTB and the relationship with the new accounting directive offer an interesting benchmark for a comparison with a country's own tax base. As a non-European country, Brazil may also have direct interest in the CCCTB format as a significant factor affecting Brazilian investment decisions in Europe. Nevertheless, these topics have not yet drawn great attention in studies published in Brazil.

Even so, it is worth mentioning that significant changes have occurred lately in the Brazilian foreign tax law and case law favoring more alignment with international

---

64. Amortizable goodwill has to be justified by the future profitability of the business acquired.

tax practice of double tax treaties[65] and taxation of foreign profits.[66] Such developments have come in good time as Brazil has increased its position as a capital exporting country. Understanding the impacts of CCCTB and the new accounting directive is also a significant step for Brazilian companies. The subsequent paragraph of this study will present a broad comparison with these sets of rules and the Brazilian system.

[A] Differences of CCCTB and Brazilian Corporate Tax Base

In this comparison more weight is given to quite dissimilar situations and also to some components of the CCCTB that, having an equivalent Brazilian rule, might have created controversies in the past.

- *Article 11, b, d, and e:* these items are subject to tax in Brazil.
- *Article 15:* benefits to shareholder are deductible, provided that the beneficiary is identified and the amounts are included as taxable income by the shareholder.[67]
- *Article 22, 1, c:* the taxation of income derived from gifts by the corporate tax is controversial in Brazil due to conflict with gift tax.
- *Article 22, 1, e and Article 23, 2:* fair value measurement does not cause taxation, even in the case of financial assets held for trading.
- *Article 24, 1:* the Brazilian rule adds the condition "predetermined prices" in the definition of "long term arrangements for the supply of goods and services."
- *Articles 25 and 27:* provisions (including losses or bad debt) are not deductible in Brazil.
- *Article 34:* economic ownership was not accepted for tax purposes, even in the cases of finance lease.[68]
- *Article 36, 2:* there is no rule for second-hand assets.
- *Article 43:* losses carried forward are not subject to a timing restriction but they can only offset 30% of any given year's profit.

[B] Fiscal Aspects of the New Accounting Directive

Brazil is obviously out of reach of the new accounting directive.[69] However, the implementation of new accounting standards in Brazil has reached an even greater

---

65. Brazilian Courts ruled in favor of the application of Article 7 (business profits) of the OECD Model Treaty Conventions refusing a long standing position of the tax authorities, that wanted to claim the application of Article 21 (other income).
66. Foreign business profits are no longer automatically taxable irrespective of their nature (passive/active) or origin (blacklisted/non-blacklisted).
67. One reason for this treatment is that taxation on the shareholder will normally overcome the benefit of deduction.
68. See specific comments on the tax treatment of a leasing transaction in section §5.03[B] below.
69. Directive 2013/34/EU.

level of complexity than that currently pursued in the EU.[70] The implementation of such a modern set of accounting rules has demanded changes in Brazilian national law and a complete reformulation of regulating acts issued by several agencies and professional bodies.[71]

One of the main changes in the prior mindset is the implementation of the substance over form principle. Brazil is a civil law country and discussions on the automatic prevalence of substance over legal form face great obstacles. The matter has drawn the attention of both accounting and tax scholars since 2008, but the discussions have been significantly influenced by tax considerations (as no adaptation law existed prior to 2013).[72]

There is great concern on how accounting rules, although not officially binding for tax purposes, may eventually influence tax decisions.[73] Tax rules prevail over accounting rules in the arena of tax computation, but the latter may contribute greatly to the clarification of those legal concepts that make reference to the economic reality of a company.[74]

In general, if the goal of "tax neutrality" is preserved, the future changes of accounting rules will not affect taxation. The case of leasing illustrates this point. Despite the accounting differentiation of operating and finance lease, the tax treatment before IFRS allowed the deduction of the rental payments for both cases.[75] After IFRS implementation, this odd situation will remain.

---

70. Please see comments above on the scale of IFRS convergence in Brazil in paragraph 2.1.
71. Every time a new IFRS is issued, the addition of regulations in the Brazilian system requires the issuance of acts by the Brazilian Securities and Exchange Commission (CVM), the National Monetary Council (CMN), the Superintendence of Private Insurance (SUSEP), the Federal Accounting Council (CFC) and agencies in their various legislative areas.
72. See comments in section §5.02[C] above on the newly enacted Law that adapted the calculation of corporate tax base to IFRS in Brazil.
73. See. R. Novais, B. Gomes, *A prevalência da forma contábil sobre a natureza jurídica e a essência econômica: o ágio nas operações dentro do mesmo grupo de empresas*, in R.Q. Mosquera, A.B. Lopes (Ed.), Controvérsias jurídico-contábeis (aproximações e distanciamentos), Dialética, 2010, pp. 396-397.
74. See A.B. Lopes, R.Q. Mosquera, *O direito contábil: Fundamentos conceituais, aspectos da experiência brasileira e implicações*, in R.Q. Mosquera, A.B. Lopes (Ed.), Controvérsias jurídico-contábeis (aproximações e distanciamentos), Dialética, 2010, p. 81.
75. Tax planning is possible when rental payments exceed the deduction obtained under a depreciation method.

CHAPTER 6

Accounting and Taxation: France

Renaud Jaune

Accounting standards have evolved considerably in the past twenty years, in Europe and elsewhere, with some effects on direct business taxation.

These two legal fields are, by tradition, strongly connected in France, implying that the corporate tax base definition is powerfully articulated to accounting principles. For example, in a country like the United States, the treatment of bad debts differs according to GAAP rules (allowance account) and to tax law (that does not allow a full deduction). In France, on the contrary, a bad debt can give way to account and tax deduction, no matter the amount, provided this deduction reflects the interest of the company's business.

Yet, both accounting standards and direct taxation tend to evolve internationally and in Europe, with a continuing risk of the two legal fields of tax and accounting drifting apart. What is the extent of the risk for the French legal system? Will profound changes be needed as the European accounting directives and the common consolidated corporate tax base project (CCCTB) evolve? Do companies face a risk of legal uncertainty?

This chapter will answer these questions by examining the considerable influence of accounting on taxation in France (§6.01), and the "réalisme" principle underlying both (§6.02). Based on these elements, we shall conclude that the evolutions in accounting and the CCCTB project are perfectly compatible with the French legal system, although some uncertainty will remain regarding the value of inner-group operations (§6.03).

§6.01 IN FRANCE, CORPORATE TAX BASE DERIVES FROM ACCOUNTING PRINCIPLES

The tax base is the same whether business is carried out individually (income tax) or through an incorporated company (corporate tax). We should point out that this stems from the schedular origin of the income tax that resulted in a series of provisions on "*industrial and commercial incomes*", notably Articles 34-45, 53 A-57 of the general tax code. Article 209 of the same code extends these provisions to corporations: "*for the purpose of the income tax on corporations, the income shall be determined according to the principles provided for by articles 34 to 45, 53 A to 57…*". This legal identity between individuals and corporate companies aims to allow firms to arbitrate their shape on a tax-neutral basis.

[A]   **The Connection between Tax and Accounting Begins with Tax Requirements**

[1]   A Tax Return That Requires Accounting Reports

Article 53 A of the general tax code makes it mandatory for companies to deliver an annual tax return, that enables the taxable income to be determined or audited. Article 54, a key article, states that "*taxpayers mentioned in Article 53 A shall, whenever requested by the administration, present whatever accounting document, inventory, copies of letters or receipts likely to establish that the profits and losses filed in the tax return are accurate*". This list obviously relates to the basic accounting documents.

Both articles illustrate the accounting influence: Article 53 A and 54 do not refer to the general notion of tax return – "*déclaration de bénéfices*" – but to a specific and very accounting-connoted notion of "*déclaration de résultats*" – literally: "*profit and loss return*". The origin of the notion dates back to the introduction of Article 54, the older of the two articles in its present wording, which stems from the schedular income tax and was codified by the Décret dated October 15, 1926. Yet quite interestingly, Article 54 is referred to by the recent Article L. 47 A of the tax procedures code, that sets rules for computerized accounting systems: "*the taxpayer shall [present] the documents mentioned at article 54 of the general tax code by providing the tax auditor, when the audit begins … with copies of the accounting files*".

[2]   Even for Small Businesses, Taxation Needs an Accounting Basis

All companies with a turnover exceeding EUR 78,300 in 2015 – EUR 27,000 if the turnover only concerns services – have to present their balance sheet and their profit and loss accounts for tax purposes (CGI, Article 53 A). Profits and losses shall be presented as a list, and the balance sheet as a chart. Of course, small businesses – under EUR 783,000 or EUR 270,000 in 2015 – do not have to present very detailed information, for example as regards amortizations and provisions. But this does not mean that there could be a threshold under which accounting disappears from tax requirements.

Indeed, even "*micro-business*" enterprises – with a turnover below EUR 78,300 or EUR 27,000 –, which do not have to present their balance sheet or profit and loss account, have to comply with the accounting principles. These include the common standards of annual and exhaustive accounts: *"The profit and loss account shall include all profits and expenses of the period, notwithstanding the date of encashment or payment"* (Commercial Law, Article L. 123-13; Plan comptable général – General Chart of Accounts –, Article 130-131).

Not fulfilling these requirements leads to tax procedure consequences. For instance, if the accounting books do not meet the standards, the tax audit may last longer – six months instead of three for small businesses. This gives the auditor time to recalculate profits and losses, in order to present the taxpayer with a complete revision of the taxable income that comes with a 10% penalty – 40% if the offense is deliberate.

Does this imply that the auditor may change the financial statements? Further developments will show that this will not happen. However, before examining this question, the moment has come to determine the extent of the legal tax/accounting connection.

[B]   The Tax Base Definition Includes Direct Reference to the Accounting Field

[1]   Profit and Loss or Balance Sheet: The Two Branches of Income

In France, the taxable income is *"the income derived ... from the exercise of a commercial, an industrial or a handicraft activity"*. The definition of the income is provided for by Article 38, which includes two sections which refer, respectively, to both the accounting result and the balance sheet. Indeed, *"the taxable income is the net profit, determined after the general result of all nature of operations carried out by enterprises, including capital gains on pieces of assets"* (CGI, Article 38.1). Second, *"the net profit is the difference between the values of the net asset at the beginning and at the end of the period covered by taxation"*,[1] with the net asset being defined as *"the exceeding part of the values of assets compared to depreciations and the liabilities toward third parties"* (CGI, Article 38.2).

The provisions of Article 38.1 determine the income from a profit and loss perspective. They have remained unchanged since first drawn up in July 1917 as a schedular tax, (codified in a Décret dated October 15, 1926). Article 38.2 also determines the income, but from a balance sheet perspective. Its provisions were created as a Vichy-Government law (Décret dated January 13, 1941) ratified by the IV Republic Government (Décret dated December 9, 1948). Article 38.1 and 38.2 together lead to a very wide notion of taxable corporate income. Article 38.2 includes as a taxable income, for example, an extinction of a company debt that does not come from a contribution of a shareholder, since such extinction results in a higher value of the net asset (Conseil d'Etat, November 19, 1976, n. 97391).

---

1. With a correction taking into account (+) the distributions to the partners and (-) their participations of the year.

[2]   Theory of a Two-Fold Legal Connection

Theoretically, one can conclude that the relationship with accounting standards works through two legal connections.

First, and quite obviously, the determination of income, in difficult cases, implies using the accounting rationale: for example, it is because of an accounting rationale that a debt extinction can be deemed to raise income through profit and loss mechanisms.

Second, the provisions of tax law quoted previously contain several words referring directly to the lexis of accountability: income, capital gains, assets, liabilities, depreciations. Interpreting each and every one of these words involves exploring accounting and influences the accounting standards. How does this influence work ?

[C]   The Key to Legal Interpretation: *"Article 38 Quater of Annex III"*

In the same way as some irregular Latin verbs bear forms deriving from ancient and forgotten rules, Article 38 quater of annex III to the CGI contains a far-reaching principle, that appears in the form of an exception. It reads: *"The enterprises shall respect the definitions included in the general accounting regulations,*[2] *unless these are incompatible with the rules applicable for tax purpose".*

[1]   An Apparent Exception

Formally, Article 38 quater of annex III is a weak one. In fact, it belongs to an annex of the code général des impôts. It is, hence, a mere regulation and not a statute whereas, pursuant to Article 34 of the V Republic Constitution, *"Statutes shall determine the rules concerning: / ... – the base, rates and methods of collection of all types of taxes ... ".* The statutory rules voted by the Parliament are, therefore, listed in the general tax code, whereas the annexes to this book, which include Article 38 quater of annexe III, are dedicated to government regulations.

Substantially, Article 38 quater of annex III means that accounting definitions and standards are generally applicable for tax purposes. The important word in the sentence is "unless". It means that tax law, when it differs literally from accounting law, prevails without accounting interference. Accordingly, ten years after the Government passed the Decree of October 28, 1965, Article 3 of which was later codified as Article 38 quater of annex III, the Conseil d'Etat took a decision according to which *"it results from the very terms of Article 3 of the Decree of 28 October 1965 that taxpayers cannot oppose tax rules by using accounting definitions. Moreover, a recommendation of the High Council of Accounting has no impact on the legal ground of taxation"* (Conseil d'Etat, November 5, 1975, n. 95015).

---

2. Litt. *"le plan comptable général"* – the general chart of accounts.

[2] ***The Actual Influence of a Broad-Spectrum Principle***

Although exceptional, Article 38 quater of annex III is necessary whenever a tax term is unclear. This is extremely important not only to the article itself but also to the principle that it encapsulates. For example, an issue was raised concerning the application of the French Local Business Tax that is based on the assets and includes a tax credit whenever the amount to be paid exceeds a certain percentage of the company's net added value – generally 3%. A section of the general tax code – Article 1647 B sexies – provides a definition of the net added value. Due to this definition, one could imagine that there is neither any need, nor much room, for applying Article 38 of annex III. Still, some civil engineering groups claimed that they were entitled to exclude some refunds their subsidiaries had allocated to one another from their net added value, since these refunds were recorded as transferred expenses in their accounting books.

The Conseil d'Etat decided that this was not the only accounting choice possible because the entities could also have recorded the refunds directly as part of the year revenue. Consequently, the Conseil d'Etat decided that "the fact that these operations have been recorded in the company books as 'transferred expenses' is no obstacle to the corresponding amounts being, pursuant to Article 1647 B sexies, *combined with* Article 38 quater of annex III, taken into account as profits to determine the net added value" (Conseil d'Etat, August 4, 2006, n. 270961). By choosing the word "combined", the Conseil d'Etat implied that accounting definitions matter in the tax field, notwithstanding the lower value of Article 38 quater of annex III.

Moreover, Article 38 quater of annex III may apply to all the tax fields and not only the income definitions in Article 38. This is why the Conseil d'Etat relates Article 38 quater of annex III to all tax provisions, and "*notably* Articles 38 and 39 of the code général des impôts" (Conseil d'Etat, June 1, 2001, n. 194699). In this case, the Conseil d'Etat decided that the tax return could not include the whole amount of an interest due one year, if part of this interest related to a contract continuing over the following years. Only the part relating to each year's obligation should be returned that same year (accrued interest).

What it reveals is that although tax law is special and superior to accounting law, interpreting the business aspects of tax law implies accounting notions and mechanisms. This, in turn, shows that however low and exceptional Article 38 quater of annex III may appear, it encapsulates the whole influence of accounting techniques on the tax matter, with accounting and commercial law working as *lex generalis*, and the tax law as *lex specialis*.

§6.02 THOUGH LEGALLY INDEPENDENT FROM TAX, ACCOUNTING LAW IS INFLUENCED BY A "REALISM" PRINCIPLE THAT APPLIES TO BOTH FIELDS

At this point, one could conclude that accounting influences tax, but not the other way around. This is all the truer in view of the fact that the tax auditor must not intervene in business. Yet to be accurate, it is interesting to note that accounting needs realism which is a key principle in business. This turns out to be a back door for tax influence on accounting.

[A]   Tax Administration Is Kept Out of Accounting by a "No Intervention" Principle

Accounting depends on the business activity, without interference from the tax law. *A contrario* proof can be found in Article 322-2.2 of the General Accounting Regulation, that states: *"Specific statutes allow or prescribe accounting rules for derogatory depreciations that do not correspond to the normal purpose of amortization and provisioning"*. Such situations where financial documents are themselves modified for tax purposes are exceptional. They relate to especially favorable tax regimes. In such situations, a company may apply the specific accounting rules, but can also decide not to. This results in a tax choice that the administration cannot criticize. The only limit is that the company, after a period of three years, is bound by its choice.

Correlatively, the administration is not to interfere in business decisions which only rest with the company's management. The decisions motivating accounting records are to be considered as stated, with two exceptions:

(1) In the case of an abuse, the administration is not bound by the operations carried out by a taxpayer. The tax auditor can, therefore, consider such operations as inexistent and assess income as though they had never occurred (Tax Procedures Code, Article L. 64; Conseil d'Etat, September 27, 2006, n. 260050, SARL Jeanfin). The possibility to use the anti-abuse device is based upon the *"sole tax purpose"* criterion, meaning that the administration must prove the taxpayer made the decision for the sole purpose of avoiding tax (i.e., the operations are fictitious or purely aimed at taking advantage of a legal loophole). Because there are usually plenty of other reasons for taking a decision, actual cases based upon the anti-abuse regime are quite scarce. The administration uses this legal device around 120 times a year, and the anti-abuse regulation authority generally rules out half of the cases – not to mention the courts' decisions afterwards.

(2) In the case of an abnormal management. The Conseil d'Etat has, over time, built case law, according to which administration can assess a company's taxable income based on the accounting consequences that should be attached to a normal management. For example, where a company had registered equity share with an overestimated value and had later depreciated the corresponding assets – thus reducing the income according to Article 38.2 –, the Conseil d'Etat decided that the administration was right to claim that this overestimation *"reflected an abnormal accounting management, whose*

consequences called for a tax assessment" (Conseil d'Etat, August 29, 1983, n. 43418).

However, assessing taxable income does not imply changing financial statements or even the tax returns. Even in cases of abuse or abnormal management, the auditor assesses the tax income but never changes the financial income itself (Conseil d'Etat, April 27, 2001, n. 212680, Sté générale de transport et d'industrie).

[B]   The Connection between Tax and Accounting Goes Back to a Common Dependence on the "réalisme" Principle

A decision by the Conseil d'Etat, dated April 28, 2006, illustrates the influence of realism as regards tax and accounting matters. Société Serip had taken control of Société Dopresse through a massive capital increase on December 17, 1992 and had, accordingly, recorded an increase in intangible assets. Shortly after, on December 31st the date of closure of the period, Serip had recorded a provision for stock depreciation in order to neutralize the value of the assets, considering that the value in use of the stock was nil. In this situation, the Conseil d'Etat refused the deduction of the provision, deciding on the grounds of accounting regulations applied to the tax matter:[3]

> According to Article 332-3 of the General Chart of Accounts, resulting from Regulation n. 99-03 dated 29 April 1999 of the Accounting Regulation Committee: 'except on the date of first booking, equity shares are to be recorded for their value in use, with this value representing what the entity would be disposed to pay to obtain the corresponding share if it were to purchase it'.

Now in this case, the company *"does not prove"* that between December 17 and 31 the same year, *"the 'value in use' of these titles had become inferior"* to the price it had just paid (Conseil d'Etat, April 28, 2006, n. 277572).

Thus, financial accounting choices that have tax impact may be criticized from an accounting perspective, if they are not suitable for truthfully reflecting a realistic image of a company's balance sheet. This is the limit to accounting independence. It stems from the very principle that organizes accounting obligations in the framework of the commercial law: *"the annual accounts shall be honest and truthful and shall ensure a fair representation of the assets, financial situation and results of the company"* (Commercial Law, Article L. 123-14). Consequently, companies may have accounting options, but filing their tax return implies making choices that fit with what an auditor from the administration considers as "realistic" *in substance*, whatever legal *form* accounting rules tolerate. For example, accounting and tax deduction is allowed if an expense corresponds to some contract, but the tax consequence of such deduction can be challenged if the contract is economically unbalanced, and should give way to accounting corrections (Conseil d'Etat, July 27, 1984, n. 34588, SA Renfort Service).

---

3. In the light of Article 38 quater of annex III.

§6.03   THE FRENCH CONNECTION FACING INTERNATIONAL CHANGES: BUSINESS AS USUAL?

Accounting directives and the CCCTB project hold changes in store across the continent. The portrait emerging from the first two sections of this paper shows that these changes are not about to upset the French tax/accounting connection. But this is not to say that there are no outstanding issues. The main question will be to account adequately for transfers within groups.

[A]   The Transposition of Accounting Innovations in the 2000s Led to No Major Change

[1]   The Introduction of the IFRS Did Not Raise Any Issues regarding Connection

The rules of consolidated accounts, deriving from IAS 12 edited in 1998, have been transposed as a regulation by the Conseil de réglementation comptable, the French regulation authority (règl. CRC n. 99-02 dated April 29, 1999). Regulation n. 1606/2002 of the European Parliament and the Council of July 19, 2002 on the application of International Accounting Standards (IAS) led to the application of the standards of the IAS Board to consolidated accounts of companies requesting public savings. Companies that are not publicly funded may also apply the International Financial Reporting Standards (IFRS), according to the Ordinance n. 2004-1382 dated December 20, 2004. As a consequence, groups in which at least one entity publishes IFRS consolidated accounts began, as from 2005, to apply the IFRS consolidated accounts to all their entities. Yet IFRS do not extend to social accounts. The 2004 Ordinance does not impose the conformity of annual accounts to the IAS. France, thus, chose a way that enabled its own accounting regulation authority to organize the process of convergence to the IAS. 2005 was *"a crucial year" for this process*, with several regulations from the French Accounting Committee and especially a new one on the Definition, Accounting and Evaluating of Assets, which includes the Fair Value principle (Règl. November 23, 2004).

The IFRS are based upon the idea that the accounting statements are part of the financial information of a company in a given economic environment. In this framework, financial statements reflect the way the economic environment and decisions influence the substance and value of the company. They appear to be constructed naturally to reflect variations, whereas old accounting standards were conceived to reflect the company's legal decisions once and for all.

The two main principles of the IFRS derive from this general philosophy: the Substance Over Form Principle, and the Fair Value Market Principle. Though the first one is quite close to the traditional idea that accountability should not only reflect the formal contracts but also the reality, the latter implies some changes in evaluating a company's assets. The values contained in the balance sheet are now accounted for on the basis of their market value, whereas they used to be accounted for at their "historical value" (e.g., the value that they had when first recorded in the balance sheet). The evolution towards a Fair Value Principle is generally related to the collapse of the Enron pension fund, where accountants had underestimated its liabilities, subjected to burdensome changes. Of course, a fair value approach can itself lead to mistakes, for example an overestimation of assets in a phase of economic expansion. In fact, no principle is sufficient to provide absolute accuracy. Still, when it comes to taking the economy into account, the Fair Value Principle is generally considered as a better proxy than the traditional "historical" value principle.

From this perspective, one can support the idea that the fair value principle promotes legal certainty through a better convergence between accounting and corporate group taxation. As regards transfer pricing, for example, the fair value principle appears to be related to the Arm's Length Principle, which implies that the relationships within a group are determined according to the values deriving from free competition mechanisms. For example, when a group owns a protected trademark for a price P and arranges royalty payments from its subsidiaries, an entity that wishes to evaluate the corresponding intangible asset is expected to account for the royalties with a function which includes the P factor,[4] same as the function deriving from an IFRS approach. The underlying reason is that both transfer pricing and the IFRS tend to take economy into account. Again the "réalisme" principle.

One remark: the IFRS were introduced at the same time as some changes regarding the process of building accounting law. Traditionally, accountability rules were prepared by a regulation committee, working as an advisory body of the Ministry of Finance. Accounting law was then wrapped up in a Plan comptable général (General Accounting Chart), a hierarchical classification of the balance sheet based on accounting criteria. The content of the "plan comptable" was enforced by the Ministry as an administrative regulation. Recently though, the regulation committee has evolved from an advisory body to a regulatory authority[5] which reflects growing responsibility and less dependence on the Ministry. Moreover, the accounting authority belongs to the IASB. The fact that the committee is part of an international body gives it the status of a sort of diplomatic representative contributing to a consensus-based standard. It makes the authority look like a sort of treaty-appointed competent authority. Writing the accounting law is no longer the sole work of the Government, but a matter for several actors.[6] This makes it necessary to monitor the quality of connection between accounting and tax law.

As a conclusion on this point, the recent accounting reforms seem to have found their equilibrium regarding tax. Although some feared that the IFRS may lead to chaos,[7]

---

4. According to the OECD guidelines, "*The general guidance set out … for applying the arm's length principle pertains equally to the determination of transfer pricing between associated enterprises for intangible property*" (OECD Transfer Pricing Guidelines for Multinational Enterprises and Tax Administrations, 2010, 6.13).
5. Statute dated April 6, 1998, after Decree of August 26, 1996.
6. Daniel Gutmann, Pluralisme juridique et fiscalité, Archives de philosophie du droit, t. 49, 2006, p. 243 s.
7. Yohann Benard, Fiscalité et comptabilité: convergence + connexion = chaos ? Revue de Jurisprudence Fiscale n. 6/2007 p. 523.

the system is now up and running and did not weaken the connection between tax and accounting.

[2]   The Transposition of Directive 2013/34 Appeared to Be Another Technical Matter

Directive 2013/34/EU, including the *"substance over form"* principle, was transposed in France without issues on tax matters. The Government considered this Directive of minor importance and grouped it together with other European Directives in Statutes n. 2014-1662 dated December 30, 2014, labeled *"On various provisions to adapt the Law to the EU's legislation as regards economic and financial rules"*. Several regulations were issued during 2015 as a consequence of this statute, on minor topics or regarding specific operators such as the French Caisse des depots et consignations, a public entity that finances a large part of public investments.

Shortly after the Directive was adopted, Anne Colmet Daâge[8] wrote it should *"not bring major changes in the French Accounting Law"*. Only two of the ten principles in the Directive, she analyzed, do not already exist in social accounts: these are first the *"material"* principle, that implies not applying the directive's requirements to mathematically negligible amounts.

This principle is quite simple and already exists in the consolidated accounts and even for the Governmental accounts, which have been reformed since 2006 and are certified annually. Being dedicated to making things simpler for the entity, the material principle does not create any problem for the French law system.

The second principle, labeled *"the Substance Over Form Principle"*, is contained in Article 5. 1. h), that states: *"items in the profit and loss account and balance sheet shall be accounted for and presented having regard to the substance of the transaction or arrangement concerned"*. However, the Directive gave the Member States the opportunity not to transpose this principle. France chose not to, as it had already taken steps to converge with the IAS that contains this principle through the action of the French Accounting Authority. On this matter, we have already quoted Article L. 123-14 of the Commercial Law, which requires *"honest and truthful"* accounts. Interestingly, this Article continues as follows:

> Where the application of an accounting requirement is not sufficient to ensure the fair representation indicated in this article, additional information must be provided in the annex. If, in an exceptional case, the application of an accounting requirement proves to be unsuitable in order to ensure a fair representation of the assets, financial situation or results, an exception must be made to this. This exception shall be indicated in the annex and duly reasoned, with an indication of its effect on the assets, financial situation and results of the company.

---

8. Anne Colmet Daâge, Comptabilité et fiscalité: retour sur l'année 2013, Droit fiscal n. 15/2014 comm. 260.

[B]   Accounting for In-Group Transfers: The Main Issue

In the French corporate tax system, in-group relationships can lead to assessments whenever there is a legal and/or economic decision center, whether the groups choose to enlist as such or not (CGI, Article 39.12). Such dependant relationships can lead, in particular, to adjustments when transfer pricing is deemed to have been determined in a way that differs from the arm's length principle (CGI, Article 57). In order to avoid such problems and make their life simpler, groups can choose to file a single tax return for all the subsidiaries, subject to a 95% capital ownership. This implies neutralizing the in-group profits and losses (CGI, Article 223 A).

[1]   Group Tax Integration Is Not More Important Than the Interest of Its Components

Consistently with these tax possibilities for groups, some taxpayers have claimed that an entity could face an expense related to the interest of the group itself, without consideration to the personal interest of the entity incurring the expense. Advertising Group SEEEE, in particular, obtained a favorable decision from the tribunal and the court against the administration, claiming that its entity Serip could bid in a capital increase organized by one of its subsidiaries, Sedep, which had bought Dopresse and then, by means of this capital increase, had handed over power and costs to Serip. The Conseil d'Etat first decided that:

> the option for the tax integration regime, as provided for by Article 223 A and the following articles of the general tax code, implies that the accounting profits of each subsidiary of the tax-integrated group, the algebric sum of which constitutes the global profit used as the tax base of the company that has exercised the option, be determined according to the common law of corporate tax, with the only exceptions included in this particular regime. None of these exceptions allows an entity of an integrated group to claim deduction, other than the ways permitted by common law, for an expense borne for the benefit of a third party.

Consequently, deduction could not be allowed on a group-interest basis. Nevertheless, the attention of the Conseil d'Etat was drawn to another circumstance of the case: the group not only claimed the interest of Sedep in Dopresse was enough in itself to allow for an expense by Serip; it also claimed that, by taking control of Dopresse through the capital increase, Serip, a holding company, gained a new subsidiary and pursued a goal of its own. The Conseil d'Etat was convinced by this different and quite interesting argument (Conseil d'Etat, April 28, 2006, n. 277572).

[2]   Implementing the CCCTB Project?

In a series of articles dedicated to the CCCTB, Prof. Daniel Gutmann analyzed the evolutions that the draft directive holds in store as regards "*the way we deal with taxable income, territoriality of taxation and tax litigation*.[9] When it comes to determining tax base, Prof. Gutmann stresses some differences compared with the present law:

- more favorable rules as regards profit distributions received, idem for proceeds from a disposal of shares, that are exempt whereas, in principle, they are taxed in France (Article 11);
- more favorable rules, concerning the costs incurred for the purpose of deriving exempt dividends such as those received from subsidiaries, which currently leads to a deduction limited to 95%: taxpayers could get a 100% deduction if they are able to prove the lower cost (Article 14);
- use of actuarial method to determine pension provisions more easily (Article 26);
- deduction of losses of a subsidiary or a permanent establishment the following years, with the sole condition of using the oldest losses first (Article 43);
- on the other side, more restrictive rules as regards entertainment costs (deduction at a rate of only 50%) and the exclusion of loss carry back (Article 14);
- last but not least, as regards intangible assets, whereas French tax law does not permit the deduction of the depreciation, the CCCTB admits deduction and provides a pragmatic rule as regards duration: *"the period for which the asset enjoys legal protection or for which the right is granted or, if that period cannot be determined, is 15 years"*.

Not all the changes contained in the CCCTB project have a clear consequence on the amount to be paid. As an example, Prof. Gutmann mentions the asset pools (Article 39), which can be depreciated as a group. CCCTB holds changes in store, but not necessarily predictable ones.

The CCCTB has been commented on in handbooks, official reports, and specific studies.

In his handbook on Financial Accounting for Tax purposes, Arnaud de Bissy[10] points to the superiority of the project compared with the French regime of tax integration that works for domestic groups whereas the CCCTB offers the possibility of a single entity treatment for Continent-sized companies carrying on their activities across the whole continent.

As for official reports, it is worth mentioning two Information Reports of the National Assembly by Representative Pierre-Alain Muet,[11] who is also an economist. For Muet, the CCCTB project is an important tool for making things easier for

---

9. L'assiette commune consolidée de l'IS: une réforme profonde de la fiscalité, Revue française de finances publiques Nov 2011 n. 116 p. 33; Les enjeux de l'ACCIS pour les groupes français, Droit fiscal n. 47/2012 comm. 528.
10. Arnaud de Bissy, Comptabilité et fiscalité, Du résultat comptable au résultat fiscal, LexNexis, 2014, n. 61 p. 40.
11. Pierre-Alain Muet, L'optimisation fiscale des entreprises dans un contexte international, Rapports d'information déposé par la Commission des finances, Assemblée nationale, n. 1243, 2013 and n. 2023, 2014.

companies, but not necessary as a legal construction for making tax laws in Europe converge, since it does not cover the problem of competition between States through tax rate differences. Nevertheless, he welcomes the project as very good news, suggesting that it should be adopted as a reinforced cooperation initiative. The second report tends to insist on the point that the CCCTB is, unfortunately, a project on the (very) long run.

In fact, the CCCTB project is not all black or white. For Prof. Gutmann,[12] it holds plenty of opportunities in store, but also some risks. It would lead to positive changes in tax law as regards several aspects of income determination, but it would also include restrictive provisions. The CCCTB would imply major changes as regards procedures, with the administrative cost dropping by 0.5% of the turnover, but this would be subject to the companies being able to choose how to proceed, which could be difficult and costly. Last but not least, the CCCTB project would change the relationships between tax administrations, since it includes the possibility for a member to litigate against the Member State sheltering the mother company.

[3]   As a Conclusion: Will International Group Economy Lead to a New Accounting Definition of Their Activities?

The fact that the CCCTB is not up and running underlines a question that has been emerging for some years regarding the in-group relationships in a global economy. Internet operators, but also financial entities and even industrial groups do not tend to carry on business on a specific territory, but on all the surface of their global presence. How can accounting and tax reflect this new trend in free trade ?

The usual answer lies in the arm's length principle with transfer pricing techniques, in an effort to adapt to the economic developments without changing the law. As we have seen, both tax and accounting laws include a principle to be adaptable to economic challenges, for the sake of being realistic. This is the strongest force that keeps both legal fields connected in spite of on-going difficulties of globalization.

But what if these difficulties were too numerous to adapt to? And, theoretically, when it comes to reflecting group activities, is the reflection provided for by tax and accounting the only one possible? IAS 18 defines revenue as *"the gross inflow of economic benefits during the period arising in the course of the ordinary activities of an entity when those inflows result in increases in equity, other than increases relating to contributions from equity participants"*. What if the *"ordinary activities"* of a world group of the Internet sector in the twenty-first century are no longer the ones that usually shaped the tools of accounting and previously designed rules of taxation? Examining the official documents that some groups draw up for their shareholders, a discrepancy is revealed between the value of their economic presence in various countries and the turnover these groups pretend derives from the corresponding territory. Is this a symptom of the concept of revenue no longer being a good indicator

---

12. Daniel Gutmann, op. cit., Revue fr. de finances publiques nov 2011 n. 116 p. 33; Droit fiscal n. 47/2012 c. 528.

of the economic activity? And if not, is there a risk that Governments may change tax law and disconnect it from the accounting revenue?

The question is open and strictly related to the economic stakes of tax evasion and adapting to globalization.

What remains is that a good connection between tax and accounting is an asset for Governments and companies, and a guarantee of legal certainty that should be preserved as much as possible.

CHAPTER 7

Accounting and Taxation: Germany

Andreas Eggert

§7.01 ACCOUNTING AND TAXATION IN GERMANY

[A] Definition of the Tax Base for a German Company

In Germany, the tax base for a company generally has to be based on its individual financial statements that have to be prepared and presented in accordance with the GAAP pursuant to the German Commercial Code (*Handelsgesetzbuch* – *HGB*). The German Commercial Code stipulates rather conservative accounting rules and does not allow the application of IFRS for a company's individual financial accounts.

[B] Connection between the Tax Base and Financial Accounting

In Germany, the link between financial and tax accounting is laid down in the statutory law. Section 5(1) sentence 1 of the German Income Tax Act (*Einkommensteuergesetz* – *EStG*) and section 8(1) sentence 1 German Corporate Income Tax Act (*Körperschaftsteuergesetz* – *KStG*) provide that a company's taxable profit has to be based on its financial accounts if the company has a legal obligation to keep accounts or does so voluntarily.

This connection dates back to the nineteenth century. In the year 1874, the state of Saxony regulated in its income tax law that a businessman's income tax should be based on the GAAP. In the same year, the Free Hanseatic City of Bremen went a step further and determined that the income tax should be levied upon the balance sheet profits. In 1891, it was regulated in the Prussian Income Tax Act that the taxable profits should be based on the GAAP under the Commercial Code.[1]

In the German Income Tax Act of 1920, the connection between the assessment of the tax base and the GAAP was established for the first time in the whole of Germany, although already in 1921 the first restrictions to the application of the GAAP to tax accounting were regulated. The courts understood reference to the GAAP as meaning that the calculation of the taxable profit had to be based on the financial statements.[2]

[C] Theoretical Justifications for the Connection between Income Taxation and Financial Accounting

The main theoretical justifications for the connection between the computation of a company's tax base and financial accounting are the following:

- Practicability: The link between financial accounting and income taxation was supposed to facilitate the computation of the taxable profit and to increase the acceptance of the relatively new income tax.[3] At least in theory it should be possible to use a single balance sheet for commercial and tax purposes (*Einheitsbilanz*).[4]
- State as silent partner: The connection between financial and tax accounting ensures that the state, similar to a silent partner, participates in the business's profits, but also in its losses. This profit and loss participation should ensure the neutrality of income taxation because it does not influence the taxpayer's risk taking.[5]
- Neutral law: Reference to the GAAP should balance the state's desire to increase revenue. Financial accounting rules are seen as 'neutral' law that provides a fair balance between the interests of the state and the taxpayer.[6]
- Conflicting interests: Taxpayers generally have an interest in showing high profits in the financial accounts and low profits in the tax accounts. These conflicting interests should balance out and lead to overall reasonable accounting policies.[7]

---

1. See for the entire paragraph: Mayer, in Schön (editor), Steuerliche Maßgeblichkeit in Deutschland und Europa, Cologne 2005, pp. 151 et seqq.
2. See for the entire paragraph: Mayer, in Schön (editor), Steuerliche Maßgeblichkeit in Deutschland und Europa, Cologne 2005, pp. 155 et seqq.
3. Weber-Grellet, Betriebs-Berater (BB) 1999, p. 2659.
4. Robisch, Das deutsche Steuerrecht (DStR) 1993, pp. 998, 999.
5. Döllerer, Betriebs-Berater (BB) 1971, pp. 1333, 1334; this idea was first mentioned by the Prussian Higher Administrative Tax Court in a judgment dated 2 July 1902 (PrOVGSt – Rep. V. A. 136/01).
6. Schön, in Schön (editor), Steuerliche Maßgeblichkeit in Deutschland und Europa, Cologne 2005, pp. 55 et seq.
7. Robisch, Das deutsche Steuerrecht (DStR) 1993, pp. 998, 999.

[D] Calculation of the Tax Base

Pursuant to section 5(1) sentence 1 of the German Income Tax Act and section 8(1) sentence 1 German Corporate Income Tax Act, the tax base of enterprises and of all corporations has to be calculated in accordance with the GAAP pursuant to the German Commercial Code. There is a rather theoretical dispute about what this reference to the GAAP means. The German Federal Tax Court, the tax authorities and most authors in tax literature understand this as a reference to the written profit calculation rules of the German Commercial Code.[8] In the case of regulatory gaps, these written rules are complemented by the unwritten German GAAP.[9]

The reference to the GAAP generally only concerns the national accounting legislation and principles. However, it is not entirely clear to what extent this reference to the national GAAP also includes the European Union Accounting Directives. In one judgment, the German Federal Tax Court did not consider the Fourth Directive 78/660/EEC to be binding for tax accounting because there were special tax accounting rules and it denied the duty to refer the matter to the CJEU.[10] Nevertheless, there are cases where German lower tax courts referred tax accounting issues to the CJEU. In those cases, the CJEU gave an interpretation of the Fourth Directive 78/660/EEC with regard to the tax accounting questions.[11] The literature is very controversial concerning a possible duty of the tax courts to present tax accounting matters to the CJEU.[12]

[E] Differences between Financial and Tax Accounting

The link between tax accounting and the GAAP is limited. According to section 5(1) sentence 1 German Income Tax Act, the financial accounts are not binding in the case that a tax option has been exercised differently. Section 5(6) German Income Tax Act stipulates that the special tax accounting rules regarding capital contributions and withdrawals, changes in the balance sheet, business expenses, valuation and amortization have to be adhered to.

There are more deviations required in the German Income Tax Act. For instance, section 5(3) to (4b) German Income Tax Act regulates restrictions for provisions. Some of these restrictions are rather clarifications that also apply for the financial statements. Other restrictions like the prohibition of provisions for onerous contracts can hardly be justified systematically and are intended to increase tax revenue.[13] Furthermore, there

---

8. Federal Tax Court, I R 103/09, 25 August 2010, Federal Tax Gazette (BStBl) II 2011, p. 215; Income tax guidance (*Einkommensteuer-Richtlinien- EStR*) 2012, H 5.2; Anzinger in Herrmann/Heuer/Raupach (editors), EStG/KStG, § 5, recital 250, with further references.
9. Anzinger in Herrmann/Heuer/Raupach (editors), EStG/KStG, § 5, recital 250.
10. Federal Tax Court, VIII R 65/91, 25 October 1994, Federal Tax Gazette (BStBl) II 1995, p. 312.
11. CJEU, 14 September 1999, C-275/97 (DE + ES); CJEU, 7 January 2003, C-306/99 (BIAO).
12. See Krumm, in Blümich (editor), EStG, KStG, GewStG, § 5 EStG, recital 99; Hennrichs, Neue Zeitschrift für Gesellschaftsrecht (NZG) 2005, pp. 783, 787; both with further references.
13. Moxter, Der Betrieb (DB) 1997, pp. 1477, 1488.

are rules for the amendment of the taxable profit outside the tax balance sheet[14] (e.g., the interest barrier rules).

[1]   Different Objectives

Variations can also result from the different objectives of financial and tax accounting (e.g., the slightly different definition of assets, see below).

In a landmark decision in 1969, the German Federal Tax Court decided that an option to capitalize an asset in the financial accounts results in a duty to capitalize the asset in the tax accounts. At the same time, an option to report a liability in the financial accounts results in the prohibition of reporting such a liability in the tax accounts.[15] For instance, there is the option for the financial statements to capitalize certain discounts as prepaid expenses.[16] This option results in a duty to capitalize those discounts in the tax accounts.[17]

The main justification for this deviation is the different purposes of the financial statements and the tax accounts. Traditionally, one of the main objectives of financial accounting in Germany is the ascertainment of the distributable profit and the protection of a corporation's creditors. This purpose allows for a fairly conservative accounting policy because the conscious creation of hidden reserves is – to a certain extent – in accordance with an accounting system that mainly aims at avoiding profit distributions that are too high. On the contrary, the purpose of tax accounting is to assess the 'full' profit. Therefore, the taxpayer must not make himself 'poorer' than he really is. Options to create hidden reserves would be contrary to the equality of taxation.[18]

These different purposes lead to many deviations when it comes to specific accounting issues. For example, it is assumed by many authors that an item must only be capitalized as an asset in the financial accounts if it can be transferred independently from the business as a whole,[19] because an item that can only be transferred together with the business as a whole cannot be sold in order to cover the business's debt.[20] For the capitalization in the tax accounts it is sufficient if the item can be transferred together with the business as a whole.[21] This wide definition of assets ensures the taxation of the full profit.

14. With regard to the separate tax balance sheet, see below §7.01[E][3].
15. Federal Tax Court, GrS 2/68, 3 February 1969, Federal Tax Gazette (BStBl) II 1969, p. 291.
16. Section 250(3) German Commercial Code.
17. Förschle/Usinger, in Beck'scher Bilanz-Kommentar, § 243 HGB, recital 114.
18. Federal Tax Court, GrS 2/68, 3 February 1969, Federal Tax Gazette (BStBl) II 1969, p. 291.
19. Acquired goodwill can only be capitalized as a fictitious asset, section 246(1) sentence 4 German Commercial Code.
20. Schön, in Schön (editor), Steuerliche Maßgeblichkeit in Deutschland und Europa, Cologne 2005, p. 74, with further references.
21. Federal Tax Court, I R 24/91, 26 August 1992, Federal Tax Gazette (BStBl) II 1992, p. 977.

[2] Reverse Authoritativeness

Until 2009, section 5(1) sentence 2 of the German Income Tax Act provided that options for the calculation of the taxable profit had to be exercised in accordance with the financial accounts. As a consequence, the financial accounts had to be adjusted to the tax rules if tax options were exercised. This so-called reverse authoritativeness principle (*umgekehrte Maßgeblichkeit*) was heavily criticized in tax and accounting literature. The criticism was that the reverse authoritative principle distorts the financial accounts. Special tax rules on depreciation and liabilities that usually serve as tax subsidies had to be taken into account for the financial statements, even though, they were not in accordance with the GAAP.[22]

The idea behind reverse authoritativeness was to maintain the one-book system as far as possible and to prevent financial means resulting from tax subsidies from being distributed to the shareholders. However, the idea of a one-book system does not justify a failure of the financial statements to provide a fair presentation. A payout block for subsidies was unnecessary because the companies had to create provisions for deferred taxes anyway.[23] In 2009, the reverse authoritativeness principle was repealed by the German Accounting Law Modernization Act (*Bilanzrechtsmodern-isierungsgesetz – BilMoG*).[24]

[3] Tax Accounting Documentation

The fact that the computation of the tax base substantially differs from financial accounting raises the question about how these deviations should be documented. Under the German Accounting Law Modernization Act of 2009, Section 5(1) sentence 2 and 3 of the German Income Tax Act were reformulated in such a way that tax options must only be exercised if the taxpayer includes assets with a tax value that deviates from their value in the financial accounts in special and regularly updated registers. Because of the many deviations between financial and tax accounting it is very common for taxpayers to maintain separate tax balance sheets.[25]

[F] The Assessment of the Financial Income by the National Tax Administration

In Germany, the tax authorities regularly audit the financial statements as the taxable profit is based on those statements. Often the tax authorities do not accept certain balance sheet items because the establishment of the item or its valuation is not in

---

22. Schön, in Schön (editor), Steuerliche Maßgeblichkeit in Deutschland und Europa, Cologne 2005, p. 56.
23. Arbeitskreis Bilanzrecht Hochschullehrer Rechtswissenschaft, Das deutsche Steuerrecht (DStR) 2008, pp. 1057, 1058 et seqq.
24. Act dated 26 May 2009, Federal Law Gazette 2009 I, p. 1102.
25. Pursuant to section 60(2) sentence 2 Income Tax Implementation Regulations (*Einkommensteuer-Durchführungsverordnung – EStDV*) taxpayers have a right, but no duty to maintain a separate tax balance sheet.

accordance with financial accounting rules. A typical example would be the incomplete capitalization of the acquisition costs of an asset.

However, this does not mean that the tax authorities can alter the financial statements.[26] In tax audits it is common for the tax official to create a so-called tax auditor's balance sheet that is binding for the tax accounts, but not for the financial statements. In these cases the taxpayer himself can amend his financial statements if he is still allowed to do so under German corporate and accounting law.[27]

§7.02   THE IMPACT OF IFRS ON FINANCIAL ACCOUNTING AND TAXATION

[A]   The Implementation of IFRS in Germany

In Germany, IFRS have only been implemented and are mandatory as required by the IAS Regulation (EC) No. 1606/2002. Consequently, in Germany IFRS are only mandatory for the consolidated accounts of publicly traded companies (Section 315a(1) and (2) German Commercial Code). Other companies are allowed to prepare their consolidated accounts in accordance with IFRS (Section 315a(3) German Commercial Code). In any case, the company's individual accounts have to be prepared in accordance with the GAAP under the German Commercial Code and not the IFRS.

[B]   Consequences of the Implementation of IFRS

Due to their narrow implementation in Germany, IFRS have no direct consequences for the company's mandatory individual financial statements and their tax balance sheets.[28] However, IFRS have important indirect consequences. For some time IFRS have been seen as a potential source of information for the interpretation of the German accounting rules, although, they are not a source of law for the individual accounts.[29] Due to their global importance, IFRS are a very valuable source of information.

In 2009, the German lawmaker made substantial changes to the German accounting rules with the German Accounting Law Modernization Act.[30] The objective of this modernization was to provide accounting rules to businesses that give a fair presentation of the company's situation, but are simpler and more cost efficient than IFRS.[31] In order to provide better information, the German accounting rules were partially oriented towards IFRS. Apart from that, there are currently no proposed national laws to change the *status quo* with regard to the implementation of IFRS.

---

26. Income tax guidance 2012, H 4.4.
27. See Rödder, in Müller/Rödder, Beck'sches Handbuch der AG, Munich 2009, § 11, recital 170, footnote 159.
28. See Krumm in Blümich (editor), EStG, KStG, GewStG, § 5 EStG, recital 105; Federal Tax Court, I R 103/09, 25 August 2010, Federal Tax Gazette (BStBl) II 2011, p. 215.
29. Hennrichs, Neue Zeitschrift für Gesellschaftsrecht (NZG) 2005, pp. 783, 787.
30. Act dated 26 May 2009, Federal Law Gazette 2009 I, p. 1102.
31. Parliament Printing 16/10067, 30 July 2008, p. 1.

To give an example, until 2009 businesses were not allowed to capitalize internally created intangible assets. Pursuant to section 248(2) sentence 1 German Commercial Code businesses are now generally allowed to capitalize such assets.[32] Nevertheless, the capitalization of internally generated brands, mastheads, publishing titles, customer lists and items similar in substance is still prohibited (section 248(2) sentence 2 German Commercial Code). This prohibition is identical to IAS 38.63. In such cases, where the wording of the German accounting rules is similar to IFRS, those international standards will regularly be used for the interpretation of the domestic rules. However, in this example the IFRS will have no effect on the tax base because internally generated intangibles must still not be capitalized in the tax accounts.[33]

Other important similarities between IFRS and the German accounting rules exist, for example, with respect to financial instruments.[34] Here it is conceivable that the IFRS have an indirect influence on the tax base because the treatment of certain financial instruments under the German financial accounting law also influences the taxation of these instruments.[35]

§7.03 DIFFERENCES BETWEEN THE CCCTB AND THE GERMAN CORPORATE TAX BASE

There are numerous publications in Germany on the CCCTB and the German tax base. Below, reference is made to only some of those publications.

The most important difference between the CCCTB and the German tax base is that the CCCTB would principally be a stand-alone tax system with no direct link to the corporation's financial statements. This has important consequences for the ascertainment of the tax base, but also for the financial statements themselves.

In Germany, the GAAP still form the basis for tax accounting. Although, there are many deviations when it comes to the details of the computation of the tax base, the taxable profit is still very much defined by the financial accounts. Even the deviations in the tax accounts can only be understood if one knows the accounting rules that are being deviated from. The link between financial accounting and tax accounting increases legal certainty for the taxpayer because the GAAP provide a basic system that can be used for the interpretation of the tax rules. This basic system also protects the taxpayer from an interpretation of the tax rules by the tax authorities and the tax courts that is biased towards increasing the tax revenue. The link between financial and tax accounting also reduces compliance costs because companies do not have to run two completely separate systems.

At the same time the link between financial and tax accounting is also beneficial for the financial statements:

32. Those assets, however, do not increase the distributable profit, see Section 268(8) German Commercial Code.
33. Section 5(2) German Income Tax Act.
34. See App/Wiehagen-Knopke, Zeitschrift für internationale und kapitalmarktorientierte Rechnungslegung (KoR) 2010, pp. 93, 95.
35. For example section 340e German Commercial Code and section 6(1) no. 2b German Income Tax Act.

- In Germany the bulk of judgments on accounting law is delivered by the tax courts and not the civil courts. The judicature of the tax courts plays a key role in the systematization of accounting law.[36] With a stand-alone tax system the number of court decisions on financial accounting law would substantially decrease.
- It is likely that many smaller businesses would neglect their financial statements if they were irrelevant for tax audits.[37]
- A stand-alone tax system would lead to higher deferred taxes in the financial statements.[38]

In my view, the link between financial and tax accounting has proven its effectiveness. Nevertheless, as long as the individual financial statements in the EU are barely harmonized – the EU accounting directives providing only a basic framework – there seems to be no alternative to the development of a CCCTB on a stand-alone basis. A direct link to IFRS would not be desirable because most businesses in Europe do not use IFRS for their individual financial statements and the IFRS accounts would need many amendments in order to be suitable for tax accounting.[39]

The studies on the CCCTB in Germany basically propose two solutions to the problems that result from the stand-alone tax accounting of the CCCTB:

(1) There is a consensus in German tax literature that the CCCTB has to be based on a foundation of principles that allow for a coherent application of the CCCTB rules. The CCCTB proposal already names some of those basic rules, but the final directive should provide a more comprehensive framework of principles.[40]

(2) Some authors suggest that there should be a reference system for the CCCTB. This system would not be the basis of the CCCTB, but a 'default position'[41] if the interpretation of the CCCTB rules alone does not provide clear results.[42] In my opinion the IFRS should serve as such a reference system.[43]

---

36. Schön, in Schön (editor), Steuerliche Maßgeblichkeit in Deutschland und Europa, Cologne 2005, p. 56.
37. Döllerer, Betriebs-Berater (BB) 1971, pp. 1333, 1335.
38. Eggert, Die Gewinnermittlung nach dem Richtlinienvorschlag über eine Gemeinsame Konsolidierte Körperschaftsteuer-Bemessungsgrundlage, Cologne 2015, p. 283.
39. See Eggert, Die Gewinnermittlung nach dem Richtlinienvorschlag über eine Gemeinsame Konsolidierte Körperschaftsteuer-Bemessungsgrundlage, Cologne 2015, pp. 118 et seqq.
40. See Herzig/Kuhr, Steuer und Wirtschaft (StuW) 2011, pp. 305, 308 et seq.; Marx, Deutsche Steuer-Zeitung (DStZ) 2011, pp. 547, 549; Herzig, Der Betrieb (DB) 2012, pp. 1, 2 et seq.; Herzig, Finanz Rundschau (FR) 2012, p. 761; Kahle/Schulz, Finanz Rundschau (FR) 2013, pp. 49, 51; Schulz, Harmonisierung der steuerlichen Gewinnermittlung, pp. 103 et seq.
41. Freedman/Macdonald, in Lang amongst others (editor), CCCTB, pp. 219, 244.
42. See Herzig, Der Betrieb (DB) 2011, Heft 15, p. M1; Wissenschaftlicher Beirat beim Bundesministerium der Finanzen: Gutachten zur Einheitlichen Bemessungsgrundlage der Körperschaftsteuer in der Europäischen Union, March 2007, p. 41; Marx, Deutsche Steuer-Zeitung (DStZ) 2011, pp. 547, 550; Kahle/Schulz, Finanz Rundschau (FR) 2013, p. 49, footnote 41.
43. Eggert, Die Gewinnermittlung nach dem Richtlinienvorschlag über eine Gemeinsame Konsolidierte Körperschaftsteuer-Bemessungsgrundlage, Cologne 2015, pp. 155 et seqq.

With regard to the other aspects of tax accounting, the CCCTB system would, in most respects, be quite similar to the German tax accounting.[44]

§7.04 FISCAL ASPECTS OF THE NEW ACCOUNTING DIRECTIVE

On 23 July 2015, the law for the implementation of the new Accounting Directive[45] (*Bilanzrichtlinie-Umsetzungsgesetz – BilRUG*) entered into force. The BilRUG does not contain many amendments of the general accounting rules that apply to all businesses. Most provisions concern the specific accounting rules for corporations (e.g., for the notes to the financial statements or the consolidated accounts) and the rules for the audit of the financial statements.

Probably, the most important general amendment is the new rule that internally generated intangible assets and acquired goodwill have to be written off in ten years if their useful life cannot be reliably estimated. However, these amendments will not have any effect on the tax accounts because internally generated intangible assets must not be capitalized in the tax balance sheet[46] and the useful life of goodwill is always fifteen years for tax purposes.[47]

Notably, the German lawmaker saw no need to amend the existing accounting laws with regard to the materiality principle and the substance over form principle that are explicitly prescribed in the new Accounting Directive,[48] but not in German law.

The materiality principle is an unwritten GAAP under German accounting law.[49] Thus, the German lawmaker saw no need to regulate it explicitly. Even if the materiality principle was explicitly implemented into the German accounting laws, this would probably have no effect on the tax accounts because the German Income Tax Act provides detailed rules with regard to materiality. For instance, assets with net acquisition costs of not more than EUR 410 do not have to be capitalized (Section 6(2) sentence 1 German Income Tax Act).

The principle that the accounting should represent the substance of the transaction or arrangement concerned is a basic principle of the German financial and tax accounting rules. It is a consequence of the necessary teleological interpretation of the accounting law. However, the presentation of the substance of a transaction does not mean that the civil law form of the transaction does not matter. The accounting of a transaction and its civil law form concur in most cases. The wording of Article 6(1)(h) of the Directive (2013/34) does not prescribe a general 'substance over form' principle.

---

44. Scheffler/Krebs, Das deutsche Steuerrecht (DStR) 2011, Beihefter zu Heft 22, p. 13; see also Spengel/Zöllkau, CC(C)TB, Heidelberg 2012.
45. Directive (2013/34) of 26 June 2013.
46. Section 5(2) German Income Tax Act.
47. Section 7(1) sentence 3 German Income Tax Act.
48. Article 6(1)(h) and (j) of the Directive (2013/34).
49. Arbeitskreis Bilanzrecht Hochschullehrer Rechtswissenschaft, Betriebs-Berater (BB) 2014, p. 2731.

It only requires that the substance be presented. Therefore, the explicit implementation of the substance principle according to Article 6(1)(h) of the Directive (2013/34) into German law is not necessary.[50] If this principle were named explicitly in the law this would have no effect on the tax accounts because it is already being adhered to.

---

50. Arbeitskreis Bilanzrecht Hochschullehrer Rechtswissenschaft, Betriebs-Berater (BB) 2014, pp. 2731, 2732; critical Lüdenbach/Freiberg, Betriebs-Berater (BB) 2014, pp. 2219, 2225.

CHAPTER 8

Accounting and Taxation: Italy

Mario Grandinetti

§8.01   INTRODUCTION

The connection between accounting and taxation is a key topic and has a central dimension in the area of company taxation. In recent years, the topic has taken on a dynamic role, due to the fact that the European Union has introduced important changes to accounting rules. Even though our analysis will concern the specific tax aspects of the determination of the companies' tax base in the Italian legal order, it is important to bear in mind some general principles as background to the topic.

Historically, accounting remains the starting point for company taxation. In point of fact, the influence of accounting rules on taxation is extremely relevant.

In this context, since 2002 (after European Regulation 1606/2002), the most important change has been the introduction of International Financial Reporting Standards (IFRS) as the mandatory standards for consolidated accounts in EU market listed companies. Furthermore, the introduction of IFRS[1] also affected financial accounting for unlisted companies. In this respect, the Italian legislator, according to Article 5 of the European Regulation 1606/2002, opted for IAS/IFRS even for the individual financial statement with the relevant tax consequences.

Moreover, after the global economic (financial) crisis, the EU Commission rethought the accounting policy and, on June 26, 2013, approved new accounting Directive 2013/34. The change of strategy adopted by the EU is described in premise

---

1. The acronym IFRS is used as a reference to both types of pronouncements: IFRS, issued by IASB, and IAS, issued by its predecessor the IASC and their corresponding interpretative acts. In our chapter we refer to "accounting" and "commercial law" as synonyms. However, in the Italian legal order, principles concerning the establishment of the balance sheet are included in the civil code. Generally accepted accounting principles (GAAP) are not legal provisions, but they are used as a tool of interpretation and integration of the legal norm contained in the civil code and in the other provisions concerning the financial statement.

Article 4 of the Directive.[2] On this ground, there are also fiscal consequences due to the change of strategies of the European Union that need to be analyzed.

So, taking into consideration the accounting implications, our research has to address the main question, i.e., the determination of the companies' tax base in the Italian legal order (theoretical aspect, main justifications of the connection, etc.) with respect to the so-called book tax conformity between the financial statement and the corporate income tax base. On this matter, an overview will be provided of the main differences between the accounting and the fiscal perspectives both for IAS/IFRS compliant companies and for non-IAS/IFRS compliant companies that continue to use the national accounting principle (GAAP).

Moreover, a specific part will be dedicated to the conformity of the corporate tax base under Italian law with the Common Consolidated Corporate Tax Base (CCCTB). Finally, the tax aspects after the implementation of the accounting Directive 2013/34 EU will be analyzed.

§8.02   GENERAL OVERVIEW CONCERNING BOOK TAX CONFORMITY. THE ITALIAN MODEL

According to the "Testo Unico delle imposte sui redditi" (hereinafter Corporate Income Tax Act, "CITA"), Corporate income tax (hereinafter, "CIT") applies to resident and non-resident companies. Resident companies are taxed on their worldwide income. Non-resident entities are subject to Italian tax only on the income derived from Italy.

With respect to resident legal entities, CIT is levied, according to Article 73 CITA, on:

(a) joint-stock companies;
(b) limited liability companies;
(c) partnerships limited by shares;
(d) cooperative societies and mutual insurance companies;
(e) public and private entities (other than companies), with or without legal personality, and trusts, whether or not their sole or main business purpose is the exercise of business activities;
(f) non-resident companies and entities of all kinds (including partnerships) subject to CIT on income derived from Italy.

Despite the name, CIT does not include all companies. For example, partnerships are companies under civil law but are not subject to CIT. At the same time, non-commercial entities are subject to CIT even if they are not companies. Italian scholars

---

2. "Annual financial statements pursue various objectives and do not merely provide information for investors in capital markets but also give an account of past transactions and enhance corporate governance. Union accounting legislation needs to strike an appropriate balance between the interests of the addressees of financial statements and the interest of undertakings in not being unduly burdened with reporting requirements". In this context see the chapter by STRAMPELLI & PASSADOR, in this book.

have clearly outlined this fundamental distinction.[3] In particular, differences are linked not only to the legal personality (partnerships do not have legal personality) but also in order to prevent tax avoidance and tax evasion.[4]

Persons subject to CITA may also be a company according to the definition of the law. In this case, there is a legal assumption that we have a company subject to CIT, but Article 73 CITA could also take into account a subject without legal personality.[5]

All income derived from companies that undertake commercial activities is qualified as business income (*reddito d'impresa*) and subject to CIT, according to Article 81.

As scholars point out,[6] in theory there are two basic models used to determine the taxable (business) income of a company: the receipts – and – outgoings system and the balance sheet system. Under the first, the determination of the taxable business income is not linked to the financial accounting, but it is based on the calculation of all recognized income amounts derived by the companies and all deductible expenses incurred during a tax period. Under the second model, taxable business income is calculated by comparing the value of the net assets in the company's balance sheet at the end of the year plus dividend distributed, with the value of the net assets in the balance sheet at the end of the previous year. As a starting point, the first model takes the gains and expenses recognized for tax purposes into consideration without any references to the accounting records. Differently, in the second model the starting point is the balance sheet drawn up by the company. However, if we take a closer look, the main difficulty is to categorize in a model the different solutions adopted by each tax law order. In that respect, in the first model it is not unusual to have accounting references within the determination of the taxable income method. At the same time, in the balance sheet model, accounting records have to be adjusted in order to take the differences between tax law and commercial accounting practices into account.

Considering this premise, a useful way of categorizing the different models in force is to distinguish between the tax law system with a "formal dependence" on one side and, on the other side, the tax law system with a "formal independence". The first situation occurs when the company tax base is fully aligned with the financial accounts. On the contrary, formal independence concerns situations in which the financial accounts are totally irrelevant for determining the company tax base. However, observing the different solutions of the European Union tax systems, it is easy to note that none fall within the two models described.[7] Consequently, the vast

---

3. In this respect, please see, among others C. SACCHETTO, *L'imposta sul reddito delle persone giuridiche*, in A. AMATUCCI (dir.), *Trattato di diritto tributario*, Vol. IV, 1994, Padua, pp. 61 and ff.; G. ZIZZO, *Reddito delle persone giuridiche (imposta sul)*, in *Digesto delle discipline privatistiche*, Sez. Commerciale, Turin, 1996, p. 1, in which it is possible to find other references to Italian scholars on this matter.
4. P. BORIA, *Il principio di trasparenza nell'imposizione delle società di persone*, Milan, 1996, p. 358.
5. See L. CASTALDI, *Soggettività tributaria*, in *Dizionario di Diritto Pubblico*, ed. S. CASSESE, Padua, 2006, p. 5612. An in-depth analysis is made by L. DI NUNZIO, M. GRANDINETTI, M. MURATORE & P. SELICATO, *Italy*, in D. GUTMANN (ed.), *Corporate Income Tax Subjects*, Amsterdam, 2015, p. 329.
6. L. BURN & R. KREVER, *Taxation of Income from Business and Investment*, in V. THURONYI (ed.), *Tax Law Design and Drafting*, The Hague-Boston, 1998, p. 599.
7. See M. BARASSI, A Comparative Survey, in this book.

majority of European tax systems starts with "practically formal dependence", in which there are no separate tax rules and the fiscal options, in order to be valid, must be applied in accordance with the financial account choices. Variations in financial accounts are permitted, but only if included in the tax legislation. Moreover, the material dependence model is a possible alternative in which the financial accounts are used as a starting point, but the fiscal options are not linked to the same choice made in the financial accounting. Finally, material independence considers financial accounting as a starting point but, in practice, tax accounts prevail in most cases.[8]

According to Article 83 of the CITA, the company tax base is the worldwide income shown in the profit and loss account drawn up for the relevant financial year according to commercial (company) law, with the adjustments required by the tax law provisions. Moreover, according to Article 109, paragraph 4, as a general rule, costs and expenses may be deducted only if they are included in the profit and loss account whereas revenues are fiscally relevant even if they are not included in the financial accounts (Article 109, paragraph 3, of the CITA).

A specific period of Article 83, CITA, concerns companies drafting financial statements according to *IAS/IFRS* (see section §8.04).

As mentioned above, the Italian legislator, historically, is anchored to the "practically formal dependence" model. The linkage between commercial law and tax law was made formally at the time of the tax reform of 1971/1973.[9] Even if the determination of the company tax base has been involved in remarkable changes following this choice, the model in force has always made reference to commercial law. In our opinion, this fact reflects the theoretical (and practical) justifications for the connection between income taxation and financial accounting. In particular, studying the evolution of the linkage between accounting and taxation, it is easy to note that even in periods in which the relationship was weak, for example when in 2004 the legislator decided to introduce the extra accounts deviation only for fiscal reasons, the dependence model has never been called into question.[10]

The value determined in the profit and loss account is just a starting point while the CITA could make a choice binding or optional within the CIT return. As scholars underline[11] in the 1971 tax reform, the Italian legislator used the word *adjustment* and not *identification* for the outcome of the profit and loss account.

---

8. For the explanation of the models, G. Falsitta, *Concetti fondamentali e principi ricostruttivi in tema di rapporti tra bilancio civile e bilancio fiscale*, in *Giurisprudenza Commerciale*, 1984, p. 877; W. Schön, *Steuerliche Maßgeblichkeit in Deutschland und Europa*, Köln, 2005, p. 4 ff.; P. Essers, *The Precious Relationship between IAS/IFRS, National Tax Accounting and the CCCTB*, in AA. VV., *The Influence of IAS/IFRS on the CCCTB, Tax Accounting, Disclosure and Corporate Law Accounting Concept*, The Hague, 2009, p. 32; P. Harris, *Corporate Tax Law*, Cambridge, 2013, p. 86; G. M.M. Michielse & V. Thuronyi (ed.), *Tax Design Issues Worldwide*, Ah Alphen aan den Rijn, 2015.
9. Delegating Law n. 825 of 9 October 1971, implemented with numerous acts of 1973. For our perspective, it is important to bear in mind Law n. 597 and 598 of 1973 concerning individual taxation (n. 597) and company taxation (n. 598).
10. The historical evolution is described by G. Tinelli, *Bilancio di esercizio, principi contabili internazionali e accertamento tributario*, in *Rivista di Diritto Tributario*, 2010, p. 164.
11. G. Zizzo, *Il reddito d'impresa*, in G. Falsitta (ed.), Manuale di Diritto Tributario, 2005, p. 230; Italian scholars have dealt with the topic in several contributions. For a general and non

One of the main theoretical justifications for the connection between the calculation of the company's tax base and the financial accounting is linked to the ability to pay principle. According to Article 53, paragraph 1, of the Italian Constitution, each taxpayer (even companies, resident and non-resident in Italy) has to be taxed according to the ability to pay principle. As far as our issue is concerned, Italian scholars[12] point out that for companies the measurement of the ability to pay should start from the profit and loss accounts. This document assures an objective calculation of the (new) income produced during the tax period. However, it is an outcome that is already available and also binding from a juridical point of view.

The choice of this kind of starting point is referred to as the need to have a "true and fair value" to tax, determined only according to the Italian civil code, in order to find an outcome that is closer to the increase of income produced by the company and taxable according to the ability to pay principle. However, in order to meet specific tax needs, an adjustment mechanism is required, both for fiscal and non-fiscal reasons.

The first category of adjustments may include, for example, all measures to contrast tax evasion and tax avoidance, while in the second one, we may consider the rules that allow special tax benefit (*agevolazione fiscale*).

As a consequence of "formal dependence", if the tax legislation provides for a different evaluation from the civil code regulation, we have to follow the first solution for the corporate tax return. On the contrary, there is an alignment between the two results only when the tax legislator does not provide any specific norm.

As far as costs are concerned, it is important to underline that in the previous tax reform (Legislative Decree no. 344 of December 12, 2003 which came into force on January 1, 2004), in order to reduce fiscal pollution within the balance sheet, the opportunity to fill out a special part of the CIT return was introduced in which it was possible to include "depreciation, amortization and other correction of value", that were deductible and not just included in the financial statement. Needless to say, this kind of element was a total breach of the dependence principle, but with the finance bill of 2008 (Law n. 244/2007) this kind of deduction was forbidden and the norm was cancelled.

Furthermore, in order to understand why the tax legislator uses the connection between accounting and taxation, we need to link this issue with the assessment of the

---

exhaustive overview see, among others, T. Di Tanno, *Brevi note a favore del doppio binario nella determinazione del reddito d'impresa*, in *Rivista di Diritto Tributario*, 2000, p. 407; F. Gallo, *Brevi note sulla necessità di eliminare le interferenze della normativa fiscale nella redazione del bilancio di esercizio*, in *Rivista di diritto tributario*, 2000, p. 3; R. Lupi, *La determinazione del reddito e del patrimonio delle società tra principi civilistici e norme tributarie*, in *Rassegna Tributaria*, 1990, p. 699; G. Falsitta, *Il bilancio di esercizio delle imprese: interrelazioni tra diritto civile e diritto tributario*, Milan, 1985; *Ibid. Il problema dei rapporti tra bilancio civile e bilancio fiscale nel progetto di riforma dell'imposta sulle società (IRES)*, in *Rivista di diritto tributario*, 2003, p. 921.

12. A. Fantozzi & M. Alderighi, *Il bilancio e la normativa tributaria*, in *Rassegna Tributaria*, 1984, page 118. I. Caraccioli, M. A. Galeotti Flori & F. Tanini, *Il reddito d'impresa nei tributi diretti*, Padua, 1990, p. 9.

taxable income by the tax administration. Only recently has this issue received some attention from scholars and then only for specific aspects of the topic.[13]

In actual fact, a tax base that starts from the outcome of the financial accounts (drawn up according to commercial law) also guarantees the tax administration an objective economic base. In the general sense, commercial law "protects" the State against taxpayers who may, generally, have an interest in showing low profits in the tax accounts (and high profits only in the financial accounts). Reference to commercial law should allow a conflict of interests between the two sides of the question. We used the word "should" deliberately because, in our opinion, this kind of justification with respect to the dependence principle is not guaranteed for all companies subject to CIT. However, as the size of the companies has become less relevant, the conflict of interest between owner, partners and other subjects may no longer be assured. Even if, in theory, the financial statement has to guarantee a true and fair view of the economic situation of the company, the small dimension of the companies might be influenced by the aim of reducing the tax burden. Conversely, in a large company, with the usual presence of statutory and the firm's own auditors, especially for companies quoted on a stock market, a major interest from the financier (banks for example) and shareholders who are more independent from the owner, it is more probable that the outcome of the balance sheet represents the real income of the company during the tax period.

We think that behind the idea of the Italian tax legislator's tax reform of 1971/73 there was this assumption: a reasonable and objective system of income determination was (and continues to be) the main reason for preferring a dependence of the tax base on the balance sheet and not on independent tax rules. Unlike the past, today it is inappropriate for the dependence model to permit a simplification of the taxable base determination process. Over the years, tax adjustments have become more numerous than the past, also because in the CITA a legislative "case by case" technique prevails over a method based on principles.

On this issue, Italian scholars[14] are unanimous in considering it a mistake to treat small and medium enterprises (SMEs) and large companies in the same way, both for the determination and for the assessment of the tax base. During the tax reform of 1971-1973, the decision to use the financial accounts for all tax subject to CIT was not in line with the tax assessment legislation. In the years immediately after the entry in force of the new tax system, the inefficiency of this model was evident. In fact, by drawing up a regular (and formal) balance sheet, all companies were protected from tax assessment by the tax administration. The latter had no possibility to go through the books for tax reasons because the dependence principle offered a safe shelter. As a

---

13. G. TINELLI, *Bilancio di esercizio, principi contabili internazionali e accertamento tributario*, in *Rivista di Diritto Tributario*, 2010, p. 163; G. ZIZZO, *Il principio di derivazione a dieci anni dall'introduzione dell'Ires*, in *Rassegna Tributaria*, 2014, p. 1311; A. CONTRINO, *Rapporti "bilancio/dichiarazione" e poteri di accertamento dell'Amministrazione finanziaria*, in *Corriere Tributario*, 2015, p. 91; A. VIOTTO, *L'accertamento sulle valutazioni di bilancio: i poteri dell'amministrazione anche alla luce della recente soppressione delle deduzioni extracontabili e delle modifiche concernenti i soggetti che adottano gli IAS*, in *Rivista di Diritto Tributario*, part I, 2009, p. 210.
14. P. BORIA, *Gli studi di settore: natura giuridica e funzione sistematica*, in P. BORIA (ed.), *Studi di settore e tutela del contribuente*, Milan, 2010, p. 2.

result, as from the end of the 1990s a different method was introduced, within the tax assessment legislation, to check the tax base of SMEs. At present, even if all companies are subject to the same legislation in order to determine the tax base, there are differences in the methods of control. For large companies, the tax administration has to start from the book accounts and only when they are not reliable is it possible to use presumptive income schemes. On the contrary, for SMEs the tax administration must not demonstrate unreliability in advance because, if necessary, it may use presumptive (inductive) income schemes.

Concluding the theoretical justifications regarding the dependence model, we may assume that the *ratio* is respected when it is possible to assure "real" financial accounts, as normally happens for large companies, while in the other case, even if the positive law, in our case Article 83, CITA, uses the outcome of the balance sheet to determine the starting point for the taxable base, this result may be disregarded by the tax administration during the tax assessment.

§8.03 DIFFERENCES BETWEEN FINANCIAL AND TAX ACCOUNTING AND THE MAIN JUSTIFICATIONS

As a consequence of the "formal dependence model", the net result of the balance sheet (profit or loss) has to be adjusted in order to take into consideration the tax provisions that, in some cases, differ from the commercial (accounting) legislation.

In this chapter, there is no need to illustrate all tax variations from commercial law, but it could be interesting to investigate the issue in general and, in this context, offer some examples.

CIT is determined on the accrual base, with some exceptions like dividends or directors' fees. As for the balance sheet, revenues are fiscally relevant only when they are realized. Diversely, costs and expenses are deductible when incurred (as in commercial law) and, moreover, in the fiscal year in which they are certain and ascertainable. The latter conditions have to be verified from a juridical point of view. "Certain" means that there must be a contract as a requirement of the existence, while "ascertainable" requires an objective (and not unpredictable) value to be included in the taxable base.

Moreover, costs are fully deductible if they are inherent to the business activity, otherwise, there are limitations as in the case of costs of acquisition, maintenance, repair and operation of vehicles or entertainment expenses.

Tax legislation also influences the choice between debt and equity. The issue, as scholars point out,[15] is a long-standing core constituent of company and taxation law the world over. Using debt or equity in order to finance companies does have not the same tax effects. According to Article 96, CITA, interest expenses are deductible up to an amount equal to interest income accrued in the same tax period. Any excess over that sum is deductible to the amount of 30% of Earnings Before Interest, Taxes,

---

15. W. Schön (et al.), *Debt and Equity in Domestic and International Tax Law – A Comparative Policy Analysis*, in *British Tax Review*, 2014, 146.

Depreciation and Amortization (EBITDA). The EBITDA is determined as the difference between the value of production and cost of production, without depreciation or amortization. On the contrary, dividends paid to shareholders are not deductible.

As scholars underline,[16] in the CIT principles, we have an "external" and "internal" accrual principle. The first occurs when costs are sustained with external subjects, i.e., suppliers. In this case, costs are, generally, fully deductible because we assume that they have been incurred for business purposes. However, tax administration may not consider this kind of cost fully deductible because, for example, the amount is not in proportion and, for this reason, considered unprofitable.

The "internal" accrual principle concerns figurative costs that are not monetary. In this case, deductions depend on a specific limit set by the tax legislator. Here, it is possible to have a discontinuity between financial account and taxation. For these reasons, for example, depreciation of tangible assets is allowed by applying a limit (as a total amount) established by the Minister of Finance and based on the cost price. According to Article 102 CITA, the method of amortization is on a straight-line basis and the limit is fixed with coefficients depending on the type of property and the sector of activity. On the contrary, in commercial law, amortization depends on the useful life of the asset which is decided by whoever prepares the financial statement. Fiscally, amortizations are the same for all assets and since the abolition of the accelerated amortization in 2008, they do not depend on the degree of utilization. This norm contrasts with a taxable base according to the ability to pay principle, but the purpose of the *ratio* is to guarantee a certainty of the determination and, consequently, to avoid an assessment by the tax administration. The latter (tax administration) permits and considers the amount in the company tax return as valid within the amount determined by coefficients.

Another case in which there is a discontinuity between accounting and taxation concerns the costs for patent rights and know-how. They are deductible in yearly installments of up to one-half of the cost. For trademarks and goodwill too, there are specific tax provisions. Both may be depreciated up to one eighteenth of their value for each tax period, but for goodwill only if it is recorded in the balance sheet.

§8.04   THE IMPACT OF IAS/IFRS ON TAXATION

Regulation (EC) n. 1606/2002 of the European Parliament and of the Council of July 19, 2002 on the application of international accounting standards stated, in Article 4, that for each financial year starting on or after January 1, 2005, companies governed by the law of a Member State shall prepare their consolidated accounts in conformity with the international accounting standards adopted in accordance with the procedure laid down in Article 6(2) if, at their balance sheet date, their securities are admitted to trading on a regulated market of any Member State within the meaning of Article 1(13) of Council Directive 93/22/EEC of May 10, 1993 on investment services in the securities field. Moreover, according to Article 5 of the regulation, Member States may,

---

16. F. Crovato, *L'imputazione a periodo nelle imposte sui redditi*, Padua, 1996, p. 60 e ff.

optionally, permit or require that (a) the companies referred to in Article 4 prepare their annual accounts, (b) companies other than those referred to in Article 4 prepare their consolidated accounts and/or their annual accounts, in conformity with the international accounting standards adopted in accordance with the procedure laid down in Article 6(2).

In a general sense, it is worth underlining that in countries in which the dependence on the financial statement is stronger, the influence of the new accounting rules will necessary influence the taxable base. Unlike the countries where "full IAS/IFRS" are mandatory, the outcome could depend on the degree to which national GAAP incorporate IAS/IFRS accounting principles in countries where "full IAS/IFRS" are not mandatory because the national GAAP might neutralize the potential impact of IAS/IFRS on tax accounting. Deviations from IAS/IFRS in national GAAP have often been encouraged by tax effects.[17]

According to Article 4 of the European Regulation n. 1606/2002, the Italian legislator opted to require some types of companies to utilize the IFRS not only for the consolidated accounts but also for the individual accounts. In a country like Italy, in which there is a link between the financial statement and the taxable base, this change might not have a neutral effect.

Initially, since this radical transformation did not involve all companies subject to tax, the main matter of concern was to ensure an equal treatment of companies which had to use the new accounting principles (IAS/IFRS) and those that continued to use the national accounting principles. The Italian legislator could adjust the national accounting framework to the IFRS or vice versa or, alternatively, create an autonomous model that could be adopted for both kinds of accounting principles. However, even if there was a formal dependence of the taxable base on the financial statement, the method in force permitting adjustment was able, de facto, to make the determination of the tax base autonomous.

If we want to conduct a systematic analysis we have to distinguish between the period before the finance bill of 2008 and the period immediately after this change.

Naturally, in the first period, in some cases reference was made within the CITA to the evaluation effected in the balance sheet (with IFRS or not) but, in a general sense, this kind of variation was not enough to put the taxable income at risk.[18] The reasons are due to the fact that the CITA only related to instruments to neutralize the effects of balance sheet evaluations. In particular, we refer to the irrelevance, from a fiscal point of view, of capital gain and capital loss not realized (Law n. 447/97). Moreover, in the previous tax reform, (Legislative Decree no. 344 of December 12, 2003 which came into force on January 1, 2004), it was possible to include "depreciation, amortization and other corrections of value", that were deductible even if they were not yet included in the balance sheet,[19] resulting for this kind of element in a total independence of the

---

17. C. NORBERG, *Accounting and Taxation, General Report Presented at the EATLP Meeting Held in Helsinki*, June 2007, p. 8.
18. See G. ZIZZO, *I principi contabili internazionali nei rapporti tra determinazione del risultato di esercizio e determinazione del reddito imponibile*, in *Rivista di diritto tributario*, 2005, p. 1166.
19. Article 109, paragraph 4 of CITA.

taxable base on the balance sheet. In 2005, in order to ensure a fiscal neutrality between IFRS companies and the rest of the tax subjects, the Italian legislator approved a Legislative Decree, n. 38 of February 2005, in which Article 11 made reference to taxation. The main aim of the new law was to neutralize the fiscal effects of IFRS in order to avoid differences of treatment between companies using IFRS compared with companies using national accounting principles. For example, with reference to the valuation of inventory, when companies replace the 'last-in, first-out' (LIFO) method with an IFRS method, 'first-in, first-out' (FIFO) or average weighted cost, they may step up the book value of their inventory. In principle, this difference is taxable. However, tax law allowed companies that had used the LIFO method for at least three financial years to retain it for tax purposes (through an option to be exercised in the relevant tax return), avoiding any taxable event in connection with the first time adoption. On the contrary, there were other cases such as the evaluation of financial asset classified in the current assets that could be taxed even if not realized. In fact, unlike the shares, in the case of bonds classified in the current asset and evaluated according to IFRS at the fair value, there was a lack of legislation and, consequently, the taxation depended on the current quotation, in other words just a hypothetical income that was not yet realized. However, this circumstance did not occur for companies using national accounting principles, with a clear discrimination between the two kinds of companies.[20] The scholars proposed to consider the income up to the old devaluation as taxable and, consequently, not to tax the revaluation up to the cost.[21] The examples demonstrate that the fiscal treatment between IAS/IFRS companies and other companies using national accounting principle was not entirely equal, but as scholars underline,[22] if the *ratio* is to ensure neutrality in respect of the accounting system, and according to Italian Constitutional principles (Article 3 and Article 53 of the Italian Constitution in particular) the Legislative Decree n. 38/2005 could be interpreted in a way as to ensure neutrality of the accounting system.

In this first period, although the tax consequences of IFRS were particularly keen in a country like Italy, using IAS/IFRS also for the annual account, they were probably overestimated, being referred to rather like a fiscal revolution. In particular, more attention has been dedicated to the fair value issue while, from a fiscal point of view, scholars have demonstrated that is not so dramatic and that the main change concerns the introduction of the substance over form principle included in international accounting principle and which is impossible for the fiscal legislator to manage with a case by case approach.[23] On this point, in a ruling issued by the Italian fiscal administration[24]

---

20. See. F. Dami, *Il rapporto tra valutazioni civilistico-contabili e fiscali delle componenti del reddito d'impresa dopo l'avvento degli IAS,* in *Tributi&Impresa,* 2005, p. 46.
21. See R. Lupi, *Ias, proposte di adeguamento fiscale e magazzino titoli,* in *Dialoghi di Diritto Tributario,* 2005, p. 87.
22. L. Salvini, *Gli IAS/IFRS e il principio fiscale di derivazione,* in *IAS/IFRS, La modernizzazione del diritto contabile in Italia,* Milan, 2007, p. 202.
23. I. Vacca, *Gli IAS/IFRS e il principio della prevalenza della sostanza sulla forma: effetti sul bilancio e sul principio di derivazione nella determinazione del reddito d'impresa,* in *Rivista di diritto tributario,* 2006, p. 757.
24. Agenzia delle Entrate, Official Interpretation ("Risoluzione"), n. 100/E of 16 May 2007, in www.finanze.it.

concerning the fiscal treatment of commercial credit, the tax authority decided that even after the introduction of IAS/IFRS, considering Article 83 of the CITA, the determination of the tax base depends on the CITA which, in the case in question, takes the formal aspect of the transaction into consideration and not the economic substance of the operation as IAS/IFRS request in the general principles (substance over form for example). The conclusion, after this first period, could be that the so-called formal dependence was able to neutralize the implications of IFRS, even in some cases requiring a special legislation or a systematic interpretation of the law. For the near future, we could say that bearing in mind that extreme solutions such as total alignment or total independence are unsuitable, it may be necessary to make more use of the instrument provided for in Article 109, paragraph 4 of the CITA, i.e., extra accounting deduction. However, as we anticipated, the finance bill of 2008 cancelled this instrument for the tax period starting from 2008 and, according to the new Article 83 of the CITA now in force, for companies adopting IFRS they can use, also for fiscal evaluations, what they decide in the balance sheet for the qualification, timing accrual and classification according IAS/IFRS. In particular, it is now stated that the latter criteria set forth by IAS/IFRS are relevant for CIT purposes and prevail over any provisions of the tax law.

According to the explanatory notes to the 2008 finance bill, the main arguments for this change are due: (1) to differences for the accrual principle; (2) to the impossibility to maintain neutrality. Ultimately, the problem is whether to create a total alignment between IFRS and CITA or separate them completely. In order to reduce compliance, it is impossible to divide the two computations and, moreover, the fiscal administration needs a valid base from which to start the calculation. A ministerial commission studied this problem and it concluded that it is not appropriate to reach a total deviation from the balance sheet, especially because an independence model does not guarantee a link with the economic standards that ensure the taxing of a "real income" produced by the company during the tax period.

Therefore, to adopt IFRS for tax purposes, it is impossible to apply a neutrality principle amongst taxpayers. IFRS has to be accepted for taxation, the dependence principle must be stressed and IFRS must be followed for qualification, accrual timing and classification of income. On the contrary, with regard to "quantification", the tax limits remain (e.g., in the case of amortization).

In a general way, the outline indicated seems clear. For IAS/IFRS subjects, there is a reduction of compliance and a single balance sheet decreases fiscal differences. For these subjects, it is easy to note the *rationes* of the dependence principle because they are, normally, large companies and, in some cases, quoted on a stock market. That is why the tax legislator decided to stress the dependence model and, consequently, identify specific provisions to determine the CIT.

In our opinion, this difference between IAS/IFRS and non-IAS/IFRS compliant subjects changes the issue concerning the ascertainability of the financial statement outcome by the tax administration. In fact, the structure of Article 83 CITA is different because the first period concerning non-IAS/IFRS subjects contained a reference to the final outcome of the financial statement (profit or loss). Differently, the second part of Article 83, CITA expressly refers to IAS/IFRS. As a result, in order to assess the CIT, tax administration has to check the proper application of the IAS/IFRS principles. For non-IAS/IFRS subjects, the borders are more blurred and, in our opinion, depend on what the tax norm said on this issue. In cases in which tax norm made reference to the financial accounting, for example for the valuation of inventory, Article 92, paragraph 4, CITA, it is hard to sustain that tax administration may change the financial statement evaluation only for tax purposes. The civil code leaves an option for the methods of evaluation and the tax norm rests on it. On the contrary, when the civil code makes a specific solution binding, tax administration may require it to be followed also in the tax return in order to avoid a breach of the dependence principle.

§8.05   (ITALIAN) CORPORATE INCOME TAX ACT AND COMMON CONSOLIDATED CORPORATE TAX BASE (CIT VERSUS CCCTB)

The Common Consolidated Corporate Tax Base (CCCTB) Directive proposal, also after the recent initiative in June 2015 by the European Commission for re-launching the project, offers us the possibility to compare the general tax principles (and the single tax provisions) included in the Directive proposal with the corresponding Italian tax rules contained in the CITA.

As already underlined by scholars[25] and the various authors in this book, the main issue concerns the separation established by the CCCTB proposal between accounting and taxation. In the explanatory memorandum of the draft Directive we read that:

> Harmonisation will only involve the computation of the tax base and will not interfere with financial accounts. Therefore, Member States will maintain their national rules on financial accounting and the CCCTB will introduce autonomous rules for computing the tax base of companies. These rules shall not affect the preparation of annual or consolidated accounts.

As Prof. Essers points out in the Netherlands report:

> because the rules concerning the calculation of the CCCTB tax base are completely separate and independent, no reference at all is made to financial accounting rules like IAS/IFRS, the system of determining the CCCTB tax base can be qualified as formal independence: a system in which no dependence at all exists between financial and tax accounting. This means that in the draft-Directive, the European Commission has introduced a taxable profit determination system that does not exist in any of the Member States of the European Union.

However, on the other side, for the European Commission, from a political point of view, it could be very hard to stress the dependence principle also because that implies harmonization from the accounting perspective that it is still a long way away.[26]

---

25. C. Ricci, *La tassazione consolidata nell'IRES*, Turin, 2015, p. 433; M. Grandinetti, *Aspetti comparati e prospettive europee (CCCTB)*, in G. Zizzo (ed.), *La fiscalità delle società IAS/IFRS*, Milan, 2011, p. 33 and ff.
26. See Strampelli & Passador, in this book.

It is true that the CCCTB does not represent the "bridge" between the tax base and the financial accounts, but, at the same time, it is also correct to point out that the elements of the future tax base, in many cases, have principles included within the IAS/IFRS structure as a starting point.

For these reasons, we think that for the purposes of this study it is more useful to describe the main differences between the principles included in the draft directive on CCCTB and the CITA rules. This level of analysis guarantees that if (in the future) an Italian company opts for the new CCCTB, we will be in a position to show which are the differences compared with the purely national situation and, moreover, from a comparative perspective, like the one of this book, we will have a "picture" of the real degree of convergence among EU countries.

Of course, within this framework, we take it for granted that some general aspects of the CCCTB, such as "the general principles" (Article 9), "elements of the tax base" (Article 10), "deductible expenses" (Article 12), or the timing and quantification of the tax base (Articles 17, 18, 19) do not differ from the CITA.

On the contrary, if we look in a more detailed manner, the norm concerning the provisions (Article 25 of the draft directive) does not contain an exhaustive list of the reserves that are allowed according to the quantitative limitations. According to Article 107, paragraph 4, of the CITA, provisions are considered fiscally relevant only when they are expressly stated in the CITA and with quantitative limits.

At the same time, one of the methods of amortization for fixed assets, the individual depreciation on a straight-line basis over useful lives, complies with the CITA. As we have pointed out in Italian legislation the tax limits of depreciation are fixed by very detailed coefficients. On the contrary, the CCCTB contain a simplification in this regard because, according to Article 36 of the draft Directive, the useful life of the fixed assets does not depend on the sector of activity, but it is always the same, unlike the Italian tax legislation. The latter, however, does not know the alternative method defined "in pooling", in which "Fixed assets ... shall be depreciated together in one asset pool at an annual rate of 25% of the depreciation base".

According to Article 29 of the draft Directive the costs of other stock items and work-in-progress shall be measured by using the FIFO or weighted-average cost method. Comparing this norm with Article 92 of the CITA, we note the lack of the LIFO method that is available to Italian companies.

Following the principle of deduction of costs in relation to the activity, in the CCCTB there are no quantitative limitations for interest expenses, unlike what was previously shown for Article 96 of the CITA.

§8.06 FISCAL ASPECTS OF THE NEW ACCOUNTING DIRECTIVE

On August 18, 2015, the law for the implementation of the new Accounting Directive[27] entered into force with the approval of Legislative Decree n. 139/2015.

---

27. Directive (2013/34) of 26 June 2013.

In a fiscal system that applies a "formal dependence model" to determine the corporate tax base, it is accepted that some tax consequences may arise.

However, in our opinion, the implementation of Directive 2013/34/EU may confirm what we have sustained in the first part of this chapter. Legislative Decree n. 169/2015, following the options offered by the European Directive, introduced provisions dedicated to different kinds of companies, i.e., micro enterprises, SMEs, and larger business concerns (Article 3). As Prof. Strampelli and Dr. Passador's chapter points out, the identification of these clusters intends to identify the beneficiaries of the simplification of administrative requirements in terms of the preparation and publication of the financial statements.

In this regard and from our (fiscal) perspective, we may note that in the implementation of the European Directive the Italian legislator decided to opt for an extension of some principles only for the medium and large companies, excluding the micro and the small ones that draw up a simplified annual balance sheet (condensed financial statement).

In particular, also for the tax aspects of the new accounting directive, the Legislative Decree obliges medium and large companies to measure the financial instruments, including derivative financial instruments at fair value, and the measurement of specified categories of assets, other than financial instruments, at amounts determined by reference to it.

Moreover, the measurement of all financial liabilities shall be performed at amortized cost, using the effective interest method, according to IAS 39. For the definition (and for the interpretation) of the amortized cost, Legislative Decree n. 139/2015 refers directly to IAS 39.

Finally, legislative Decree n. 139/2015 clarifies the implementation in the Italian civil code of the substance over form principle.

As a general consideration, it seems that for large and medium companies there is an alignment to the equivalent tax measurements dedicated to IAS/IFRS subjects. However, in this case, unlike Legislative Decree n. 138/2005 that introduced the IAS/IFRS in Italy, there is a lack of specific tax provisions. In some cases, it is possible to establish a fiscal treatment using the general principles, but it is not always the case. In this context, also to guarantee a certainty, prompt legislative measures would be desirable. During the next months, according to Legislative Decree n. 139/2015, the Italian Accounting Standard Setter ("Organismo Italiano di Contabilità") will publish an updated version of the Italian GAAP and, consequently, it will be possible to make in-depth considerations from the fiscal point of view.

However, a preliminary evaluation would involve, for the CIT, the tax treatment of the research and development expenses (R&D), advertising costs, the consequences of the utilization of the amortized cost and, finally, the fair value for the financial instrument measurement.

With the implementation of the Accounting Directive, the Italian legislator modified the civil code for the treatment of the R&D and advertising costs. In particular, for these expenses, starting from 2016, research and advertising expenses may not be capitalized and, consequently, have become elements of the year, relevant in the profit and loss account as costs (and not as fixed assets).

138

On the contrary, expenses concerning development may be fixed assets, capitalized within a period on the basis of the useful life and under specific conditions. Under previous legislation, development costs could be amortized over five years, as a maximum period, in the same way as goodwill.

For R&D and advertising costs, there is a tax provision (Article 108, paragraphs 1 and 2, CITA) that ensures a fiscal treatment that, according to scholars[28] (and contrary to the opinion of the tax administration), does not depend on the accounting perspective, in breach of the dependence principle. In this regard, Article 108 CITA, says that research and development expenses are deductible in the financial year in which they are incurred or in equal proportion in that year and the following years, but for no more than 4 years. Advertising and other publicity expenses are deductible in the financial year in which they are incurred or in equal proportions in that year and the following 4 years. If the tax legislator does not modify this provision, bringing Article 108 CITA into force, we may assume that scholars were thinking in the right direction and, de facto, the tax administration should change its rulings.

The use of amortized cost for the evaluation of all financial liabilities is relevant, because at the end of each financial year, the value of trade receivables (i.e., debt-claims arising from goods whose sale or disposal gives rise to gross receipts) can be reduced by setting aside in a provision for bad debts 0.5% of the total amount of such accounts not covered by any form of guarantee. Allocations to the provision are deductible until the total provision reaches 5% of qualifying receivables at the end of the financial year. According to Article 106, paragraph 2, the value relevant (and recognized) for tax purposes starts from the nominal value. The latter is not equal to the value calculated by applying the amortized cost according to IAS39. At present, if we follow the CITA for non-IAS/IFRS compliant companies there is an objective difference compared with CIT subjects applying Article 106, paragraph 2. On the contrary, for those adopting IAS/IFRS, we can solve the issue in advance because it is a question of accounting qualification that, according to Article 83 CITA, prevails over tax legislation.

Finally, for the financial instruments, and in particular for derivative ones, the evaluation has to be done at fair value with a possible impact, in the following years, on the profit and loss account or, under certain conditions, on the net equity. In our opinion, for this kind of question, CITA is already covered by Article 112 that is dedicated to companies adopting IAS/IFRS, in this case, and which may also be considered for companies using GAAP.

In conclusion, the implementation of the Directive 2013/34/EU could represent an opportunity to rethink the Italian model in order to determine the CIT and, in particular, to define specific rules for SMEs and, conversely, to maintain a strong link between accounting and taxation only for large companies. At present, in the CITA we may refer to three different methods for determining the CIT: the first, dedicated to IAS/IFRS subjects, the second for non-IAS/IFRS subjects that may use some general

---

28. M. Leo, *Le imposte sui redditi nel testo unico*, Milan, 2007, p. 1936.

principles linked to IAS/IFRS (such as fair value and amortized cost 'method') and, the last, concerning SMEs.

However, Article 83 treats large companies (non-IAS/IFRS) and SMEs in the same manner, even if the financial accounts (drawn up according to commercial law), especially after the implementation of the Accounting Directive, do not follow the same principles.

As scholars point out, even recently,[29] it is time to change the method used to determine the CIT and follow the evolution of accounting legislation. For SMEs, in general, financial accounts do not allow the *rationes* on which the dependence model is based to be observed. So, for this kind of tax subject, it is preferable to identify a method to determine the tax base in advance *(ex ante),* in collaboration and in agreement with the taxpayer.

In other respects, the dependence principle could be strengthened for large companies with a system of cooperative compliance for specific tax matters.[30]

---

29. A. Giovannini, *Il Re Fisco è nudo,* Franco Angeli, 2016, p. 135.
30. Recently the Italian legislator approved a new tax regime called "Adempimento collaborativo", dedicated to large companies (Legislative Decree n. 128/2015). It is not a new topic for the Italian scholars that, in the past, proposed this kind of tax regime, R. Lupi, *Le illusioni fiscali,* Il Mulino, 1996, p. 97.

CHAPTER 9

Accounting and Taxation: Luxembourg

Charlène van Eysinga

§9.01 INTRODUCTION

Corporate Income Tax (*'CIT'*) is governed by the Luxembourg Income Tax Law of 4 December 1967 (*'LITL'*).[1]

Under Article 159 LITL, companies having their statutory seat or their central administration within the territory of the Grand Duchy of Luxembourg are subject to taxation on their worldwide income unless an applicable tax treaty provides otherwise. Under Article 160 LITL, non-resident companies are only taxable in Luxembourg on their Luxembourg derived income.

The Luxembourg corporation tax rate for domestic companies is levied at the rate of 20% on taxable income which does not exceed EUR 15,000[2] and at 21% on taxable income exceeding this amount. The solidarity surcharge of 7% must be added to this, and all together the applicable rate is set at 22.47%.

Municipal business tax (*'MBT'*) is governed by a law dated 1 December 1936 (*Gewerbesteuergesetz,* hereafter *'GewStG'*), which became applicable in Luxembourg during World War II and has remained in effect ever since.

MBT is levied at a basic rate of 3% which is to be multiplied by a factor that varies between 225% and 400% depending on the municipality. In Luxembourg city, this leads to an effective MBT rate of 6.75% (i.e., 225% * 3%) for 2014. MBT is due on profits derived from commercial activities carried out by Luxembourg resident companies. As a matter of principle, Luxembourg commercial companies (having a legal form including amongst others *société anonyme* or *société à responsabilité limitée)* are

---

1. Law dated 4 December 1967 *Concernant l'impôt sur le revenu* Mémorial A n° 79, 6 December 1967.
2. Article 174 LITL.

deemed to be subject to MBT. MBT is determined on a basis essentially similar to the basis applied for CIT purposes. Certain items are, however, added back for MBT purposes, while others are deductible only for MBT. For example, based on paragraph 9 *GewStG*, adjustments are made to avoid MBT from applying both to a partnership as well as its members.

The overall income tax rate for Luxembourg resident companies including the MBT is 29.22% (for the city of Luxembourg).

Luxembourg also applies a minimum taxation for corporations, which – as of 2013 – varies according to the assets of the company, as provided by Article 174(6) LITL. This tax amounts to EUR 3,000, increased by the solidarity surcharge for companies for which the sum of the fixed financial assets, transferable securities, receivables on affiliated companies and cash at bank represents more than 90% of total assets. Otherwise, the minimum taxation for companies varies between EUR 500 (for companies with a total balance sheet of less than, or equal to, EUR 350,000) and EUR 20,000 (for companies with a total balance sheet which is equal, or higher than, EUR 20 million). Taking into account the solidarity surcharge, this brings the maximum amount of minimum taxation to EUR 21,400. It should also be noted that assets which, according to an applicable tax treaty, are not subject to taxation in Luxembourg (such as, for example, real estate located outside the Grand Duchy of Luxembourg), will not be taken into account for the purpose of this calculation.

In order to address the European Commission's criticism that the minimum CIT might infringe on the EU Parent Subsidiary Directive,[3] a bill is currently pending to replace this tax with a minimum net wealth tax. As per the tax bill, both the fixed and the contingent minimum CIT will become a minimum net wealth tax, and the existing minimum net wealth taxes of EUR 25 and EUR 62.5 respectively will be abolished. The tax bill also increases the range for the contingent minimum tax to EUR 32,100 for a balance sheet total exceeding EUR 30 million.

In contrast to the current minimum CIT, the minimum net wealth tax will not be an advance tax and, therefore, not be creditable to future net wealth tax.

An annual net wealth tax ('*NWT*'), governed by two laws of German origin dated 16 October 1934 (*Vermögenssteuergesetz* and *Bewertungsgesetz*,) is due by Luxembourg resident companies. NWT applies to the unitary value of the company and is determined as of 1 January of each year at a rate of 0.5%. The unitary value, that is the net asset value of the company, is to be determined on the last closing commercial balance sheet of the company and is subject to some specific adjustment (e.g. exemptions) provided for in the law.

A pending tax bill foresees the introduction as from January 2016 of a reduced net wealth tax rate of 0.05% for the net wealth in excess of EUR 500 million. The taxable net wealth will then be taxed with an amount of EUR 2.5 million (i.e., 0.5% of EUR 500 million) plus 0.05% on the taxable wealth exceeding the EUR 500 million.

---

3. Council Directive 2011/96/EU of 30 November 2011 on the common system of taxation applicable in the case of parent companies and subsidiaries of different Member States *OJ L 345, 29.12.2011, pp. 8-16.*

§9.02 CONNECTION BETWEEN FINANCIAL ACCOUNTING AND TAX BASE

In Luxembourg, the relationship between the commercial accounts and the computation of the taxable basis is fundamental. The financial statements constitute the basis of the tax computation under the principle of linking the tax [...] balance sheet to the commercial balance: the '*théorie de l'accrochement du bilan fiscal au bilan commercial*' or '*Maßgeblichkeitsprinzip*'. This principle is laid down in tax law:

> Article 40 LITL
> '1. When the valuation rules for tax purposes do not demand that another value be used, the values in the tax balance sheet should be those of the commercial balance sheet or should approximate to these as far as possible within the constraints of the rules mentioned above, depending upon whether or not the values of the commercial balance sheet comply with these rules.
> 2. The useful economic life used to calculate the depreciation for the tax balance sheet must be consistent with that used to calculate the depreciation for the commercial balance sheet, unless this latter period is calculated in a manifestly inexact manner or a manner that is contrary to the requirements of Art. 22, paragraph 1.'
>
> Article 22, paragraph 1 LITL
> 'the entrepreneur should carry out the valuation in a consistent manner unless economic reasons justify a modification'.[4]

When no specific provisions regulating fiscal evaluation require an evaluation at a given time, the values to be retained for tax purposes must conform to those of the commercial balance sheet, or be as close as possible.

The fundamental principle of linking the tax balance sheet to the commercial balance sheet governs business taxation in Luxembourg and has its origin in German law. At the time of World War II, Germany introduced its legislation in Luxembourg and this legislation was maintained by the Luxembourg government until completion of the new tax code, the LITL. However, even with the adoption of the LITL and the several tax reforms adopted since 1967,[5] that widened the gap between tax legislations in Germany and in Luxembourg[6] the current tax code is still strongly influenced by German tax principles as illustrated by the permanence of the principle of linking the tax balance sheet to the commercial balance sheet.

A jurisprudential example of the principle was provided no later than on 21 May 2015, by the Luxembourg Higher Administrative Court.[7] The Court ruled that when the balance sheet is modified as per Article 41(2) LITL, although it is not expressly required by the law, the parallel modification of the commercial balance sheet has to be performed further to the principle of 'accrochement'.

---

4. Translation by the author.
5. Jean Schaffner, 'General principles of Luxembourg taxation' (1.2 Governing laws), 9.
6. *Ibid.*
7. Administrative Court, Case number 34531C, free translation by the author: '*the appellant respected the requirement to make a parallel change in the commercial balance sheet, albeit not formally stated by Article 41 of the law, but directly arising from the principle of "accrochement".*'

A distinction between the material link (*accrochement matériel*) and the formal link (*accrochement formel*) can be made. The former means that, at the time of the determination of the income, the taxpayer has to respect the abstract rules of commercial law, in particular, to identify the elements to be recorded on the asset or liability side of the balance sheet. The latter requires that the values recorded in the accounts are booked identically in the tax balance sheet.

The Luxembourg use of the principle of '*accrochement*' shows that the legislator has opted for a relationship which is neither one of full dependence nor of total independence of business taxation with regard to financial accounting. Instead, the said dependence is affected and overruled by the imperative character of certain tax rules.[8]

In that context, the evaluation rules of Article 23 LITL have to be envisaged as they illustrate the dependence part of the relationship.

Through Article 23 LITL, Luxembourg tax law refers to accounting valuation principles such as the precautionary principle, one aspect of which is the imparity principle (or *Imparitätsprinzip*). It also refers to the principle of a regular accounting policy for the purpose of corporate taxation. This article also mentions that profits realized at the closing date of the balance sheet have to be recorded, whereas unrealized profits should not be taken into account.

Article 18 LITL requires the determination of the taxable profit through the comparison of the net assets invested at the beginning and at the end of the accounting period considered. In that respect, the fundamental accounting principle known as the 'historical cost accounting' is applicable to tax law: it requires the valuation of the recorded assets on the balance sheet to be realized on the basis of the acquisition/historical cost or on the lower market value and keeping this same cost as an upper limit of taxation.[9]

Article 22 LITL also provides valuation rules applicable for taxation purposes which derive from Luxembourg accounting rules and principles. The continuous evaluation principle which implies that a company cannot arbitrarily change its valuation principle, except when justified by economics reasons, is an example of such valuation rules.

The principle of linking the tax balance sheet to the commercial balance sheet constitutes a simplification measure to the extent that, in most cases, the values recorded in the financial accounts are copied in the tax balance sheet. Therefore, the practical implementation of this principle is that it avoids having the obligation to establish a separate tax balance sheet which would be based on rules diverging from the accounting rules.

The Circular enacted by the Luxembourg tax authorities ('*LTA*') on 5 November 1985[10] refers to the dependence of the tax balance sheet on the commercial one. It

---

8. Article 40 – paragraph 2.
9. Article 23 LITL.
10. Circular of the Director of contributions L.I.R. N°101 dated 5 November 1985.

underlines the necessity to preserve the link between these two balance sheets otherwise taxpayers' accountancy work would be made much more complex and LTA's tax would become overburdened. The LTA consider that, through the creation of imperative tax rules – which are sometimes necessary to take into account specific tax treatment that could occur – the purpose is to adapt them as much as possible to the commercial balance sheet in order to avoid causing 'injuries' to the tax system.

If Luxembourg has kept the traditional link between commercial and tax accounts for its simplicity, other factors would have played a role. Among those factors is the fact that a tax balance sheet corresponding to the commercial balance sheet is perceived as a rule moralizing business life: by preventing a diverging approach toward the creditors and towards the LTA, the principle prevents taxpayers from privileging one over the other.

§9.03 PERMITTED DEVIATIONS

As a general rule the taxable profits are determined on the basis of the accounting profits as established in accordance with the Luxembourg Generally Accepted Accounting Principles ('*Lux GAAP*'), except when the valuation rules for tax purposes demand otherwise.

Under the application of the *accrochement du bilan fiscal au bilan commercial* and as previously mentioned, the tax balance sheet is, in principle, similar to the commercial balance sheet, but for special tax rules. In this instance, a separate tax balance sheet may have to be prepared in order to take into account these derogating rules.

The commercial result on the commercial balance sheet is thus not necessarily the result that is subject to taxation.

The primary reasons for such deviations to the accounting treatment are the avoidance of economic double taxation, the facilitation of tax neutral corporate restructuring, and the elimination of non-arm's length transactions between related parties.

An example of such deviation from the commercial result is the so-called participation exemption.[11] Further to the participation exemption, results need to be added back to the commercial result (non-deductible expenses) or deducted from them (tax exempt amount). These amendments are, however, generally made in the tax return itself and do not require the establishment of a separate tax balance sheet.

Generally speaking, LITL follows the economic approach. This means that when making a tax qualification of the assets in the commercial accounts, the LTA are not bound by the mere legal qualification of the transaction. Instead, the LTA take into account the economic circumstances of a transaction and the LITL follows the so-called substance over form principle (*Prinzip der wirtschaftlichen Betrachtungsweise*). An example concerns the qualification of certain instruments as 'debt' or as 'equity'. The

---

11. Article 166 LITL and Article 45(2) LITL.

legal form of the funding instrument is not the only element considered. To the contrary, the funding instrument is assessed on the basis of its economic nature and feature.

Another example of permitted deviation is the case of hidden capital contribution.[12]

While Lux GAAP does not recognize hidden contribution as contribution to the capital, but rather report it as a profit, Luxembourg tax law has a wider approach of the concept of capital contributions: when hidden capital contributions increase the asset side or reduce the liability side, Luxembourg tax law requires a correction for tax purposes to be made to reduce the amount of profit reported or to be reported in the commercial accounts.[13]

The capital contribution's mechanisms under Luxembourg tax law is based on the separation between the company's sphere and the shareholder's sphere (*Trennungsprinzip*): any element in the commercial accounts which have been driven by shareholders' reasons should not be considered when determining the taxable amount. This means that only the profit related to the economic activity of the company should be subject to CIT and MBT but that, the 'profit' resulting from a contribution by the shareholder should not be subject to CIT and MBT. Therefore, the tax treatment of the 'ordinary contribution' and those of the 'hidden capital contribution' should be similar.[14]

These changes may require a separate tax balance sheet to be drawn up.

Another example of permitted derogation concerns the expenses of Luxembourg companies.

From a Luxembourg tax perspective, not all commercially recorded expenses can be deducted, only those expenses linked exclusively to business activities are to be treated as deductible expenses.[15] If LTA are not entitled to assess the viability of an expense and therewith whether it is deductible or not, the company is responsible for establishing the causal link between its activity and the expense incurred.

Other derogating rules requiring the establishment of a separate tax balance sheet are, for example, mergers, demergers and share for share exchange.[16] It should be noted that some of these derogations may only attain their desired tax effect subject to being recorded in the commercial accounts (e.g., a gain roll-over). This mechanism has been defined by the *principe de l'accrochement à l'envers (Umgekehrte Massgeblickeit)* which is demonstrating a certain dominance of the tax rules over commercial accounting rules.[17]

---

12. Luxembourg tax law does not provide for a definition of hidden capital contribution (*Verdeckte Einlage* or *apport cache*) but in the absence of such a definition, the German jurisprudence (Reichsfinanzhof and the Bundesfinanzhof) has often been referred to.
13. Article 18 LITL.
14. The same approach is taken towards (hidden) dividend distributions. Amounts paid by a Luxembourg company as (hidden) distribution shall be added to the taxable basis as a non-deductible distribution. Article 164 LITL.
15. Article 45(1) LITL.
16. Article 22*bis* LITL.
17. Jean-Pierre Winandy 'Les impôts sur le revenu et sur la fortune', 403.

§9.04 CCCTB

In order to tackle fiscal impediments to growth, in 2001 the European commission proposed the implementation of a common consolidated base for corporate income tax at the European level ('*CCCTB*').[18]

The CCCTB, once in force, will allow taxpayers to compute their tax base across the European Union based on a common set of rules. It will also allow multi-jurisdictional businesses ('*MJB*') to determine a sole tax base for the whole group and to file a single consolidated tax return. An apportionment formula will allocate taxable profits to an MJB member and to the respective Member States. To put it differently, profits of an MJB are consolidated and apportioned across Member States according to a formula. Once apportioned to each Member State, the profits are taxed at the national corporate tax rates.

In spite of the good intensions of the CCCTB, the criteria (also called the keys) for the allocation of profit (three equally weighted factors: labour, assets and sales[19]) are likely to create unfairness in Luxembourg in respect of the aim to ensure that profits are taxed where they are earned.[20] A consequence of applying this method is that Luxembourg companies will probably not be allocated with an appropriate share of the profit. The sale factor is bound to be underestimated as Luxembourg companies are usually merely intermediaries, but based on the CCCTB draft directive, the sales factor is determined by reference to the Member State of the client. However, the asset factor is likely to suffer the opposite fate since on the one hand the allocation keys should not take the economic owner of the intangibles into account when allocating the profits and on the other hand financial services represent a large sector of the Luxembourg economy even if they do not reflect the value created in Luxembourg. As for the labour factor, since Luxembourg businesses employ a relatively small number of employees which represent high value-added functions, it is deemed to be underestimated.[21]

The Luxembourg government has appointed a dedicated committee to deal specifically with further investigation and research related to the CCCTB proposals.

§9.05 LUX GAAP VERSUS IFRS

The connection in Luxembourg between the commercial accounts and the tax base computation is fundamental. Therefore, the accounting method used for the purpose of establishing the commercial accounts (which is based on Lux GAAP) is very relevant for taxation purposes.

---

18. Proposal for a Council Directive on a Common Consolidated Corporate Tax Base (CCCTB), COM(2011) 121/4, 2011/0058 (CNS).
19. Council Directive, recital 21.
20. *Ibid.*
21. Wim Piot, Begga Sigurdardottir and Marc Rasch – Impact of the European Commision's Common Consolidated Corporate Tax Base Proposals – International Transfer Pricing Journal, 2011 (Volume 18), N°6, 415.

Since 2005, (IAS/IFRS) apply to the consolidated accounts of the EU listed companies as well as to credit institutions and insurance companies.[22] In Luxembourg, the law was amended in 2006 in order to transpose the major changes in relation to the accounting regime of accounts published by credit institutions.[23] It gave credit institutions the choice to publish their annual accounts, or their consolidated accounts, in accordance with the Lux GAAP, the 'mixed' accounting regime (Lux GAAP with IFRS options) or the 'full' IFRS accounting regime (IFRS as adopted by the EU).

In 2010, international accounting standards were introduced in Luxembourg.[24] Despite this introduction and the never-ending discussion about amending it, Luxembourg tax law has not yet been adapted to accounting frameworks other than to the Lux GAAP.

In 2008, a draft law aimed at adopting the IFRS standards for tax purposes led to a belief in an impending change. The draft law's commentaries stated that the principle of *accrochement* would also apply to IFRS accounting standards. Therefore, a Luxembourg company having its financial accounts in IFRS would not need to adapt them to Lux GAAP for tax purposes. A provision was also planned to allow a '*décrochage ponctuel*', that is a one-time break-off between the tax and the accounting balance sheet, in order to ensure tax neutrality in case of the adoption of IFRS standards. Moreover, the draft envisaged introducing an obligation to evaluate the financing instruments at their fair value, if this value was higher than the acquisition price and if the evaluation at fair value was prescribed by the accounting standards of the company. The purpose of this provision was to prevent Luxembourg companies from being forced to adopt Lux GAAP standards for tax purposes in order not to recognize fair values and latent capital gains that the fair value evaluation would otherwise attract.[25]

As far as Article 18 LITL was concerned with regard to the draft legislation, the principle for determining the commercial profit remained the same, i.e., the difference between the net assets invested at the beginning and at the end of the exercise plus the levies and minus the contributions of the exercise. It could, however, be subject to adjustments in order to neutralize the effects related to the adoption of the IFRS accounting standards.

The downside of the evaluation at fair value of the financing instruments as provided for by draft Article 23 LITL was to lead Luxembourg companies to the

22. 'Agreement on International Accounting Standards will help investors and boost business in EU' – Brussels, 7 June 2002 – European Commission – IP/02/827 07/06/2002.
23. Law dated 16 March 2006 *relative à l'introduction des normes comptables internationales pour les établissements de crédit*, Mémorial A N° 55, 28 March 2006.
24. The law of 10 December 2010 *relative à l'introduction des normes comptables internationales*, Mémorial A – N° 225, 17 December 2010 transposed into national law the Directives 2001/65/EC and 2003/51/EC.
25. It is worth mentioning that the provision of draft Article 23 LITL did not intend to apply to the other assets and liabilities held by a Luxembourg company. The assets and liabilities (other than the financing instruments) would have remained subject to the existing (and largely unchanged) rules of Article 23 LITL. If the accounting rules adopted by the company are different from the tax evaluation rules, it would be necessary to make the appropriate tax adjustments for these other assets and liabilities (one-time break-off pursuant to Article 40 LITL).

realization (and taxation) of latent capital gains. Therefore, a proposal was made to amend Article 18 LITL partially in order to neutralize the effects of these new evaluation rules. The adjustments allowed by Article 18 LITL have been described in depth in the draft Grand Ducal regulation ('*RGD*') which explained the methods of non-accounting neutralization of the (non-intended) tax effects generated by the evaluation of the financing instruments at fair value. According to the RGD, the tax effects connected to the new evaluation rules of the financing instruments should be neutralized as follows:

- RGD Article 4: non-realized capital gains are temporarily immunized (tax deferral) if these latent capital gains are booked at a fair value in a reserve account in the company's balance sheet (i.e., if the booking of these latent capital gains does not have any effect on the profit and loss account of the company).
  On the contrary, the latent capital gains resulting from the fair value evaluation and booked in the profit and loss account would be taxable. The commentaries to the project specify that the allocation of the re-evaluated capital gains to a fair value reserve account (balance sheet) or to a profit and loss account depend on the accounting standard of the company (no tax choice or *décrochement* of the tax balance sheet in relation to the commercial balance sheet seems to be possible in the case at hand).
- RGD Article 6: the capital gains realized at the time of the first adoption of the fair value could, on demand, be spread over a period ranging from two to five years on a linear basis. This provision seems to aim at the case where, depending on the accounting standard applied by the company, the re-evaluation of the latent capital gains on the financial instrument is directly booked in the company's profit and loss account. The part of the capital gain which has not yet been spread will remain a special entry in the balance sheet.

This proposal was heavily disputed and then imperceptibly withdrawn. As of today, Luxembourg companies still need to file their tax return based on Lux GAAP which for companies applying IFRS means two sets of accounts. However, the Luxembourg tax authorities tend to informally accept a simplified tax balance sheet when drawn up according to IFRS to the extent that it clearly indicates the differences between IFRS and Lux GAAP and how the Luxembourg tax position is affected.

§9.06 NEW ACCOUNTING DIRECTIVE

The Directive 2013/34/EU ('*New Accounting Directive*') needed to be implemented prior to July 2015 to enable application as from 2016.[26] However, a delay occurred: a

---

26. Directive 2013/34/EU of the European Parliament and of the Council of 26 June 2013 on the annual financial statements, consolidated financial statements and related reports of certain types of undertakings, amending Directive 2006/43/EC of the European Parliament and of the Council and repealing Council Directives 78/660/EEC and 83/349/EEC Text with EEA relevance *OJ L 182, 29.6.2013, pp. 19-76.*

draft bill[27] was presented to the Luxembourg Chamber of Deputies in 2014 but is was adopted only on 9 December 2015.

The objective of this Directive is to simplify the accounting requirements for SME and to improve both the clarity and the comparability of companies' financial statements within the European Union. By means of bill 6718, changes should be brought to Luxembourg accounting law in accordance with the Directive requirements but those changes should not interfere '*too significantly with Luxembourg companies or their providers, as the models of balance sheets and profits and losses remain close enough to the old patterns*'.[28] It notably abolishes the horizontal layout of the profit and loss and introduces a new presentation as a list. It also introduces changes to the notes to the annual account (definition of the materiality concept, obligation to present the notes in a specific order, obligation to disclose exceptional items, etc), and it increases the threshold for medium and large-sized companies to 20 million for the total balance sheet and 40 million for the turnover. With the aim of combating bribery, it also obliges large and public interest entities of the extractive industry and loggers of primary forests to report payments made to governments.

All things come to those who wait!

---

27. Draft bill 6718.
28. Explanatory memorandum to the draft bill 6718, translation by the author.

CHAPTER 10

Accounting and Taxation: Netherlands[*]

Peter H.J. Essers

§10.01 THE SYSTEM

The starting point for calculating taxable profit in the Netherlands, both for individual entrepreneurs and for companies, is the concept of total profit mentioned in Article 3.8 *Wet inkomstenbelasting 2001* (Personal Income Tax Act 2001). According to Article 8, section 1 *Wet op de vennootschapsbelasting 1969* (Corporate Income Tax Act 1969) this provision is also applicable to corporate income tax. Total profit is the aggregate amount of benefits, in any name or form, obtained from trade or business. This total profit, received during the existence of the enterprise, must be attributed to the various years in which the company exists. The sum of the annual profits equals the total profit. In the Netherlands, annual fiscal profit accounting is determined by the concept of *goed koopmansgebruik* (in German: *guter Kaufmannsbrauch*; in English: *sound business practice*) in Article 3.25 *Wet inkomstenbelasting 2001* (Personal Income Tax Act 2001): the annual profit is determined according to *goed koopmansgebruik*, involving consistent behaviour that is independent of the probable outcome and which can only be changed if this is justified by *goed koopmansgebruik*. In its landmark case decision of 8 May 1957, BNB 1957/208, the Dutch Supreme Court (*Hoge Raad*) clearly indicated the relationship between the concept of *goed koopmansgebruik* and the principles of business economics: the starting point is that a system of fiscal profit determination

---

[*] See also: Peter Essers and Ronald Russo, The Precious Relationship between Tax Accounting and Financial Accounting, in: Peter Essers, Theo Raaijmakers, Ronald Russo, Pieter van der Schee, Leo van der Tas en Peter van der Zanden (eds), *The Influence of IAS/IFRS on the CCCTB, Tax Accounting, Disclosure, and Corporate Law Accounting Concepts ('A Clash of Cultures')*, Kluwer Law International, EUCOTAX Series on European Taxation, 2009, pp. 29-86 and Goed koopmansgebruik Quo Vadis? (De mogelijke invloed van IFRS en CCCTB op GKG), Rapport van de Commissie GKG en IFRS, Geschriften van de Vereniging voor Belastingwetenschap nr. 254, Vereniging voor Belastingwetenschap, The Hague, 2015.

must be assumed to be in accordance with *goed koopmansgebruik* if this system is based on proper business economics views of profit determination. Exceptions to this rule, however, have to be included if these views are in conflict with any regulation in a tax law, a general intention or principle of the relevant tax law. Therefore, in principle, every method that is in line with business economics can also be in accordance with *goed koopmansgebruik*. However, the views of business economics must always be tested against the fiscal concept of *goed koopmansgebruik*.

The same is true with respect to the relationship between financial (based on national GAAP, IAS/IFRS) and tax accounts since financial accounting rules also reflect the views of business economics.

This concept has led to a system of fiscal profit accounting that, in practice, is almost completely independent from financial profit accounting. In this respect, the Dutch system differs completely from dependence systems, like those in Germany and France. It also means that the national tax administration is entitled to assess the taxable financial income without considering the financial accounts. This does not mean that GAAP/IAS/IFRS have no influence at all on fiscal profit accounting. In the Netherlands, national GAAP permit IAS/IFRS for the annual accounts of both listed and non-listed companies. Small companies are allowed to use tax accounts for their financial accounts.

IAS/IFRS can be seen as a starting point for fiscal profit determination. However, specific regulations in a tax law, the general intention or principles of taxation can forbid the application of GAAP/IAS/IFRS in fiscal profit accounting. Until now, the *Hoge Raad* has not yet ruled explicitly on the influence of IAS/IFRS on *goed koopmansgebruik*. In its case law on hedge accounting, the *Hoge Raad* links up with elements that can be found in IAS 39.[1] However, at the same time for tax purposes the *Hoge Raad* explicitly accepted the base stock system, although this system is not allowed by IAS/IFRS. In my view, in the future we may expect more and more alignment between IAS/IFRS and *goed koopmansgebruik*.

In general, the rules of *goed koopmansgebruik* for determining the annual taxable profit are more flexible than those regarding the total profit. This is because questions dealing with the total profit are connected to characterization issues (does it or does it not belong to the taxable profit?), whereas questions concerning the annual profit mostly refer to timing issues (is it taxed now or later?). In the concept of total profit, a strict nominalism is applied. In principle, inflation accounting is not allowed. By calculating annual profit, however, some inflation accounting systems for certain assets are allowed, such as the base stock system and 'last-in first-out' (LIFO). In fact, *goed koopmansgebruik* offers minimum and maximum rules allowing various systems all of which fit within the concept of *goed koopmansgebruik*. No later than at the end of an enterprise's existence are all hidden reserves and goodwill taxed as a final annual profit. Finally, the sum of all annual profits ideally equals the total profit. Most of *goed koopmansgebruik* has been developed in case law by tax judges. However, the law also contains many provisions with respect to *goed koopmansgebruik*. These legal

---

1. HR 10 April 2009, nr. 42916, BNB 2009/271 and HR 21 March 2014, nr. 12/02793, BNB 2014/116.

provisions are mostly meant to repair decisions by the *Hoge Raad* which were considered to be too costly for the State's budget. These unfavourable budgetary decisions of the *Hoge Raad* provoked the legislator to interfere by introducing legislation that overrules case law with respect to *goed koopmansgebruik*, sometimes even with retroactive effect. As of 1 January 2007, the Dutch legislator introduced several regulations leading to restrictions on depreciation possibilities with respect to, *inter alia*, real estate[2] and goodwill[3] and on profit deferrals with respect to work-in progress.[4] The budgetary revenue of these restrictions was used to finance the reduction of the tax profit rates in the Netherlands.

§10.02 PRINCIPLES OF *GOED KOOPMANSGEBRUIK*

The principles of *goed koopmansgebruik* are to be found in the extensive case law of the *Hoge Raad*. An analysis of this case law demonstrates that most decisions of the *Hoge Raad* can be related to an area of tension between the principles of reality, prudence and simplicity. These main principles match the character of fiscal profit determination in the Netherlands. Although *goed koopmansgebruik* is a legal concept and as such regards legal reality as a starting point, the calculation of the tax base is rooted in economic reality. 'Substance over form' is very much applicable to *goed koopmansgebruik*. Another principle that results from the reality principle is the matching principle: expenses have to be allocated as much as possible to the years in which the revenues resulting from these expenses, are presented. If expenses cannot be allocated in this way to revenues (e.g., because the relationship with yearly revenues is too remote), according to the 'principle of cause' these expenses are presented in the year in which they have been accrued. In general, all revenues and expenses have to be allocated to the year to which they belong. Therefore, the reality principle prohibits unmotivated profit shifting to the future.

The recognition of revenues and costs according to *goed koopmansgebruik* is governed by the realization principle. In practice, because of reasons of liquidity, the moment of realization will mostly be chosen as the ultimate acceptable moment of profit taking. For goods, normally, this moment is the moment of delivery, meaning the moment when the asset changes from 'stock' to 'debtors' in the balance sheet. For services, this is normally the moment the service is performed. Under some conditions, in the case of goods, taxpayers may also take profits into account earlier than the moment of delivery, e.g., at the moment the purchase/sale agreement is signed. A reason for this early profit taking could be that a taxpayer wants to credit losses from the past with these profits within the sometimes limited legal loss compensation period.

---

2. According to this regulation (Article 3.30a *Wet inkomstenbelasting 2001*) real estate can no longer be depreciated for tax reasons as long as the book value does not exceed half of the real market value. For real estate investment, the threshold is the full real market value.
3. Article 3.30 *Wet inkomstenbelasting 2001* (Personal Income Tax Act 2001).
4. Article 3.29b *Wet inkomstenbelasting 2001* (Personal Income Tax Act 2001).

The *Hoge Raad* is fully aware that because of the special character of taxation, the consequences of profit calculation according to *goed koopmansgebruik* differ from the consequences of profit calculation according to financial rules. In general, the determination of taxable profit in a year will have immediate consequences on the distribution of the profit in that year considered to the tax administration as a special stakeholder of the business, paying personal income tax or corporate income tax. For tax purposes, this means that the *Hoge Raad* will allow the entrepreneur to calculate the yearly fiscal profit within the boundaries of reality with a certain degree of prudence. For example, an entrepreneur is not obliged to take into account the profits made on goods sold belonging to the stock for tax reasons before the moment of delivery of these goods. Losses, however, can already be taken into account in the year in which these losses were caused, provided there was a fair probability in that year that these losses would occur in the near future. This is the so-called principle of prudence.

The process of taxation also demands that it should be taken into account that not all taxpayers have access to sophisticated accounting techniques. As a result, for tax purposes, it is sometimes possible that accounting systems can be allowed which, from a business-economics point of view, are not regarded as acceptable (like a cash accounting system). However, the tax administration must be able to check the accounting systems applied by taxpayers. This means that the most sophisticated accounting systems might not always be in line with *goed koopmansgebruik*, simply because they cannot always be checked adequately by a tax inspector. This is the principle of simplicity: both for the taxpayer and for the tax inspector an accounting system must be manageable so as to be in line with *goed koopmansgebruik*.

The main principles of *goed koopmansgebruik* – reality, prudence and simplicity – guarantee the calculation of the yearly fiscal profit according to economic reality, but adjusted by the special characteristics of taxation. These special characteristics justify a prudent attitude on the part of the taxpayer and an accounting system that is adjusted to the possibilities of his or her enterprise and that is also fit for being checked by the tax administration. This 'fiscal reality' also reflects the different goals of profit calculation for financial or tax purposes. Profit calculation for tax purposes is primarily meant to report the taxable yearly profit to the tax authorities. Profit calculation for financial purposes is mainly meant to report the wealth and profit of a company to the external stakeholders of the company. Both reports take economic reality as a starting point, however elements like prudence and simplicity play a greater role in reporting for tax purposes. In this respect, *goed koopmansgebruik* is really an autonomous tax concept. Thus, also the new accounting Directive 2013/34/EU has only limited influence on the determination of the tax base in the Netherlands. The same goes for IFRS-SME.[5]

IAS/IFRS are primarily focused on the balance sheet, the presentation of assets and liabilities. However, the determination of the taxable year profit according to *goed koopmansgebruik* is primarily orientated towards the profit and loss account and the profit determining balance sheet relating to this profit and loss account. The function

---

5. In the Netherlands IFRS-SME is not often used.

of this balance sheet is primarily to achieve a correct allocation of revenues and expenses in time. Because of the different treatment of several assets and liabilities according to *goed koopmansgebruik,* it can be worthwhile to know which category (stocks, work-in-progress, fixed assets, financial instruments) the different balance sheet items belong. This classification is not necessarily the same as the classification used in financial accounting as in IAS/IFRS.

§10.03 ADVANTAGES AND DISADVANTAGES OF *GOED KOOPMANSGEBRUIK*

The fact that *goed koopmansgebruik* has mainly been developed by case law offers the advantage of flexibility: it offers the opportunity to adapt the concept of *goed koopmansgebruik* to new financial and technical developments. However, this system also has disadvantages. It might lead to legal uncertainty. From time to time, the *Hoge Raad* changes its mind. These swings in decisions – sometimes due to changes in objective external circumstances, but mostly because the *Hoge Raad* simply changes its mind – may affect the legal security of taxpayers and cause transitional problems. Furthermore, in spite of the hundreds of decisions with respect to *goed koopmansgebruik,* many unanswered questions exist with respect to the range of this concept in areas like intangibles, hedge accounting, leasing and work-in progress.

§10.04 A COMPLETELY DIFFERENT SYSTEM COMPARED TO OTHER COUNTRIES

A frequently asked question concerns the reason for – what at first sight appears to be – the completely opposite positions in Germany and the Netherlands in the field of fiscal profit accounting. One of the answers to this question can be found in the historical differences in the character of the financial accounting systems in both countries. Together with countries like France and Italy, the German commercial accounting system is an example of the *continental approach.* This approach has always been characterized by the strong emphasis on creditor protection and maintenance of company capital. In the continental system, the prudence principle has always been the most important principle to ensure these goals. For this reason, the *Maßgeblichkeitsprinzip* guaranteed a moderate taxation of business profits, in such a way that profits were not taxed before they had been realized and losses were already taken into account at the moment that a fair probability existed that they would occur (*Imparitätsprinzip*). Thus, the *Maßgeblichkeitsprinzip* used to protect the taxpayer against the administration.[6]

The Dutch system of financial accounting has always been more oriented towards the *Anglo-Saxon approach* in countries like the UK and Ireland, characterized by a focus on the interests of the shareholders rather than those of the creditors. In such

---

6. For the history of the *Maßgeblichkeitsprinzip,* see: Stefan Mayer, in: *Wolfgang Schön*, Steuerliche Maßgeblichkeit in Deutschland und Europa, Verlag Dr. Otto Schmidt, Köln, 2004, pp. 147-168.

a system, the emphasis is on providing information to the capital market based on a *true and fair view*. IAS/IFRS also disclose their roots in this Anglo-Saxon approach, by prescribing, for example, fair value accounting for some assets.[7] This explains why, in the past, in countries like the Netherlands,[8] the UK[9] and Ireland, linkage between fiscal and financial accounts, in general, was not necessarily regarded as advantageous for taxpayers. Therefore, for a long time these countries have been known for their more or less independent system of fiscal profit accounting leading to a conservative way of determining fiscal profits.[10] A striking difference between the Dutch accounting concept and the traditional Anglo-Saxon approach was the absence in the Netherlands till the 1970s of detailed legal rules. Another difference was the strong link between financial accounting in the Netherlands and the science of business economics, of which *Meij*, *Limperg* and *Van der Schroeff* were the most important Dutch representatives.

Thus, the underlying goals of the Netherlands, UK and German concepts of fiscal profit accounting are basically the same: to protect the taxpayer against an overly eager tax inspector who wants to tax profits too early.

§10.05   CCCTB[11]

A very relevant question in the perspective of this book is, to what extent is the proposal for a Council Directive on a Common Consolidated Corporate Tax Base (CCCTB) connected to the globally accepted IAS/IFRS?[12] In first instance, the European

---

7. See also: Philippe Bielen, International Accounting Standards/International Financial Reporting Standards and Corporate Tax Base Design, in: Michael Lang, Christine Obermair, Josef Schuch, Claus Staringer, Patrick Weninger, *Tax Compliance Costs for Companies in an Enlarged European Community*, Linde Verlag, Vienna, 2008, p. 482.
8. Another reason for the rather autonomous concept of fiscal profit in the Netherlands is that, unlike Germany, before the Second World War this country did not have a profit tax but a distribution tax for corporations. This has probably also contributed to the relatively restricted influence of the financial accounting concept of profit on the tax concept of profit for corporations.
9. However, at present a tendency exists in the UK to increase the catenation between tax accounts and financial accounts. See: Graeme Macdonald, *Taxation of Business Income: Aligning Taxable Income with Accounting Income*, The Institute for Fiscal Studies, London, 2002; Judith Freedman, Aligning Taxable Profits and Accounting Profits: Accounting Standards, Legislators and Judges, *eJournal Tax Research* 71(2), 2004. See also: Wolfgang Schön, The Odd Couple: A Common Future for Financial and Tax Accounting?, The David R. Tillinghast Lecture, *Tax Law Review*, 58(2), New York University School of Law, pp. 118-119 and Christopher Nobes, *A Conceptual Framework for the Taxable Income of Business, and How to Apply it under IFRS*, London, 2004.
10. See: Wolfgang Schön, International Accounting Standards – A 'Starting Point' for a Common European Tax Base?, *European Taxation*, October 2004, p. 431, and Peter Essers, De toekomst van goed koopmansgebruik na de invoering van International Financial Reporting Standards in 2005, Kluwer, Deventer, 2005, Geschriften van de Vereniging voor Belastingwetenschap, no. 224, pp. 9 and 10.
11. See P.H.J. Essers, De winstbepaling in de Conceptrichtlijn CCCTB, WFR 2011/6927, p. 1395 and further.
12. See also: Andreas Eggert, Die Gewinnermittlung nach dem Richtlinienvorschlag über eine Gemeinsame Konsolidierte Körperschaftsteuer-Bemessungsgrundlage (Vergleich mit der Gewinnermittlung nach dem HGB, EStG und den IFRS), Köln: Verlag Dr. Otto Schmidt KG, Köln, 2015 and R. Russo, CCCTB: General Principles and Characteristics, in D.M. Weber (ed.), *Eucotax*

Commission considered IAS/IFRS as a *starting point* for the application of CCCTB. Gradually, this position has been abandoned. In a *Working Document* of 26 July 2007[13] the following was said about this issue:

> In the work on the CCCTB constant reference has been made to IAS/IFRS. As the Commission has stressed in the past (Com (2006) 157, page 7), it is not possible to make a formal link between the base and IAS/IFRS. Such a link would, it is true, provide a common starting point and have the advantage of allowing the base to evolve over time in line with IAS/IFRS. However, many Member States currently do not permit the use of IAS/IFRS for individual company accounts and not all IAS/IFRS are considered suitable for tax purposes. One therefore has to accept that most companies would start from accounts prepared in accordance with a number of different national GAAP (General Accepted Accounting Principles) and would be required to make a number of adjustments on key elements to satisfy the rules and definitions on the CCCTB in arriving at uniform base. The rules for the CCCTB in the Directive would therefore define the tax base itself but would not define the methodology for adjusting the accounts (sometimes called the 'bridge') to arrive at the tax base – this is not possible as companies will potentially be starting from accounts prepared under twenty-seven different national GAAP.

This statement already implied that the CCCTB-Directive would contain an autonomous concept of taxable profit without any reference to IAS/IFRS. In that same *Working Document* of 26 July 2007, the impossibility to include every detail in the Directive was recognized. However, there would be space for further possible implementation by using the so-called comitology-procedure, in which the Council of Ministers delegates the authority to implement and specify certain rules to the European Commission. In the Lisbon Treaty, this comitology-procedure has been changed by the delegated acts-procedure of Article 290 TFEU.

In the draft-Directive on CCCTB, a decision was taken not to refer to IAS/IFRS. This is also confirmed in the explanatory memorandum to this draft-Directive (page 5):

> Harmonisation will only involve the computation of the tax base and will not interfere with financial accounts. Therefore, Member States will maintain their national rules on financial accounting and the CCCTB will introduce autonomous rules for computing the tax base of companies. These rules shall not affect the preparation of annual or consolidated accounts.

Contrary to expectations, the draft-Directive uses the delegated acts-procedure only in a very limited way. This procedure is only applicable to the list of non-deductible taxes (Article 14, section three, draft-Directive), leasing – with respect to the definition of legal and economic ownership, the calculation of the capital and interest elements of the lease payments and the calculation of the depreciation base of a leased asset (Article 34, section 5) –, and for the precision of categories of fixed assets (Article 42). For the interpretation of all the other rules relevant for the CCCTB tax base, only the wording of the Articles of the draft-Directive can be used. These rules can be found

---

Series on European Taxation. Eucotax Series on European Taxation, Kluwer Law International, Alphen aan de Rijn, 2012, pp. 67-79.

13. Common Consolidated Corporate Tax Base Working Group, CCCTB: possible elements of a technical outline, Working Document, CCCTB/WP057, 5.

mainly in Chapter IV ('Calculation of the tax base'), Chapter V ('Timing and quantification'), Chapter VI ('Depreciation of fixed assets') and Chapter VII ('Losses'). In Chapter II ('Fundamental concepts') Article 4, sections 8-10 and Article 4, sections 14-20 are relevant for the determination of the tax base. In addition to this, at the beginning of the draft-Directive some general considerations have been introduced. Considerations 10-15 and 19 are relevant for the determination of the tax base.

Because the rules concerning the calculation of the CCCTB tax base are completely separate and independent, no reference at all is made to financial accounting rules like IAS/IFRS, the system of determining the CCCTB tax base can be qualified as formal independence: a system in which no dependence at all exists between financial and tax accounting. This means that in the draft-Directive, the European Commission has introduced a taxable profit determination system that does not exist in any of the Member States of the European Union. I would have preferred a system in which IAS/IFRS were used as a reference in such a way that, principally, the calculation of the tax base in line with IAS/IFRS is also regarded to be in line with the CCCTB rules with respect to the tax base, unless specific provisions in the CCCTB-Directive deviate from IAS/IFRS or the object and purpose of the determination of the CCCTB tax base justify such a deviation. If, as is the case in the draft-Directive, no reference at all is made to already well-known concepts like IAS/IFRS, national judges have no frame of reference to base their judgments on in cases where the wording of the Directive is not clear. In such cases it can be expected that national judges will be influenced by their own national legal culture in the field of fiscal profit determination. This would mean that a Dutch judge would be inclined to follow the concept of *goed koopmansgebruik* and that a German or French judge would rather look for a connection with financial accounting rules. Of course, national judges may ask preliminary questions to the ECJ on the interpretation of concepts in the CCCTB-Directive, but it will take a very long time before practice is clear about this. As a comparison, it has taken the *Hoge Raad* more than a century to clarify *goed koopmansgebruik*, and, moreover, many questions have still not been answered and new questions arise regularly. Besides, in my opinion, in order to make the CCCTB tax base sufficiently flexible and dynamic in order to respond to new future developments, the delegated act-procedure should be used more often.

§10.06   NO EXPLICIT CONCEPT OF TOTAL PROFIT

The draft-Directive does not use the Dutch structure that makes a clear distinction between the concept of total profit and the concept of annual profit, determined by *goed koopmansgebruik*. Instead of the concept of total profit, Article 10 of the draft-Directive contains a definition of the elements of the tax base: 'The tax base shall be calculated as revenues less exempt revenues, deductible expenses and other deductible items'. This lack of a concept of total profit could explain why the draft-Directive only offers a few options to taxpayers in determining the CCCTB tax base. In the Netherlands, taxpayers can easily change their system of profit determination as long as the new system is also in accordance with *goed koopmansgebruik*. In

Article 9, section 3 of the draft-Directive a change in the calculation system of the tax base is not allowed, 'unless exceptional circumstances justify a change'.

§10.07 GENERAL PRINCIPLES WITH RESPECT TO THE CALCULATION OF THE TAX BASE

Article 9 of the draft-Directive contains four general principles regarding the calculation of the tax base:

(1) In computing the tax base, profits and losses shall be recognized only when realized (Article 9, section 1).
(2) Transactions and taxable events shall be measured individually (Article 9, section 2).
(3) The calculation of the tax base shall be carried out in a consistent manner unless exceptional circumstances justify a change (Article 9, section 3).
(4) The tax base shall be determined for each tax year unless otherwise provided. A tax year shall be any twelve-month period, unless otherwise provided (Article 9, section 4).

The main elements on which the case law on *goed koopmansgebruik* is based in the Netherlands, i.e., reality, prudence and simplicity, have not been used explicitly in the wording of the draft-Directive. This sometimes complicates the interpretation of the general principles and their effects. The prudence principle of *goed koopmansgebruik* states that losses can already be taken into account before the year in which they are realized, provided that these losses are linked to the current year and a fair probability exists that these losses will occur. This is different for profits: they are not taxable before they have been realized. Based on Article 9, section 1 of the draft-Directive, I assume that this 'Imparity-principle' is not valid for the application of CCCTB. This means that only if specific rules apply, can losses be taken into account before they have been realized; see, e.g., Article 25 (Provisions), Article 27 (Bad debt deductions) and Article 41 (Exceptional depreciation). Another exception is Article 22(e), which states that for the purposes of calculating the tax base, transactions shall be measured at the fair value of financial assets and liabilities held for trading. Article 23 indicates when financial assets and liabilities are considered to be held for trading.

The realization principle of Article 9, section 1, is further developed in Articles 17, 18 and 19. Article 17 prescribes that 'revenues, expenses and all other deductible items shall be recognized in the tax year in which they accrue or are incurred, unless otherwise provided for in this Directive'. On the basis of Article 18, revenues accrue 'when the right to receive them arises and they can be quantified with reasonable accuracy, regardless of whether the actual payment is deferred'. Article 19 prescribes that a deductible expense is incurred at the moment the following conditions are met: 'a. the obligation to make the payment has arisen; b. the amount of the obligation can be quantified with reasonable accuracy; c. in the case of the trading of goods, the significant risks and rewards of ownership over the goods have been transferred to the taxpayer and, in the case of supplies of services, the latter have been received by the taxpayer.'

Article 18 raises the question concerning what should be done if a revenue is received which relates to future costs, e.g., compensation for damage due to land subsidence caused by mining, to be used for future restoration work. In the Netherlands, this compensation can be allocated to the years in which the costs occur (see Tax Court of Den Bosch 8 November 1957, nr. 130/1956R, BNB 1958/266).[14] Considering the wording of Article 18 of the draft-Directive, in CCCTB the compensation for future costs has to be taken into full account at the moment in which the right to receive this compensation arises. This is due to the fact that the draft-Directive does not contain a general matching principle. A similar problem arises with regard to Article 19 in the case of payments relating to costs concerning the previous year (like phone and energy costs) which have to be made after the balance day. It seems that for these future payments Article 25 is applicable. On the basis of this Article, a provision can be created, provided, *inter alia*, there is a future legal obligation to do so. Probably, on the basis of Article 19(c), advance payments can be allocated to the moment that 'the significant risks and rewards of ownership over the goods have been transferred to the taxpayer and, in the case of supplies of services, the latter have been received by the taxpayer'.

Separate rules exist with respect to, *inter alia*, hedge accounting, stocks and work-in-progress and depreciation of fixed assets and provisions. They give rise to many differences compared with *goed koopmansgebruik*..[15]

§10.08   HEDGE ACCOUNTING

For hedging relationships, Article 28 makes an exception to the general principle of Article 9, section 2 in which transactions and taxable events shall be measured individually. In the Netherlands, in general, for tax purposes taxpayers want to prevent an integral valuation of losses and profits. The imparity principle often makes it possible for losses to be taken into account already when there is a fair probability that they will occur, whereas profits have to be taken into account not earlier than the moment of realization. From a commercial perspective however, hedge accounting is attractive because this prevents losses from having to be presented separately. Then, only the net result of losses and profits has to be presented. IAS 39 makes sure that hedge accounting is only possible under very strict conditions.

In the Netherlands, in the decision of 10 April 2009, nr. 42916, BNB 2009/271, the *Hoge Raad* ruled that for tax purposes hedge accounting is obligatory if: (1) there is a connection between the hedging instrument and the hedged item, to be ascertained by the specific circumstances, *inter alia* the answer to the question whether the mitigation

---

14. See also HR 20 April 1977, nr. 1017, BNB 1978/195.
15. Other differences can be found in, *inter alia*, the anti-abuse provisions and in the roll-over relief for replacement assets (Article 38).

of risks was aimed at; and (2) the hedge is expected to be highly effective in such a way that on the balance date it is to be expected that the developments in value of the relevant items will correlate within a range of 80% to 125%. This range has been derived from IAS 39. As the imparity principle is not applicable under CCCTB, the importance of hedging is not very significant. At the same time, Article 22, section 1, e, and Article 23 prescribe valuation at the fair value of financial assets and liabilities held for trading. According to Article 28, there is a hedging relationship where both the following conditions are met: (1) the hedging relationship is formally designated and documented in advance; and (2) the hedge is expected to be highly effective and the effectiveness can be measured reliably. These criteria also seem to be derived from IAS 39, but there is no certainty about this. In any case, Article 28 offers sufficient possibilities for taxpayers to decide whether or not hedge accounting is desired, since the absence of a formal designation of the hedging relationship already prevents the application of hedge accounting.

§10.09 STOCKS AND WORK-IN-PROGRESS

The draft-Directive on CCCTB treats stocks and work-in-progress in the same way. In the Netherlands, different rules exist for stocks and work-in-progress. In Article 4(19), stocks and work-in-progress are defined as: 'assets held for sale, in the process of production for sale or in the form of materials or supplies to be consumed in the production process or in the rendering of services'. This definition is more or less the same as the definitions used in the Netherlands. Article 29, section 4, prescribes valuation at the lower of cost and net realizable value. The net realizable value is the estimated selling price in the ordinary course of business less the estimated costs of completion and estimated costs necessary to make the sale. In the Netherlands, this is the same with respect to goods. This means that profit is taken into account no earlier than the moment of sale or delivery. However for work-in-progress, the percentage of completion method is obligatory (Article 3.29b *Wet inkomstenbelasting 2014*; Personal Income Tax 2001). Under CCCTB, only revenues relating to a long-term contract shall be recognized at the amount corresponding to the part of the contract completed in the respective tax year (Article 24, section 2).

The cost of stock items and work-in-progress that are not ordinarily interchangeable and goods or services produced and segregated for specific projects shall be measured individually. The costs of other stock items and work-in-progress shall be measured by using the first-in-first-out (FIFO) or weighted-average cost method (Article 29, section 1). Application of the base stock system and LIFO is not permitted. In the Netherlands, both methods are still allowed. Only direct costs have to be included in the cost price (Article 29, section 2). This is, in general, also the case in the Netherlands. However, under CCCTB, a taxpayer who has also included indirect costs in valuing stocks and work-in-progress before opting for CCCTB may continue to apply the indirect cost approach (Article 29, section 2).

§10.10   FIXED ASSETS/DEPRECIATION

Chapter IV of the draft-Directive contains rules for the depreciation of fixed assets. In the Netherlands, the economic lifetime is decisive for the depreciation. Under CCCTB, the term useful life is applied. For the determination of the useful life a distinction is made between new and second-hand assets (Article 16). Furthermore, a distinction is also made between individually depreciable assets and assets to be depreciated in one asset pool (Articles 36 and 39). In the Netherlands, other distinctions are used. According to Article 36, under CCCTB only depreciation on a straight-line basis is allowed. In the Netherlands, under certain conditions other depreciation methods, like the degressive method (fixed percentage of the book value), are possible as well. Finally, it seems that under CCCTB a residual value is not recognized. This also differs from the Dutch system.

§10.11   PROVISIONS

Article 19 states that a deductible expense is incurred at the moment the following conditions are met: '(a) the obligation to make the payment has arisen; (b) the amount of the obligation can be quantified with reasonable accuracy'. In Article 25, section 1, a provision can be made:

> Notwithstanding Article 19, where at the end of a tax year it is established that the taxpayer has a legal obligation, or a probable future legal obligation, arising from activities or transactions carried out in that, or previous tax years, any amount arising from that obligation which can be reliably estimated shall be deductible, provided that the eventual settlement of the amount is expected to result in a deductible expense.

Where the obligation relates to an activity or transaction which will continue over future tax years, 'the deduction shall be spread proportionately over the estimated duration of the activity or transaction, having regard to the revenue derived therefrom'.

Similar conditions have been formulated by the *Hoge Raad* in its decision of 26 August 1998, nr. 33147, BNB 1998/409. The only significant difference is that in the draft-Directive a legal obligation is required, whereas the *Hoge Raad* only demands that the cause for the provision should be found in the tax year or in the previous years.

CHAPTER 11

Accounting and Taxation: Portugal

Nina Aguiar & Júlio Tormenta

---

§11.01   THE RELATIONSHIP BETWEEN THE TAX BASE AND COMMERCIAL ACCOUNTING

[A]   The Definition of the Tax Base

According to Article 17 of the Corporate Income Tax (CIT) Code,[1] the tax base of an undertaking is the profit disclosed in the profit and loss account, adjusted (for tax purposes only) under specific rules provided for in the CIT. Article 17(1) of the CIT reads as follows: "the taxable income of [corporations] will be computed via an algebraic addition of the net profit of the period with decreases and increases in assets recorded in the same period and not evidenced in the profit and loss account, determined on the basis of accounts and adjusted whenever necessary under this law" (CIT).[2]

   The "net profit", as referred to in Article 17(1) of the CIT, is the net (after tax) profit disclosed in the commercial profit and loss account and in the balance sheet. The expression "decreases and increases in assets recorded in the same period and not evidenced in the profit and loss account" refers to possible variations, either positive or negative, in the corporation's assets recorded directly as capital and, thus, not disclosed in the profit and loss account. In fact, commercial accounting rules contemplate situations where variations in asset value can be recorded directly as capital and are not, consequently, disclosed in the profit and loss account. This is the case of contributions from shareholders, withdrawals by shareholders, amounts paid to collaborators based on profits, etc. Not all increases or decreases in assets are taken

---

1. Código do Imposto sobre o Rendimento das Pessoas Coletivas (CIRC), Law nr. 2/2014, of January 16.
2. Translated by the authors.

into account to calculate the taxable profit and, in fact, there are very few that fall within this provision.[3] In short, the provision aims to assure that any liquid asset increase is subject to tax, according to the Schanz-Haig-Simons concept of income.[4]

The expression "adjusted whenever necessary under this law" refers to specific rules of the CIT Code that either set methods and rules for the calculation of the taxable profit that are divergent from those provided for in commercial accounting law or set quantitative limits to costs or income determined on the basis of commercial accounting rules.

[B]   The Connection between the Corporations' Tax Base and Financial Accounting: Characterization

[1]   *The Preclusive Effect of Judgments and Choices Made in Commercial Accounts for the Calculation of Taxable Profit*

The relationship between the tax base and the financial accounts is a complex one. This relationship is not entirely, but only partially established in the aforementioned Article 17 of the CIT. Some important aspects of that connection have been defined by case law and by the administration *modus operandi*.

The first aspect of that connection, set forth in Article 17(1) of the CIT, is that the commercial accounts (financial accounts prepared in compliance with commercial law requirements) "form the basis" for calculating the taxable profit.[5] "Forming the basis" for calculating the taxable profit is a common expression used to refer to the fact that the taxable profit is calculated by means of an algebraic operation in which the commercial net profit appears as the first term. Translated into proper legal terminology, the expression means that any discretionary choices or subjective judgments made in the commercial financial accounts regarding the treatment of any financial facts are preclusive for calculating the taxable profit.[6] For instance, if, regarding the treatment of certain investment-related expenses, commercial accounting rules allow the manager to elect between capitalizing such expenses or treating them as costs, the choice made in commercial accounts cannot be changed for the purpose of calculating the taxable profit, even if the tax law expressly grants the possibility of treating those expenses in a different way (a different situation is where the tax law *imposes* a different treatment).

It is a fact that the calculation of the taxable profit usually implies some adjustments or modifications of the profit disclosed in the commercial balance sheet. However, the taxpayer is not free to introduce adjustments that they may consider as more favorable for taxation purposes or even as more adequate from the point of view

---

3. Morais, R. D., *Apontamentos ao IRC*, Almedina, Coimbra, 2007, p. 63.
4. Pereira, M. H. F, *A Periodização do Lucro Tributável*, Cadernos de Ciência e Técnica Fiscal, nr. 152, 1988, p. 28.
5. Morais, R. D., *supra*, p. 63.
6. Aguiar, N., *Tributación y Contabilidad, Una Perspectiva Histórica y de Derecho Comparado*, Granada, 2011, p. 464.

of taxation, even when that different treatment may seem to be legitimate under tax law. Even when tax law seems to allow a treatment that is more favorable than the one adopted in commercial accounts for a given financial fact – e.g., a certain expense, the taxpayer is, in principle, not allowed to modify that treatment for tax purposes. Just to give a simple example, if the taxpayer accounted for an amortization of 100 (discretionary choice) in their commercial accounts, even when the tax provision – a special provision concerning amortization included in the CIT – would allow them to account for an amortization of 150, the taxpayer will not be able to deduct a 150 amortization, having deducted only a 100 amortization in their commercial accounts, because they are bound by the discretionary choice they made in their commercial accounts. In order to be able to use the 150 amortization granted by tax law, they should have used a 150 amortization in their commercial accounts.

This is a consequence of the probative value of the commercial accounts.[7] If the taxpayer, in their commercial accounts, registered an amortization of 100, this means that this figure represents the real asset depletion in the period and, therefore, any other amortization they may want to deduct for tax purposes will not correspond to the real depletion of the asset. The same reasoning applies to most accounting choices or judgments about the time of recognition of financial facts, to inventories, to provisions, and any aspects of commercial accounts where commercial accounting rules require the manager to make a discretionary choice or judgment instead of following rigid rules in evaluating or qualifying any financial fact.

This first aspect of the connection between commercial accounts and taxation can be designated as the "preclusive effect of the commercial accounts to the calculation of the taxable profit". This preclusive effect concerns exclusively accounting choices, which take place whenever there is a range of discretionary possibilities of accounting treatment for one single financial fact according to tax rules.[8] These discretionary possibilities of treatment may concern either the qualification of financial facts (e.g., qualifying some expenses as assets or as costs, qualifying a debt as bad debt, etc.), the quantification of financial facts (e.g., quantifying the depreciation of an asset and the consequent amortization, quantifying the value of inventories, etc.) or the timing of financial facts (e.g., deciding whether the rents paid in a leasing contract are attributable to year 1 or to year 2). In order to simplify the text, we will refer hereinafter to this principle as "formal connection."[9]

A relevant note to help clarify the content of the formal connection between commercial accounts and the tax base is that it acts as a limitation on the taxpayers' ability to shape the tax base in their favor. Therefore, it does not prevent the taxpayer from changing their tax accounts *in peius*. Thus, if the taxpayer adds to the tax base (annuls) a cost deducted in their profit and loss account or adds to the tax base some income not recognized in the profit and loss account, the formal connection rule will not be affected. Similarly, if the tax rules determine that a cost deducted or some

---

7. Aguiar, N., *supra*, p. 378.
8. Aguiar, N., *supra*, p. 305.
9. The term is used by García-Moreno, V. A., *La Base Imponible del Impuesto sobre Sociedades*, Madrid, 1999, p. 34.

income that has not been recognized must be added to the tax base, the formal connection rule will not be affected. The formal connection rule will be affected only when the taxpayer is allowed to deduct any costs not recognized in the profit and loss account or to erase from the tax base any income recognized in the profit and loss account, because in that case the taxpayer will be modifying the tax base *in melius*, i.e., in their favor.

[2]   The Binding Effect of the Formal Connection regarding Tax Administration Powers

Regarding tax administration powers, the formal connection rule explained above means that the tax administration cannot reject the taxpayer's commercial accounts prepared in accordance with commercial accounting regulations in force. Moreover, as long as commercial accounts are prepared in accordance with commercial accounting law, the tax administration is bound to accept the discretionary choices and judgments that the taxpayer has made in their commercial accounts. This rule has never been expressly enunciated, either by courts or the legislator, but it is implicit in Article 17(1) of the CIT. It is an important rule that was only able to materialize after commercial accounting regulation reached a certain degree of consolidation. Up until the mid-1970s in Portugal, commercial accounting regulations were not solid enough for the taxpayer to make use of them against the tax authorities. As a consequence, the tax authorities had significant discretionary powers in assessing the accuracy of the taxpayer's accounts. In practice, taxpayers felt compelled to follow the tax authorities' opinions and conceptions regarding accounting methods.[10]

[3]   The Adjustment Mechanism

The second structural element of the connection between commercial accounts and the calculation of the taxable profit is the one concerning adjustments, which must be viewed as modifications of qualifications, valuations and timing judgments made in commercial accounts. As a general rule, adjustments of qualifications, valuations and timing judgments determined by tax provisions are mandatory adjustments. In other words, the majority of adjustments are not left to the discretion of the taxpayer but the taxpayer is required, in these situations, to modify the net profit for taxation purposes. Adjustments take place whenever the values, qualifications or timing judgments made in commercial accounts are not accepted for tax purposes.

Therefore, after saying that the taxpayer must take the commercial financial accounts as a basis for calculating their taxable profit, the tax law determines that the taxpayer must, in some situations, modify the qualifications, valuations and timing judgments made in their accounts, without giving them the choice of not doing so.

---

10. Until 1998, the courts endorsed the view that the accounting rules enshrined in the tax laws were mandatory for commercial accounting (Supreme Administrative Court, Sentence of 18 November 1998, Process nr. 21703.

As will be explained in further detail below, these adjustments have different rationales and can be grouped in various categories. The most important category of adjustments concerns those adjustments resulting from the application of rules of tax law defining accounting criteria or methods. Unlike the adjustments of other categories, the adjustments of this category aim to determine the undertaking's real profit. The norms at the origin of these adjustments are intended to limit the manager's discretional powers allowed by commercial accounting rules concerning the timing, the valuation and qualification of financial facts.

Such adjustments are also frequently misunderstood, as they are seen as exceptions to the rule that we have designated as the formal connection between commercial accounts and the calculation of the tax base. Nevertheless, these adjustments cannot be viewed in most cases as exceptions to that rule, since they operate inside the formal connection principle.[11]

A brief example may help to illustrate the idea: if a loss in inventories occurs in a given undertaking, that loss can be computed as a negative component of the profit. However, accounting rules leave significant discretion as to the method on which to calculate the loss. What the tax rule does in this case is to set some limits to that discretion, in order to prevent the taxpayer from using discretion to distort their taxable income. However, the taxpayer will never be able to deduct a loss on inventories for tax purposes if they have not deducted the same loss in their commercial accounts owing to the formal connection. In other words, the fact that the tax law contains an accounting rule that apparently diverges from the corresponding commercial accounting rule does not mean that the taxpayer is allowed to make a valuation, qualification or timing judgment of the same financial fact for tax purposes that differs from that made in the commercial accounts. It only means that the valuation or the qualification made in the commercial accounts may need to be modified in order to be brought to within certain limits. It is still the commercial valuation, qualification or timing judgment that is being used for tax purposes.

[4]   Referral to Commercial Accounting Law

A third element of the connection between commercial accounting and the tax base concerns not the commercial accounts but the commercial accounting rules. The above-mentioned Article 17(2) of the CIT says: "To allow the computation referred to in paragraph 1, the [commercial] accounts must be organized in accordance with accounting standards and other legal provisions applicable to the sector of activity, subject to compliance with the provisions of this Code".

The provision is fairly ambiguous. The first part contains a referral to the commercial accounting rules. The provision does not mention the legal character of the rules referred to, but there can be no doubt that the accounting rules currently in force are of a legal nature. So the CIT, in its Article 17(2) refers to the commercial accounting law. This means that the net profit to be taken as a basis for the computation of the tax

---

11. Aguiar, N., *supra,* p. 359.

base is a profit calculated according to the commercial accounting rules in force. This norm could be described as a "connection between the calculation of the tax base and the commercial accounting rules".

The last part of the provision ("subject to compliance with the provisions of this Code") suggests that the commercial accounts must be prepared in accordance with the commercial accounting rules only to the extent to which the rules do not contravene the accounting rules provided for in tax law. Nevertheless, the provision is not applied with this meaning by the tax administration and, therefore, the courts have not been called to pass judgment about the interpretation of the norm, since there are no litigations arising from its application.[12] In practice, the tax administration accepts that commercial accounts are prepared following commercial accounting rules only. Therefore, the last part of Article 17(2) could be considered as a "dead letter." This being said, it is worth mentioning that taxpayers tend to make their commercial accounts conform to the accounting methods dictated by the tax law, whenever there is a divergence, in order to avoid conflicts with the tax administration. Thus, the last part of Article 17(2) of the CIT, although a "dead letter" in the sense that it is not applied by the tax administration, can be said to have a subtle deterrent effect on the taxpayers, giving rise to an effect that can be described, after the Italian doctrine, as reverse dependence.[13] This reverse dependence has to be understood as not expressly laid down in tax law, but rather as a consequence of the ambiguity of the norm referred to in Article 17(2) and the natural unbalance of positions between the taxpayer and the tax administration.

[5]   The Requisite of Commercial Account Accuracy

Finally, a fourth structural element of the formal connection between the determination of taxable profit and the commercial accounts concerns the requisite of commercial account accuracy. The formal connection between the calculation of the taxable profit and the commercial accounts will only apply whenever the commercial accounts are considered accurate. Otherwise, the tax administration will be authorized to disregard the commercial accounts and use different methods to calculate the taxable profit.[14] As explained above, the accuracy of commercial accounts is to be assessed on the basis of the commercial accounting rules only.

The connection described between the commercial accounts and the calculation of the tax base of the CIT (formal connection principle) has existed in the Portuguese

---

12. Under the previous CIT of 1963, the Supreme Administrative Court issued a sentence which declared the right of the taxpayer to prepare their commercial accounts based on unwritten commercial accounting standards, disregarding the unwritten criteria propounded by the tax administration (Supreme Administrative Court, 10 February 1971, Process nr. 16314, in www.dgsi.pt.
13. Falsitta, G., *Il bilancio di esercizio delle imprese*, Milan, Giuffrè, 1985, p. 10; Grandinetti, M., *La Determinazione della base imponibile delle società ai fini delle Imposte sui Redditi*, Rubbettino, Soveria Mannelli, 2009, p. 47.
14. Sentence of the Supreme Administrative Court, 27 April 1988, process nr. 4694.

tax system since 1963.[15] Before then the taxation of business profits was based exclusively on deemed income. The formal connection system was subsequently established in the 1988 CIT. Thus, a system where the tax base was formed by the real profit and the calculation of the taxable profit not connected with the commercial accounts has never existed in the Portuguese legal system.

However, the system in force from 1963 to 1988 showed some differences compared to the system instituted in 1988. These differences mainly concerned the mandatory character of the accounting rules for the commercial accounts. As in the 1988 CIT, the 1963 CIT contained numerous norms defining the accounting treatment of financial facts. However, there were practically no written accounting rules in commercial law. As a consequence, the tax administration saw the accounting rules contained in the CIT as mandatory for the commercial accounts, and occasionally, if these norms were not observed in the commercial accounts, the tax administration could repute the commercial accounts to be inaccurate. This situation was not the result of an express legal provision but rather an administrative practice sanctioned by the courts in particular aspects, such as inventories.[16]

[C] Theoretical Justifications for the Connection between the Corporations' Tax Base and the Financial Accounts

In the 1963 CIT Act, in which the taxation based on the profit disclosed in the commercial balance sheet was introduced for the first time just for a group of taxpayers formed by the largest corporations, the legislator expressed very clearly the view that the purpose of that novelty was to guarantee that taxation was imposed on the "real profit" of the business.[17] Moreover, the legislator additionally stated that a tax that guarantees the taxation on real profit instead of on a deemed profit, is a tax that satisfies the ability to pay principle[18] better. So the theoretical justification of the formal connection in the 1963 CIT was based on the idea that the profit disclosed in commercial accounts is the income measurement that fits the taxpayer's ability to pay more closely.

The principle of corporate taxation on real income, as opposed to the taxation of deemed income, was expressly declared by the Portuguese Constitution of 1976, which gives an idea of the importance devoted to this principle at that time. Twelve years

---

15. "Código da Contribuição Industrial", Article 6(1).
16. For example the sentences of the Supreme Administrative Court of 23 May 1979, process nr. 1226; of 11 January 1995, process nr. 18499 (where the taxpayer applied, in their commercial accounts, timing criteria that differed from those laid down in the tax statute and, consequently, the tax administration reputed the commercial accounts to be inaccurate); of 5 April 1989, process nr. 5799 (where the taxpayer used an inventory method different from that permitted by the 1963 CIT); and of 16 June 1971, process nr. 16394, in www.dgsi.pt.
17. There seems to be a coincidence in this aspect with the Italian legal system (Grandinetti, M., *supra*, p. 31) as well as with the Spanish legal system (Báez-Moreno, A., *Normas Contables e Impuesto sobre Sociedades, Thomson/Aranzadi*, Cizur Menor, 2005, p. 129.
18. The first CIT entitled "Contribuição Industrial" was enacted in 1963 by the Decree Law nr. 45103 of 1 July 1963 and entered in force on 31 July 1963.

later, the 1988 CIT extended the system of calculating the taxable income based on commercial accounts to all forms of businesses.[19]

There is, therefore, no doubt that the principle of taxation of companies on their real profit is the main dogmatic basis of the current principle of connection between the determination of taxable profit and commercial accounts, complemented by the idea that the profit disclosed in commercial accounts is the figure that fits the taxpayer's ability to pay better.

Another dogmatic basis of the "formal connection" principle lies in the probative value of commercial accounts.[20] The principle was already recognized in case law before the 1988 CIT was approved[21] but has been developed since then.[22] This aspect needs further explanation. Most negative components of the profit – costs – need to be substantiated by external commercial documents (invoices and receipts). Income, on the contrary, does not need to be proven by any documents, as it is sufficient for the income to be evidenced in the accounts. However, regarding costs, sometimes their recognition is not based on invoices or other documents. This is the case of provisions, amortization and losses on inventories, just to mention the most common situations. In these situations, the accounts prove, as a general rule, that the managers believe that the cost occurred in the period. Inversely, if the cost was not registered in the accounts of the period, this proves that the cost did not actually occur. In this situation, even if the tax rules allowed the deduction of a cost, the taxpayer would not be able to deduct the cost, because this is not disclosed in the accounts.[23] Regarding income, the probative value of commercial accounts will apply mainly on the time of recognition. If some income was recognized in the commercial accounts in year N1, it will not be possible to claim that the income should only be recognized in year N2 for tax purposes, because the accounts prove that the income accrued in year N1.

[D]   The Role of GAAP

At present, Portuguese tax law does not lay down a referral to any national generally accepted account principles (GAAP) nor to the international generally accepted accounting principles. There was a referral to the national generally accepted accounting principles until 1988, but this referral was then abandoned when the current Corporate Tax Act was passed. Since then, corporate tax refers to the legislated accounting rules only.

---

19. Today, the principle applies to all corporations and partnerships, regardless of their dimension, and also to sole proprietor businesses with an annual income above EUR 200,000 and sole proprietor businesses with an annual income of less than EUR 200,000 if the proprietor declares that option.
20. Báez-Moreno, A., *supra*, p. 71.
21. Sentence of the Supreme Administrative Court of 30 March 1966, process nr. 15325, in *www.dgsi.pt*.
22. Sentences of the Supreme Administrative Court of 9 February 2000, process nr. 22208; of 21 November 2001, process nr. 26080; of 30 April 2003, process nr. 101/03; of 18 May 2005, process nr. 0132/05; of 18 October 2006, process 0668/06; of 25 January 2006, process nr. 0830/05; of 18 June 2014, process nr. 1463/12, in *www.dgsi.pt*.
23. Supremo Tribunal Administrativo, Ruling of 10 June 2014, Process nr. 1463/12.

[E] Deviations Permitted in the Financial Statement for Fiscal Purposes

As stated above, Article 17(1) of the 1988 CIT stipulates that the tax base encompasses some deviations regarding the net profit disclosed in commercial accounts. Depending on the type of deviation, some are allowed while others are imposed. Sometimes the deviations entail an exception regarding the formal connection rule while most often such an exception does not occur. As also mentioned above, deviations between the commercial net profit and the taxable profit have different rationales. It is possible to group these deviations into five different categories. Understanding these different categories facilitates an understanding of why the deviations sometimes involve an exception to the formal connection principle and other times they do not.

[1] Technical Deviations

Some of these adjustments are of a technical nature:

– *The deduction of the estimated corporate tax and other direct or indirect taxes on income*
 The net profit referred to in Article 17(1) is an after (estimated) corporate tax profit. Therefore, in order to calculate the taxable profit, which is a before tax profit, it is necessary to add the deducted estimated corporate tax.
– *Losses of previous years*
 Article 52 of the CIT allows the taxpayer from 2014 onwards to deduct from their current net profit the losses of the previous twelve years. It is well known that any income needs to be ascertained by reference to a given period. Thus, the income of a period will not be influenced, in principle, by the income ascertained in other periods. This said, it is also commonly understood that losses registered in a year have a reflection on the ability to pay of the corporation in future years, where the profits are necessarily used to cover those profits and, hence, cannot be distributed to shareholders. For this reason, the deduction of previous years' losses cannot be said to be aimed at determining the real income of the year, but it is still aimed at determining the taxpayer's ability to pay.

The adjustments of this type – technical adjustments – are not mandatory, but are a taxpayer's option.

These adjustments do not encompass an exception to the formal connection principle, because all the valuations, qualifications and timing judgments made in the commercial accounts are left unchanged.

[2] Deviations Based on Considerations of Good Management

Other adjustments are based on considerations of good management. In general, these deviations concern costs. For instance, penalties of whatever kind cannot be deducted.

These adjustments are mandatory. They do not encompass an exception to the formal connection either, since all accounting choices and judgments made in commercial accounts remain unchanged.

[3]   Tax Incentive-Related Deviations

Other adjustments are related to tax incentives. For instance, it is possible to exclude from the net profit capital gains that have been reinvested in some defined conditions. It is also possible to increase some socially-related costs above the nominal value, etc.

These adjustments are not mandatory. They are optional for the taxpayer.

These adjustments encompass exceptions to the formal connection rule: income that has been recognized in the commercial balance sheet shall not be recognized for tax purposes; or costs that have not been recognized in the balance sheet shall be recognized for tax purposes.

These exceptions to the formal connection principle are justified because the tax law rules applied are not intended to determine the entity's real profit, but rather to allow the exclusion of parts of the profit from taxation, this being the method in which the tax incentive operates.

The present CIT contains the following tax incentives operating by means of a deduction in the tax base:

- Capital gains:[24] the deduction of 50% of capital gains obtained with the sale of fixed and biological assets and reinvested in new assets of the same categories.
- Research and development expenditure:[25] research and development expenses may be deducted in the tax base in the year in which the expense has occurred, even when it was not accounted for as a cost in the commercial accounts but was recognized as an asset.
- Expenditure on nurseries, kindergartens and breastfeeding facilities:[26] these expenses may be deducted as costs up to 140% of their nominal amount.
- Membership fees paid to business associations:[27] these expenses may be deducted as costs up to 150% of their amount.

[4]   Deviations Aimed at Preventing Tax Evasion

In these situations, the tax rules are based on the assumption that the expenses are not related to business costs and are intended to obtain tax advantages. These deviations are mandatory and do not encompass exceptions to the formal connection principle.

---

24. CIT, Article 48.
25. CIT, Article 32.
26. CIT, Article 43(9).
27. CIT, Article 44.

Some of these deviations are:

- Costs that are not connected with the income generating process cannot be deducted in the tax base.[28]
- Non-documented expenses cannot be deducted in the tax base.[29] Expenses not documented in conformity with the VAT legislation cannot be deducted either.[30]
- Fuel expenses cannot be deducted in the tax base when the taxpayer does not prove that the fuel was used as a business asset and does not exceed the normal consumption.[31]
- Interests paid to shareholders by the company over a certain rate cannot be deducted in the tax base.[32]
- Amounts paid to any entities resident in a low tax territory cannot be deducted in the tax base.[33]

[5] Deviations Aimed at Determining the Real Income by Limiting Discretion

These form the large majority of deviations between commercial accounts and tax accounts. In a way, the tax rules applicable in these cases are also aimed at preventing tax evasion. However, unlike the preceding situations, these rules do not rely on the assumption that the accounting records in question are untrue. The tax legislator just assumes that in the absence of limits to discretionary criteria, the taxpayer may use discretion to minimize the tax burden in detriment of a true and fair view.[34] So these rules set limits to discretion allowed by commercial accounting rules, with a view to inducing the taxpayer to declare the real income.[35] These deviations do not encompass exceptions to the formal connection principle, because the taxpayer cannot deduct any unaccounted costs nor reduce or eliminate income accounted for in commercial accounts. Moreover, the taxpayer is not allowed to change any accounting choices made in commercial accounts.

---

28. CIT, Article 23(1).
29. CIT, Article 23-A(1)(b).
30. CIT, Article 23-A(1)(c).
31. CIT, Article 23-A(1)(j).
32. CIT, Article 23-A(1)(m).
33. CIT, Article 23-A(1)(r).
34. Báez-Moreno, A., *supra,* p. 55, using the reasoning in relation to the Spanish system, refers to this type of "adjustment rules" as limitative adjustment rules, a concept to which we adhere completely. Grandinetti, M, *supra,* p. 37 also stresses that most of the adjustment tax rules aim at avoiding an abusive use of discretion. The two Authors agree in that the rationale of tax adjustment rules does not lie in the different purposes of the commercial accounting or the tax base, but rather in the need to limit/neutralize accounting discretion for tax purposes, a concept that the Authors of this article fully heed.
35. Supreme Administrative Court, Sentence of 11 February 2009, Process nr. 862/08.

The adjustments of this category are not only the most important in number but they are also the most important because they are perceived by the taxpayer as liable to curtail the free judgment of the manager.

The list of deviations of this type includes:

- Methods of inventory measurement and inventory loss computation.[36]
- Criteria for the deduction of losses related to bad debts.[37]
- Criteria for the deduction of specific bank provisions.[38]
- Amortization allowances.[39]
- Provisions for predictable future losses.[40]
- Environmental damage repairing provisions.[41]
- Irrecoverable debt.[42]
- Calculation of capital gains and losses.[43]
- Gains and losses resulting from the application of the criterion of fair value to financial derivative instruments.[44]
- Income from industrial property.[45]

[F]   The Tax Administration Powers regarding the Assessment of Financial Income for Tax Purposes

As explained above, according to Article 17(2) of the CIT, the formal connection between the calculation of the taxable profit and the commercial accounts will only apply whenever the commercial accounts are considered accurate. Concerning the basis on which commercial account accuracy is assessed, the legal provision is ambiguous. It says: "To allow the computation referred to in paragraph 1, the [commercial] accounts must be organized in accordance with accounting standards and other legal provisions applicable to the sector of activity, *subject to compliance with the provisions of this Code.*"

The provision suggests very clearly that commercial accounts must be in conformity with commercial account rules *only to the extent* to which commercial accounting rules are in accordance with the tax accounting criteria. As we said above too, the administration practice does not go in this direction and courts have never applied the provision with this meaning. Considering, thus, this part of the provision as a dead letter, we can say that the tax law contains a referral to commercial accounting law. The profit and loss account that serves as a basis for calculating the taxable base

---

36. CIT, Articles 26 and 28.
37. CIT, Articles 28-A and 28-B.
38. CIT, Article 28-C.
39. CIT, Articles 29-34.
40. CIT, Article 39.
41. CIT, Article 40.
42. CIT, Article 41.
43. CIT, Articles 46-47-A.
44. CIT, Article 49.
45. CIT, Article 50-A.

is a profit and loss account prepared in accordance with the commercial accounting legislation in force.

According to the literal meaning of the legal rule quoted, if the commercial accounts are not in full compliance with the commercial legal rules applicable, the formal connection rule would not be applicable. The administration could disregard the commercial accounts and use different methods to calculate the taxable profit.[46]

However, this rule has not been applied in this strict sense. If the tax administration detects mistakes, inaccuracies or any deficiencies in the taxpayer's commercial accounts, during an inspection procedure or by simply cross-checking data within the services, the tax authorities may make the necessary corrections for tax purposes only (commercial accounts are not changed by the tax administration).

These corrections may be made using various methods. If the accounting books contain the elements needed to make the corrections, i.e., if the taxpayer registered in his accounting books all financial facts relevant for determining the annual profit, albeit with accounting errors, the tax authorities will just make "technical corrections".[47] "Technical corrections"[48] are based on a strict application of accounting rules which do not entail the exercise of discretionary judgments.[49] The formal connection rule will apply to the parts of the accounts considered accurate. If the accounting books and documents do not contain the elements needed to make the necessary corrections, but the majority of the accounting information contained in the accounting books is valid, the tax authorities will make use of indirect methods to correct the deficiencies that cannot be fixed otherwise and will apply the formal connection rule to those parts of the accounts deemed accurate.[50] If the commercial accounts are inexistent or are inaccurate as a whole and there are no elements to evaluate the profit directly, the tax authorities may apply indirect methods to estimate the taxable profit as a whole, disregarding the commercial accounts. In any of these cases, the tax authorities need to substantiate thoroughly the corrections made.

§11.02 THE IMPACT OF IFRS ON *FINANCIAL ACCOUNTING* AND TAX CONSEQUENCES

The Portuguese commercial accounting law underwent a thorough reform in 2009,[51] aimed at adapting it to EC Regulation 1606/2002. Although the Regulation was mandatory only for the consolidated accounts of the entities mentioned in Article 4 (companies governed by the law of a Member State whose securities are, at the date of the balance sheet, admitted to trading on a regulated market of any Member State) the

---

46. Sentence of the Supreme Administrative Court of 27 April 1988, process no. 4694.
47. Sentences of the Supreme Administrative Court of 7-05-2003, process no. 0243/03 and of 26 April 2007, process no. 37/07.
48. The term "technical correction" is not a legal term but an expression used by the tax authorities in audit reports.
49. Sentence of the Supreme Administrative Court of 5 February 1997, process no. 21176.
50. Sentence of the Supreme Administrative Court of 19 March 2009, process no. 890/08.
51. The reform of the commercial accounting law was undertaken through Decree Law nr. 158/2009.

fact that there were two very distinct sets of accounting rules for different companies operating in the same domestic market was seen as undesirable, impairing the comparability of accounts. Therefore, it was understood that the domestic commercial accounting law should be amended in order to incorporate the international accounting standards, as implemented through the Commission Regulation (EC) 1126/2008. The 2009 reform implemented the International Financial Reporting Standards (IFRS) 2007[52] in the domestic legal order for companies and other forms of business not covered directly by the EC Regulation 1606/2002.

The accounting legislation passed in 2009 provides two accounting schemes, one applicable to small and medium enterprises (SME scheme) and a second one (general scheme), applicable to all other businesses regardless of their legal form. The general scheme is just a condensed version of the international accounting standards (in their 2007 version), with no relevant differences regarding the content of the norms. The SME scheme is a slightly simplified version of the general scheme and only with regard to disclosure duties. In both schemes the categories, the concepts, the principles and the valuation rules are thoroughly coincident with the international accounting standards that were in force in 2009 (IFRS 2007).

In short, business entities in Portugal may apply three different sets of accounting rules in their commercial accounts: companies admitted to listing on the stock exchange apply the Commission Regulation (EC) 1126/2008 in their consolidated accounts directly; they may also apply the Regulation in their individual accounts; SME apply the simplified SME accounting scheme; all the other companies apply the general accounting scheme. In the last two cases, although companies do not formally apply the international accounting standards, because they apply the domestic accounting law, the content of their accounts is in conformity with the 2007 IFRS, since the commercial accounting law is a simplification of these international accounting standards.

Notwithstanding this, it is relevant to note that the IFRS enshrined in the Portuguese commercial accounting regulation of 2009 were the IFRS in force in 2007. Since 2007, IFRS have undergone numerous changes that have not been assimilated by the Portuguese accounting legislation. This illustrates the difficulty arising from establishing a link between the IFRS, with their peculiar issuing system, and the accounting law or the tax law.

From the point of view of commercial accounting, the accounting regulation reform of 2009 that incorporated the 2007 IFRS had important consequences. In general, subjectivity and discretion in accounting qualifications and valuations have increased significantly. The present net value and the fair value criteria have replaced historical costs in a number of situations, such as financial instruments, derivatives, liabilities and investment property.[53] Concerning inventories, the last-in-first-out

---

52. International Financial Reporting Standards in force in 2007.
53. Vasconcelos, A., *O Justo Valor e o Código do IRC*, Revista de Finanças Públicas e Direito Fiscal, IV (1), 2012, p. 196.

(LIFO)[54] method ceased to be accepted.[55] Amortization of goodwill ceased to be obligatory or even possible in some cases, with the consequence that companies who have a goodwill registered in their balance sheet will show a better financial position than before.

Meanwhile, a new provision was introduced in the Companies Act, prohibiting the distribution of any profits resulting from the application of the fair value method.[56]

From the point of view of taxation, the main consequence of the accounting regulation reform of 2009 was a slight increase in discrepancy between the profit calculated for commercial law purposes and the taxable profit.[57]

This happened despite some modifications to the tax law aimed at adapting it to the new accounting regulation.[58] It was the case, for example, with the net current value criterion, which is now accepted for tax purposes in line with the commercial balance sheet for some categories of assets, like inventories and liability instruments for medium /long term. The same did not happen, however, in other aspects, like the fair value criterion, which is in general not relevant for tax purposes. There was also a deep change in the terminology used by the tax law,[59] in order to align it with the accounting regulations.

However, due to the formal connection between the tax balance sheet and the commercial balance sheet, on the one hand, and the referral made by the tax law to commercial accounting law, on the other, the tax law followed the transformation undergone by the commercial accounting law.

§11.03 THE COMMON CONSOLIDATED CORPORATE TAX BASE (CCCTB)[60]

[A] Main Differences between the CCCTB and the National Tax Base

[1] *Relationship between the Tax Base and the Commercial Balance Sheet and Commercial Accounting Rules*

The first difference between the CCCTB Directive proposal and the national legislation regarding the tax base concerns the relationship between the tax base and commercial accounts. Unlike the Portuguese law, the Directive proposal does not provide explicitly

---

54. LIFO, Last-in-first-out.
55. Carlos, M. A., *O Impacto do IAS 2 nas Sociedades Comerciais – Reflexões a Propósito do Novo Regime Fiscal*, Revista de Finanças Públicas e Direito Fiscal, IV (4), 2012 p. 107.
56. Article 32(2) of the Companies Act 1986.
57. Guimarães, J. C., *Reflexões sobre o SNC*, Contabilidade e Empresas, nr. 8, 2011, p. 13; Lérias, A. G., *Contabilidade vs. Fiscalidade: Reorientações?*, Revista de Finanças Públicas e Direito Fiscal, IV (1), 2011, p. 85.
58. Guimarães, J. C., *supra*, p. 12.
59. Guimarães, J. C., *supra*, p. 12.
60. Proposal for a Council Directive on a Common Consolidated Corporate Tax Base (CCCTB) European Commission COM (2011) 121 Final.

or implicitly for any connection between the tax base and commercial accounting.[61] The proposal does not provide for a referral to commercial accounting rules either.[62]

This omission is expected to give rise to difficulties. For instance, the definition of revenues in Article 4 seems insufficient.[63] The question of what should be considered revenue is resolved in the Portuguese tax law by the normative referral to the accounting law and by the formal connection rule, which is not the case with the CCCTB proposal.

Inevitably, in the author's opinion, the question will be raised as to whether, on this particular point, the proposal contains an implicit reference to the commercial accounts and what kind of reference it is.

In general, in the author's opinion, there is less coordination with the rules of the European commercial accounting law, compared to what happens under Portuguese law.

[2]   Realization Principle (Article 9 of the Proposal)

The realization principle is laid down in Article 9 of the proposal, which says: "In computing the tax base, profits and losses shall be recognized only when realized". The realization principle is also the general principle applicable in the domestic tax law.[64] The only exception to this principle regards derivatives. Value increases in derivatives resulting from the application of fair value are taxed without realization. In this particular aspect, the CCCTB Directive proposal is more favorable for taxpayers than the domestic tax law.

[3]   Charitable Bodies (Article 16 of the Proposal)

It will be necessary to adapt the Portuguese law with regard to the concept of "charitable bodies" referred to in Article 16 of the proposal, since there is no such concept in Portuguese law. In domestic law, there is a bottom line distinction between for-profit and non-profit organizations. The latter may additionally fit into four different legal statuses – public utility, administrative public utility, social solidarity institutions and non-profit organizations without public utility. None of these legal statuses exactly match the common-law concept of "charity".

[4]   Timing General Principle and Timing General Rules (Articles 17-19 of the Proposal)

The timing rules of Articles 17, 18 and 19 of the proposal are similar to the timing rules of the Portuguese CIT. However, the Portuguese timing rules are more detailed,

---

61. Freedman, J. and Macdonald., *The Nature of the Directive: Rules or Principles?, in "The KPMG Guide to CCCTB"*, I, KPMG International Cooperative, 2012, p. 20.
62. KPMG'S EU Tax Centre, *Calculation of the Tax Base, in "The KPMG Guide to CCCTB"*, KPMG International Cooperative, II, KPMG International Cooperative, 2012, p. 33.
63. Freedman, J. and Macdonald, G., *supra*, p. 21.
64. CIT, Article 18.

whereas the proposal rules have a higher degree of indeterminacy. This means that, although the timing principles are the same, the proposal provides more room for discretion with respect to timing judgments.

The proposal, unlike the CIT, does not provide any rules for the timing of income or losses unknown at the competent accrual moment. It is possibly another case in which the proposal makes implicit reference to commercial accounting rules.

[5]   Costs Related to Non-depreciable Assets (Article 20 of the Proposal)

According to the proposal, costs relating to the acquisition, construction or improvement of fixed assets not subject to depreciation can only be deducted in the tax year in which the fixed assets are disposed of, provided that the disposal proceeds are included in the tax base. In the domestic legislation these costs can be deducted in the tax year in which they have been incurred. The proposal rule seems more adequate, although it is less favorable from the taxpayer's point of view.

[6]   Pensions (Article 26 of the Proposal)

The rule of Article 26 of the proposal is significantly less restrictive than the Portuguese legislation.

[7]   Bad Debt Deductions (Article 27 of the Proposal)

The proposal is much more flexible compared to the Portuguese rule, as regards the burden on the taxpayer in respect of collection efforts required in order for the taxpayer to be able to deduct bad debt losses. In the domestic legislation, in order to be able to deduct a bad debt provision, the taxpayers must prove that they have endeavored to collect the debt and that they have done it in due time. Since this is one of the aspects of the tax base that has caused more problems for taxpayers,[65] they should welcome the proposed rule with gratitude.

[8]   Amortizations (Articles 32-42 of the Proposal)

For individually depreciable assets, the useful lifetime differs significantly between the proposal and the Portuguese tax law. The depreciation periods in general are significantly shorter in the proposal. Compared to a taxpayer taxed under the Portuguese CIT currently in force, a taxpayer taxed under the proposed CCCTB will be able to deduct buildings, long-life tangible assets and other depreciable assets other than intangible assets in a period that is on average 20% shorter. In general, the amortization rules and

---

65. Supreme Administrative Court: Sentence of 18 June 2014, Process nr. 1463/12; Sentence of 4 September 2013, Process nr. 164/12; Sentence of 30 April 2003, process nr. 0101/03; Sentence of 18 October 2006, process nr. 668/06; Sentence of 24 January 2007, Process nr. 491/06; Sentence of 18 May 2005, Process nr. 132/05; Sentence of 21 November 2001, Process nr. 26080.

methods of depreciation are also much simpler in the proposal compared to the domestic tax law.

[9]   Rollover Relief for Replacement Assets (Article 38)

Under the proposal, taxpayers are allowed to deduct 100% of the proceeds from the disposal of an individually depreciable asset when those proceeds are to be reinvested in an asset used for the same or a similar purpose before the end of the second tax year after the tax year in which the disposal took place. Under the Portuguese legislation, the taxpayer is only allowed to deduct 50% of the gain obtained with the sale.

Under the proposal, the acquisition of replacement assets may take place up to one year before the disposal of the replaced assets, whereas under the Portuguese legislation the acquisition occurs after the disposal.

In contrast, the rollover relief under the proposal applies to fewer categories of assets, compared to the domestic Portuguese legislation. The Portuguese rollover relief for replacement assets applies to fixed tangible assets, intangible assets and non-consumable biological assets, whereas under the proposal the rollover relief covers individually depreciable assets, which excludes intangible assets and at least some biological assets.

In case of failure to reinvest the disposal proceeds, under the Portuguese legislation these are increased by 15%, whereas under the proposal they are increased by 10%.

[10]   Loss Carryforward (Article 43)

Under the Portuguese CIT from 2014 onwards, there has been a twelve year limit for loss carryforward, whereas under the proposal there is no time limit for loss carryforward, which can lead to a shrinkage of the tax base, in the opinion of some authors.[66]

§11.04   FISCAL ASPECTS OF THE NEW DIRECTIVE 2013/34/EU

The Directive 2013/34/EU[67] encompasses some relevant differences regarding IFRS or even the Portuguese accounting regulations. Under IFRS, the fair value measurement method is mandatory for certain assets, like derivative financial instruments. Under the new Directive, it is an option of the Member States to determine the obligatory application of the fair value on those assets. As to liabilities, which are measured at net

---

66. Lopes, C., and Rodrigues, A. M., A Base Comum Consolidada na União Europeia e as Regras Substantivas de Determinação da Matéria Colectável, *in* Rodrigues, A. M., Lopes, C. e Tavares, T. (eds), "Os Grupos- Uma Perspectiva Crítica e Multidisciplinar", Editora Almedina, Coimbra, (forthcoming).
67. Directive 2013/34/EU of the European Parliament and of the Council of 26 June 2013, on the annual financial statements, consolidated financial statements and related reports of certain types of undertakings, amending Directive 2006/43/EC of the European Parliament and of the Council and repealing Council Directives 78/660/EEC and 83/349/EEC.

present value under the Portuguese accounting regulations, it seems that historical cost will be the only measurement method applicable under the new Directive. Another major difference regards the treatment of goodwill. Under the Portuguese accounting regulations, the goodwill should never be written off, but it can be amortized for tax purposes. Under the new Directive the goodwill must always be written off over a period from five to ten years. Moreover, any intangible assets must be written off over their useful economic life, which differs from what happens under the Portuguese accounting regulations, e.g., with development expenses, trademarks, etc. Regarding the measurement of stocks and work-in-progress, the last-in-last-out (LIFO) method is permitted under the new Directive, which is not the case under both the Portuguese legislation and the CCCTB.

Concerning the substance over form principle, it has a long tradition in Portuguese accounting law, since it was already enshrined in the 1977 legislation. However, the Portuguese tradition is that the principle is materialized through specific norms and not left to the discretion of the undertakings. It is, thus, conceivable that the Portuguese State will use the option provided for in Article 6(3) of the Directive.

The implementation of the Directive will require the Portuguese Government to reflect on whether the Portuguese State should opt for minimum adaptation regarding the existing SME accounting rules (quite similar to the general accounting rules) or should opt for a steadier differentiation. The extent of legislative modification to accounting regulations will depend on the result of this reflection. If the Portuguese Government opts for a steady differentiation between SMEs and general accounting rules, it is predictable that the CIT must undergo significant modifications.

REFERENCES

Aguiar, N., *Tributación y Contabilidad, Una Perspectiva Histórica y de Derecho Comparado,* Granada, 2011.

Báez-Moreno, A., *Normas Contables e Impuesto sobre Sociedades, Thomson/Aranzadi,* Cizur Menor, 2005.

Carlos, M. A., *O Impacto do IAS 2 nas Sociedades Comerciais – Reflexões a Propósito do Novo Regime Fiscal,* Revista de Finanças Públicas e Direito Fiscal, IV (4), 2012, pp. 89-107.

Falsitta, G., *Il bilancio di esercizio delle imprese,* Milán, Giuffrè, 1985.

Freedman, J. and Macdonald, G., *The Nature of the Directive: Rules or Principles?, in* "The KPMG Guide to CCCTB", I, KPMG International Cooperative, 2012.

García-Moreno, V. A., *La Base Imponible del Impuesto sobre Sociedades,* Madrid, 1999.

Grandinetti, M., *La Determinazione della base imponibile delle società ai fini delle Imposte sui Redditi,* Rubbettino, Soveria Mannelli, 2009.

Guimarães, J. C., *Reflexões sobre o SNC,* Contabilidade e Empresas, nr. 8, 2011.

KPMG'S EU Tax Centre, *Calculation of the Tax Base, in* "The KPMG Guide to CCCTB", KPMG International Cooperative, II, KPMG International Cooperative, 2012.

Lérias, A. G., *Contabilidade vs. Fiscalidade: Reorientações?,* Revista de Finanças Públicas e Direito Fiscal, IV (1), 2011, pp. 75-91.

Lopes, C., and Rodrigues, A. M., A Base Comum Consolidada na União Europeia e as Regras Substantivas de Determinação da Matéria Colectável, *in* Rodrigues, A. M., Lopes, C. e Tavares, T. (eds), "Os Grupos- Uma Perspectiva Crítica e Multidisciplinar", Editora Almedina, Coimbra, (forthcoming).

Morais, R. D., *Apontamentos ao IRC,* Almedina, Coimbra, 2007.

Pereira, M. H. F, *A Periodização do Lucro Tributável,* Cadernos de Ciência e Técnica Fiscal, nr. 152, 1988.

Proposal for a Council Directive on a Common Consolidated Corporate Tax Base (CCCTB) European Commission COM (2011) 121 Final.

Vasconcelos, A., *O Justo Valor e o Código do IRC,* Revista de Finanças Públicas e Direito Fiscal, IV (1), 2012, pp. 191-208.

CHAPTER 12

Accounting and Taxation: Spain

Andrés Báez Moreno

§12.01 GENERAL PRESENTATION OF THE TOPIC IN SPAIN

After having a confusing system of relations between commercial and tax accounting[1] for nearly twenty years, the Spanish Parliament passed the *Ley 43/1995, de 27 de diciembre, del Impuesto sobre Sociedades* (hereinafter CITA 95) thanks to which Spain could count, for the first time, on a more or less clear set of rules regarding these relations. The new synthetic tax approach is illustrated in the regulation of its taxable event[2] and, particularly, in those new provisions generally devoted to the tax base for Corporate Tax Purposes that we quote below due to their particular importance:

Article 10.1 CITA 95:

'*The tax base is the amount of the fiscal year taxable income reduced by negative tax bases of previous fiscal years*'.

Article 10.3 CITA 95:

'*In the direct assessment system[3] the taxable base will be determined by correcting, according to the special provisions of this law, the accounting profit or loss*

---

1. The *Ley 61/1978, de 27 de diciembre, del Impuesto sobre Sociedades* (CITA 78 hereinafter) contained a very complicated, uncoordinated and primitive set of rules on these issues which enabled different Spanish scholars to label the system as book-tax conformity or independent tax accounting rules. On this controversy, concluding that these rules lead to an independent tax accounting rules system: Báez Moreno, Andrés. *Normas Contables e Impuesto sobre Sociedades.* Pamplona: Aranzadi, 2005, pp. 30-45.
2. Article 4.1 CITA 95 defines it as: *The obtaining of income by the taxpayer whatever its source and origin.*
3. The direct assessment system (*estimación directa*) is the general regime for the assessment of taxable bases founded upon real data of revenue and expense. According to the *Ley General Tributaria* (hereinafter General Tax Code, GTC 2003) also presumptive systems exist in the Spanish tax legislation but they are rather exceptional in Corporate Income Tax (actually

calculated in accordance to the Commercial Code, other laws relevant for that calculation and the regulations implementing the former'.

Following the German concepts and after some discussion, there seems to be a general agreement among scholars (accepted, if not explicitly at least implicitly, by the Tax Authorities) that, according to the previous rule, the relationship between commercial and tax accounting in Spain is based upon three main principles.

[A]   Material Book-Tax Conformity[4]

In accordance with this first principle, commercial accounting rules (hereinafter Spanish GAAP) have become a part of the set of rules according to which the taxable base of the Spanish Corporate Income Tax is determined. The object of the reference to accounting rules operated by Article 10.3 of the CITA is extraordinarily broad insofar as it embraces not only the *Commercial Code* and further formal accounting legislation[5] but also, and most importantly, regulations implementing the former legislation of which the so-called *Plan General de Contabilidad* (hereinafter PGC) is of paramount importance. The fact that the PGC[6] and further relevant rules for commercial accounting[7] purposes lack formal legal rank has generated heavy criticism, inasmuch as some Spanish scholars have interpreted this as a violation of the rule of law principle contained in the Constitution.[8]

The theoretical justifications upon which the material book-tax conformity system is based have never been a clear issue in the Spanish system. The Explanatory Memorandum of the CITA 95, which introduced the current system in Spain, justified the connection on the basis that, as the Corporate Tax is a tax on income, the latter should be construed according to the rules and principles that govern the determination of profits or losses for accounting purposes. Besides, and again according to the Memorandum, the book-tax conformity system would lead to greater legal certainty for the tax payer. I have always found these alleged justifications less than persuasive. As regards the first reason, it involves assuming the existence of a pre-normative concept of income valid for both commercial and tax purposes; the fact that commercial and tax

---

concentrated in the Spanish Tonnage Tax, Articles 113-117 of the current CITA the *Ley 27/2014, de 27 de noviembre, del Impuesto sobre Sociedades*, hereinafter CITA 2014).

4. *Determinación material* in Spanish as a direct translation of the German term *Materielle Maßgeblichkeit*.
5. The accounting law reform passed in Spain in 2007 took away much of the importance of Company Law Acts (*Ley de Sociedades Anónimas* and *Ley de Sociedades de Responsabilidad Limitada*) for commercial accounting purposes as the determination rules were eliminated completely and moved to the Commercial Code.
6. *Real Decreto 1514/2007, de 16 de noviembre.*
7. See in great detail: Cobo de Guzmán Pisón, Juan. *La base imponible.* /En/ Impuesto sobre Sociedades. Régimen General. Tomo I. (Eduardo Sanfrutos Gambín, dir.). Segunda Edición. Pamplona: Thomson Reuters-Aranzadi, 2013, pp. 364-369.
8. On this constitutional issue see: Báez Moreno, Andrés. *El principio de reserva de la ley tributaria y la base imponible del Impuesto sobre Sociedades: una reflexión sobre la institucionalidad del artículo 10.3 del TRLIS.* /En/ Revista Española de Derecho Financiero, n° 128, 2005, pp. 851-896.

accounting are geared towards (partially) different objectives[9] suffices to call the bases of the argument into question.[10] As far as the argument regarding legal certainty is concerned, I find it difficult to understand why a book-tax conformity system provides more certainty than an autonomous set of pure tax accounting rules,[11] especially if we take into account that many of the legal controversies involving the tax base in conformity systems arise from the fact that it is not always easy to determine whether a factual constellation might be resolved according to the commercial accounting rule or the special tax deviation rule.[12] This does not mean, in my view, that the Spanish Book-Tax Conformity system lacks any technical justification. In the current legal situation, as in 1995 when the system was created, the general remission to commercial accounting rules serves the purpose of simplification avoiding the necessity of a double set of accounting rules and documents.[13] In my opinion, the fact that deviations from commercial accounting rules have dramatically increased over the last few years – as argued below – does not jeopardize this justification as it will always be easier to determine the tax base in a book-tax conformity system than to apply two whole sets of commercial and tax accounting rules.[14]

However, Spain has never had a full book-tax conformity system. Since the creation of the system in 1995, the CITA has always regulated a significant number of deviations. Nevertheless, if these deviations have been growing gradually over the last three years since the introduction of the system,[15]– concurring, not by chance, with the financial crisis – this progressive separation of commercial and tax accounting might well be labelled dramatic. Traditionally, these deviations were based upon a rather

---

9. As explained in other contributions, a commercial accounting system aimed essentially at providing financial information about the reporting entity that is useful to existing and potential investors, lenders and other creditors will suit tax requirements better (Báez Moreno, Andrés. *Normas contables, supra* pp. 469-485. Zornoza Pérez, Juan José & Báez Moreno, Andrés. *Modelos comparados de relación entre normas contables y normas fiscales en la imposición sobre el beneficio de las empresas.* /En/ El impuesto sobre la renta y complementarios (Edit. Julio Roberto Piza Rodríguez y Pedro Enrique Sarmiento Pérez). Bogotá: Universidad del Externado de Colombia, 2010, p. 448). Nevertheless, a full identification of aims has never been achieved.

10. On this issue in detail: Báez Moreno, Andrés. *Normas contables, supra* pp. 97-146.

11. Even if in the origin of the book-tax conformity in the XIX century this might have been true. On this justification, in a historical perspective: Báez Moreno, Andrés. *Normas contables, supra* pp. 146-148.

12. As regards *sale and lease back transactions* and long-term contracts in the Spanish system: Zornoza Pérez, Juan José& Báez Moreno, Andrés. *Modelos comparados … supra* pp. 449-454.

13. On this ground in the Spanish system: Zornoza Pérez, Juan José & Báez Moreno, Andrés. *Modelos comparados … supra* pp. 434-435. On this ground in the historical and current German literature: Báez Moreno, Andrés. *Normas contables, supra* p. 148.

14. As the Spanish pre-1995 situation has shown, this also holds true for those cases in which commercial and tax accounting rules are identical or almost identical, as far as the hypothetical divergence of interpretations of literally similar rules might be possible according to teleological arguments generating significant legal uncertainty. Additional arguments in this respect for the German experience in: LINK, Simon. *Die Maßgeblichketsdiskussion angesichts der Einführung von IAS/IFRS in die Rechnungslegung.* /En/ Steuerliche Maßgeblichkeit in Deutschland und Europa (ed. W. Schön). Köln: Otto Schmidt, 2005, pp. 212-213.

15. As sustained elsewhere, this gradual introduction of deviations is the consequence of a regular process to correct defects and problems of a pure book-conformity system: Báez Moreno, Andrés. *Normas contables, supra* p. 149.

excessively prudent approach of the commercial accounting model (rules for provisions and contingent liabilities[16] or valuation of certain transactions at historic value[17]), the uncertain content of accounting regimes (rules for depreciation[18] or impairment of assets[19]) or the introduction of tax benefits for Corporate Income Tax Purposes (as for example accelerated or free depreciation rules[20]).[21] Despite being present already in the original formulation of the Spanish book-tax conformity system (thin capitalization[22] or transfer pricing rules[23]), in the last few years we have experienced an exponential growth in deviation rules aimed theoretically at the prevention of tax evasion and avoidance. Only this objective might explain the limitation or prohibition on the deduction for tax purposes of impairments of tangible assets, intangible assets, immovable property, equity and financial debt instruments, customer or suppliers care expenses, severance payments and, most importantly, financial expenses. All these rules are either total prohibitions of deductibility or, more often, limitations built upon objective thresholds. The deviations do not discriminate between domestic and cross-border situations – the Spanish legislator seems to be particularly aware of EU-Law constraints – but they pose very serious concerns as regards constitutional limits for taxing powers. Even though the Spanish Constitutional Court has been extremely acquiescent with the tax legislator, limitations to the net taxation principle based upon objective thresholds, without escape clauses,[24] seem difficult to justify strictly from the point of view of proportionality.[25]

[B]   Formal Book-Tax Conformity[26]

In this case, we are dealing with a second and less evident relationship between commercial and tax accounting. If, according to the material book-tax conformity principle, commercial accounting rules are the starting point for the taxable base, the question that this new principle tries to answer is whether the profit or loss actually calculated by the taxpayer for commercial purposes must also be decisive for tax purposes. If the profit or loss has been calculated correctly, according to commercial

---

16. According to Article 14 of the current *Ley 27/2014, de 27 de noviembre del Impuesto sobre Sociedades* (hereinafter CITA 2014).
17. According to Article 17 of the CITA 2014.
18. According to Article 12 of the CITA 2014.
19. According to Article 13 of the CITA 2014.
20. According to Articles 12.3, 102 and 103 of the CITA 2014.
21. This list of deviations might by no means be considered exhaustive. It merely aims to show, as requested by the questionnaire, the main justifications for these deviations in the Spanish system.
22. Thin capitalization rules were repealed in 2004 just for EU lenders and then generally in 2012.
23. Contained today in Article 18 of the CITA 2014.
24. Many of these new deviations do not allow the tax payer to prove that the expense is real and/or not abusive.
25. The Spanish tax legislator does not understand that the reasons that might lead to an infringement of EU-Law in relation to the fundamental freedoms might also be applicable to a purely domestic judgment of the rule on the basis of the ability-to-pay principle.
26. *Determinación formal* in Spanish as a direct translation of the German term *Formalle Maßgeblichkeit*.

rules, both principles (material and formal book-tax conformity) might appear to be identical. Nevertheless, this first impression would be wrong if we analyse the problem taking into consideration options granted by commercial and tax accounting rules. Let us start with an example from the Spanish regulation of depreciations for tangible assets. The commercial accounting regulation of this depreciation in Spain allows the alternative use of the straight-line method, the diminishing balance method and the unit of production method.[27] For tax purposes, the CITA also offers a list of methods available – literally methods that lead to an effective and, therefore, tax deductible depreciation – of which Article 12 of the CITA 2014 recognizes the straight-line method, the constant percentage method, the sum of the year's digit method, depreciation rulings and even the particular proof of reduction in value. Of course, the question is whether once an acceptable method has been used for commercial purposes – assuming this method is also acceptable according to the special tax deviation rule on depreciations – the tax payer may use a different acceptable method exclusively to determine his taxable base. Tax payers might be keen to exercise these asymmetrical option rights as far as they allow the determination of higher profits for commercial purposes – by means of straight-line methods – and a reduction of the taxable base using, for example, the declining balance method. There is no explicit solution for this problem in the Spanish Tax system,[28] but the need to exercise concurrent commercial and tax accounting option rights has been inferred for other provisions contained in the CITA as for example Article 11.3.1 of the CITA 2014[29] or, more correctly in my view, Article 10.3 of the CITA.[30] Whatever the legal basis might be for this formal book-tax conformity principle in Spain, there are I believe strong teleological arguments to defend it.[31]

[C]   Book-Tax Conformity and the Powers of Assessment of the Tax Administration

Since the introduction of the book-tax conformity system in Spain, the CITA has always empowered the Tax Administration to assess the financial income according to the

---

27. Rule 3.5 of the *Resolución del Instituto de Contabilidad y Auditoría de Cuentas de 1 de marzo que diCITA normas de registro y valoración del inmovilizado material y de las inversiones inmobiliarias.*
28. As, for example, the one provided, before its reform, by § 5.1.2 of the German *Einkommensteuergesetzt* and according to which: '*Tax options for the purposes of the determination of the taxable base must be exercised in accordance with commercial accounts*'.
29. According to this provision: '*Expenses will not be deductible for tax purposes if they have not been recorded in the profit or loss account or, in those cases in which this might be allowed by legal provisions or regulations, in a reserves account, except as provided in this act for those assets that may be depreciated freely or according to accelerated methods*'. The Spanish Tax Administration has derived the existence of a formal book-tax conformity principle in the system according to this provision (Response to a consultation submitted by a tax payer to the Spanish General Tax Directorate on 27 July 1999). More recently, the Spanish Courts in the decisions of the *Audiencia Nacional* (hereinafter AN) of 9 December 2008 and *Tribunal Supremo (Supreme Court)* of 19 January 2012 decided in a similar way.
30. As defended in: Báez Moreno, Andrés. *Normas contables, supra* pp. 63-68.
31. Báez Moreno, Andrés. *Normas contables, supra* pp. 48-63.

applicable commercial accounting rules. According to the current formulation of this empowerment in Article 131 of the CITA 2014: *'For the sole purpose of determining the taxable base, the Tax Administration will apply all those rules referred to in Article 10.3 of this Act'*.[32] As previously reported, these rules embrace all those commercial accounting rules to which the CITA makes an explicit remission. In the old days, when the provision was first introduced in the Spanish system – together with the very institutionalization of the book-tax conformity – it caused quite a commotion amongst certain Spanish scholars who wanted to see the recognition of exorbitant powers for the Tax Administration in this rule and a consequent regression of tax payers' rights.[33] I have always been very critical of these alarmist voices believing that this empowerment is just the logical procedural consequence of the book-tax conformity system. Indeed, if commercial accounting rules integrate the provisions upon which the determination of the taxable base for CITA purposes is based, it seems logical that the Tax Administration should be enabled to control the proper application of these rules and, if required, correct it.[34] This does not necessarily imply that this empowerment is trouble-free, and at least three legal problems should be emphasized: (1) The fact that the tax administration is allowed to assess the financial income of the taxpayer does not mean that tax authorities may arbitrarily change accounting option rights attributed by commercial accounting provisions. On the contrary, as demonstrated in a previous work,[35] the vast majority of (supposed) accounting options cannot be considered unconditional and merely allow the accounting treatment of a transaction to be adapted according to the particular facts and circumstances of the case. An appropriate interpretation of this power can be illustrated with an example. According to the Spanish commercial accounting rules,[36] the cost of stock items and work in progress that are ordinarily interchangeable, shall be measured by using the first-in first-out (FIFO) or weighted-average cost method. As the latter method is labelled by these rules the *'general method'* and as FIFO is an *'acceptable method that might be used if the Company considers it more appropriate for its management'* all this could lead to the consideration that this amounts to an unconditioned option that the tax payer might exercise without any sort of administrative scrutiny. Nevertheless, in my view, the *true*

---

32. Some Spanish case law has seen a radical difference between the original wording of the provision, introduced in 1995 and applicable until 2001, and according to which *'For the sole purpose of determining the taxable base, the Tax Administration will determine the profit or loss for commercial accounting purposes applying all those rules referred to in article 10.3 of this Act'*. According to the decisions of the Spanish Supreme Court of 22 December 2011 and 17 and 31 January 2012 the new wording introduced in 2001 prevents the tax authorities from determining the profit or loss for commercial purposes being entitled only to adjust the taxable base. It is true that the reform in 2001 is difficult to understand. However, it is equally true that the interpretation defended by the Supreme Court does not make any sense.
33. Ferreiro Lapatza, José Juan. *Sobre la Ley 43/1995, de 27 de diciembre, del Impuesto sobre Sociedades*. /En/ Quincena Fiscal Aranzadi, n° 5, 1996, pp. 13-15. Esteban Marina, Ángel. *Impuesto sobre Sociedades: cálculo de la base imponible*. /En/ Carta Tributaria, n° 239-240, pp. 2-11.
34. Báez Moreno, Andrés. *Normas contables, supra* pp. 318-330.
35. Báez Moreno, Andrés. *Normas contables, supra* pp. 217-258.
36. *Norma de Valoración* (Valuation rule) 10ª 1.3 from the PGC 2007.

and fair view principle[37] may be crucial for determining the exercise of this option as far as the FIFO method might not be used if the physical flow of stock does not follow a FIFO pattern. I do not mean that the tax authorities might physically check this flow and exclude the FIFO method, but just that for certain goods or warehouses the FIFO pattern is simply unthinkable. A case in point would be the flow in a mine in which the ore is deposited physically on top of previous stock and, therefore, the first to be sold and removed is actually the last to have been stored ('last-in first-out' (LIFO) pattern).[38] Now, comparing the problem at stake with this example, I do not think that the tax authorities would be able to correct the financial statements by changing an option exercised by the tax payer in these cases in which the selected alternative clearly opposes the facts and circumstances of the case at hand. However, those options cannot always be considered as unconditional by the taxpayers.[39] (2) From the literal wording of the CITA, it is clear that the effects of this administrative calculation do not reach accounting figures for strictly commercial purposes as far as the application of accounting rules and principles is *for the sole purpose of determining the taxable base*. Even though this interpretation is undisputed in Spanish literature, certain conflicts have arisen on the secondary tax effects of this administrative prerogative. To this respect Tax Authorities have used Article 131 of the CITA to determine that a company is involved in a winding-up cause for Company Law purposes and subsequently excluded from the Tax Consolidation Regime according to the Corporate Tax Act.[40] Even if this position was initially accepted by the Tax Courts in Spain,[41] this interpretation was later overruled by those same Tax Courts[42] and more recently by the Spanish Supreme Court.[43] In short, the empowerment recognized under Article 131 of the CITA can be used exclusively to determine the tax base and not for other (Corporate Tax) purposes. (3) There is a general consensus in Spain that the Tax Administration is not bound by the contents or opinions of the audit report.[44] The strongest evidence of this

---

37. Its general and overriding function is recognized in Article 34.2 and 34.4 of the *Código de Comercio*.
38. The same rationale was used to deny the application of the LIFO method (acceptable according to the PGC 1990) to perishable goods. See Báez Moreno, Andrés. *Normas contables, supra* p. 237 and the German literature quoted there.
39. In the same way: Blázquez Lidoy, Alejandro. *La base imponible.* /En/ Impuesto sobre Sociedades (coord. Eva María Cordero González). Pamplona: Thomson Ruters-Civitas, 2010, p. 242. In disagreement with this position: Cobo de Guzmán Pisón, Juan. *La base...supra* p. 538.
40. According to Article 67.4.d of the Spanish CITA (before its 2015 version) a Company involved in a winding-up cause in accordance with Article 363.1.d) of the *Ley de Sociedades de Capital* (Law on Corporations) could not integrate a fiscal group for the purposes of the Tax Consolidation Regime.
41. Resolución del Tribunal Económico Administrativo Central (hereinafter TEAC) of 23 November 2006. The Spanish Tax Courts (*Tribunales Económico-Administrativos*) are not real Courts but a part of the Tax Administration.
42. Resoluciones del TEAC of 25 July 2005, 14 February 2008, and 3 July 2014.
43. Decision of the Supreme Court of 11 February 2013. It was the CITA 2014 which, in its Article 58.4.d), settled the controversy definitively.
44. Gota Losada, Alfonso. *La Base Imponible del Impuesto sobre Sociedades.* /En/ Documentos de Trabajo del Instituto de Estudios Fiscales, n° 29, 2003, p. 35. Cobo de Guzmán Pisón, Juan. *La base...supra* p. 538.

consensus is the almost entire absence of controversies regarding this relationship, but even in those strange cases in which the Courts have faced the problem, the submission of the Tax Administration to the opinions of the auditors has been a no-go from the start.[45]

§12.02   THE IMPACT OF IFRS ON FINANCIAL ACCOUNTING AND TAX CONSEQUENCES

Article 5 of the EU Regulation (EC) No. 1606/2002 of the European Parliament and of the Council of 19 July 2002 on the application of international accounting standards (hereinafter Regulation 1606/2002) gave Member States the option to permit or require publicly traded companies to prepare their annual accounts in conformity with International Accounting Standards (IAS) adopted in accordance with the procedures laid down in the Regulation and to extend this requirement to other companies as regards the preparation of their consolidated accounts and/or their annual accounts. Before making the final decision, the Spanish Authorities commissioned a report from a Committee of experts together with academics and practitioners on the situation of the Spanish Accounting System and guidelines for its reform.[46] Despite recognition of the benefits derived from an *en bloc* incorporation of IAS/IFRS[47] for the regulation of annual accounts of publicly traded companies and, in general, of large companies or companies integrated in consolidated groups,[48] the Report finally recommended, on the basis of strict legal considerations,[49] that annual accounts be further elaborated in accordance with the Spanish Accounting Standards. Nevertheless, the Report strongly recommended an in-depth reform of the Spanish Accounting system which was still based, in 2002, on a rather conservative (prudent) orientation of the annual accounts.

The outcome of this process of modernization was the Ley 16/2007, of 4th July.[50] This Act introduced some general rules and principles in the Spanish Commercial Code and, basically, implied the incorporation of the IASB Conceptual Framework for Financial Reporting in the Spanish legal system. Nevertheless, the core of the reform was the enactment of the PGC 2007, a Royal Decree which contains the detailed regulations of the Spanish Commercial Accounting regime. It is difficult to determine whether these new accounting rules are closer to the European accounting tradition or to the whole IAS/IFRS acquis. The new rules are based on two main principles:

---

45. More precisely, Decision of the *Tribunal Superior de Justicia de Madrid*, 18 July 2007.
46. *Informe sobre la situación actual de la contabilidad en España y líneas básicas para abordar su reforma (Libro Blanco para la reforma de la Contabilidad en España)*. Madrid: Instituto de Contabilidad y Auditoría de Cuentas, Madrid, 2002, 374 p.
47. Following the same pattern as for the consolidated accounts of listed groups.
48. *Informe sobre la situación actual ... supra* pp. 90-91.
49. One of the principal disadvantages of this *en bloc* incorporation, again according to the Report, would be that IAS/IFRS could not be used for tax accounting purposes (*Informe sobre la situación actual ... supra* pp. 91-92).
50. The so-called Act for the reform and adaptation of the national commercial accounting regulation for its international harmonization on the basis of the EU rules.

(1) IAS/IFRS are not incorporated *en bloc* in the Spanish commercial accounting rules; and (2) the new rules, as regards particularly the PGC, take the IAS/IFRS as a starting point. This international inspiration for the Spanish accounting rules explains why the PGC 2007 has been labelled as a *'Spanish version of IAS/IFRS'*.[51]

Amazingly enough, the accounting reform in 2007 did not provoke a deep revision of the book-tax conformity system in Spain. In fact, many of the reforms made in the deviation rules in the CITA are either just focused on purely terminological issues,[52] or merely state the validity of accounting rules for tax purposes[53] or, even imply a further approach to commercial and tax accounting rules,[54] The tax legislator's lack of reaction to a whole new accounting regime suggests that the idea, according to which accounting rules aimed essentially at information (IAS/IFRS) are better equipped for tax purposes than traditional rules targeted at the protection of creditors, may be right.[55]

However, this improved alignment of commercial and tax accounting rules must not lead us to think necessarily that the new normative landscape, as regards the relationship between commercial and tax accounting rules, is less complex than it was prior to the accounting reform of 2007. Even if it is true that certain problems disappeared, it is equally true that the reform, operated by the Spanish legislator, generated other highly problematic issues; we will focus on one of them that appears to be particularly worrying.

As stated before, the new accounting rules were supposed to take IAS/IFRS as a starting point. It is far from clear what this should mean in legal terms but it suggests that the Spanish commercial accounting rules should somehow be inspired by the concepts and solutions of IAS/IFRS. Even if this inspiration is undeniable in the current Spanish commercial accounting rules, one should not lose track of the fact that: (i) Sometimes the Spanish accounting rules deviate totally or partially from the

---

51. Calderón Carrero, José Manuel & Báez Moreno, Andrés. *La armonización contable europea. Las NIC/NIIF y su influencia en la base imponible del Impuesto sobre Sociedades.* /En/ Impuesto sobre Sociedades. Régimen General. Tomo I (Eduardo Sanfrutos Gambín, dir & Domingo Carbajo Vasco, coord.). 2ª edición. Pamplona: Thomson Reuters-Aranzadi-Ernst & Young Abogados, 2013, p. 109.
52. Like those referring to depreciation.
53. The taxability of *fair value revaluations* is explicitly recognized according to Law 16/2007. This recognition, without further analysis, seems particularly surprising taking into account the huge amount of concern generated by the taxation of non-realized income in literature. On this issue: Báez Moreno, Andrés. *El 'valor razonable' y la imposición societaria: un apunte sobre la idoneidad fiscal de las normas internacionales de información financiera.* /En/ Nueva Fiscalidad, 2006, nº 10. Báez Moreno, Andrés & Kaiser, Thomas. *Fair value' und die Körperschaftsteuer aus spanischer Sicht. Anmerkungen zur steuerlichen Geeignetheit der IFRS.* /En/ Steuer und Wirtschaft, Nr. 2., 2007.
54. This is the clear case of provisions. Under Article 13 of the CITA (until the accounting reform) just those provisions explicitly mentioned in the deviation rule were deductible for tax purposes. According to the new rule, introduced by Law 16/2007, all accounting provisions acceptable for commercial purposes were deductible with the exception of those mentioned explicitly in Article 13 of the CITA.
55. Defended – in minority – by this author in previous works: Báez Moreno, Andrés. *Normas contables, supra* pp. 467-470.

IAS/IFRS solution.[56] (ii) For a good number of reasons that would be too long to list here, the rules contained in IAS/IFRS go into much more detail than those of the Spanish commercial accounting regime. This will cause no problems if the local accounting rule is clear, as far as no resource to the 'inspiring rule' will be needed. However, in those frequent cases in which the Spanish accounting rule is either open to interpretation or contains a loophole, things may be more complicated.

These two possibilities – partial deviations from the IAS/IFRS regime and, especially, doubts over interpretation and loopholes in the Spanish commercial accounting rules – have recently generated two interesting legal problems:[57] (a) The role of IAS/IFRS rules for the interpretation and integration (loopholes) of Spanish GAAP. In principle, it might seem reasonable to exclude this role entirely, insofar as the Spanish legislator decided to elaborate an autonomous set of rules just affected in legal terms, by the European Accounting Directive.[58] Nevertheless, the practice in Spain, particularly that of the Tax Authorities, shows a clear de facto influence of IAS/IFRS in the interpretation of current Spanish GAAPs.[59] The most serious problem of this influence is the fact that the administrative practice seems to be inconsistent, giving rise to a sort of 'selective approach' according to which IAS/IFRS are only invoked when those rules seem to be in line with the interests of the Treasury. The Spanish Courts do not seem to be providing a strong response to this 'cherry-picking' approach. In a recent decision,[60] the Spanish Supreme Court stated that:

> IAS were not formally incorporated into our legal system until the enactment of the EU Regulation (EC) No 1606/2002 of the European Parliament and of the Council of 19th July 2002, being applicable as from January 1st 2005. Therefore, all references to IAS in 2002, the period under scrutiny, cannot be considered as applicable law; they can hardly be considered more than guiding principles of a future regulation.

This decision clearly excluded the application of IAS/IFRS in 2002,[61] but also clearly implies, *a contrario*, their crucial interpretative influence in 2005 and subsequent financial years. (b) It is established case law of the ECJ that where questions

---

56. To mention just one, but relevant example, IAS 38 forbids the capitalization of research expenses allowing it, under rather strict circumstances, for development expenses, whereas the Spanish accounting rule (Valuation Rule 6.a of the PGC 2007) allows the capitalization for both kinds of expenses. Further elaboration on this difference and its consequences in: Calderón Carrero, José Manuel & Báez Moreno, Andrés. *La armonización contable ... supra* pp. 153-154.
57. More in depth on both issues in: Calderón Carrero, José Manuel & Báez Moreno, Andrés. *La armonización contable ... supra* pp. 140-155.
58. This also seems to be the position of the Spanish Accounting regulator (*Instituto de Contabilidad y Auditoría de Cuentas*) who in a Decision issued in 2008 (BOICAC núm. 74/2008) literally stated: ' ... *in the absence of a rule or interpretation in the Spanish GAAP, the directors should use their professional judgement in order to define a criterion for interpretation that is as respectful as possible to the Framework contained in the PGC and the Spanish GAAP'*.
59. See: Calderón Carrero, José Manuel & Báez Moreno, Andrés. *La armonización contable ... supra* pp. 146-147.
60. Decision of the Spanish Supreme Court of 6 November 2014.
61. Contradicting previous decisions of the ECJ, even if not mentioned explicitly. In its decision of 7 January 2003 (C-306/99, *BIAO*) the Court indicated: 'As for the questions seeking to obtain clarification regarding the criteria for assessing the degree of likelihood of a risk, the legitimacy

submitted by national courts concern the interpretation of a provision of Community law, the Court is, in principle, obliged to give a ruling. According to the ECJ, neither the wording of the Treaty nor the aim of the procedure indicates that the Treaty makers intended to exclude requests for a preliminary ruling on a Community provision from the jurisdiction of the Court where the domestic law of a Member State refers to that Community provision in order to determine the rules applicable to a situation which is purely internal to that State. Applying that case law, the Court has repeatedly held that it has jurisdiction to give preliminary rulings on questions concerning Community provisions in situations where the facts of the cases being considered by the national courts are outside the scope of Community law, but the provisions have been rendered applicable either by domestic law or merely by virtue of terms in a contract (*Dzodzi case law*).[62] However, in its *Kleinwort Benson* decision, the Court observed that, unlike the situation in the previous line of cases, the provisions of EU-Law which the Court was asked to interpret had not been rendered applicable as such by the law of the contracting State concerned. The Court pointed out that the Act of Parliament in question took EU-Law only as a model and only partially reproduced its terms, thus denying its jurisdiction (*Kleinwort* exception).[63] This case law of the ECJ has been subject to harsh criticism both from scholars and Advocates General.[64] Leaving this criticism to one side, the truth is that the option of the Spanish legislator raises a doubt as to whether the ECJ would admit a preliminary question in relation to a provision contained in Spanish GAAP and based upon IAS/IFRS endorsed in EU-Law for the purposes of EU Regulation 1606/2002. In short, the doubt is whether these '*Spanish IAS/IFRS*' follow a '*Dzodzi*' or rather a '*Kleinwort*' structure. I myself believe that the boundaries between those structures are not at all clear according to the current case law of the ECJ[65] and, therefore, a clear conclusion might prove difficult to achieve but, in any case, the aim here was just to point out the legal difficulties created by the peculiar way of introducing IAS/IFRS in Spain as regards individual accounts.

---

of taking country risk and the risk of insolvency into account simultaneously, and the ways of avoiding risks being taken into account twice over, it is sufficient to point out that the Fourth Directive merely sets out general principles without seeking to regulate all their possible applications. In the absence of such particulars, *that assessment is a matter for national law, read, where appropriate, in the light of the international accounting standards (IAS) as they are applied at the time of the facts in the main proceedings*, provided always that the general principles set out by the Fourth Directive, as referred to in paragraphs 72 to 75 of this judgement, are fully complied with'. Even if I do not think that the Spanish Supreme Court even considered this previous decision, I also believe that, in the end, the Court got it right as the BIAO decision, as regards this particular issue, was simply wrong from a legal perspective.

62. This position of the ECJ is actually not confined to tax law cases; nevertheless, it is also true that in the field of tax law this case law has acquired increasing significance. See: Calderón Carrero, José Manuel & Báez Moreno, Andrés. *La armonización contable ... supra* pp. 11-125.
63. Decision of 28 March 1995, C-346/93, *Kleinwort Benson*.
64. I myself have been very critical in this regard: Báez Moreno, Andrés. *Normas contables, supra* pp. 442-447. Calderón Carrero, José Manuel & Báez Moreno, Andrés. *La armonización contable ... supra* pp. 125-140.
65. Calderón Carrero, José Manuel & Báez Moreno, Andrés. *La armonización contable ... supra* p. 130.

§12.03   THE CCCTB

To the best of my knowledge, there has been no academic work in Spain comparing the CCCTB rules[66] and the corresponding Spanish national Tax Base for CIT purposes.[67] The work has focused so far on either a descriptive approach to the CCCTB proposal itself or a critical revision of the project all together or of specific rules contained in the proposal.

In the following paragraphs I will try to describe briefly the fundamental differences between those sets of rules, bearing in mind that a comprehensive, detailed comparison is well beyond the scope and aim of this Report. Two main groups of differences must be highlighted for the sake of clarity:

(1) Differences in the legal structure to determine the taxable base. As described in section §12.01[A], the taxable base for CIT purposes in Spain follows a partial book-tax conformity system, according to which Spanish GAAP become part of the set of rules to determine this taxable base, but the CITA regulates a significant number of deviation rules. Under the CCCTB proposal, the approach is from a radically different starting point inasmuch as it introduces autonomous rules for computing the tax base of companies.[68] This seemingly formal difference has far-reaching implications as regards interpretative and procedural issues of both sets of rules.[69] Of course this does not mean that the final solution to a specific problem offered by the CCCTB proposal and the Spanish rules need necessarily be different; if the rule for CCCTB purposes and the Spanish GAAP or CITA deviation rule coincide there would be no significant differences, at least at first glance. As we will verify below this coincidence is not uncommon.

(2) Differences in specific registration, valuation or timing issues. At a very general normative level, the principles upon which the CCCTB is based (realization, separated valuation and consistency[70]) do not differ significantly from those inspiring the Spanish GAAP[71] and accepted for CITA purposes

---

66. I refer to the Proposal for a Council Directive on a Common Consolidated Corporate Tax Base (CCCTB) COM(2011) 121/4 2011/0058 (CNS) (hereinafter CCCTB proposal).
67. Perhaps with one exception: Mora Aguado, Leonor (et al.). Base imponible común consolidada v. normativa fiscal española: *una aproximación a su impacto fiscal.* /In/ Crónica Tributaria, nº 144, 2012, pp. 89-110.
68. As stated in the Explanatory Memorandum of the Project: 'Harmonization will only involve the computation of the tax base and will not interfere with financial accounts. Therefore, Member States will maintain their national rules on financial accounting and the *CCCTB system will introduce autonomous rules for computing the tax base of companies. These rules shall not affect the preparation of annual or consolidated accounts'.*
69. See, in this respect, the problems of the current Spanish system described in section §12.02. Of course, these problems could also arise in the context of the CCCTB proposal – although in a more moderate manner – if the proposed rules were to be considered based upon IAS/IFRS.
70. Article 9 of the CCCTB proposal.
71. All those principles are also recognized by the Spanish Commercial Accounting Rules (Article 38 of the Spanish Commercial Code, and Rule 3, Part I of the PGC 2007).

according to the rules described above. From the foregoing, it may be wrongly concluded that identical principles lead to identical or very similar detailed rules. This is obviously not the case. (Tax) accounting principles provide just a basis for a further specification of accounting rules and might serve in addition to resolve interpretative issues.[72] However, two (tax) accounting systems might evolve with very different rules departing from identical principles. We might illustrate this statement with a case in point regarding the different development of the realization principle both in the CCCTB proposal and the Spanish taxable base. According to both systems, profits shall be recognized only when realized.[73] Both systems also give a very similar rule on when revenues might accrue and might, therefore, be recognized for (tax) accounting purposes: it is when the right to receive them arises and they can be quantified with reasonable accuracy, regardless of whether the actual payment is deferred.[74] Nevertheless, departing from the same principle and giving a very similar definition of accrual, both systems reach diametrically opposed results as regards long-term contracts – i.e., a contract concluded for the purpose of manufacturing, installation or construction or the performance of services whose term exceeds, or is expected to exceed, twelve months.[75] While Article 24.2 of the CCCTB proposal imposes that revenues relating to a long-term contract shall be recognized, for tax purposes, at the amount corresponding to the part of the contract completed in the respective tax year (so-called *Percentage of Completion Method*), the Spanish system adheres unconditionally to the general timing rule considering that the revenues do not accrue until the contract has been fulfilled and the construction or asset has been delivered to the purchaser (*Completed Contract Method*).[76] This is just an example of how identical principles, even those such as realization, that have a precise content,[77] might result in very different rules.

However, having said that, there are significant coincidences between the CCCTB proposal and the Spanish rules on the CIT taxable base as regards elements of the tax

---

72. As stated by Freedman & Macdonald '[...] *(principles) will apply at three stages in formulating and implementing a tax system: first the policy stage of setting the overall tax objectives, second at the design and legislative stage of determining the tax structure and setting the rules and third, at the stage of interpreting and applying the tax rules'* (J. Freedman & G. Macdonald. *The Tax Base for CCCTB: The Role of Principles.*In *Common Consolidated Corporate Tax Base* (M. Lang, P. Pistone, J. Schuch & C. Staringer eds, Wien: Linde, 2008) p. 221).
73. Article 9.1 of the CCCTB proposal and Article 38.c) of the Spanish Commercial Code.
74. Article 18 of the CCCTB proposal and Valuation Rule 14.2 of the PGC 2007.
75. According to the definition contained in Article 24.1 of the CCCTB proposal.
76. Even if, in my view, this is not the correct approach according to the Spanish GAAP, the Spanish Accounting regulator (*Instituto de Contabilidad y Auditoría de Cuentas*) has defended this interpretation. On this particular problem see: Zornoza Pérez, Juan José & Báez Moreno, Andrés. *Modelos comparados ... supra* pp. 452-453.
77. Let alone for other (tax) accounting principles with a more ambiguous legal content.

base (such as non-deductible expenses[78] or provisions[79]), timing (such as rules on accrual of revenues and incurrence of deductible expenses[80]) and valuation issues (such as general rules on measurement of transactions[81] or valuation rules for stock and work-in-progress[82]). Despite these coincidences, there are also crucial disparities between the systems.[83] However, the most interesting phenomenon in this respect might be the dramatic separation of the CIT taxable base and the Spanish GAAP that has occurred over the last few years. As mentioned before, since 2011, the Spanish CITA has experienced an exponential growth of deviation rules, theoretically aimed at the prevention of tax evasion and avoidance; these new special tax accounting rules not only take [...] the taxable base even further away from the Spanish GAAP, but also from the CCCTB proposal. In this respect, the limitation or prohibition on the deduction for tax purposes of impairments of tangible assets, intangible assets, immovable property, equity and debt financial instruments, customer or suppliers care expenses, severance payments and, most importantly, financial expenses, strongly contrast with the current rules of the CCCTB proposal, firmly based upon the 'net taxation principle' and, therefore, granting a deduction, prima facie, for whatever costs of sales and expenses are incurred by the taxpayer with a view to obtaining or securing income.[84] In short, it might well be said that the greatest difference between the CCCTB rules and the current Spanish system, is that the former strictly respects the 'net taxation

---

78. With several nuances, the list of non-deductible expenses in the CCCTB proposal (Article 14) and the Spanish CITA (Article 15) share common features.
79. Even if Article 14 of the Spanish CITA introduces several restrictions for the deduction of particular kinds of provisions, the general rule is of deductibility, and the concept of provision is very similar in the Spanish GAAP and the CCCTB proposal (Article 25) both being definitions clearly influenced by IAS 37.
80. With several nuances, one of which has already been mentioned before, the rules on this crucial problem are very similar in the CCCTB proposal (Articles 17-19) and the Spanish CITA (Article 11).
81. The general historic value rule (price of acquisition or cost of production) supplemented by a market value rule for certain transactions (wholly or partly non-monetary transactions and gifts made or received by a tax payer) and financial assets and liabilities held for trading are almost identical in the CCCTB proposal (Articles 22 and 23) and the Spanish CITA (Article 17).
82. The rules contained in the CCCTB proposal (Article 29) and the Spanish GAAP (Valuation Rule 10.1.3 of the PGC) on this issue (individual measurement and FIFO or weighted-average cost method for ordinarily interchangeable goods or services) are actually identical.
83. The disparities have always been very clear as regards depreciation rules. The CCCTB proposal imposes the depreciation on a straight-line basis (Article 36.1) whereas the Spanish tax rules also allow non-linear methods of depreciation (Article 12.1 of the CITA). The Spanish rules contemplate a good number of assets that might be depreciated without restrictions (actually a tax incentive for certain kinds of transactions or undertakings); these allowances do not exist under the CCCTB proposal. Finally, Article 39 of the CCCTB proposal contemplates an asset pool for depreciation purposes which is totally alien to the Spanish tax depreciation rules.
84. In this regard: deductibility of 50% of entertainment costs (Article 14.1.b of the CCCTB proposal), non-deductibility of costs incurred by a company for the purpose of deriving income which is exempt (Article 14.1.g of the CCCTB proposal) – instead of a lump sum non-deductibility of financial expenses as contemplated in the Spanish CITA (Article 17), deductibility of impairments of financial assets and liabilities held for trading (trading book), (Article 23.2 of the CCCTB proposal), deductibility of impairments of stock and work in progress (Article 29.4 of the CCCTB proposal), and impairments of fixed assets (Article 41 of the CCCTB proposal) even if, in this last case, the content of the rule is not clear at all.

principle', introducing very targeted special anti-avoidance or anti-evasion rules when necessary,[85] whereas the Spanish CITA is based upon a radical lack of faith in different and crucial categories of expenses and, in general, in impairments; this distrust leads to upfront prohibitions or severe limitations for deductions.

§12.04 FISCAL ASPECTS OF THE NEW DIRECTIVE 2013/34/EU

At the time of writing this chapter, Spain has not yet transposed the Directive 2013/34/EU. Nevertheless, the rumour has spread in professional circles that the Spanish Accounting Regulator (*ICAC*) is still considering a new *Plan Contable para PYMES* (Accounting Plan for Small and Medium-Sized Enterprises) Of course the details remain unknown, but some possible contents of this new regulation have been leaked to the public. On the basis of these potential amendments we will try to identify the tax effects[86] of this future reform:

(1) The depreciation of goodwill in a period that shall not be shorter than five years and shall not exceed ten years. This change might be crucial for commercial accounting purposes in Spain, inasmuch as, in the current situation, the depreciation of goodwill is not allowed.[87] Nevertheless, its importance for the taxable base of the CIT will be less significant insofar as the CITA has always contemplated the depreciation of goodwill,[88] for tax purposes, even after the accounting reform of 2007 when the current accounting rule was first introduced. If the Spanish legislator (re)introduces this rule, the final outcome will be rather shocking: goodwill will be depreciated (in five to ten years) and impaired (without reversal) for commercial accounting purposes; for tax purposes it will be depreciated (in twenty years or more) and never impaired. Whether or not these different useful lives are justified might depend very much on the very concept and legal nature of goodwill itself;[89] what is clear though, to give a clear example, is that the Spanish legislator is

---

85. For example the rule, already mentioned above, on entertainment costs or the special rule on expenditure incurred for the benefit of shareholders, contained in Article 15 of the CCCTB proposal.
86. We will focus on 'material changes' and leave formal issues apart, such as simplified presentation layouts for the balance sheet and the profit or loss account, reduction of the information required for the notes to the financial statements and the suppression of the statement of changes in equity all referred to small and medium-sized enterprises. It must be stated, however, that most of these material changes are not in fact a result of innovations in the Directive but just the result of the Spanish legislator holding back from some of the rules introduced in the Accounting Reform of 2007 and actually not imposed by the Directive, but inspired by the idea of a convergence with IAS/IFRS.
87. According to Article 39.4 of the Commercial Code.
88. According to Article 13.3 of the CITA, goodwill will be depreciated in a period that shall not be shorter than 20 years. From the beginning of 2015 the CITA (Article 13.2.a) has made it clear that impairments of goodwill (that have always been deductible for commercial accounting purposes) will not be deductible for tax purposes. Before this rule was introduced in 2014 this was a contended issue in the Spanish practice.
89. On the nature of this peculiar intangible: Báez Moreno, Andrés. *Normas contables, supra* pp. 170-171.

stating implicitly that if a renowned company that produces beverages is found to be using dioxins in its production, this will only affect its sales but not its goodwill, at least for tax accounting purposes. This outcome is certainly untenable, but it is just a clear reflection of the distrust in which the Spanish legislator seems to have been involved recently.

(2) Capitalization of formation expenses (start-up costs).[90] After the Spanish Accounting Reform in 2007, these expenditures, which had traditionally been capitalized according to Spanish Commercial and Tax Accounting Rules, had to be deducted immediately when incurred;[91] as long as the rules in the CITA did not mention these expenses, the rule also applied for tax accounting purposes. Even if this is not a direct consequence of the new Accounting Directive,[92] it seems the Spanish legislator will use the transposition to restore the traditional capitalization of these expenses. The convenience, for commercial and tax accounting purposes, of this 'ideal asset' is in fact a very old question that I have considered in more detail in previous works.[93]

(3) Cost of stock items and work in progress that are ordinarily interchangeable. As a result of the Spanish Accounting Reform in 2007, a new rule was introduced according to which the cost of stock items and work in progress that are ordinarily interchangeable, shall be measured using the first-in first-out (FIFO) or weighted-average cost method.[94] Up until then, and following the rule contained in the Directive,[95] other methods, such as LIFO or similar, had also been admitted by the traditional Spanish Accounting rules. Apparently, the Spanish legislator will use the transposition of Directive 2013/34/EU to restore the traditional rule and make LIFO or any method reflecting generally accepted best practice available. Inasmuch as the Spanish CITA has never contemplated particular rules on this issue, the new methods will also be admitted for tax accounting purposes. Readers are referred to a previous work by the author on these options and the particular problems of the LIFO method for tax accounting purposes.[96]

As can be seen from the previous statements, apart from merely formal (purely informative) changes and some steps backwards, with regard to some amendments

---

90. This is the term used traditionally by the IV Directive (in Directive 2013/34/EU see Article 12.11.4). They are commonly known in the profession as start-up costs.
91. According to Valuation Rule 5.1 of the PGC 2007.
92. The rule on the capitalization of these expenses has not actually changed since the original version of the IV Directive: '*Where national law authorizes the inclusion of formation expenses under "Assets", they must be written off within a maximum period of five years*'.
93. Báez Moreno, Andrés. *Normas contables, supra* pp. 172 et seq. Báez Moreno, Andrés & Zornoza Pérez, Juan José. *Definition of Assets and Capitalization Problems for CCCTB Purposes*. In *Common Consolidated Corporate Tax Base* (M. Lang, P. Pistone, J. Schuch & C. Staringer eds, Wien: Linde, 2008) pp. 294-295.
94. Valuation rule 10.1.3 of the PGC 2007.
95. Article 40.1 of Directive 78/660/EEC (now Article 12.9 of Directive 2013/34/EU).
96. Báez Moreno, Andrés. *Normas contables, supra* pp. 232-241.

introduced in 2007,[97] the transposition of the new Accounting Directive will not dramatically affect current tax accounting rules in Spain. There is a change though in the Directive to which the Spanish legislator does not seem to be paying further attention; we refer to the *substance over form* principle now contained in Article 6 of Directive 2013/34/EU as a 'General financial reporting principle'.[98] There is a very easy explanation for this failure to address the issue: the substance over form principal in commercial accounting had already been incorporated in Spanish Law in the Accounting Reform of 2007. According to Article 34.2 of the Spanish Commercial Code: '*Transactions must be accounted according to their substance and not just according to their legal form*'. This 'new principle', either in its premature incorporation in the Spanish GAAP or in its current recognition under Directive 2013/34/EU, demands further clarification:

(1) In my view, an explicit recognition of the substance over form principle was not necessary, either in the domestic law of a Member State or at the level of the Directive, inasmuch as it could be directly inferred from the *true and fair view principle*[99] (hereinafter TFV) and especially from the so-called *true and fair view override* (TFO).[100] Even if this may be contended among European scholars, TFV and TFO amalgamate, in my view, three different legal mandates: to interpret accounting rules according to the purpose of these provisions;[101] to limit the options granted by accounting rules if the selected alternative is not consistent with a true and fair view of the undertaking's assets, liabilities, financial position and profit or loss;[102] and, finally, to override (disapply) a commercial accounting provision when its strict application results in an abusive outcome.[103] There may be several reasons why these well-known legal instruments (purposive interpretation, restriction of

---

97. In fact all the amendments made in 2007 were not a result of changes in the Directives but only an intent to make the Spanish GAAP converge with IAS/IFRS.

98. According to Article 6.1.h of the Directive: '*... items in the profit and loss account and balance sheet shall be accounted for and presented having regard to the substance of the transaction or arrangement concerned*'.

99. Contained in both, Directive 78/660/EEC (Article 2.3) and Directive 2013/34/EU (Article 4.3) with the following wording: '*The annual financial statements shall give a true and fair view of the undertaking's assets, liabilities, financial position and profit or loss*'.

100. Contained in both Directive 78/660/EEC (Article 2.5) and Directive 2013/34/EU (Article 4.4) with the following wording: '*Where in exceptional cases the application of a provision of this Directive is incompatible with the obligation laid down in paragraph 3, that provision shall be disapplied in order to give a true and fair view of the undertaking's assets, liabilities, financial position and profit or loss. The disapplication of any such provision shall be disclosed in the notes to the financial statements together with an explanation of the reasons for it and of its effect on the undertaking's assets, liabilities, financial position and profit or loss*'.

101. Further elaboration on this first function in: Báez Moreno, Andrés. *Normas contables, supra* pp. 381-385; Calderón Carrero, José Manuel & Báez Moreno, Andrés. *La armonización contable ... supra* pp. 137-140.

102. Further elaboration on this second function in: Báez Moreno, Andrés. *Normas contables, supra* pp. 402-415.

103. Further elaboration on this third function in: Báez Moreno, Andrés. *El caso GIMLE: una nueva oportunidad perdida para aclarar el sentido del principio de imagen fiel y sus consecuencias fiscales. /En/ Revista Técnica Tributaria*, n° 106, 2014, pp. 29-52.

options, and anti-avoidance rules) were merged and framed with the rather untelling expressions, at least according to the European legal tradition, of TFV and TFO[104] but, in any case, what is quite clear is that, having a TFO at the level of the Directive and/or domestic law renders the additional codification of the *substance over form* principle useless and confusing.[105]

(2) Even if previous decisions of the ECJ as regards TFV,[106] strongly indicated a bias of the Court towards a broad interpretation of TFO – as a powerful anti-avoidance device – the recent decision in the GIMLE case[107] seems to suggest quite the opposite. In a case in which associated companies manipulated the prices in several transfers of shares, in order to shift profits to Belgium and thereby gain a tax exemption on the capital gains, the Court clearly stated that: *'the principle that a true and fair view must be given, set out in Article 2(3) to (5) of the Fourth Directive, does not permit the principle of valuation of assets on the basis of their acquisition price or their production cost, contained in Article 32 of that directive, to be departed from in favour of a valuation on the basis of their real value, where the acquisition price or the production cost of those assets is manifestly lower than their real value'.*[108] It is true that the decision itself poses serious arguable defects;[109] but it is by no means less true that it also seriously questions the role and practical relevance of the TFV and its corollaries, the TFO/substance over form principle.

(3) Whatever the content and scope of the TFO/substance over form principle might be for strict commercial accounting proposals, in those systems, such as the Spanish one, based upon a partial book-tax conformity rule, its tax consequences should be limited or none at all. As stated before, the Spanish CITA has always regulated a significant amount of deviations for tax accounting purposes. In my view, those deviations should not be limited to the ones explicitly contained in the CITA; if, as is the case in Spain and other countries following a partial book-tax conformity system, a statutory (Tax) General Anti-Avoidance Rule[110] (GAAR) exists, then abuses, even at a purely commercial accounting level, must be corrected when determining the taxable base of CIT resorting to said GAAR, and not by means of the TFO or the general substance over form principle. This would refrain Tax Authorities

---

104. As the cohabitation of different legal traditions in Europe and the importance of the profession in standard setting is the most relevant; see: Grossfeld, Bernhard. *Common Roots of the European Law of Accounting.* In International Lawyer, n° 4, 1989, p. 871. Alexander, David & Eberhartinger, Eva. *The True and Fair View in the European Union.* In European Accounting Review, n° 3, 2009, p. 575.

105. A clear and additional sign of the confusion, among the drafters of Directive 2013/34/EU, is the fact that Article 6.3 of the same now envisages the possibility for Member States to exempt undertakings from the requirements of the substance over form principle. It is evident that if TFO and substance over form actually embody an anti-avoidance device, this exemption does not make any sense.

106. C-275/97 *DE + ES Bauunternehmung*; C-306/99 *BIAO*; and especially C-234/94, *Tomberger*.

107. C-322/12 *État belge v. GIMLE SA.*

108. C-322/12 *État belge v. GIMLE SA*, paragraph 42.

109. Báez Moreno, Andrés. *El caso GIMLE...supra* pp. 31-52.

110. Contained in Article 15 of the Spanish *Ley General Tributaria* (General Tax Code).

from leaving the GAAR apart and opting for the easy way out of the TFO/substance over form principle which might be procedurally easier, practically lacks conditions of applicability[111] and, in many cases, as opposed to GAARs, entails the imposition of tax fines or might even result in criminal offences.

---

111. As defended elsewhere: 'Substance over form is just the description of a legal consequence according to which two substantially equal arrangements, regardless of their legal form, must be treated equally for tax purposes. With this approach, the technique does not differ essentially from analogy or the general constitutional principle of equality. It does not differ either from the legal consequences of the GAAR as previously described. The difference, and this is the crucial issue, lies in the fact that substance over form lacks legal conditions of application; formulated as a question: what must happen in order to disregard the legal form and tax the arrangement according to its substance? Substance over form works more as a principle than as a rule' (Báez, Andrés & Zornoza, Juan José. 'General Anti-Avoidance Rules (GAARs) – A Key Element of Tax Systems in the Post-BEPS Tax World?' Spanish Report. (http://papers.ssrn.com/sol3/papers.cfm?abstract_id = 2559817 accessed 9 June 2015).

CHAPTER 13

Accounting and Taxation: UK

Simon James

§13.01   ACCOUNTING AND TAXATION IN THE UK

[A]   Definition of the Tax Base for a UK Company

In general, corporation tax is levied on companies resident in the UK and on other companies on their profits generated in the UK. The tax base of a company is the company's income and chargeable capital gains calculated in accordance with the relevant legislation, case law, administrative statements of practice and extra-statutory concessions. The primary legislation relating to corporation tax was formerly found in the Taxes Act 1988. This has now been rewritten as part of the Tax Law Rewrite project set up to make tax legislation 'clearer and easier to use, without changing or making less certain its general effect'[1] and is now included in the Corporation Tax Act 2009, the Corporation Tax Act 2010 and the Taxation (International and Other Provisions) Act 2010 though other legislation may also be relevant.

   The precise definition of the tax base is, of course, complex. In addition it should be noted that the definition of the tax base may be modified by the UK Government's plans regarding the reform of corporation tax. Some of these are described in the Government's 'road map' for corporation tax as laid out in a policy paper published by

---

1. Antony Seely, *Tax Law Rewrite: The Final Bills*, House of Commons Library, Standard Note SN5239, 21 April 2010, p. 1, available at: *researchbriefings.files.parliament.uk/documents/ SN05239/SN05239.pdf (accessed 3 January 2016).*

HM Treasury in 2010.[2] This chapter states that there are four main ways in which business is affected by the corporation tax system namely:

- The main rate of corporation tax.
- The definition of the tax base.
- The quality of tax policy development.
- The administration and collection of corporation tax.

In terms of the definition of the tax base this chapter states:[3]

> The definition of the corporation tax base is important as it determines the burden placed on businesses to compute their liabilities and also the scope and reach of the UK tax system. As such it has a significant impact on the decisions of global business based and investing here. The Government wants to deliver a simpler tax system and ensure that the corporation tax system continues to place a relatively low compliance burden on business. In addition, its aim of creating the most competitive corporate tax system in the G20 means it should look at areas where the UK legislation is uncompetitive or where it has not kept pace with wider developments. Two particular areas where business has concerns are the taxation of income that is earned abroad and income from intellectual property (IP).[4]

Progress was made by the Government of 2010 to 2015 as described and evaluated, for example, by the Oxford University Centre for Business Taxation.[5] Perhaps the most high profile change related to the rates rather than the tax base with a series of reductions in the main rate of corporation tax taking it from 28% in 2010 to 20% in 2015. However, there were also developments regarding the tax base, for example with respect to writing-down allowances for plant and machinery, the annual investment allowance and the controlled foreign company regime. Further changes are to come. Following the general election in May 2015 the new Government reaffirmed its support for reform in the subsequent Summer Budget Statement[6] which announced that a new business tax road map will be published in 2016 and this will set out plans for business tax reform over the period of the new Parliament – that is to 2020. Furthermore in 2015 the Office of Tax Simplification began a review of the taxation of smaller companies with the aim of simplifying the system and this may also have implications for the tax base.[7]

---

2. HM Treasury, The Corporate Tax Road Map, 2010, available at: https://www.gov.uk/govern ment/uploads/system/uploads/attachment_data/file/193239/Corporation_tax_road_map.pdf (accessed 10 January 2016).
3. *Ibid.* paragraph 1.5.
4. *Ibid.* paragraph 1.7.
5. Giorgia Maffini (eds) *Business Taxation under the Coalition Government*, Oxford University Centre for Business Taxation, 2015, available at: https://www.sbs.ox.ac.uk/sites/default/files/ Business_Taxation/Docs/Publications/Reports/cbt-coalition-report-final.pdf (accessed 10 January 2015).
6. HM Treasury, *Summer Budget 2015*, HC 264, paragraph 1.244.
7. Office of Tax Simplification, simplification review of small company taxation, further information available at: https://www.gov.uk/government/publications/ots-review-of-small-company-taxa tion-tor (accessed 22 January 2016).

[B]   The Connection between the Tax Base and Financial Accounting

The relationship between accounting principles and taxation in the UK has been examined before and is more complex than may at first appear.[8] This may be partly because in the UK financial accounting has developed more independently from tax legislation than in some other countries.[9] As Nobes and Parker[10] make clear, tax legislation has only a small effect on financial reporting by companies in the UK and it is not a major consideration in the preparation of unconsolidated financial statements as it is in many parts of continental Europe. However, the connection between the tax base and financial accounting is also complex because the basic nature and purpose of both accounting and taxation are different – as examined in section §13.01[E] below. Furthermore, accounting is in a continual process of development. Sir Thomas Bingham put it well in the case of *Gallagher v. Jones*[11] with respect to accepted principles of commercial accountancy by saying that: 'as has often been pointed out, such principles are not static: they may be modified, refined and elaborated over time as circumstances change and accounting insights happen.'

Cases form an important part of the UK tax system and accounting principles are often accepted for the purposes of taxation. Again, as Sir Thomas Bingham suggested in *Gallagher v. Jones:*[12]

> I find it hard to understand how any judge-made rule could override the applica-tion of a generally accepted rule of commercial accountancy which (a) applied to the situation in question (b) is not one of two or more rules applicable to the situation and (c) was not shown to be inconsistent with the true facts or otherwise inapt to determine the true profits of losses of the business.

The UK situation is that financial statements are usually the starting point for taxation but the figures are modified by the requirements of tax legislation. For example, the depreciation of capital assets is an important inclusion in financial accounts but in the UK it is not deductible against taxable income. Instead companies can claim capital allowances, the rates of which are laid down by law. There may be other divergences between accounting and taxation for matters such as the timing of receipts and when unpaid accounts become allowable as bad debts. Another example is that in running a business all legitimate costs should be deducted before profits are calculated but in the UK some costs such as those incurred in entertaining customers are disallowed for tax purposes. The original reason for this seems to have been to

---

8. For example, see Simon James, 'The Relationship between Accounting Principles and Taxation: A UK Perspective', *Asia-Pacific Journal of Taxation*, 2002, 6(3), 84-97.
9. Margaret Lamb, 'The Relationship between Accounting and Tax: The United Kingdom'. *European Accounting Review*, 1996(5) 1996, 933-949 and Margaret Lamb, Christopher Nobes and Alan Roberts, 'International Variations in the Connections between Tax and Financial Reporting'. *Accounting and Business Research*, 1998, 28(3), 173-188.
10. Christopher Nobes and Robert Parker, *Comparative International Accounting*, 12th ed., Pearson, 2012.
11. [1993] STC 537 at 555.
12. [1993] STC 537 at 555-556.

prevent extravagance and tax avoidance but such expenses could be very important to the commercial success of the company.

There are also, of course, changes taking place as the former UK GAAP is being replaced by new arrangements influenced by International Financial Reporting Standards (IFRS) and these are summarized in section §13.02 below.

[C]   Theoretical Justifications for the Connection between Income Taxation and Financial Accounting

There are theoretical justifications for linking taxation and financial accounting. Clearly in terms of efficiency it is preferable to have the same figures serve more than one purpose provided there are no compelling reasons why they should be different. Furthermore, using the same figures might make taxation simpler and therefore perhaps more acceptable to taxpayers as well as saving administrative and compliance costs.[13]

A related argument is certainty in taxation. Macdonald[14] set out the issue as to whether it is possible to increase certainty in the tax system 'by legislating for accounting principles which are appropriate for tax purposes and not inconsistent with those on which accounting practice is based.'

A further theoretical justification is that a single set of figures might reduce the scope for taxpayers to manipulate them for the purposes of avoiding tax.

Another justification relates to advantages of taxation being more aligned with the realities of business so that the government shares fairly in both profits and losses.[15] This requires the tax system to take account of genuine business losses as well as profits as far as possible.

[D]   Calculation of the Tax Base

In the UK the calculation can often be a complex process not only because tax legislation is very detailed but also because case law is extensive. The UK tax authority, HM Revenue and Customs (HMRC),[16] also issues a large number of statements of practice and extra-statutory concessions which may be relevant to the calculation of chargeable profits.

---

13. Simon James, Adrian Sawyer and Tamer Budak (eds) *The Complexity of Tax Simplification: Experiences from Around the World*, Palgrave Macmillan, 2016.
14. Graeme Macdonald, *The Taxation of Business Income: Aligning Taxable Income with Accounting Income*, 2002, Tax Law Review Committee Discussion Paper No. 2, p. 52, available at: http://www.ifs.org.uk/comms/dp2.pdf (accessed 6 January 2016).
15. See, for example, Richard A. Musgrave and Peggy B. Musgrave, *Public Finance in Theory and Practice*, McGraw-Hill, 1989, 5th ed., Chapter 17, section C.
16. Further information is available at https://www.gov.uk/government/organisations/hm-revenue-customs (accessed 2 January 2016).

[E] Differences between Financial and Tax Accounting

Although it might be thought that the calculation of variables such as income, expenditure and profits should be the same for both accounting and taxation, this is not always true. Different figures might be appropriate in different circumstances[17] and tax systems and financial reporting have different purposes.[18] Taxation is raised, of course, to pay for public expenditure but such is the pervasiveness of taxation in modern economies that it may also be used as an instrument for a whole range of government policies such as the redistribution of wealth and other social objectives, to influence the economy and for political purposes. In terms of principles, a good tax system should be economically efficient, equitable, certain and not unduly costly to administer and comply with[19] but sometimes there are tensions between such criteria and government objectives which may result in even more complications for the tax system.[20] In contrast, the general purpose of financial accounting is to provide information for the purposes of control and decision-making. It is important to a range of interests – managers, investors and creditors – and their need for financial information may not be the same as that of the tax authorities.

Specifically in the UK, the impact of accounting practice on the definition of taxable trading profit has been an issue for a very long time.[21] The situation was made clear by Whittington who combines distinction in both tax policy and accounting. In the field of tax policy he was a member of the Meade Committee on the reform of direct taxation and subsequently of the IFS Tax Law Reform Committee: in the field of accounting he was a member of the Accounting Standards Board and later a full-time member of the International Accounting Standards Board. Whittington's[22] view was that principles of taxation would not lead to the adoption of accounting policy as a basis for corporation tax. As he pointed out, it is possible to incorporate accounting standards into revenue law but, after examining different aspects of the issue, he concluded that 'financial reporting to investors and accounting for tax purposes are distinct objectives which are not always consistent with each other.' The discussion has continued, for example, with Macdonald's Tax Law Review Committee paper[23] which examined some of the basic issues that arise in considering the alignment of

17. See, for example, Clinton Alley and Simon James, 'The Use of Financial Reporting Standards Based Accounting for the Preparation of Taxation Returns', *International Tax Journal*, 2005, 31(3), 31-48.
18. Thomas M. Porcano and Alfred V. Tran, Relationship of Tax and Financial Accounting Rules in Anglo-Saxon Countries, 1998, 33(4), 433-454. DOI: 10.1016/S0020-7063(98)80003-4.
19. Simon James, and Christopher Nobes, *The Economics of Taxation: Principles, Policies and Practice*, 15th ed. Fiscal Publications, 2015.
20. Simon James and Alison Edwards, 'Developing Tax Policy in a Complex and Changing World', *Economic Analysis and Policy*, 2008, 38(1), 35-53.
21. See, for example, Judith Freeman, 'Defining Taxable Profit in a Changing Accounting Environment', *British Tax Review*, 1995, 5, 434-444.
22. Geoffrey Whittington, 'Tax Policy and Accounting Standards', *British Tax Review*, 1995, 5, 452-456.
23. Graeme Macdonald, *The Taxation of Business Income: Aligning Taxable Income with Accounting Income*, 2002, Tax Law Review Committee Discussion Paper No. 2, available at: http://www.ifs.org.uk/comms/dp2.pdf (accessed 6 January 2016).

accounting and taxable profits and whether or not a more consistent alignment of the two would be appropriate. These matters form part of the background of the Common Consolidated Corporate Tax Base (CCCTB) examined in section §13.03 below.

[F]   The Assessment of the Financial Income by the National Tax Administration

In the UK, corporation tax has had a full self-assessment system since 1998 and each company is responsible for making the assessment.[24] As the self-assessment must include the tax payable, HM Revenue and Customs (HMRC) does not need to raise an assessment, though it has the powers to do so in certain cases where the company does not submit a return or the authorities are not satisfied with the return that was submitted. After the return has been received HMRC usually has a period of twelve months within which formal enquiries are to be carried out. These enquiries are often resolved by correspondence and further information. HMRC has the power to require information and to enter premises in some circumstances but this power is not often used and tax officials do not routinely visit the premises of taxpayers.

There is a requirement to disclose certain tax planning arrangements under the Disclosure of Tax Avoidance Schemes (DOTAS) requirements.[25] There are also many penalties for failure to comply with the self-assessment system, for example by failing to submit tax returns on time, maintain required records and unreasonably failing to report errors in HMRC assessments.

§13.02   THE IMPACT OF IFRS ON FINANCIAL ACCOUNTING AND TAXATION

[A]   The Implementation of IFRS in the UK

Moves towards International Accounting Standards, or IAS as they were then called, have been going on in the UK for some time. A difficulty with IAS, and more recently IFRS, was that the great majority of UK companies are small or very small enterprises without either the need or capability to implement IFRS. The process of convergence with international standards was delayed for a while and a new document was developed – IFRS for SMEs – intended as an international standard for non-publicly accountable enterprises. Standards in the UK continued to be revised and, largely with effect from 1 January 2015, the 'old GAAP' has been replaced by a 'New GAAP'[26]

---

24. John Tiley and Glen Loutzenhiser, *Advanced Topics in Revenue Law*, Hart Publishing, 2013, p. 33.
25. HM Revenue and Customs, Draft legislation: Disclosure of Tax Avoidance Schemes (DOTAS), July 2015, available at: https://www.gov.uk/government/publications/draft-legislation-disclo sure-of-tax-avoidance-schemes-dotas (accessed 7 January 2016).
26. Financial Reporting Council, 'The New UK GAAP' available at: https://www.frc.org.uk/Our-Work/Codes-Standards/Accounting-and-Reporting-Policy/New-UK-GAAP.aspx (accessed 10 January 2016).

consisting of financial reporting standards FRS 100 to 105. IFRS is required for the consolidated financial statements of all companies whose securities are listed on a regulated market. It is also permitted for other consolidated financial statements and for separate or individual financial statements. It does not apply directly to unlisted entities for which there is a new accounting standard FRS 102[27] based on IFRS for SMEs. There is also FRS 105[28] for micro-entities.

One example of the way IFRS has converged with accounting standards in the UK is the issue of substance over form. The Financial Reporting Council[29] presents the issue clearly as follows:

'IFRS and new UK GAAP, unlike the standards it replaces, do not contain separate standards that require accounts to reflect the substance of a transaction rather than its legal form where this is different. However, this does not mean that substance over form has no place in IFRS or new UK GAAP.

'It would be difficult for accounts to present a true and fair view if form had overridden substance. IAS 8 states that for information to be reliable, it must be reported in accordance with economic substance, rather than strictly in adherence to its legal form. Indeed if material transactions are not accounted for in accordance with their substance it is doubtful whether the accounts present a true and fair view.'

The position is also made clear in FRS 102[30] which states: 'Transactions and other events and conditions should be accounted for and presented in accordance with their substance and not merely their legal form.'

[B] Consequences of the Implementation of IFRS

Although IFRS represents an important initiative to reduce international differences in accounting rules, it is not necessarily true that its implementation will always result in uniform accounting practices. In an influential paper Ball[31] suggested that there might be significant differences between countries in the implementation of IFRS which might be hidden by a veneer of uniformity and that it was unlikely that uniform

27. Financial Reporting Council, *FRS 102 The Financial Reporting Standard applicable in the UK and Republic of Ireland*, 2015, available at: https://www.frc.org.uk/Our-Work/Publications/Accounting-and-Reporting-Policy/FRS-102-The-Financial-Reporting-Standard-applicab.pdf (accessed 10 January 2016).
28. Financial Reporting Council, FRS 105 *The Financial Reporting Standard applicable to the Micro-entities Regime*, 2015, available at: https://www.frc.org.uk/Our-Work/Publications/Accounting-and-Reporting-Policy/FRS-105-The-Financial-Reporting-Standard-applicab.pdf (accessed 10 January, 2016).
29. Financial Reporting Council *True and Fair*, June 2014, p. 3, available at: https://www.frc.org.uk/FRC-Documents/Accounting-and-Reporting/True-and-Fair-June-2014.pdf (accessed 22 January 2016).
30. Financial Reporting Council, FRS 102 The Financial Reporting Standard applicable in the UK and Republic of Ireland, *supra*, p. 29, paragraph 2.8.
31. Ray Ball, 'International Financial Reporting Standards (IFRS): Pros and Cons for Investors', *Accounting and Business Research*, 2006, 36(1), 5-27. DOI: 10.1080/00014788.2006.9730040.

standards would produce uniform financial reporting. Callao et al.[32] found that the first application of IFRS had different effects on financial reporting in different countries. Kvaal and Nobes[33] presented evidence that different national accounting practices before IFRS continued where it was allowed within IFRS. They were also able to document the existence of national patterns of accounting within IFRS. In examining the costs and benefits of the implementation of IFRS Fox et al.[34] explained similarities and differences from an Anglo-Saxon and an EU continental perspective. Another contribution[35] compared the implementation of IFRS in the UK as an example of the Anglo-Saxon accounting model and Spain as a representative of the continental model. This study was also concerned with possible effects of the level of enforcement which previous research had indicated was higher in the UK than in Spain. The research examined the quantitative impact of IFRS on financial reporting by first-time adopters and the results indicated that the quantitative impact was significant in both countries but higher in the UK. The authors also found evidence of negative effects on the relevance of financial reporting though this effect was only significant in Spain.

A study by the Institute of Chartered Accountants in Scotland[36] of the implementation of IFRS in the UK, Italy and Ireland found that it has not always been easy. However, although the financial impact has often been negligible, there have been substantial changes to systems and processes in organizations. The study also found that there had been an increase in internationally-orientated disclosures in corporate annual reports.

Two other areas are worth mentioning. One is the application of IFRS to the public sector which followed the private sector in the UK in adopting IFRS. The other aspect in the UK context is devolution. Connelly and Wall[37] studied the implementation of IFRS in the central government departments in the devolved administrations of Northern Ireland, Scotland and Wales. They found that the implementation of IFRS was smoother than expected but that the effects on management information systems and other aspects were limited.

---

32. Susana Callao, Cristina Ferrer, José I. Jarne and José A. Laínez, 'The Impact of IFRS on the European Union: Is it Related to the Accounting Tradition of the Countries?', *Journal of Applied Accounting Research*, 2009, 10(1), 33-55.
33. Erlend Kvaal and Christopher Nobes, 'International Differences in IFRS Policy Choice: A Research Note', *Accounting and Business Research*, 2010, 40(2), 173-187. DOI: 10.1080/00014788.2010.9663390.
34. Alison Fox, Gwen Hannah, Christine Helliar and Monica Veneziani, 'The Costs and Benefits of IFRS Implementation in the UK and Italy', *Journal of Applied Accounting Research*, 2013, 14(1), 86-101.
35. Susana Callao Gastón, Cristina Ferrer García, José Ignacio Jarne Jarne and José Antonio Laínez Gadea, 'IFRS Adoption in Spain and the United Kingdom: Effects on Accounting Numbers and Relevance', *Advances in Accounting*, 2010, 26(2), 304-313.
36. Institute of Chartered Accountants of Scotland, *The Implementation of IFRS in the UK, Italy and Ireland*, Edinburgh, 2008, available at: https://www.icas.com/__data/assets/pdf_file/0013/10 552/17-The-Implementation-of-IFRS-in-the-UK-Italy-and-Ireland-ICAS.pdf (accessed 6 January 2016).
37. Ciaran Connolly and Tony Wall, *The Implementation of IFRS in the UK Devolved Administrations*, 2013, ICAS, Edinburgh, available at: https://www.icas.com/__data/assets/pdf_file/0004 /7789/99-The-Implementation-of-IFRS-in-the-UK-Devolved-Administrations-ICAS.pdf   (accessed 6 January 2016).

§13.03   DIFFERENCES BETWEEN THE CCCTB AND THE UK CORPORATE TAX BASE

There has not been a great deal of scholarly literature published in the UK on the CCCTB but there have been some significant contributions. Freedman and Macdonald[38] indicated the importance of principles in designing a new tax base and argued that to be successful the CCCTB must contain a comprehensive and autonomous set of rules. As the authors put it, the CCCTB 'must be a Comprehensive Common Consolidated Corporate Tax Base (CCCCTB or C4TB)'.[39] Fuest[40] discussed the implications of the CCCTB proposal for the efficiency and fairness of the tax system and concluded that for the proposal to receive widespread support there would have to be more evidence of economic benefits. Devereux and Fuest[41] examined the economic advantages and disadvantages of the CCCTB concept concluding there were advantages but also some significant drawbacks. The authoritative volume by Tiley and Loutzenhiser[42] contains only a few passing references to the CCCTB but includes doubts that the UK would find the CCCTB acceptable.

However, the basic features as contained in the draft CCCTB Directive of 16 March 2011 and the possible effects of these on the UK tax system have been analysed by Panayi.[43] She compared the proposed rules with UK provisions and concentrated on issues such as anti-abuse rules, formulary apportionment, loss relief, intra-group transfers, the taxation of inbound and outbound investment and the administration of the new system.

As Panayi points out, features of the CCCTB that differ from the UK arrangements may influence tax planning on the part of multinational companies. For example, domestic tax incentives are not allowable under the CCCTB. She also suggested that all Member States should look again at whether to adopt the CCCTB on the basis of legal and economic grounds rather than on the basis of political factors and reminded us that there are other developments in the international tax field which are leading to closer tax integration between countries anyway.[44]

The progress of the CCCTB has been held back by a lack of support in various quarters so further developments were initiated in 2015 when the European Commission relaunched its proposal for the CCCTB and published an Action Plan for 'A fair and Efficient Corporate Tax System in the European Union'.[45] One of the difficulties for the

---

38. Judith Freedman and Graeme Macdonald, *The Tax Base for CCCTB: The Role of Principles*, 2008, Oxford Centre for Business Taxation, WP 08/07.

39. *Ibid.*, p. 1.

40. Clemens Fuest, 'The European Commission's Proposal for a Common Consolidated Corporate Tax Base', *Oxford Review of Economic Policy*, 2008, 24(4), pp. 720-739.

41. Michael P. Devereux and Clemens Fuest, 'Corporate Income Tax Coordination in the European Union', *Transfer: European Review of Labour and Research*, February 2010, 16(1), 23-28. DOI:002010.1177/1024258909357699.

42. John Tiley and Glen Loutzenhiser, *Advanced Topics in Revenue Law*, Hart Publishing, 2013.

43. Christiana HJI Panayi, *The Common Consolidated Corporate Tax Base and the UK Tax System*, London: Institute for Fiscal Studies, TLRC Discussion Paper No. 9, 2011.

44. *Ibid.*, p. 96.

45. European Commission, Communication from the Commission to the European Parliament and the Council, COM(2015) 302 final, 17 June 2015.

UK is that the CCCTB is designed to reduce tax competition between countries but tax policy in the UK endorses tax competition, not only by cutting the rate of corporation tax but also by making the UK tax regime more favourable for multinational companies in other ways. The UK Government therefore is reluctant to adopt the CCCTB. In June 2015, David Gauke, financial secretary to the Treasury, said: 'The CCCTB has been around a very long time. It is a proposal still looking for a justification.'[46] Later David Gauke told representatives from the European Parliament that the UK would not adopt the latest proposals[47] and the Treasury said in a statement 'Direct taxation is a matter for EU countries, and any direct taxation matters require unanimity across all EU countries. We're fully involved in international discussions on tax issues and have consistently supported global measures, through the EU, G20 and OECD, which will strengthen international rules to prevent corporate tax avoidance.'[48]

§13.04 FISCAL ASPECTS OF THE NEW ACCOUNTING DIRECTIVE

The effects of the EU's new accounting Directive – 'EU Directive 2013/34/EU on the annual financial statements, consolidated statements and related reports of certain types of undertakings' were relatively limited in the UK as much had already been implemented.[49] The aims of the Directive were to simplify the accounting requirements for small companies and improve the clarity and comparability of financial statements. They were therefore supported by the UK Government which stated that:

> The Government has a strong and on-going commitment to reducing unnecessary administrative burdens, in particular for small businesses. These changes in European Law provide an opportunity for the Government to further reduce the administrative burdens associated with the preparation and publication of statutory accounts, especially for small companies.[50]

The Government set up a consultation exercise on its approach to implementing the new Directive and all the responses were published.[51] There was broad support for the Government's proposals[52] which were implemented in the form of a UK Statutory

---

46. Quoted in the *Financial Times*, 1 June, 2015.
47. Reported in *The Guardian*, 21 June 2015.
48. *Ibid.*
49. Department for Business Innovation & Skills, *UK Implementation of the EU Accounting Directive*, Chapters 1-9: Annual financial statements, consolidated financial statements, related reports of certain types of undertakings and general requirements for audit, first published on 29 August 2014 and most recently updated on 17 September 2015, p. 4, available at: https://www.gov.uk /government/uploads/system/uploads/attachment_data/file/350864/bis-14-1025-implemention-of-eu-accounting-directive-chapters-1-to-9-consultation.pdf (accessed 5 January 2016).
50. *Ibid.*
51. *Ibid* and also Department for Business Innovation & Skills, *UK Implementation of the EU Accounting Directive*, Chapter 10: Extractive industries reporting – Government response to consultation, available at: https://www.gov.uk/government/uploads/system/uploads/attach ment_data/file/343599/bis-14-1006-eu-accounting-directive-implementation-extractive-industr ies-reporting-response.pdf (accessed 5 January 2016).
52. Department for Business Innovation & Skills, *UK Implementation of Chapters 1-9 of the EU Accounting Directive: Government response to the consultation*, January 2015, available at:

Instrument.[53] There do not appear to be any major tax implications and the present author was unable to find any scholarly work in the UK on the subject. There may be a reduction in the administrative and compliance costs of taxation in the UK but it is unlikely these would be substantial.

https://www.gov.uk/government/consultations/eu-accounting-directive-smaller-companies-reporting (accessed 5 January 2016).
53. The Companies, Partnerships and Groups (Accounts and Reports) Regulations 2015, No. 980, available at: http://www.legislation.gov.uk/uksi/2015/980/pdfs/uksi_20150980_en.pdf (accessed 15 January 2016).

CHAPTER 14

Accounting and Taxation: United States

Steven J. Willis

§14.01 INTRODUCTION

Defining the U.S. corporate tax base is complicated by many factors:

(1) General Legal Restrictions
(2) Type of Entity
(3) Basic Rules
(4) Arbitrary Exceptions
(5) Ease of Avoidance.

[A] General Legal Restrictions

The U.S. corporate tax is an excise[1] and thus subject only to the constitutional requirements that it be uniform among the states[2] and be justified as "for the general welfare."[3] Neither restriction is particularly stringent as long as the rates do not vary from state to state.[4] Because it is technically not an "income tax,"[5] it need not meet the

---

1. *Flint v. Stone Tracy Co.*, 220 U.S. 107 (1911).
2. U.S. CONST. ART. I section 9.
3. *Ibid.*
4. *Flint* at 142.
5. The U.S. corporate tax is styled as a tax on "income" and always has been; however, because, under constitutional principles, it is an excise on the privilege of doing business as a corporation, it *could be* very different. For example, it could be a tax on gross receipts or cash flows. No constitutional requirement of any deductions for costs exists. In contrast, the U.S. tax on individual income exists under 16th Amendment restrictions that place two significant requirements: that it be on "income," which the Supreme Court has held refers to an "undeniable

215

"derived" and "accession to wealth" requirements of the 16th Amendment to the U.S. Constitution.

Arguably tax on non-corporate income must satisfy the requirements of the 16th Amendment to the constitution: "derived" and an "accession to wealth clearly realized."[6] Hence, fair value reporting is questionable for that, though it would be constitutional for a corporate tax.

Most of the fifty states[7] (and many cities or localities) have a tax on corporate income and many on non-corporate business income. Although many unify their systems as "piggy-back codes,"[8] not all do. Further, most states modify state-level corporate tax base at least minimally, if not substantially. Unification of state and local corporate tax systems would be difficult under the 10th Amendment.[9]

Nevertheless, Congress has chosen since the first enactment of a corporate income tax to lay it upon "income" as opposed to gross receipts or some other measure. Further, the U.S. has used an annual, rather than transactional, system of tax accounting. That the system was annual was not fully decided until 1931 and 1932 in *Sanford & Brooks*[10] and *North American Oil.*[11] This is critical because without an annual system, we would have a transaction-based income tax that would lay taxes on each transaction separately. An income tax system would not likely be feasible in such a case.

[B]   Type of Entity

The U.S. taxes the income from different persons and entities differently, which makes defining a "corporate tax base" problematic. Publicly-traded companies,[12] including publicly-traded partnerships,[13] are subject to the basic rules described below. But, different rules apply to farming,[14] which uses a hybrid method of accounting and many aspects of the cash receipts and disbursements method; hence, for corporations

---

accessions to wealth, clearly realized, and over which the taxpayers have complete dominion." *Comm'r v. Glenshaw Glass*, 348 U.S. 426, 431 (1955); *but see, Cottage Savings Association v. Comm'r*, 499 U.S. 554 (1991) (which arguably limited *Glenshaw Glass* to a rule of administrative convenience rather than constitutional significance.) The individual income tax is also subject to the "derived" requirement that imposes a realization event principle. *See, Eisner v. Macomber*, 252 U.S. 189 (1920) (holding stock dividends did not result in gross income because they were not derived.)

6. *Ibid.*
7. According to the Tax Foundation, forty-four states generally have a corporate income tax with Texas and Ohio being major exceptions. Ohio has a commercial activities tax, which is similar to an income tax but which also has elements of a gross receipts tax.
8. Such states adopt the federal system as their own, albeit often with modifications.
9. U.S. Const. Amend. X reserves powers not otherwise granted to Congress to the States. The power to tax for state purposes is almost certainly one of those powers.
10. *Burnet v. Sanford & Brooks. Co.*, 282 U.S. 359 (1931).
11. *North American Oil v. Burnet*, 298 U.S. 417 (1932).
12. Per I.R.C. section 448, all C Corporations must use the accrual method of accounting. All publicly-traded corporations would be C Corporations as they cannot satisfy the section 1362 election for S status (a flow-through entity taxed at the shareholder level).
13. Per I.R.C. section 7704, publicly-traded partnerships are taxed as C Corporations.
14. See, I.R.C. § 448(b)(1).

engaged in farming, the tax base is closer to annual receipts minus costs paid. Many businesses, including some very large ones, operate as S corporations, partnerships, or LLCs and may use the cash method,[15] unless they have inventories.[16] For those using the cash method, the tax base is not well defined because it is easily subject to easy manipulation through acceleration of income or expenses, or through the assignment of such items to a later period.[17] Subchapter L also taxes "insurance companies" quite differently in how they handle future costs: they may deduct the present value of expected future costs attributable to current revenues for risks undertaken.[18]

[C] Basic Rules

In general, publicly-traded companies or publicly-traded partnerships must use the accrual method for measuring income and expenses.[19] Very generally, this creates a tax base comparable to financial or accounting income – income results from accessions to wealth clearly realized over which the taxpayer has dominion and control.[20] Similarly such a base, for general principles, allows ordinary and necessary deductions[21] that properly match with[22] the reported income.

Still, the U.S. corporate tax base generally has a poor intellectual foundation. As explained by the Tax Foundation:

> The federal tax system is built on a poor intellectual foundation; it relies heavily on a definition of income developed by economists Robert Haig and Henry Simons

---

15. I.R.C. § 448. Under the cash method, income arises only upon "receipt" and expenses are deductible only when "paid."
16. I.R.C. section 472 requires the inventory method of accounting, which generally follows accrual principles.
17. Many doctrines and code provisions exist to preclude such manipulation, but they are of questionable effectiveness. *See* the doctrines of constructive receipt (Treas. Reg. §1.451-2(a)), economic benefit (*Reed v. Comm'r*, 723 F.2d 138 (5th Cir. 1983)), and cash equivalence (*Cowden v. Comm'r*, 289 F.2d 20 (5th Cir. 1961)), as well as economic substance/business purpose doctrine (I.R.C. §7701(o)) exist to overcome these manipulations however, they are complicated and often easily avoided. *See*, Willis, *Top 50 U.S. Tax Doctrines*, INTRODUCTION TO TAX SCHOOL (2015) (available at http://www.ufcle.com/willis/willis.htm).
18. This deduction, while consistent with financial accounting and U.S. GAAP, is inconsistent with the treatment of many similarly incurred but deferred costs. *See* I.R.C. § 461(h) deferring the accrual of deductions until the later of "all events" under traditional accrual or "economic performance" (which often means payment). *See also* the often-conflicting rules of sections 467 (pre or post-paid rent or service costs), 468 (mining and solid waste reclamation costs), 468A (nuclear power decommissioning costs), and 468B (tort liability costs), which substantially vary the treatment of similar expenses by industry.
19. I.R.C. §§ 448, 7704.
20. *Comm'r v. Glenshaw Glass*, 348 U.S. 426, 431 (1955).
21. I.R.C. §§ 162 (allowing ordinary and necessary business expenses), 263 (requiring capitalization of many costs, generally which are material and have future effects). *See, Welch v. Helvering*, 290 U.S. 111 (1933) (declining to define "ordinary and necessary" and instead imposing a subjective test); *Gregory v. Helvering*, 293 U.S. 465 (1935) (generally allowing taxpayers to arrange affairs so as to minimize tax liabilities, except when they cannot do so, without providing any principles).
22. *But see, Albertson's Inc. v. Comm'r*, 42 F.3d 537 (9th Cir. 1994) (in which both the Tax Court and the Court of Appeals for the Ninth Circuit declined to follow the traditional "matching principle" of U.S. GAAP).

almost a century ago. The Haig-Simons definition of income is that income equals the sum of your consumption plus your change in net worth. While this is a useful accounting identity, it is a poor tax base, because it is not neutral between immediate consumption and future consumption.[23]

[D]   Arbitrary Exceptions

The U.S. tax system is riddled with many seemingly arbitrary and politically motivated provisions that erode the corporate tax base. These include accelerated depreciation[24] (with zero salvage, arbitrarily short lives, rates far more rapid than economically justifiable), Internal Revenue Code ("Code") section 179,[25] deduction of interest,[26] and Code section 1031.[27] They also include special deductions for particular investments (e.g., a variety of credits, (e.g., low-income housing credit in section 42, and including section 611 for depletion).

[E]   Ease of Avoidance

The U.S. corporate tax system is easily avoided through transfer pricing and unclear source rules. "It is also due to our deferral-based international tax system, which generally allows U.S. companies operating through foreign subsidiaries to if and when foreign profits are subject to U.S. tax. This can result in lower effective tax rates on U.S. companies investing abroad rather than in the United States."[28] Sections 881-882 describe the tax on income not connected with a U.S. trade or business and income effectively connected with a U.S. trade or business, which together form the basic source rules.

Because the U.S. corporate income tax rate is high (35% plus various state and local rates), entities arguably have a strong incentive to "allocate" as much income as possible to operations in low-tax countries (which comprise most of the planet). Financial and tax accounting techniques involving intra-company and inter-company

---

23. Alan Cole, *Corporate v. Individual Tax Expenditures*, TAX FOUNDATION SPECIAL REPORT NO. 218 (April 2014) at 2.
24. I.R.C. §§167, 168.
25. I.R.C. §179. Although section 179 is available to C corporations, it has "phase-out" rules that make it inapplicable to entities with annual capital expenditures significantly greater than USD 200,000; however, for years 2009 through 2015, the phase-out rules began at USD 2,000,000.
26. I.R.C. §163. The deduction of interest presents two often discussed problems. First, it favors debt financing over equity financing, and second, when coupled with rapid depreciation rules, it materially subsidizes capital expenditures. Edward Kleinbard, *How Tax Reform Can Happen*, 146 TAX NOTES 91, 97 (2015).
27. I.R.C. §1031 excludes from the tax base any transactions involving "like-kind" exchanges. As a result, many corporations never suffer a tax on gains involving real (immovable) property and some personal (movable property). Through complicated deals involving multiple parties, they sell the assets and re-invest in other broadly defined "like-kind" assets. As a result, they may exclude any resulting gains, though they must transfer their tax basis (tax value) to the new asset. As a result, they effectively postpone such gains for the life of the entity.
28. U.S. Senate Committee on Finance, *Summary of Staff Discussion Draft: International Business Tax Reform* at 1 (2013).

transactions (through overtly or covertly related entities) permit the allocation. Common techniques involve the place of ownership for intangibles as well as product pricing. The same problem exists within the U.S. at the state and local level, with corporations allocating earnings to operations in lower-taxed states. Despite many government efforts to overcome such allocations, the problem appears entrenched.

As explained by the Tax Foundation:

> Deferral here means that the additional domestic tax on foreign earnings (*i.e.,* the repatriation tax), which is over and above what is paid abroad, can be deferred as long as the earnings remain invested abroad. Indefinite deferral approaches a territorial tax system of full exemption of foreign earnings, although it involves excessive tax planning and administrative costs and also results in the problem of locked out profits.[29]

Many studies have called for reform either through:

- Reduction of corporate tax rates (to discourage abuse and to enhance competitiveness).[30]
- Repatriation Amnesty.[31]
- Elimination of the corporate income tax.[32]
- Integration of the corporate tax with shareholder taxes.[33]

§14.02 CONNECTION BETWEEN ACCOUNTING AND TAXATION. MAIN THEORETICAL JUSTIFICATIONS. ROLE OF U.S. GAAP AND OTHER NATIONAL LEGISLATION ON THIS ISSUE

Very generally, the U.S. corporate income tax system relates to financial accounting. The relationship, however, is fraught with exceptions. Section 446(c)(2) of the Internal Revenue Code *permits* (but does not require) the use of the accrual method of accounting. Similar provisions have existed since the adoption of the first broad-based U.S. income tax in 1913 after enactment of the 16th Amendment (generally authorizing

---

29. Alan Cole, *Corporate v. Individual Tax Expenditures*, TAX FOUNDATION SPECIAL REPORT No. 218 (April 2014) at 6; *see*, Robert Carroll, *The Importance of Tax Deferral and a Lower Corporate Tax Rate*, TAX FOUNDATION SPECIAL REPORT No. 174 (2010).
30. Several prominent politicians have recently favored lowering U.S. corporate tax rates, Donald Trump, *Tax Reform for Security and Prosperity*, WALL STREET JOURNAL (September 29, 2015) (arguing for a 15% corporate rate); *Jeb Bush: Everyone Gets a Tax Cut*, WALL STREET JOURNAL (September 8, 2015) (proposing a 20% corporate rate with full expensing of all capital investment); *Obama Proposes Lowering Corporate Tax Rate to 28%*, WASH. POST (February 22, 2012). See, Michael L. Graetz, Address at the National Press Club in Washington, D.C. (June 17, 2013), available at http://media.law.columbia.edu/specialevents/EconomyInCrisis.mp4.
31. Twenty-four International Tax Experts Address Current Tax Reform Efforts in Congress, Open Letter September 29, 2015, Tax Analysts, Doc. 2015-21649.
32. Chris Edwards, *Replacing the Scandal-Plagued Corporate Income Tax With a Cash-Flow Tax*, CATO POLICY ANALYSIS No. 484 (August 2003).
33. George K. Yin, Corporate Tax Integration and the Search for the Pragmatic Deal, 47 TAX L. REV. 431 (1992); *but see*, Karen Burke & Grayson McCouch, Turning Slogans into Tax Policy, 27 VA. TAX REV. 747 (2008) (opposing integration).

an income tax). For corporate income tax purposes (which transcend the 16th Amendment), a relationship to financial income has existed since the adoption of the first corporate income tax in 1894.[34]

Treasury Regulations interpreting section 446 permit any method of accounting, but with the following restrictions:

> No method of accounting is acceptable unless, *in the opinion of the Commissioner*, it clearly reflects income. The method used by the taxpayer in determining when income is to be accounted for will generally be acceptable if it accords with *generally accepted accounting principles*, is consistently used by the taxpayer from year to year, *and* is consistent with the Income Tax Regulations.[35]

Similarly, taxpayers with "inventories" must use the inventory method of accounting provided for in section 471 and related regulations, which provides:

> Whenever in the opinion of the Secretary the use of inventories is necessary in order clearly to determine the income of any taxpayer, inventories shall be taken by such taxpayer *on such basis as the Secretary may prescribe* as conforming as nearly as may be to the *best accounting practice* in the trade or business and as most clearly reflecting the income.[36]

Although those Code and regulation provisions appear to coordinate tax accounting with financial accounting, they actually grant substantial power to the Secretary of the Treasury to require accounting methods materially different from financial accounting and U.S. GAAP. Indeed, as the Supreme Court explained in 1979:

> It is obvious that on their face, §§ 446 and 471, with their accompanying Regulations, vest the Commissioner with wide discretion in determining whether a particular method of inventory accounting should be disallowed as not clearly reflective of income. This Court's cases confirm the breadth of this discretion. In construing §446 and its predecessors, the Court has held that "[the] Commissioner has broad powers in determining whether accounting methods used by a taxpayer

---

34. The first U.S. corporate income tax (at a 2% rate) was part of Wilson-Gorman Tariff Act of 1894, but was declared unconstitutional because an integral part of the act (applying to individuals) violated the constitutional requirement that direct taxes be apportioned. *Pollock v. Farmer's Loan and Trust Co*, 158 U.S. 601, 639 (1895) (emphasis added), ("By section 27 of the act of August 28, 1894, known as the Wilson Tariff act, and entitled 'An act to reduce taxation, to provide revenue for the government, and for other purposes'," it was provided: "That from and after the first day of January eighteen hundred and ninety-five, and until the first day of January nineteen hundred, there shall be assessed, levied, collected, and paid annually upon the gains, profits, and income received in the preceding calendar year by every citizen of the United States, whether residing at home or abroad, and every person residing therein, whether *said gains, profits, or income* be derived from any kind of property, rents, interest, dividends, or salaries, or from any profession, trade, employment, or vocation carried on in the United States or elsewhere, or from any other source whatever, a tax of two per centum on the amount so derived over and above four thousand dollars, and a like tax shall be levied, collected, and paid annually upon the gains, profits, and income from all property owned and of every business, trade, or profession carried on in the United States by persons residing without the United States." *Flint v. Stone Tracy Co.*, 220 U.S. 107 (1911) (upholding the second U.S. corporate tax enacted in 1909).
35. Treas. Reg. §1.446-1(a)(4)(C) (emphasis added).
36. I.R.C. §471 (emphasis added). See also, Treas. Reg. section 1.471-2(c)(1) (adding consistency as an over-riding principle for inventory accounting, as well as "best practices.").

220

clearly reflect income." **** Since the Commissioner has "[much] latitude for discretion," his interpretation of the statute's clear-reflection standard "should not be interfered with unless clearly unlawful." *Lucas* v. *American Code Co.*, 280 U.S. 445, 449 (1930). To the same effect are *United States* v. *Catto*, 384 U.S. 102, 114 (1966); v. *Commissioner*, 372 U.S. 128, 133-134 (1963); *American Automobile Assn.* v. *United States*, 367 U.S. 687, 697-698 (1961); *Automobile Club of Michigan* v. *Commissioner*, 353 U.S. 180, 189-190 (1957); *Brown* v. *Helvering*, 291 U.S. 193, 203 (1934). In construing **** a predecessor of § 471, the Court held that the taxpayer bears a "heavy burden of [proof]," and that the Commissioner's disallowance of an inventory accounting method is not to be set aside unless shown to be "plainly arbitrary." *Lucas* v. *Structural Steel Co.*, 281 U.S. 264, 271 (1930).[37]

Many of the cases cited by the Court involved inventories, but many also involved other areas of accounting. For example, *Schlude*, *American Automobile Assn.*, and *Automobile Club* form a famous "trilogy" in which the Court refused to permit the accrual method of accounting for income if related payments were either due or received prior to earning of the items. As a result, U.S. taxpayers must use a modified cash method for "pre-paid" items, effectively increasing their tax base through acceleration of such items to years earlier than appropriate under financial accounting.[38]

In contrast, Congress enacted Code section 461(h)[39] in 1982, effectively removing nearly all expenses from traditional financial accounting rules. Under that section, a purported accrual method taxpayer may not deduct an item until the later of the "all events test"[40] being met or economic performance. "All events" follows traditional financial accounting, but "economic performance"[41] does not. As a result, the trilogy of cases removes material items of income from financial accounting rules, and section 461(h) removes a very large portion of expenses from traditional financial accounting rules.

Another important aspect of the U.S. tax base involves the Legislative Grace Doctrine,[42] under which Courts broadly construe code provisions involving income inclusion, but narrowly construe deduction and exclusion provisions. Though not universally followed, the doctrine places the burden on taxpayers to cite and to defend the application of specific allowance provisions for deductions. No general principle

---

37. *Thor Power Tool, Co.* v. *Comm'r*, 439 U.S. 522, 532 (1979). *Cf.*, *INDOPCO, Inc.* v. *Comm'r*, 503 U.S. 79 (1992) (which generally follows traditional accounting rules, but which prompted Treasury Regulations under section 263 (dealing with capitalization of costs) that deviate substantially from financial accounting.

38. *See*, Steven J. Willis, *It's Time for Schlude to Go*, 93 Tax Notes 127 (2001); *Show Me the Numbers Please*, 93 Tax Notes 1321 (2001); *but see*, Deborah Geier, *Taxing Advance Payment: Choosing Among Imperfect Alternative*, Tax Notes, October 8, 2001, p. 285 (arguing against using financial accounting as the tax base); Calvin Johnson, *The Illegitimate "Earned" Requirement in Tax and Nontax Accounting*, 54 Tax L. Rev. 373 (1995); Daniel Halperin, *Financial Accounting Is Not Always the Best Measure of Taxable Income*, Tax Notes, July 2, 2001, p. 131.

39. I.R.C. § 461(h).

40. I.R.C. §461(h)(4): the test is met if "all events have occurred which determine the fact of liability and the amount of such liability can be determined with reasonable accuracy."

41. I.R.C. §461(h)(2) (listing four instances of economic performance).

42. *See*, *Interstate Transit Lines* v. *Comm'r*, 319 U.S. 590 (1943); *but see*, *King* v. *Burwell*, ___ U.S. ___, 135 S. Ct. 2480 (2015) (reading a tax credit broadly without citation to the tradition doctrine that such laws are read narrowly).

exists that would allow costs of producing income as deductions, either currently or over time. Thus, although U.S. tax law generally allows "ordinary and necessary" business expenses, and thus tends to mirror financial accounting in that respect, this is not because of any entrenched principle of law.

U.S. law has followed financial accounting for timing since 1931 when the Supreme Court upheld the statutory use of an annual tax system rather than one based on transactions. It has required the accrual method of accounting[43] for C corporations since 1986 and for publicly-traded partnerships[44] since 1986, as well.

The principle theoretical justifications for generally – at least as a starting point – relating corporate income for tax law purposes to financial income involve the stated desire to "clearly reflect income" and to do so "consistently" from year to year. Both justifications appear in Code section 446.

Under the Securities Acts of 1933 and 1934, the Securities and Exchange Commission (SEC) has statutory authority to create accounting principles.[45] The SEC delegated that authority to the private sector, initially to the AICPA.[46] However, in 1973 the Financial Accounting Standards Board (FASB) came into existence and the SEC delegated its authority to the FASB for the creation of U.S. GAAP.[47] Thus U.S. GAAP are not government-created rules, except through the broad delegation from the SEC to the FASB. Occasionally, however, the SEC has imposed rules supplementary to U.S. GAAP for publicly-traded companies.

§14.03   PERMITTED DEVIATIONS AND MAIN THEORETICALLY JUSTIFICATIONS

U.S. tax law permits or requires many deviations from U.S. GAAP financial accounting. Some significant examples (and related justifications) applying to corporations include:

- Accelerated depreciation. Sections 167 and 168 permit rapid depreciation of most capital investments. The justification, given since the 1960s, has been for the stimulation of the economy. By allowing deduction of capital investment earlier than economically justified, the government essentially subsidizes such investment hoping to encourage more investment and thus higher levels of employment and income. For example, per section 168(e)(1), property with an economic life of four years depreciates for tax purposes in three; property with an economic life of five to ten years depreciates in five years; property with an

---

43. I.R.C. §448(a)(1), P. L. 99-514 (Tax Reform Act of 1986).
44. I.R.C. §7704.
45. Section 10A of the Securities Exchange Act of 1934.
46. American Institute for Certified Public Accountants. This body, which promulgates Generally Accepted Auditing Standards, and aids in the regulation of the accounting profession, adopted the FASB rules as authoritative for U.S. GAAP in 1973. *Rule 203, Rules of Professional Conduct, as amended May 1973 and May 1979.*
47. SEC Financial Reporting Release No. 1, Section 101 (1973) (reaffirmed in April 2003 Policy Statement).

economic life of ten to sixteen years depreciates in seven years. The section also defaults to a double-declining balance method and assumes zero salvage value, which also increases the depreciable cost. Prior to 2015, the section[48] also permitted "bonus depreciation" permitting taxpayers to deduct an additional 50% of capital costs.

- Expensing of capital costs. Section 179, in coordination with section 38 (the general business credit) permits taxpayers to expense USD 25,000 of capital investment each year. Prior to 2015, the amount allowed was USD 500,000. The stated justification was to subsidize investment so as to stimulate employment.
- Code section 46 permits a significant tax credit for the production and use of alcohol as a fuel. The stated justification centered on the stimulation of the production of alternative fuels. As a practical matter, the State of Iowa is a major corn producer and it hosts the first presidential primary election every four years; as a result, the corn lobby is very strong.
- Code section 448(b)(1) permits the cash method for farms. The stated justification is to subsidize the production of food as a necessary part of national defense. Additionally, the farm lobby is very powerful in many U.S. states that comprise a substantial number of electoral votes.
- Interest is fully deductible per Code section 163[49] subject to some restrictions.[50] This arguably presents a serious corporate tax base problem because a corporation could borrow funds in the U.S., deduct the interest, but effectively use the liquidity to fund non-U.S. operations. Because money is fungible, allocation of such funds is not simple. This arguably seriously erodes the corporate tax base because it effectively permits excessive deductions more properly attributable to non-U.S. operations that produce deferred income for tax purposes.[51] No fiscal policy justification exists for this anomaly. Code section 482[52] provides the government with the power to re-allocate various items (income or expense) among related entities or operations. U.S. GAAP, to the extent it measures domestic and international operations separately, would properly apportion interest and similar costs to various operations. Appropriate allocation techniques might involve comparative receipts, employees, profits, or capitalization. Direct sourcing of funds would seem to be a poor allocation method, as the fungible nature of money would open such a

---

48. I.R.C. §168(k) (applying to years 2007 through 2014).
49. I.R.C. §163.
50. Section 163(j) limits "excess interest expense" for corporations (if interest expense exceeds 50% of "adjusted taxable income" and the debt to equity ratio exceeds 1.5:1); section 163(d) limits investment interest expense to the amount of investment income; section 265(a)(1) denies a deduction for interest allocable to wholly exempt income (arguably this should be amended to defer interest allocable to deferred income, including non-repatriated foreign income); section 465 limits deductions for activities in which the taxpayer is not "at risk"; section 469 limits deductions for passive activities.
51. *See* Kleinbard, *supra* note 26.
52. I.R.C. §482.

technique to manipulation. Why the U.S. tax authorities have not required proper allocation is a mystery.

– Code section 1031[53] excludes from the tax base any transactions involving "like-kind" exchanges. As a result, many corporations never suffer a tax on gains involving real (immovable) property and some personal (movable property). Through complicated deals involving multiple parties, they sell appreciated assets and re-invest in other broadly defined "like-kind" assets. As a result, they may exclude any resulting gains, though they must transfer their tax basis (tax value) to the new asset. As a result, they effectively postpone such gains for the life of the entity.

– Code sections 661-663 allow percentage depletion for extraction industries, ranging from 5% to 22% of the production income. This exists to subsidize the domestic production of natural resources, particularly oil and gas. Similarly sections 616-617 permit the current deduction of some otherwise capitalizable development and exploration costs.

– Section 199[54] permits a deduction equal to 9% of taxable income for domestic production (excluding services) to encourage domestic production.

§14.04   RELATIONSHIP BETWEEN ACCOUNTING AND TAXATION: IS THE TAX ADMINISTRATION ASSESS THE FINANCIAL INCOME?

Generally speaking, the Tax Administration does not assess the financial income. The Code defines the tax base (income and expenses) and U.S. GAAP defines financial income. Nevertheless, the Treasury Department has considerable power to define income and expenses. If the issue is litigated, the burden of proof to determine the proper amount of income and expense is on the taxpayer; hence, the Internal Revenue Service could, at least theoretically, issue a notice of deficiency to a corporate taxpayer based solely on financial statement income and thereby force the taxpayer to prove the amounts were not appropriate for tax purposes.

As a more practical matter, a taxpayer must "conform" its financial books to its tax income and thus justify any discrepancies. In some specific instances, the Treasury has overtly exercised its power to impose full conformity between financial and tax accounting.[55] Per general legal principles, the Treasury may force any taxpayer to use a particular method of accounting if, in the opinion of the Commissioner, the method used does not "clearly reflect income."[56] Although the Commissioner has not used this power broadly to force taxpayers to use financial accounting for tax purposes, the possibility remains.

---

53. I.R.C. §1031. *See*, Steven J. Willis, *Of Permissible Illogic and Section 1031*, 34 U. FLA. L. REV. 72 (1981).
54. I.R.C. §199.
55. For example Treas. Reg. §1.263(a)-1(f)(i) permits a safe harbor capitalization rule only if the taxpayer uses the same method for financial accounting. Section 472 permits the use of a LIFO inventory system, but only if the taxpayer also uses the same method for financial accounting.
56. Treas. Reg. §1.446-1(a)(4)(C).

An important issue involves the power of the government to obtain tax accrual work papers prepared by accountants either in the reconciliation of book/tax discrepancies or for internal evaluation of risky tax positions. Generally, communications between a CPA and a client are not privileged; hence, the government may obtain them. However, also generally, a lawyer may seek to place a CPA (and his or her analysis) under the attorney's confidentiality privilege. To do so, the attorney must carefully draft a "*Kovel*[57] Letter" or "*Kovel* Engagement". It should provide:

- The accountant works for the lawyer.
- The accountant reports directly to the lawyer or members of his/her firm.
- The accountant must keep all work papers, opinions, and information confidential. The work papers belong to the lawyer and will be turned over to the lawyer upon request, including all copies.
- The accountant will provide advice to the lawyer, and not to the client directly without the express permission from the lawyer. The accountant generally should bill the lawyer, not the client. The lawyer can then pass on the charge.
- If the accountant separately advises the client on other matters, the accountant agrees to bill the client separately. Generally, however, a lawyer may prefer to not use an accountant with either a pre-existing or other relationship to the client.

In recent years, the IRS has aggressively sought to limit the *Kovel* Doctrine, with some success, particularly in relation to tax accrual work papers[58] and in the preparation of tax returns.[59] As a result, the government has had greater success in obtaining internal, traditionally confidential, financial information and analysis. With that access to information, the government has a greater practical ability to effectively assess financial income.

§14.05 THE IMPACT OF IFRS ON FINANCIAL ACCOUNTING AND TAX CONSEQUENCES

IFRS has not been adopted in the U.S.; however, the FASB and the SEC have continued efforts to conform U.S. GAAP to IFRS, at least in part. For example, a current exposure draft on "materiality" addresses the IFRS treatment and proposes a U.S. GAAP modification to partially reconcile the two.[60]

---

57. *United States v. Kovel*, 296 F.2d 918 (2d Cir. 1961).
58. *See, United States v. Deloitte LLP*, 610 F.3d 129 (D.C. Cir. 2010). *See also* FASB 48 relating to accounting for tax/book differences: tax accrual work papers arise from it.
59. *United States v. Gurtner*, 474 F.2d 297 (9th Cir. 1973) (attorney sent client to CPA for preparation of tax returns. CPA did not come under the attorney's privilege.) *See,* Kossman, *CPAs and Privileged Communications*, THE TAX ADVISOR (October 1, 2013), http://www.aicpa.org/publications/taxadviser/2013/october/pages/tpp_oct2013-story-03.aspx. *See also*, Denzil Causey & Frances McNair, *An Analysis of State Accountant-Client Privilege Statutes and Public Policy Implications for the Accountant-Client Relationship*, 27 AM BUS. L. J. 535 (1990).
60. FASB Exposure Draft, *Notes to Financial Statements* (Topic 235) (September 24, 2015) at 14-15.

The SEC has examined the adoption of IFRS for many years, beginning as early as 1981.[61] In 1997, the SEC issued a Report to Congress that "encouraged the efforts of the International Accounting Standards Committee [succeeded by the IASB] to develop a core set of accounting standards that could serve as a framework for financial reporting and cross-border offerings."[62] The Report promised the continued cooperation of the SEC. IFRS resulted from those efforts. In the 2002 Norwalk Agreement, the FASB and the IASB issued a joint memorandum to converge the two systems.[63] Indeed, the 2002 Sarbanes-Oxley Act required an SEC study on the adoption by the U.S. of a principles-based accounting system.[64] Again, in 2008, the SEC issued a proposed "roadmap" for a "possible path" to a single set of globally accepted accounting standards.[65] In 2010, the SEC reiterated, "a single set of high quality globally accepted accounting standards would benefit U.S. investors."[66] It thus continued to encourage convergence of U.S. GAAP and IFRS (which arose, at least in part, from U.S. efforts and encouragement). The Report called for a work-plan, which the SEC issued in 2012.[67] However recent public statements[68] suggest the adoption is not contemplated in the foreseeable future. Because the SEC has statutory authority to adopt U.S. accounting principles,[69] no additional legislation would be required. That said, such a large change in accounting rules would seem to raise at least some political questions: the Administrative Branch of the U.S. government would need to be motivated such that it was willing to change the basic working rules of over 400,000 accounting professionals,[70] a group that very recently completed a major overhaul and codification of U.S. GAAP.

---

61. *See, e.g., Integrated Disclosure System for Foreign Private Issuers*, Release No. 33-6360 (November 20, 1981) [46 Fed. Reg. 58,511 (December 2, 1981)].
62. "Pursuant to Section 509(5) of the National Securities Markets Improvement Act of 1996 Report on Promoting Global Preeminence of American Securities Markets" (October 1997).
63. "Memorandum of Understanding, 'The Norwalk Agreement,'" (September 18, 2002).
64. Section 108(d) of Sarbanes-Oxley.
65. *See, Roadmap For the Potential Use of Financial Statements Prepared in Accordance with International Financial Reporting Standards by U.S. Issuers*, Release No. 33-8982 (November 14, 2008) [73 Fed. Reg. 70,816 (November 21, 2008)].
66. *See* SEC Release No. 33-9109 (February 24, 2010), Commission Statement of Support of Convergence and Global Accounting Standards [75 Fed. Reg. 9,494 (March 2, 2010)].
67. *See, Work Plan for the Consideration of Incorporating International Financial Reporting Standards into the Financial Reporting System for U.S. Issuers Final Staff Report* (July 2012).
68. "Securities and Exchange Commission chief accountant James Schnurr is rethinking a proposal he made last December that the SEC allow U.S. companies the option of providing some information, such as revenues, using International Financial Reporting Standards as a supplement to U.S. U.S. GAAP without requiring reconciliation." ACCOUNTING TODAY (May 7, 2015), http://www.accountingtoday.com/news/audit-accounting/sec-chief-accountant-backs-away-from-ifrs-proposal-74553-1.html; "Kara Stein, a commissioner with the Securities and Exchange Commission, appeared to reject the need for convergence with International Financial Reporting Standards in a speech last week." ACCOUNTING TODAY (March 30, 2015) http://www.accountingtoday.com/news/audit-accounting/sec-commissioner-rejects-ifrs-74128-1.html.
69. Section 10A of the Securities Exchange Act of 1934.
70. Most, but not all, CPAs in the United States belong to the AICPA, which has over 400,000 members in 2015. http://www.aicpa.org/Membership/Pages/Membership.aspx.

Two significant issues arise: the unification of U.S. GAAP/IFRS and the unification of U.S. GAAS/IAS, with the second being much easier to imagine in the near term. Most international accounting firms are already in compliance with both U.S. Generally Accepted Auditing Standards (GAAS) (now PCAOB Auditing Standards) and International Auditing Standards. With effective unification of auditing standards, a reinvigorated attempted to unify substantive standards is at least plausible.

From an accounting standpoint the practical consequences are significant for CPAs and for companies with international operations. U.S. CPAs must begin to learn both systems, which complicates both academic programs and practitioners; unfortunately, IFRS is not typically taught in many U.S. accounting programs. In many states, accounting is a five-year degree program leading to the CPA exam. Requiring students (and faculty) to learn two systems presents practical problems: a point militating in favor of ultimate unification, but against doing it quickly.

Very generally, U.S. GAAP is a rules-based system with a recently adopted extensive codification. In contrast, IFRS are principles-based with greater discretion allowed to management and accountants. The philosophical underpinnings differ substantially, which likens the practicalities to learning two different languages. Fundamentally, the IFRS principles are very similar to U.S. GAAP principles underpinning very detailed interpretive rules; nevertheless, keeping track of two systems is very difficult. The existence of the recent codification – finalized in 2014 – suggests little sympathy within the U.S. accounting profession for a wholesale change in rules.

Investors, however, must be able to compare operations audited under two different systems. In a general macro-economic sense, the two systems likely produce very similar results. But, in a specific, micro-economic sense involving particular companies being compared, the differences can be profound, making comparisons risky. Reconciliation is difficult, if not impossible in practical terms: no one can seriously expect full financial statements prepared under both systems. Simply obtaining qualified persons to audit such statements would be a daunting task. As a result, the current divergent system seems unsustainable. Nevertheless, inertia to change is daunting.

From a tax perspective, the lack of LIFO inventories in IFRS is a substantial difference. U.S. companies may use LIFO for tax accounting if they also use it for financial accounting.[71] If the U.S. adopts IFRS, all taxpayers previously using LIFO will need to change their inventory accounting method, which will require substantial section 481[72] adjustments. This alone has been a significant obstacle.

---

71. I.R.C. §472(c). Paragraphs 330-10-35-1C through 35-7 of the FASB Codification provide for LIFO under U.S. GAAP (2015).
72. I.R.C. §481. This requires complicated adjustments if a taxpayer changes an accounting method. very generally, the taxpayer must adjust all years since 1954 (the date of enactment) as if the new method had been used at all times. *See*, Michael B. Lang, Elliott Manning & Steven J. Willis, Federal Tax Accounting at 541-567 (Lexis 2006).

§14.06   THE CCCTB (U.S. POINT OF VIEW)

U.S. scholarship on the CCCTB is limited; however, there has been some discussion.[73] Differences fall into three categories:

(1) Structural
(2) Theoretical
(3) Substantive.

[A]   Structural Differences

 – The CCCTB 2011 proposed Directive comprises approximately 34 substantive pages. Some rules are specific, while others are more principle-based. In contrast, the U.S. tax system, as it applies to taxation of income, comprises many hundreds of pages (quantification is difficult because how one defines a page and what one might include is subjective). But, the difference in complexity is striking.
 – A material portion of the U.S. tax base for corporations is at the state or local level, which has its own divergent rules and levels of complexity. Although many states adopt the federal system, many have significant differences. The CCCTB would not permit such differences among members.
 – U.S. tax laws overwhelmingly, at least as far as the tax base is concerned, apply the same rules to corporations, partnerships, trusts, individuals, and other types of entities. For example, the definition of business expenses, depreciation, income, gains and similar generally applicable rules apply exactly the same regardless of the taxpayer's form. In contrast, the CCCTB appears to propose one unified tax base for corporations, but to permit (*but see* the 2013 accounting directive) the use of a different tax base for individuals or non-corporate commercial activities.

[B]   Theoretical

 – The CCCTB formulary approach is roughly similar to the "subnational" U.S. system, which is also mostly formulary.[74] The formula components – labor,

---

73. *See*, CORPORATE INCOME TAXATION IN EUROPE: THE COMMON CONSOLIDATED CORPORATE TAX BASE (CCCTB) AND THIRD COUNTRIES (Edward Elgar Publishing 2013) (edited and written, in part, by U.S. scholars); Peter Harris, CORPORATE TAX LAW: STRUCTURE, POLICY AND PRACTICE (Cambridge 2013) (not U.S.); Walter Hellerstein, A COMMON CONSOLIDATED CORPORATE TAX BASE FOR EUROPE (2008) at 150-154; Ann Holley, THE KPMG GUIDE TO THE CCCTB (2012); *Cf.*, Joann M. Weiner, *Redirecting the Debate on Formulary Apportionment*, TAX NOTES INTERNATIONAL at 1213 (June 18, 2007) (not discussing the CCCTB, but generally discussing the topic and presenting a useful bibliography); Reuven S. Avi-Yonah, *Globalization, Tax Competition, and the Fiscal Crisis of the Welfare State*, 113 HARV. L. REV. 1575 (2000) (not discussing the CCCTB, but discussing the topic and related/earlier proposals).
74. *See generally*, Walter Hellerstein, A COMMON CONSOLIDATED CORPORATE TAX BASE FOR EUROPE (2008) at 150-154.

assets, and sales – are generally the same factors used by most U.S. states; however, many states define[75] and weigh[76] the factors differently.

[C] Substantive Differences

- Article 10 generally corresponds to U.S. law; however, it lists no credits, which the U.S. frequently uses.
- Article 12 allows charitable deductions for 0.5% of revenues; in contrast, U.S. corporate charitable contributions are limited to 5% of taxable income.[77]
- Article 14(a)(g) permits a small deduction for expenses attributable to exempt income; I.R.C. section 265 disallows all such costs.
- Article 16 describes exempt organizations; in contrast, U.S. charity tax law is far more complex.[78]
- Articles 17-18 impose the accrual method of accounting. U.S. law imposes a similar rule on some corporations, but it differs substantially in the treatment of pre-paid but unearned items.[79]
- Articles 19 and 25 generally require the accrual method for expenses, including deferred-but-incurred future costs. In contrast, the U.S. defers almost all such costs to the year of "economic performance" which can be substantially later than the CCCTB system.[80]
- Article 26 permits accrual of pension costs without discussion of funding; U.S. law regarding deferred compensation is very complicated and generally requires funding.[81] For some "non-qualified" deferred compensation, no deduction is allowed until the employee/contractor includes the deferred item.[82]
- Article 29 requires FIFO inventories; U.S. law permits LIFO inventories.[83]
- Article 33 defines the depreciable base very briefly; in contrast, U.S. capitalization rules span more than 220 pages of detailed, complex rules.[84]

---

75. For example, many states focus on compensation rather than the number of employees. States also tend to eliminate the involvement of independent contractors. See, Ann Holley, The KPMG Guide to the CCCTB (2012) at 3.
76. *Id. See, Moorman Mfg. Co. v. Bair*, 437 U.S. 267 (1978) (holding that Iowa's allocation of far greater weight to sales than did other states was not in violation of due process, although Congress could require formula uniformity under the commerce clause).
77. I.R.C. §170(b)(2).
78. *See*, Jones, Willis, Brennen & Moran THE TAX LAW OF CHARITIES (2014). U.S. charity law has extensive rules on lobbying, unrelated business activities, and private foundations.
79. *See* the text accompanying notes 37-38 *infra*.
80. See I.R.C. §461(h) (deferring most accrued costs to the later of "all events" or economic performance), §468 (allowing deferred-but-incurred costs for mining operations, but without a provision for the time value of money). *See*, Willis *supra* note 38.
81. I.R.C. §§401 *et. seq.*
82. I.R.C. §404.
83. I.R.C. §472. Taxpayers using LIFO must also use LIFO for financial reporting.
84. Treas. Reg. §§1.263, 1.263A.

- Article 36 lists depreciable lives of 15 and 40 years and allows straight-line depreciation. In contrast, U.S. law permits accelerated depreciation with arbitrarily shortened lives, including some expensing of capital investments.[85]
- Article 37 allows a full year of depreciation in the acquisition year. In contrast, U.S. law generally imposes a mid-year convention for movable property and a mid-month convention for immovable property.[86]
- Article 41 allows exceptional depreciation. U.S. tax law has no such provision. Section 165[87] allows a sustained loss for property not sold or exchanged only if it results from a casualty such as a fire, storm or shipwreck.
- Article 43 has no apparent time limitation on loss carryovers; in contrast, U.S. law permits a two-year loss carryback and limits carryovers to 18 years.[88]
- Article 54 provides consolidation rules beginning at 50% control. In contrast, U.S. rules require 80% ownership.[89]
- Article 68 speaks of capitalization for certain self-generated intangibles. U.S. law would expense nearly all such items.[90]

§14.07   EU DIRECTIVE AND U.S. SIMILARITY AND DIFFERENCES

The U.S. already has, for example, the statutory substance over form principle.[91] Similarly, the U.S. effectively uses the materiality principle for both tax law and U.S. GAAP. Full disclosure of bribery[92] and other payments to governments is also an aspect of U.S. tax and accounting rules.

Requiring financial audits for non-publicly-traded entities would be an enormous change in the U.S. I doubt the U.S. has sufficient CPAs to provide the needed services. I understand the Directive has, as a goal, lessening burdens on SME's, but as stated, it would seem to be a substantial increase in the U.S. to the extent of required audits.

The Corporate Social Responsibility (CSR) movement is active in the U.S.[93] As a result, many entities, particularly publicly-traded ones, already include non-financial statements regarding social and environment issues affecting sustainability.[94] FASB

---

85. I.R.C. §§179, 167, 168.
86. I.R.C. §168.
87. I.R.C. §165(h).
88. I.R.C. §172.
89. I.R.C. §1563.
90. Treas. Reg. §1.263 generally expenses research & development costs as well as marketing and advertising. I.R.C. §174 (research and experimental expenditures are currently deductible). Treas. Reg. § 1.263(a)-1(c)(3) (current deduction of intangibles acquired from an employee); 1.263A-1(l)Example 7 (Product launch costs are currently deductible).
91. I.R.C. §7701(o).
92. I.R.C. §162(c)(1); Foreign Corrupt Practices Act.
93. See, Steven J. Willis, *Corporations, Taxes, and Religion: The Hobby Lobby and Conestoga Contraceptive Cases*, 65 S. Car. L. Rev. 1, 44-55 (2013), discussing the corporate social responsibility movement, and the social entrepreneurship movement, as well as the spread of L3C and Benefit Corporations.
94. *CR Magazine* annually lists the "100 Best Corporate Citizens," as noted in *Forbes*. Jacquelyn Smith, *The 100 Best Corporate Citizens*, Forbes (April 18, 2012), http://www.forbes.com/sites/

rules do not generally cover relevant issues, however, accounting for contingencies (such as environmental cleanup costs) is required by FASB 5. Broader requirement of non-financial disclosures would likely take legislation, as it appears to be beyond the financial regulatory powers of the SEC.

While many people may cynically believe that corporate support of "good causes" is purely the result of profit-seeking motives,[95] others appear to believe that such support has elements of reality – as opposed to public relations – suggesting that imposing a moral code is relevant to corporations.[96]

As a practical matter, most persons and most businesses in the U.S. are not audited for tax purposes. Requiring financial audits of closely-held small and medium-sized entities would provide a wealth of new information to taxing authorities. Presumably, a financial audit would require reconciliation of book and tax discrepancies, which would present the government with a tax audit roadmap.

Unification of accounting rules for privately held entities is a difficult undertaking in the U.S. for several reasons:

- The costs and burdens of an audit.
- The wide-spread desire for privacy of proprietary information.
- The divergent financial and tax law rules as well as the broadly divergent accounting rules for other legal areas. For example, accounting for family matters (division of property, alimony, and child support needs varies from state to state and also varies widely from financial accounting: typically it focuses on tax rules), and accounting for trusts (rules vary by state and are often unsophisticated) differ substantially from U.S. GAAP. Unification of tax law and financial accounting could help alleviate such discrepancies.
- The divergent tax bases used in various state laws.

---

jacquelynsmith/2014/04/18/the-100-best-corporate-citizens/. Listed number one, Bristol-Myers told *Forbes*: "Our top ranking on this list and similar lists year after year recognizes the positive impact our company's commitments to promoting economic, social and environmental sustainability are having on our patients and customers, our employees, our shareholders, our global communities, and our environment." *Id.* The company lists this, and similar rankings, prominently on its website. *Achievements*, BRISTOL-MEYERS SQUIBB, http://www.bms.com/ responsibility/Pages/achievements.aspx (last visited September 24, 2013). The company also emphasizes its responsibility culture on its website, consistently using jargon such as "sustainability," doing the "right thing," being a "good neighbor," "public trust," "personal integrity," "values," and "ethical business practices." *Responsibility Message from the CEO*, BRISTOL-MEYERS SQUIBB, http://www.bms.com/responsibility/Pages/responsibility-message-from-CEO.aspx (last visited September 24, 2013). Further, the company maintains the Bristol-Myers Squibb Foundation, which it presents as a legitimate philanthropic institution. *How to Apply for Bristol-Meyers Squibb Foundation Grants*, BRISTOL-MEYERS SQUIBB, http://www.bms.com/ foundation/Pages/bristol_myers_squibb_foundation_grants.aspx (last visited September 24, 2013). The foundation website, however, closely connects to the commercial website, raising questions about its legitimacy.

95. *See* Steven J. Willis, *People in Glass Houses*, 113 TAX NOTES 477, 477 (2006) (arguing that the Bank of America Charitable Foundation "lacks a valid charitable purpose and thus should be denied exempt status … ").

96. Willis, *supra* note 93 at 46; *Increasing Impact, Enhancing Value: A Practitioner's Guide to Leading Corporate Philanthropy*, COUNCIL ON FOUNDS. 8 (http://www.cof.org/files/Bamboo/ whoweserve/corporate/documents/corporateguide.pdf (September 24, 2013) (citing Citizens Engage! Edelman "goodpurpose" Global Study, 2010" Edelman, 2010).

Many scholars have studied corporate transparency and social responsibility.[97] Recent U.S. litigation has focused on the religious and moral responsibilities of corporations and employers.[98] The topic is fraught with emotion and strong, opposing positions. See the many studies cited in my articles.

As far as unification of accounting and tax law,[99] I have long argued for the unification of accounting and tax law; however, most U.S. academics strongly oppose the idea.

The requirements of Directive 2014/95/EU regarding non-financial reporting present fascinating issues. The U.S. has an entity that calls itself the SASB, or Social Accounting Standards Board. It has proposed expanding social audits and reporting, largely on a piecemeal basis, recognizing the political realities and difficulties. I am unclear how auditors would examine – let alone express an opinion on – social and environmental responsibilities to the extent they are non-financial.

Unification of financial accounting and tax accounting, which is what I would propose, would involve an enormous undertaking and many years to phase-in the process. The U.S. attempted a limited project along these lines in 1954 with the enactment of sections 454 and 464; however, Congress repealed the sections within a year because of the huge, albeit temporary, loss of revenues. Most U.S. tax lawyers, as well as most U.S. tax academics and tax judges are not trained in financial accounting. Unification of tax law and accounting rules would require what would probably be an insurmountable amount of re-education for tax professionals. A gradual phase-in involving particular accounts (such as I have recommended involving deferred-but-incurred costs and pre-paid receipts) would be feasible. Opposition to such proposals, however, is extensive.

---

97. Susan Ariel Aaronson, Corporate *Strategy and Inadequate Governance: The Pitfalls of CSR* (2009).
98. *Burwell v. Hobby Lobby*, 573 U.S. (2014) (deciding that closely-held corporations may assert religious rights of owners). Interestingly, the government argued, in brief, that corporations are amoral entities. Defendants' Memorandum in Opposition to Plaintiff's Motion for Preliminary Injunction at 304, *Hobby Lobby District* I, 8790 F. Supp. 2d 1278 (W.D. Okla. October 22, 2012) (No. Civ. 12-1000-HE).
99. *See* the discussion accompanying notes 34-43 *supra*.

Part IV CCCTB and Federal Income Tax: A U.S. Lesson for the European Union? (From U.S. to EU)

CHAPTER 15

The Harmonization of Corporate Income Taxation. The CCCTB and the Lessons from the U.S.

Gianluigi Bizioli

§15.01 INTRODUCTION

The purpose of this chapter is slightly different from the others published in this book. Whereas the latter aim at describing the relations and the connections between accounting and tax rules in the computation of the taxable base, this contribution tries to explore the future backdrops of corporate income taxation in the European Union ("EU"). More precisely, it deals with the "comprehensive" solutions proposed by EU Institutions to cope with cross-border tax obstacles for corporations and the lessons (if any) which can be learnt from the experience of the United States of America ("U.S.").

According to these objectives, the chapter is structured in three main parts. The first briefly outlines the evolution of EU policies in the corporate income taxation field, focusing on the recent "Communication on a Fair and Efficient Tax System in the European Union".[1] The second part introduces the general features of the Common Consolidated Corporate Tax Base ("CCCTB") and, finally, an attempt at comparison with the U.S. experience will be provided. Some conclusions close the chapter.

---

1. European Commission, "A Fair and Efficient Corporate Tax System in the European Union: 5 Key Areas for Action", Communication to the European Parliament and the Council of June 17, 2015, COM(2015) 302 final.

§15.02   THE EVOLUTION OF THE EU POLICIES IN CORPORATE INCOME TAXATION

The early stage of the EU approach to corporate income taxation is well-known and does not need any particular analysis. Although this period can be divided into various sub-stages, the common feature was the "top-down" or "harmonization from above" approach. Rooted on the need to create a European common market similar to the national markets and/or the approach employed in the building of the monetary union, the EU tried to introduce a corporate tax harmonization (or tax standardization) which also included centrally-mandated tax rates. Similarly to the indirect tax field, the goal of the Commission was to create a Community corporate tax with common rules, uniform tax rates and a credit system to avoid double taxation.[2]

This idea was officially abandoned, and the normative project withheld only in 1990 when it was sufficiently clear that, in the short term, the tax harmonization perspectives should be strictly connected with the realization of the internal market without (fiscal) barriers.[3]

The late 1990s inaugurated the season of the unfair tax competition and of the coordination approaches.[4] On the assumption that "[t]here is a need for action at the European level in order to reduce distortions to the Single Market; to prevent significant losses of tax revenue; and to reverse the trend of an increasing tax burden on labour as compared to more mobile tax bases",[5] the Commission presented a series of measures based on different approaches (the so-called Tax Package). The "Code of Conduct for Business Taxation", which directly targeted "potentially harmful" tax measures, contained recommendations directed at the Member States, with the purpose of coordinating national corporate income taxation. The Code was an instrument of the so-called soft-law that does not directly bind the Member States, but whose implementation would have fostered the tax coordination of the Union. On the side of the cross-border obstacles and distortions to the taxation of capital income and of interest and royalties payments between companies, the 1997 Communication undertook the traditional "hard-law" approach proposing the adoption of two Directives.

This tax policy was, therefore, based on two features which marked the change from the past. The need to curb harmful tax competition, i.e., to prevent the erosion of tax bases within the Union, was added to the traditional aim of the creation and the

---

2. The topic is treated in depth by A.J. Martín Jiménez, *Toward Corporate Tax Harmonization in the European Community. An Institutional and Procedural Analysis* (Kluwer Law International, London-The Hague-Boston, 1999), pp. 105 ff. See, also, W.W. Bratton & J.A. McCahery, "Tax Coordination and Tax Competition in the European Union: Evaluating the Code of Conduct on Business Taxation", 38 *Common Market Law Review* (2001), p. 677, at p. 681 ff.
3. Commission of the European Communities ("EC"), "Guidelines on Company Taxation", Communication to Parliament and the Council of April 20, 1990, SEC(90) 601 final, which justified the decision according to the principle of subsidiarity: "[m]ember States should remain free to determine their tax arrangements, except where these would lead to major distortions" (paragraph 5.).
4. Commission of the EC, "Towards tax co-ordination in the European Union. A package to tackle harmful tax competition", Communication to the Council of October 1, 1997, COM(97) 495 final.
5. "Towards tax co-ordination in the European Union. A package to tackle harmful tax competition", *supra* note 4, paragraph 2.

functioning of the internal market. It is worth noting that this change has been strongly influenced by the evolution of the international tax policy and, in particular, by the publication of the OECD Report on Harmful Tax Competition.[6]

On the other side, these objectives were carried out not only through the traditional harmonization method, i.e., not only within a pure EU legal context but also vesting Member States with the task of adapting the domestic corporate tax systems to the internal market (and to a *fair* tax competition). This approach shifted from a top-down law-making process (harmonization) to a bottom-up legal cooperation (coordination). The legal basis of this shift was founded in the general principle of cooperation between the Member States and the EU, now stated by Article 4(3) of the Treaty on the European Union (TEU).

It is within the context of the "Tax Package" that the idea for a single consolidated corporate tax base has crept in. The Vienna European Council of December 11 and 12, 1998 called for a comprehensive study on company taxation in the EU with the role of emphasizing:

> the need to combat harmful tax competition whilst taking into account that cooperation in the tax policy area is not aiming at uniform tax rates and is not inconsistent with fair tax competition but is called for to reduce the continuing distortions in the single market also in view of stimulating economic growth, and enhancing the international competitiveness of the Community, to prevent excessive losses of tax revenue or to get tax structures to develop in a more employment-friendly way.[7]

The outcomes of this study and, in particular, the accompanying Communication of the Commission,[8] highlighting "the importance of all the features of the company tax systems" (p. 5) and considering the influence of those systems on the "international competitiveness of the EU companies" (p. 8), proposed a return to the past through the adoption of a comprehensive harmonization in the field of corporate income taxation. In particular, the Commission put forward the idea of a common consolidated tax base for the EU-activities of multinational companies based in Europe which allows them to (i) compute the income of the entire group according to one set of rules; and (ii) establish consolidated accounts for tax purposes (thus eliminating the potential tax effects of purely internal transactions within the group) (p. 15).

The importance of this Communication has to be appreciated in two different directions. On one hand, the Commission considered that "[o]nly providing multinational companies with a consolidated corporate tax base for their EU-wide activities will really, through a single framework of company taxation, systematically tackle the

---

6. OECD, *Harmful Tax Competition. An Emerging Global Issue*, (OECD Publications, Paris, 1998).
7. Commission of the EC, "Company Taxation in the Internal Market", Commission Staff Working Paper of October 23, 2010, SEC(2001) 1681, p. 2.
8. Commission of the EC, "Towards an Internal Market without tax obstacles. A strategy for providing companies with a consolidated corporate tax base for their EU-wide activities", Communication to the Council, the European Parliament and the Economic and Social Committee of October 23, 2001, COM(2001) 582.

majority of the tax obstacles to cross-border economic activity in the Single Market".[9] In other words, there was the awareness that only the replacement of the existing national corporate income tax systems with one EU regulation would have resolved the major tax obstacles for multinational corporations.

On the other hand, the same Communication proposed a piecemeal approach for tackling the most critical tax obstacles. In comparison with the comprehensive approach, this method revealed the urgency of some threats which affected the internal market. Based on the tax study, the Commission identified five different critical areas: transfer pricing, cross-border payments of dividends, interest and royalties, cross-border loss relief, cross-border restructuring operations and double taxation.

In conclusion, on this matter that aimed at relaunching corporate income tax cooperation, the Commission presented two objectives and two means. Besides the ambitious project to introduce a common consolidated tax base, the Commission was aware of the existence of immediate problems which were affecting the circulation of the productive factors within the internal market. As to the means, the traditional harmonization approach was supported with the coordination action carried out by each single Member State.

Once the objective had been presented, four technical solutions were identified: (i) Home State Taxation; (ii) Common Consolidated (Base) Taxation; (iii) European Corporate Income Tax; and (iv) an harmonized single tax base in the EU.[10] After restricting the choice to the solutions *sub (i)* and *sub (ii)*[11] and a decade of preparation, on March 16, 2011 the Commission finally presented the Directive for a CCCTB.[12]

The opposition of some Member States – for instance, Germany, Ireland, the Netherlands and the United Kingdom[13] – and the emerging problems of the EU – in particular, the financial and budgetary crisis – has consigned this project to oblivion.

The CCCTB was relaunched at the beginning of 2015 as part of the Action Plan for a fair and efficient corporate tax system.[14] Based on the assumption that "[t]he current rules for corporate taxation no longer fit the modern context [since] [c]orporate income

---

9. M. Aujean, *The CCCTB Project and the Future of European Taxation*, p. 13, at p. 30, in M. Lang, P. Pistone, J. Schuch and C. Staringer (eds), *Common Consolidated Corporate Tax Base* (Linde Verlag, Wien, 2008).
10. COM(2001) 582, pp. 16-17.
11. Commission of the EC, "An internal market without internal tax obstacles. Achievements, ongoing initiatives and remaining challenges", Communication to the Council, the European Parliament and the Economic and Social Committee, COM(2003) 726, p. 11 ff.
12. European Commission, "Proposal for a Council Directive on a Common Consolidated Corporate Tax Base (CCCTB)", COM(2011) 121 final.

    In 2005, the Commission presented a Home State Taxation pilot project in favor of Small and Medium-Sized enterprises ("SMEs") which, however, did not receive any interest from Member States. The detailed proposal is contained in "Tackling the corporation tax obstacles of small and medium-sized enterprises in the Internal Market – outline of a possible Home State Taxation pilot scheme [...]", Communication to the Council, the European Parliament and the Economic and Social Committee of December 23, 2005, COM(2005) 702 final.
13. On this point, see E.C.C.M. Kemmeren, "CCCTB: Enhanced Speed Ahead for Improvement", 20 *EC Tax Review* (2011), p. 208.
14. European Commission, "A Fair and Efficient Corporate Tax System in the European Union: 5 Key Areas for Action", Communication to the European Parliament and the Council of June 17, 2015, COM(2015) 302 final.

is taxed at national level, but the economic environment has become more globalised, mobile and digital" (p. 2), the Commission has addressed five different areas of action, which affect the EU and global contexts. Among these actions, the first mentioned concerned the relaunching of the CCCTB, targeting a reduction of the administrative burdens and a simplification of the Single Market, the prevention of profit shifting and corporate tax abuse and the offsetting of cross-border losses within the EU.

There are substantially two key changes compared to the original 2011 version. On the first side, the Commission aims at rendering the regulation mandatory, "at least for multinational enterprises" (p. 8). On the other side, in view of the practical difficulties connected with the implementation of the proposal, "the Commission is advocating a step-by-step approach to agreeing on the different elements of the CCCTB" (p. 5). In particular, according to the Communication, this step-by-step route will be organized as a two-prong approach. Primary focus will be given to the common tax base and, in particular, to the "beneficial treatment of Research and Development expenses". The consolidation of the base will be deferred "until after the common base has been agreed and implemented".

The other actions considered in the Plan involve specific aspects of corporate income taxation, according to the (already highlighted) piecemeal approach. The actual improvement of the Communication provides the proposal with some measures to "provide the foundation for a more coherent and competitive EU approach in the global context" (p. 6).

§15.03   AN OUTLINE OF THE CCCTB REGULATION

As already stated in the previous paragraph, the CCCTB proposal forms part of the traditional process of EU tax harmonization. Although over the years this process has been enriched with other objectives – fair competition and coherence of the EU initiatives in the international tax context –, the legal basis still remains the functioning of the internal market. According to this conclusion, the legal competence for this regulation shall be founded in Article 115 of the Treaty on the Functioning of the European Union ("TFEU") and, in particular, the need to prevent tax distortions which hamper the movement of the productive factors and the fair competition.

The CCCTB introduces a revolution in the computation of the tax base of multinational enterprises. The current method employed considers each taxable subject separately in its state of residence on its individual profits. According to that method, these profits are determined by means of the arm's length principle. On the contrary, the CCCTB proposal provides for a system of common rules for computing the tax base of multinational enterprises. In this sense, each company belonging to the same group, computes the tax base according to a common set of tax rules and then consolidates the different tax bases. Since treasuries, budgets and competences remain at national level, the consolidated tax base shall be apportioned among the different Member States in which the companies reside according to a specific formula. In synthesis, therefore, the proposal is based on three different stages: (i) computation of individual results according to common tax rules; (ii) consolidation of the individual tax results; and (iii) apportionment of the consolidated tax base. As to *sub (i)*, the determination of the taxable unit, i.e., according to which criteria the subsidiaries and the branches should be comprised in the global taxable subject, is of fundamental relevance.

The revolution is, therefore, the consequence of the shift from the arm's length/separate entity approach to a formulary apportionment. According to the Commission in fact, "transaction-by-transaction pricing based on the 'arm's length' principle may no longer be the most appropriate method for profit allocation" of an integrated economy.[15] On the contrary, "[a]llowing the immediate consolidation of profits and losses for computing the EU-wide taxable base is a step towards reducing over-taxation in cross-border situations and thereby towards improving the tax neutrality conditions between domestic and cross-border activities to better exploit the potential of the Internal Market".[16]

It is well-known that OECD opposes these conclusions, for (at least) two different reasons. First, "[t]he transition to a global formulary apportionment system (…) would present enormous political and administrative complexity and require a level of international cooperation that is unrealistic to expect in the field of international taxation".[17] Second, the protection against double taxation "would require substantial international coordination and consensus on the predetermined formulae to be used and on the composition of the group in question".[18]

The second element of the proposed regulation which deserves attention is the dual track approach concerning the computation of the tax base. The CCCTB sets national rules on financial accounting aside and computes the taxable base wholly according to the fiscal profit-and-loss account. More precisely, the common tax base is defined as the sum of all revenues "less exempt revenues, deductible expenses and other deductible items" (Article 10 of the proposed Directive) and these concepts are autonomously provided for by the proposed Directive.[19]

In this sense, the CCCTB tax base is not influenced by the accounting standards adopted by the national jurisdictions which, as already stressed, "more or less ignores the balance sheet for tax purposes, possibly to avoid disagreement not absolutely necessary".[20]

Two final points should be further considered.

Eligibility of subsidiaries for consolidation is determined on the basis of two elements: (i) the right to exercise more than 50% of the voting rights; and (ii) the ownership right amounting to more than 75% of the company's capital or more than 75% of the rights giving entitlement to profit (Article 54, paragraph 1, of the proposed

---

15. COM(2011) 121 final, p. 4.
16. COM(2011) 121 final, p. 5.
17. OECD, *Transfer Pricing Guidelines for Multinational Enterprises and Tax Administrations* (OECD Publications, Paris, 2010), p. 39.
18. OECD, *supra* note 17, p. 38.
19. Revenues are defined by Article 4, n. 8, and all revenues should be taxable (recital n. 10); exempt revenues are listed in Article 11, whereas the deductible expenses are referred to in Articles 12 and 13.
20. B.J.M. Terra & P.J. Wattel, *European Tax Law* (Wolters Kluwer Law & Business, Alphen aan den Rijn, 2012), p. 800.

Directive). In addition, consolidation ignores any transactions between group members.

Finally, the apportionment formula is connected equally to sales, labor and assets (Article 86 of the proposed Directive). The most problematic aspect of the formula involves the scope of application of the assets, since the proposal excludes intangibles and financial assets "due to their mobile nature and the risks of circumventing the system" (Proposed Directive, recital n. 21). Although the justification for this solution can be shared, it is nonetheless not neutral, because it favors those economies based on traditional industry.

In conclusion, the CCCTB proposal is the most ambitious tax project after the Value Added Tax ("VAT") harmonization. With the latter, it shares the common set of rules throughout the EU and the discretionary power enjoyed by Member States. However, it also differs completely, since VAT is fastened to a transaction-based allocation of tax base to separate taxing jurisdictions.[21]

§15.04 LESSONS FROM THE U.S.

Due to its federal structure, the U.S. has an extensive experience in the field of taxation of multijurisdictional enterprises.[22] Even if there are significant differences between the U.S. and the EU legal contexts, the lessons from the U.S. may be somewhat useful for this stage of relaunching of the CCCTB project.

Based on the book, the main difference lies in the power of Congress to regulate intrastate commerce (Article I, § 8 of the U.S. Constitution). According to this provision, labeled "Commerce Clause", Congress is empowered to require that state tax power be exercised consistently with both the federal government's international and domestic responsibilities.[23] In this sense, even if federal and state tax authority can be understood as concurrent, the former is vested with an unlimited power to coordinate the latter. Differently, as is well-known, the EU Member States retain taxing powers in the field of direct (income) taxation, since the European Treaties do not attribute any competence to the supranational level. The legal basis of the direct taxation Directives is traced back to Article 115 TFEU, whose scope of application is general – "the approximation of such laws, regulations or administrative provisions of the Member States" – and restricted to the "establishment or functioning of the internal market".

However, the actual application of the mentioned provisions has significantly reduced the genetic difference between the two legal systems. With regard to the U.S. experience, Congress has rarely exercised the power to regulate interstate commerce; however, the steady European Court of Justice ("ECJ") case law binds the exercise of

---

21. The point is highlighted by B.J.M. Terra & P.J. Wattel, *supra* note 20, p. 800.
22. Although similar experiences can also be found in Canada and Switzerland, the comparison will be restricted to the U.S. case.
23. W. Hellerstein, *The United States*, p. 25, at p. 47 ff., in G. Bizioli and C. Sacchetto (eds), *Tax Aspects of Fiscal Federalism. A Comparative Analysis* (IBFD, Amsterdam, 2011).

the national tax authority in direct taxation, since "the powers retained by the Member States must (...) be exercised consistently with Community law".[24]

The very difference between the two experiences lies in the budgetary dimension. Differently from the EU, which has only spending authority, U.S. Congress has the power to "lay" and "collect" taxes (Article I, § 8, U.S. Constitution), even on income without any apportionment among the States (XVI Amendment). In this sense, the U.S. federal expenditures are funded directly by the taxpayers. In other words, the huge difference between the EU and U.S. experiences is that only that latter has two autonomous budgets entirely financed by taxes.

According to this background, the U.S. State power to levy (corporate income) tax is restrained by two limits, generally attributed to the Commerce and the Due Process Clauses.[25] The first limit is the well-known economic link between the territory and the economic activity carried out by the company. The second, "the state may tax only the portion of the corporation's income that is fairly attributable to the corporation's income producing activities in the state".[26] This apportionment must be grounded on factors which reflect "a reasonable sense of how income is generated"[27] and may not produce "a grossly distorted result".[28]

In conclusion, therefore, the U.S. Constitution, as interpreted by the Supreme Court, does not provide any specific solution for the method of apportionment of income among the different States, leaving them free to choose the proper solution. The adoption of a formulary apportionment has occurred substantially at the same time as the development of the transcontinental railroad system and the need to allocate the relative property and capital. Since the property value arose from a sole activity, as a single unit, and it could be distributed according to the value of the railway lines allocated to each state out of the total value, for the measurement of the results a comprehensive solution was chosen. In this sense, the adoption of the formulary apportionment does not lay in "its theoretical superiority (...) but rather because of practical necessity".[29] Therefore, the lesson for the EU is that any highly integrated economy requires the introduction of methods of consolidation and apportionment of the corporate income tax in order to reduce the compliance costs connected with the taxation of the single entities of multinational groups.

A second lesson concerns the definition of the formula of the apportionment. As already pointed out,[30] this is mainly a political affair. Nevertheless, the political choice

---

24. ECJ, February 14, 1995, case C-279/93, *Finanzamt Köln-Altstadt v. R. Schumacker,* in ECR I-225, paragraph 21.
25. The point is developed in detail by W. Hellerstein, "State Taxation of Corporate Income From Intangibles: Allied-Signal and Beyond", 48 *Tax Law Review* (1993), p. 739, at p. 743 ff.
26. W. Hellerstein, *supra* note 25, p. 744.
27. U.S. Supreme Court, *Container Corp. of America v. Franchise Tax Bd.,* 463 U.S. 159, 166 (1983).
28. U.S. Supreme Court, *Norfolk & W. Ry. v. Missouri State Tax Comm'n,* 390 U.S. 317, 326 (1968).
29. W. Hellerstein, *Lessons of US Subnational Experience for EU CCCTB Initiative,* p. 150, at p. 151, in W. Schön, U. Schreiber and C. Spengel (eds), *A Common Consolidated Corporate Tax Base for Europe. Eine einheitliche Körperschaftsteuerbemessungsgrundlage für Europa* (Springer, Berlin, 2008).
30. By W. Hellerstein, *supra* note 29, p. 151 ff.

must consider the legal framework which may be summarized as the allocation of the income according to the place where the production occurs.

§15.05   CONCLUSIONS

This analysis leads to two different conclusions.

The adoption of the CCCTB depends mainly on practical and political choices, rather than technical ones. The U.S. experience demonstrates that integrated economies, governed by one currency, demand a coordinated corporate income taxation based on a formulary apportionment. In other words, the choice is between the strengthen of the internal market or the submissive acceptance of one currency in a divided economy. As to the practice, the tax design involves two delicate points: the definition of the group and the apportionment formula.

In addition, the CCCTB also brings a great opportunity: to provide the EU with its own real resource. This issue requires a specific and separate analysis; however, the improvement of the harmonization of the corporate income taxation may be the opportunity to rethink the current structure of the EU budget, in order to make the Union representative vis-à-vis the European citizens.

PART V   Comparative Survey

CHAPTER 16

A Comparative Perspective

Marco Barassi

§16.01 THE METHOD OF TAX COMPARATIVE LAW: A BRIEF INTRODUCTION

Only recently have scholars started to consider the theoretical issue of comparison applied to tax law.[1] Accordingly, one of the main points relates to the method to be applied in comparing tax law.[2] So, before outlining a comparative synthesis based on the reports from different countries concerning the relationship between accounting and taxation, it is worthwhile looking at the comparative approach on this subject with particular reference to the method, that is to say *how one should compare*. This is a very important issue because, as Prof. Mössner rightly remarks:

> legal comparison represents an instrument of knowledge with an extraordinary power and effectiveness. Through the comparative analysis it is possible to identify characteristics common to different legal systems and, with taxonomic function, these are divided into "families"; comparison allows to discover legal transplants and movement of models from a system to another; it is the necessary preamble to introduce a foreign model in national law.[3]

---

1. MOESSNER J.M., *Why and How to Compare Tax Law*, in *Liber Amicorum Luc Hinnekens*, J.M. Smits ed., Brussels, 2003, pp. 306 et seq.; BARASSI M., *Comparazione (Dir. Trib.)*, in Cassese, S. ed., *Dizionario di Diritto Pubblico*, II, Milan, 2006, p. 1070; BARASSI M., *Comparazione giuridica e studio del diritto tributario straniero*, in Uckmar, V. ed., *Diritto Tributario internazionale*, 2005, pp. 1499 et seq.; BARASSI M., *La comparazione nel diritto tributario*, Bergamo, 2002; TURONYI V., *Comparative Tax Law*, The Hague, 2003, and AULT H.J. & ARNOLD B.J., *Comparative Income Taxation. A Structural Analysis*, 3rd ed., Alphen aan den Rijn, 2010.
2. Se the Authors quoted in the previous footnote.
3. MOESSNER, J.M., *supra* n.1, and now also in SACCHETTO, C. & BARASSI, M. ed., *Introduction to Comparative Tax Law*, Soveria Mannelli, 2008, pp. 13 et seq.

The first thing a comparatist has to do is to choose the object of comparison, that is to say an issue that a tax legal order has to face. The choice of the object must not be influenced by the conceptualism or dogmatism of the comparatist's own legal culture. According to this approach, the relation between accounting and taxation is a problem that most countries have to face in establishing the rules of business income taxation. In fact, commercial law usually obliges companies and entrepreneurs to perform accounting and draw up financial statements that show profits, losses, assets and liabilities for each year. Tax is applied on business income. So the problem is how to determine business income. Does tax law consider the balance statement's profit or loss as business income or is the financial accounting profit or loss only considered to be a starting point for determining business income? There again, must business income be calculated according to specific tax rules? Furthermore does the tax administration have the power to assess data included in financial statements that affect the tax base? All these questions represent a good topic for comparative tax law. The reports from different countries included in this book, answer these questions and others concerning the relationship between tax law and the CCCTB draft directive and the new accounting directive.

After choosing the object of comparison, the tax comparatist has to face other methodological problems: he has to study a foreign law and, in so doing, has to face many problems.[4] The comparatist has to find the sources of – foreign – law considering the two points that follow.

First, the sources of law have to be chosen, bearing in mind that source of law, under a comparative perspective, is everything that affects the actual working of law (law in action). For example statutes, court cases, opinions of scholars, opinions of tax administration. In other words, sources of comparative law are not only formal sources of law. Then, the sources of law have to be interpreted according to the criteria applicable under the foreign law and not according to the criteria of the comparatist's own law.

Second, tax law rules often refer to other areas of law (civil law, administrative law, etc.). So the tax comparatist who usually studies and compares foreign laws, not only has to know about foreign tax law but also areas of foreign law that do not concern tax law and sometimes even disciplines other than the law. This kind of knowledge is not easy to achieve.

So, when accounting and taxation is at stake, a knowledge of accounting rules is usually necessary: these rules may be included in accountancy law and/or in Generally Accepted Accounting Principles (GAAP). This point would be easier if accounting rules were standardized as in the case of IFRS, although IFRS are not always applicable to the determination of the tax base.

---

4. It is not possible to describe in this chapter the problems arising when studying a foreign law. On the method of comparing tax law, see THURONYI V., *Comparative Tax Law*, in *Encyclopedia of Comparative Law*, J.M. Smits ed., Cheltenham, Northampton (Mass.), Elgar, 2006.

As regards the subject of this book, the knowledge of foreign legal systems has been acquired through questionnaires prepared by the coordinator of the research.[5] The formulation of each question is crucial as they need to be interpreted in precisely the same way by each Scholar; moreover abstract categories should be avoided in order to prevent misunderstanding, as the same words may have different meanings in different legal orders. The answers should point to the rules actually applied even if they differ from those described by the statutes: in fact, the reports clearly show which are the rules applied by Courts, taxpayers and tax administration.

§16.02 ACCOUNTING AND TAXATION: THE ISSUE

Commercial law usually obliges companies to prepare financial statements that must represent the net worth and profits and losses of the financial year, thus giving a true and fair view of the financial performance and position of the entity. Rules applicable to financial statements are not only established in commercial law, but also in accountancy law and GAAP. Moving on from this assumption, the question is: can financial statements be useful for calculating taxable income as well?

The answer to the question above is the starting point of the relationship between accounting and taxation.

The issue involves various elements.

The first one is the existence of GAAP, their level of development and their legal relevance (in other words their inclusion in statutes or regulations or reference to them in statutes, their issuance by Governments or by independent entities), since nowadays it may be assumed that GAAP exist in every State considered here. For instance, from a legal perspective, IAS/IFRS have the highest value in EU Member States since they are included in the Regulation (EC) No. 1606/2002 but they usually apply only to a limited number of companies and to consolidated accounts and not to individual accounts.

The second element is the method of calculation of accounting profit and of taxable profit. This point is a consequence of the purposes pursued by rules governing financial statements and those governing the tax base. This point may be analyzed from different perspectives:

(a) The main difference among the various accounting systems is maybe the attitude to protect creditors and company capital instead of shareholders; in the first case the system follows a conservative approach in which the historic cost is the reference value of the different items, legal reality is very important (instead of economic reality), the principle of prudence tends to make revenues to be recognized only when realized, while costs are included in the financial statements when they are likely to occur; in the second case the true

---

5. Mario Grandinetti, University of Turin, prepared the questionnaires. The method followed in the research refers to the so-called factual approach that is based on questions, submitted to people from different legal systems that focus on concrete problems and not on theoretical categories. On the factual approach, see Sacco R., *Legal Formants. A Dynamic Approach to Comparative Law*, *The American Journal of Comparative Law*, 39(1), 27 seq.

and fair view is very important and the reference value is, for certain items, the fair value; of course, these different kinds of approach usually determine different profits. The different accounting systems include, on one side, countries like Germany, France, Italy, Spain and, on the other side, countries like U.K., Ireland and the Netherlands.

(b) The systems of calculation of financial profit and of taxable profit pursue different aims. Those of financial statements are explained above while, those of taxable profit are the calculation of taxable income according to the principles that characterize the tax system: for example, taxation must affect ability to pay (that may have a different legal relevance in different States), the system must consider the tendency of taxpayers to reduce taxable income deferring the realization of profits and anticipating expenses, including costs not related to the business, avoiding and evading tax), the system must be manageable for the taxpayer and for the tax authority; the different aims of the financial system and the tax system are the reason, at least in part,[6] of the adjustments of financial profit required by tax law.

The third element is the link between financial statements and taxable income.

Moving to the reports from different countries, the idea that the starting point for calculating taxable income in every system is the financial profit, seems to be correct. Then, from a theoretical and general point of view three models are possible: (a) a full dependence of taxable income on financial profit; (b) a partial dependence of taxable income on financial profit with adjustments required by tax law; (c) a complete independence of taxable income on financial profit. Since no State, from amongst those examined, uses model a), that is to say considering the financial profit as taxable income, most of the States adopt a kind of partial dependence or complete independence. Accordingly, it is worth following the classification provided by Scholars in which three groups of models are identified: formal dependency, material dependency and material independency.[7] Formal dependency relates to a close connection between financial accounts and taxable income and, usually, in order to deduct expenses in the taxable base, they must be included in the financial statements. Adjustments of the financial profit apply to calculate taxable profit. Material dependency refers to a looser connection since financial profit is the starting point for calculating taxable profit, but it is not necessary to include tax options in the financial statements as well. Material independency refers to a weak connection between financial profit and taxable profit: the two areas are governed by different rules.

The examination of the different systems enables them to be grouped into one of the models above. It is worth noting that the law changes constantly and so the legal system belonging to the same group may differ from that belonging to the same group

---

6. Some adjustments, like the exemption of dividends and capital gains according to the participation exemption, are due to specific reasons belonging to the tax system such as avoiding economic double taxation.
7. ESSERS P. & R. RUSSO, *The Precious Relationship between IAS/IFRS, National Tax Accounting Systems and the CCCTB*, in AA. VV., *The Influence of IAS/IFRS on the CCCTB, Tax Accounting, Disclosure and Corporate Law Accounting Concept*, AA.VV, The Hague, 2009, p. 32.

at a different time. An example is provided by the U.K. that referred to the material independence system in the past, but now belongs to the material dependence system, in the same way as the German system that moved from the formal dependence to the material dependence model.[8]

The grouping together of systems with common features is based on the actual working of the system itself, that is to say looking at the *law in action* and not at the law *in the book*. Therefore, in Luxembourg, for example, the financial statement constitutes the base of the tax computation according to the principle of *Maßgeblichkeitsprinzip* that is explicitly included in tax law.[9] In Belgium, the calculation of taxable income is based on the results of the financial statement and adapted according to specific tax law provisions.[10] This principle is not settled in the statute (Belgian Income Tax Code), but contains a few references to accounting law. In addition, the Supreme Court has confirmed the principle. Therefore, the same principle is applied, but in one case it is included in tax law and, in the other, it is set by case law.

§16.03 RELEVANT FEATURES OF THE DIFFERENT SYSTEMS: CONVERGENCES AND DIVERGENCES

Below, the different systems are examined, searching for the main characteristics of each one and without a close reference to the classification of formal dependency, material dependency or material independency, as mentioned above.

The leading system that represents a high level of dependency of the taxable base on financial statements, is perhaps the German one. It has a long tradition of such a dependency (*Maßgeblichkeitsprinzip*) since the German Report explains that the origin of the connection between the tax base and financial accounting goes back to the nineteenth century. The German system has been followed by Luxembourg[11] and Spain;[12] also Italian, French and Portuguese systems are similar to the German one.

This model is characterized by a high influence of accounting on the tax base since taxable income is calculated starting from financial statements and with the adjustments required by tax law. The principles on which the relationship is based are:

- obviously, the difference between financial profit and taxable profit is not so wide as to need a complete separate balance (for financial and tax purposes);
- a reference included in tax law to financial accounts; in some cases, as in Spain, the reference is very wide-reaching because it includes regulations (*Plan General de Contabilidad*) implementing the legislation. A similar reference to *le plan comptable général* also exists in France: "*Les entreprises doivent respecter les définitions édictées par le plan comptable général, sous réserve que celles-ci ne soient pas incompatibles avec les règles applicables pour l'assiette de*

---

8. The movement goes back to 2009 when the law changed.
9. Article 40 Luxembourg Income Tax Law; see Luxembourg report p. 143.
10. Belgium report, p. 68.
11. As explicitly referred to in the Luxembourg Report, 143.
12. The Spanish Report refers to the German system: see 184 and note 4.

l'impôt.[13] These references to regulations, in tax law, make such regulations become legally relevant. This is also the case in the U.K. where reference to accounting principles was made in tax cases that are part of tax law, and such reference was afterwards included in the statute;

- the fewer the adjustments required to calculate taxable profit, the simpler the system is, requiring only one balance and not two separate ones; this implies low compliance costs for the taxpayer and a manageable system for the tax authority; the system is, as a result, simple and manageable;

- the existence of only one balance resolves the conflicting interest of the taxpayer to show high profits in the financial accounts and low profits in the tax accounts.[14]

The last principle is linked to another. Since financial accounts show the "real profit" of the company, it is not possible to reduce this "real profit" only in respect to the tax administration, i.e., the taxable income may not be lower than the financial profit, unless the tax law explicitly allows it (e.g., exempting some items). This means that financial accounts compliant with GAAP bind the taxpayer who may not depart from them in calculating taxable income. This seems to be a common ground of different States. In Portugal it is designated as the *"preclusive effect of the commercial accounts to the calculation of the taxable profit"*[15] and is a consequence of the probative value of the commercial accounts.[16] In Belgium, the commentary of the tax administration to the Income Tax Code mentions: *"The annual account approved by the general meeting of shareholders irrevocably binds the company, except when it concerns material mistakes and errors"*.[17] In other countries, the same rule seems to be applicable and especially with reference to options provided by tax law. In Germany until 2009, Italy, Spain,[18] Luxembourg (for some specific tax measures[19]) and to some extent Brazil,[20] an item must be recorded in the books in order to take advantage of the same for tax purposes. The principle is known as *reverse authoritativeness (umgekehrteMassgeblichkeit)*. Therefore, items may be included in the financial statements only to have a tax advantage and this may lead to a distortion of the financial statements. The justifications for the reverse authoritativeness in Germany should be to maintain the one-book system and not to distribute means arising from tax subsidies to the shareholders, but these reasons have been criticized.[21]

---

13. Article 38 quater of Annex III to the Code Genéralé des Impots; see France Report, p. 104.
14. German report p. 116.
15. Portuguese report p. 165.
16. Portuguese report p. 165.
17. Belgian Report pp. 72.
18. Spanish Report quoting Article 11.3.1. of the Corporate Income Tax Act p. 187.
19. Luxembourg report p. 146.
20. Brazilian Report, p. 91: according to case law the deduction of expenses for tax purposes requires the prior registration of these expenses in the financial accounts. Moreover, taxpayers tend to comply with tax law options in financial accounts too, thus gaining tax advantages at the expense of a fair representation of economic reality in financial statements.
21. German report p. 119; the Reporter and the Authors quoted therein criticize these justifications as the one-book system does not justify an unfair presentation in the financial statements and the caution on the distribution of subsidies is secured by deferred taxes.

Another issue arises from the linkage of financial accounts and taxable income and it concerns the legal value of financial accounts and the GAAP on which it is based, *vis-à-vis* the tax authority. If this value is strong enough, the consequence should be that the tax authority will be bound by the financial accounts to the extent that they *comply* with GAAP.[22] As a principle, if financial accounts are the starting point for calculating the taxable income, since the law gives legal value to financial accounts and the link between them and the tax base, the binding effect of financial accounts should be effective both for the taxpayer and the tax administration. This is, for example, what happens in Belgium.[23] Moreover, if GAAP allow different options and tax law does not provide differently, the taxpayer should be free to choose from amongst the options and the choice should bind the tax administration.[24] The same result seems to have been reached by the Spanish system where tax statute gives power to the tax administration to apply all the accounting rules to which the Corporate Income Tax Act makes explicit remission, for the sole purpose of determining the taxable base:[25] this power of assessment affects the proper application of accounting rules that are relevant in determining the taxable base.[26] This idea does not seem to be followed by German tax cases where options provided in preparing financial accounts have no effect on taxable base that is to say the taxpayer may not choose the more favorable option in calculating the taxable income.[27] The justification is the different purposes of the financial accounts and the tax accounts: the latter aim to assess the "full" profit and the creation of hidden reserves does not comply with this objective.[28] In fact, the prudential approach of GAAP is not, as it happens, acceptable under a tax law perspective even in Spain or Italy. In France, as in the afore-mentioned countries, companies may exercise choices provided by accountancy without interference from tax administration except in the case in which abuse or abnormal management occur.[29] Moreover, tax administration may assess accounting choices that have an impact on taxable income if those choices do not give a true and fair view of the company, as commercial law requires.[30]

Belgium and Germany are examples of two systems that belong to the general model of "dependence" of taxable income on financial accounts, but that diverge as regards the actual application of the model itself. The GAAP of the two systems mentioned above, Belgium and Germany, do not seem to differ substantially as neither applies IFRS to individual accounts of publicly traded companies but only to consolidated accounts.[31] Thus, the Belgian system seems to prefer legal certainty (binding

---

22. Of course, unless tax law states different rules.
23. Belgian report, quoting a judgment of the Belgian Supreme Court of 20 February 1997 p. 70.
24. For example see Belgian Report p. 73.
25. Spanish Report p. 188.
26. Similarly Spanish Report p. 188.
27. German Report p. 118 with the following example: an option to capitalize an asset in the financial accounts results in a duty to capitalize the asset in the tax account.
28. German Report, p. 118.
29. French Report, p. 106.
30. French Report, p. 107.
31. The German case law mentioned refers to GAAP prior to the changes in the accounting rules introduced in 2009.

effect of financial accounts if the conditions explained above are satisfied) and simplicity, while the German one stresses the correct determination of taxable profit in order to apply equality and ability to pay principles.

Generally, although tax administration can access the tax base, it has no power to change the financial income.

The U.K. system may be grouped with those of (material) dependence since Section 46 of the Corporation Tax Act 2009 states, "*The profits of a trade must be calculated in accordance with generally accepted accounting practice, subject to any adjustment required or authorized by law in calculating profits for corporation tax purposes*". This rule was included in the statute as from the Finance Act 1998, Section 42 of which states that trading profits "*must be computed in accordance with generally accepted accounting practice*". This is the point of arrival of a course that starts from principles stated by cases. In fact, the relevance of accounting principles for the purpose of taxation has already been pointed out by case law.[32] So statute has been changed in order to include a principle stated by judges.[33] As scholars pointed out, reference to adjustment required or authorized by law means not only statute law but also common law, that is to say to case law; this is the rule in a common law system though the more detailed the GAAP become, the lower the need for court intervention seems to be.[34] Therefore, the U.K. system moved to a material dependence system.

The system of determination of taxable income for businesses in the Netherlands is described as a completely independent one from financial accounting, thus differing from the dependence systems of Germany, France, Italy and others. Annual fiscal profit accounting is determined by the concept of *sound business practice*, a legal concept developed by case law, characterized by prudence, reality and simplicity.[35] A system of fiscal profit determination is in accordance with sound business practice if it is based on proper business economic views of profit determination.[36] Nevertheless, there are exceptions to this rule if any regulation in tax law or principles of tax law provide differently. The reason for such a different system compared to the other European ones seems to be the Anglo-Saxon orientation of the Dutch financial accounting system towards the interest of shareholders instead of that of creditors, providing information to the capital market based on a true and fair view.[37] As the taxable profit is calculated in a more conservative way, it is independent from financial accounting.

As noted above, the afore-mentioned classification of formal dependence, material dependence and material independence shows a movement of some countries from one group to another: the United Kingdom moved from independence to material dependence and Germany from formal dependence to material dependence. The first

---

32. In *Gallagher v. Jones* [1993] STC 537 at 555-556.
33. The evolution of the relationship between accounting and taxation is analyzed in depth by Grandinetti M., *Il principio di derivazione nell'IRES*, forthcoming and the Authors quoted therein.
34. GRANDINETTI M., *Il principio di derivazione nell'IRES*, forthcoming, pp. 240-241, and the Authors quoted therein.
35. Netherlands Report p. 153.
36. Netherlands Report, p. 152.
37. Netherlands Report, p. 156.

movement could be justified by an increasing value of GAAP, partly due to their development and completeness; the second, by the modernization of the accounting rules in order to give a fair presentation of the company's situation[38] that is likely to be achieved without tax interference in the financial accounts.

§16.04   TAX IMPLICATIONS OF IAS/IFRS

This paragraph only deals with the different approach followed by the States as concerns the link between financial statements and taxable base, once IFRS have been implemented.[39]

IAS/IFRS generally apply to publicly traded companies and to consolidated accounts, but not to companies' individual accounts. Therefore, they do not seem to have a direct impact on the taxable base that is usually calculated starting from individual accounts.

IAS/IFRS do not have an impact on the application of Common Consolidated Corporate Tax Base (CCCTB) either. Since most Member States adopt a dependence model – formal or material – it could be expected that the draft directive on a CCCTB would also share a dependence pattern. Under this perspective, the IAS/IFRS could have represented a common financial base from which to start in order to calculate taxable income. After a first approach in this direction however, the European Commission abandoned this position and the draft directive follows an independence system since IAS/IFRS are not always permitted for individual accounts and are not all considered suitable for tax purposes.[40]

As far as the link between financial accounts and taxable base is concerned, States had a different approach to IAS/IFRS. The implementation of IFRS has been different. In most States, IAS/IFRS apply only to the consolidated account of listed companies and other companies (such as banks and insurances), while, in some cases, they are permitted for other companies. As taxation usually applies to the income of each company, except group taxation, IAS/IFRS has no effect on the calculation of the tax base that is frequently determined starting from financial statements with the adjustments required by tax law. In a few cases, for example Brazil, IAS/IFRS, with some modification, apply to all types of companies, for consolidated and individual accounts but, after a transitional period during which national GAAP applied for tax purposes and IAS/IFRS applied to financial statements, now income tax is not affected by many innovations brought by IAS/IFRS. States like Spain, that considered a full incorporation of IAS/IFRS, abandoned this path, one reason being that IAS/IFRS could not be used for tax accounting purposes.[41] What transpires from a comparative perspective is that, after the implementation of IAS/IFRS, national GAAP were often modified becoming closer to IAS/IFRS: although to differing extents, this seems to be

---

38. German report, p. 120.
39. The relationship between IFRS and taxation is dealt with by Harris P., *IFRS and the Structural Features of an Income Tax Law*, and by Hrdinkova M., *IFRS Any Good for Tax?*, both in Michielse G. & Thuronyi V., *Tax Design Issues Worldwide*, Alphen aan den Rijn, 2015.
40. Available at: http://ec.europa.eu/taxation_customs/resources/documents/taxation/company_tax/common_tax_base/ccctbwp057_en.pdf.
41. Spanish Report, p. 190 (note 49).

the case for example in Portugal, Spain, Germany and the U.K.[42] Therefore, the tendency seems to be towards some kind of uniformity, partially IAS/IFRS oriented.[43] The impact of the introduction of IAS/IFRS or GAAP partially IAS/IFRS oriented, on taxation is not unique. In some States, it causes a weaker link between financial statements and taxable base, in other words it involves more adjustments to the financial profit in order to determine taxable income (Portugal and Brazil). In other cases, as in Germany, the modification of accounting rules was partially oriented towards IAS/IFRS, considering a fair presentation of the company situation but simpler and more cost efficient than IFRS:[44] the examples quoted in the German report show no influence of IAS/IFRS partially oriented accounting rules in some cases and their influence in others on taxation.[45] In other States, like Spain, the link between the (new) accounting rules (labeled Spanish version of IAS/IFRS[46]) and the taxable base did not change, so scholars argued that accounting rules based on IAS/IFRS (but not conforming fully to them), aimed at information, are better equipped for tax purposes than traditional rules, aimed at protecting creditors.[47] In Italy, IAS/IFRS apply to listed companies and other companies and, generally speaking, financial profit is also assumed to calculate taxable profit. Instead, in other States, like Belgium, IAS/IFRS have no influence on taxation. Luxembourg is a peculiar model since different accounting rules apply (GAAP, mixed GAAP with IFRS options, IFRS, hybrid) but tax law has not yet been amended in order to adapt to the new accounting standards; as a result, companies still have to file tax returns based on GAAP but it seems that the tax authority accepts a tax balance sheet based on IFRS giving clear indications of the differences between GAAP and IFRS and their effect on the tax position.[48]

In conclusion, it seems that States have shown different approaches to the implementation of IAS/IFRS. Although limited in scope, these approaches have in some cases determined a convergence of national GAAP towards IAS/IFRS and this allows a dependence model of determination of taxable income starting from financial accounts to be maintained that does not require too many adjustments and is suitable both for the taxpayer and the tax administration.

§16.05   THE NEW ACCOUNTING DIRECTIVE 2013/34/EU

The Accounting Directive clearly shows the leaving, by the EU, of the idea of accounting harmonization based on IAS/IFRS that started with Directives 2003/51/EC

---

42. Since the new accounting standards applicable to unlisted companies are based on IFRS for SMEs; see the U.K. Report, p. 209.
43. This tendency is, to some extent, confirmed by the Directive 2013/34/EU; concerning the directive, see STRAMPELLI G., *Legal Aspects of the New Accounting Legislation*, in this book.
44. German Report, p. 120.
45. German Report p. 121 with some exceptions, under the accounting rules it is possible to capitalize internally generated intangibles while the possibility does not exist in tax accounts; on the other side, the accounting treatment of financial instruments also influences the taxation of these instruments.
46. Spanish Report, p. 191.
47. Spanish Report, page 191.
48. Luxembourg Report, p. 149.

and 2001/65/EC. The new perspective emerges from the recital no. 4 of the Directive, which states that financial statements pursue various objectives and do not merely provide information for investors in capital markets. As a result, the European legal rules of financial statements divide enterprises on the basis of their dimension: listed and financial companies apply IAS/IFRS, while others apply the new accounting directive.

Nevertheless, the new accounting directive includes some rules that belong to IAS/IFRS standards. These principles are substance over form, evaluation at fair value for derivative instruments and rules on evaluation of credits and debts based on 'amortized cost' method). They are not compulsory but Member States have options to implement them.

There are principles – like those just mentioned – and rules in the Accounting Directive that could have an impact on the determination of the tax base insofar as the latter is linked to the financial profit. The principle of substance over form, the materiality principle, the evaluation criteria of financial instruments with particular reference to derivative instruments and the evaluation of goodwill are a few examples of these principles and rules. Owing to the various options that the Accounting Directive grants to the Member States, implementation may differ in each State.[49] From a fiscal perspective, the prevailing model for calculating the tax base seems to be the one of partial dependence, that is to say the taxable income is calculated modifying the financial profit according to the adjustments required by tax law. Therefore, the rules that are not suitable for tax law will be overridden in the calculation of the tax base. Treatment of goodwill is an example: usually tax law establishes the useful life, so when it is different from the one set by accounting rules, an adjustment is required.

For this reason the implementation of the Accounting Directive does not seem to have been critical from a tax perspective.[50]

Such an idea seems to be confirmed as regards the substance over form principle, since most States have already included it in their law. This is the case of Spain where it was included in the accounting reform of 2007,[51] of France,[52] and of Germany where it is a basic principle of the financial and tax accounting rules[53] and of Luxembourg where the principle is already embedded in accounting legislation;[54] in Portugal, the principle has a long-standing tradition in accounting law.

In conclusion, the implementation of the Accounting Directive does not seem to be critical for tax purposes because of the many options left to the States, the purpose

---

49. According to STRAMPELLI G. & PASSADOR M.L., *The Unfinished Harmonization of the Accounting Law in the EU*, in this book, page 3-4, the adoption of the new Accounting Directive (2013/34/EU) does not seem to have led to a harmonization of accounting rules in the EU also because of the several choices granted to the Member States.
50. See, for example, the English report, p. 213, French report, p. 110.
51. Spanish report p. 199.
52. French report p. 110.
53. German Report p. 123.
54. Luxembourg report p. 150.

of these options being not to interfere with the determination of the taxable income that, according to the prevailing model, is the one of partial dependence. The cost of this choice is the lack of comparability of financial statements of European companies.[55]

---

55. STRAMPELLI G. & PASSADOR M.L., *The Unfinished Harmonization of the Accounting Law in the EU*, in this book.

Index

EUCOTAX Series on European Taxation

(1) Peter HJ Essers, Guido JME de Bont & Eric CCM Kemmeren (eds), *The Compatibility of Anti-Abuse Provisions in Tax Treaties with EC Law,* 1998 (ISBN 90-411-9678-1).

(2) Gerard TK Meussen (ed.), *The Principle of Equality in European Taxation,* 1999 (ISBN 90-411-9693-5).

(3) Michael Lang (ed.), *Tax Treaty Interpretation,* 2001 (ISBN 90-411-9857-1).

(4) Pasquale Pistone, *The Impact of Community Law on Tax Treaties: Issues and Solutions,* 2002 (ISBN 90-411-9860-1).

(5) René Offermanns, *The Entrepreneurship Concept in a European Comparative Tax Law Perspective,* 2002 (ISBN 90-411-9887-3).

(6) Michael Lang & Mario Züger, *Settlement of Disputes in Tax Treaty Law,* 2002 (ISBN 90-411-9904-7).

(7) Carlo Pinto, *Tax Competition and EU Law,* 2003 (ISBN 90-411-9913-6).

(8) Michael Lang, Hans-Jörgen Aigner, Ulrich Scheuerle & Markus *Stefaner, CFC Legislation, Tax Treaties and EC Law,* 2004 (ISBN 90-411-2284-2).

(9) Mattias Dahlberg, *Direct Taxation in Relation to the Freedom of Establishment and the Free Movement of Capital,* 2005 (ISBN 90-411-2363-6).

(10) Michael Lang, Judith Herdin & Ines Hofbauer, *WTO and Direct Taxation,* 2005 (ISBN 90-411-2371-7).

(11) Dennis Weber, *Tax Avoidance and the EC Tray Freedoms: A Study of the Limitations under European Law for the Prevention of Tax Avoidance,* 2005 (ISBN 90-411-2402-0).

(12) Félix Alberto Vega Borrego, *Limitations on Benefits Clauses on Double Taxation Conventions,* 2005 (ISBN 90-411-2370-9).

(13) Michael Lang, Josef Schuch & Claus Staringer, *ECJ-Recent Developments in Direct Taxation,* 2006 (ISBN 90-411-2509-4).

(14) Reuven S. Avi-Yonah, James R. Hines Jr. & Michael Lang, *Comparative Fiscal Federalism. Comparing the European Court of Justice and the US Supreme Court's Tax Jurisprudence,* 2007 (ISBN 978-90-411-2552-1).

(15) Christiana HJI Panayi, *Double Taxation, Tax Treaties, Treaty-Shopping and the European Community,* 2007 (ISBN 978-90-411-2658-0).

(16) Dennis Weber, *The Influence of European Law on Direct Taxation: Recent and Future Developments,* 2007 (ISBN 978-90-411-2667-2).

(17) Michael Lang & Pasquale Pistone, *The EU and Third Countries: Direct Taxation,* 2007 (ISBN 978-90-411-2665-8).

(18) Oskar Henkow, *Financial Activities in European VAT: A Theoretical and Legal Research of the European VAT System and Preferred Treatment of Financial Activities,* 2007 (ISBN 978-90-411-2703-7).

(19) Michael Lang (ed.), *Tax Compliance Costs for Companies in an Enlarged European Community,* 2008 (ISBN 978-90-411-2666-5).

(20) Michael Lang (ed.), *Source versus Residence. Problems Arising from the Allocation of Taxing Rights in Tax Treaty Law and Possible Alternatives*, 2008 (ISBN 978-90-411-2763-1).

(21) Ioanna Mitroyanni, *Integration Approaches to Group Taxation in the European Internal Market*, 2008 (ISBN 978-90-411-2779-2).

(22) Rolf Eicke, *Tax Planning with Holding Companies. Repatriation of US Profits from Europe:Concepts, Strategies, Structures*, 2008 (ISBN978-90-411-2794-5).

(23) Peter Essers et al. (ed.), *The Influence of IAS/IFRS on the CCCTB, Tax Accounting, Disclosure and Corporate Law Accounting Concepts: 'A Clash of Cultures'*, 2008 (ISBN 978-90-411-2819-5).

(24) Tonny Schenk-Geers, *International Exchange of Information and the Protection of Taxpayers*, 2009 (ISBN 978-90-411-3142-3).

(25) Raymond Adema, *UCITS and Taxation: Towards Harmonization of the Taxation of UCITS*, 2009 (ISBN 978-90-411-2839-3).

(26) Michael Lang, Jianwen Liu & Gongliang Tang (eds), *Europe–China Tax Treaties*, 2010 (ISBN 978-90-411-3216-1).

(27) Michael Lang, Pasquale Pistone, Josef Schuch & Claus Staringer (eds), *Procedural Rules in Tax Law in the Context of European Union and Domestic Law*, 2010 (ISBN 978-90-411-3376-2).

(28) Sjaak J.J.M. Jansen, *Fiscal Sovereignty of the Member States in an Internal Market: Past and Future*, 2011 (ISBN 978-90-411-3403-5).

(29) Dennis Weber & Bruno da Silva, *From Marks & Spencer to X Holding: The Future of Cross-Border Group Taxation*, 2011 (ISBN 978-90-411-3399-1).

(30) Claus Bohn Jespersen, *Intermediation of Insurance and Financial Services in European VAT*, 2011 (ISBN 978-90-411-3732-6).

(31) Sabine Heidenbauer, *Charity Crossing Borders: The Fundamental Freedoms' Influence on Charity and Donor Taxation in Europe*, 2011 (ISBN 978-90-411-3813-2).

(32) Michael Lang, et al., *The Future of Indirect Taxation: Recent Trends in VAT and GST Systems around the World*, 2012 (ISBN 978-90-411-3797-5).

(33) Harm van den Broek, *Cross-Border Mergers within the EU: Proposals to Remove the Remaining Tax Obstacles*, 2012 (ISBN 978-90-411-3824-8).

(34) Michael Lang, et al. (eds), *Tax Treaty Case Law around the Globe – 2011*, 2012 (ISBN 978-90-411-3876-7).

(35) Dennis Weber (ed.), *CCCTB: Selected Issues*, 2012 (ISBN 978-90-411-3872-9).

(36) Daniël Smit, *EU Freedoms, Non-EU Countries and Company Taxation*, 2012 (ISBN 978-90-411-4041-8).

(37) Rita de la Feria, *VAT Exemptions: Consequences and Design Alternatives*, 2013 (ISBN 978-90-411-3276-5).

(38) Karin Simader, *Withholding Taxes and the Fundamental Freedoms*, 2013 (ISBN 978-90-411-4842-1).

(39) Madeleine Merkx, *Establishments in European VAT*, 2013 (ISBN 978-90-411-4554-3).

(40) Carla De Pietro, *Tax Treaty Override*, 2014 (ISBN 978-90-411-5406-4).

(41) G.K. Fibbe & A.J.A. Stevens (eds), *Hybrid Entities and the EU Direct Tax Directives*, 2015 (ISBN 978-90-411-5942-7).

(42) Gerard Staats, *Personal Pensions in the EU*, 2015 (ISBN 978-90-411-5953-3).

(43) Michael Lang & Ine Lejeune (eds), *VAT/GST in a Global Digital Economy*, 2015 (ISBN 978-90-411-5952-6).

(44) Massimo Basilavecchia, Lorenzo del Federico & Pietro Mastellone (eds), *Tax Implications of Environmental Disasters and Pollution*, 2015 (ISBN 978-90-411-5611-2).

(45) Cristina Trenta, *Rethinking EU VAT for P2P Distribution*, 2015 (ISBN 978-90-411-6137-6).

(46) Marie Lamensch, Edoardo Traversa & Servaas van Thiel (eds), *Value Added Tax and the Digital Economy: The 2015 EU Rules and Broader Issues*, 2016 (ISBN 978-90-411-6612-8).

(47) Raffaele Petruzzi, *Transfer Pricing Aspects of Intra-Group Financing*, 2016 (ISBN 978-90-411-6732-3).

(48) Mario Grandinetti (ed.), *Corporate Tax Base in the Light of the IAS/IFRS and EU Directive 2013/34: A Comparative Approach*, 2016 (ISBN 978-90-411-6745-3).